K

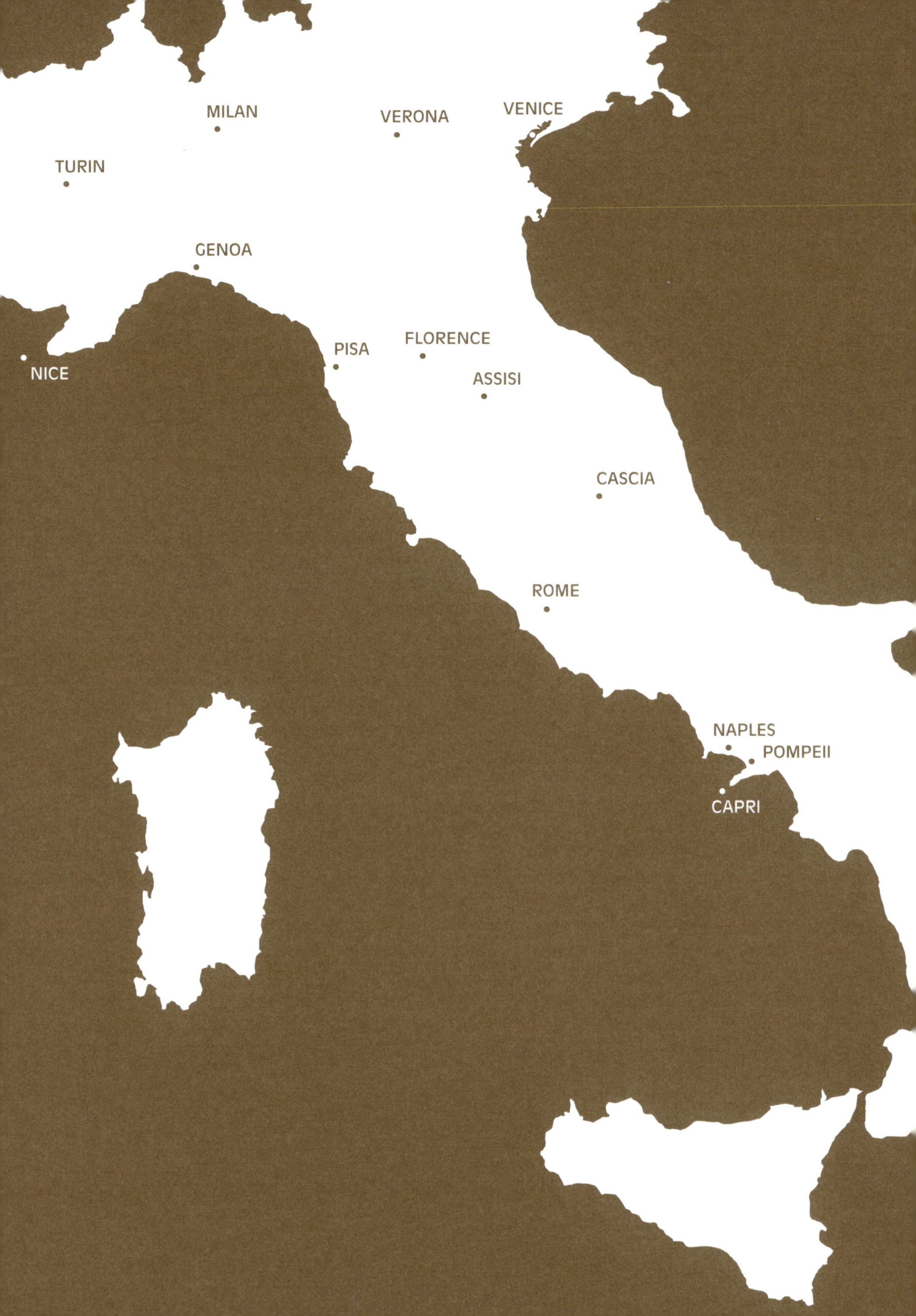

TURIN
MILAN
VERONA
VENICE
GENOA
NICE
PISA
FLORENCE
ASSISI
CASCIA
ROME
NAPLES
POMPEII
CAPRI

CECILIA BRASCHI

YVES KLEIN

ITALY

BRUNO CORÀ

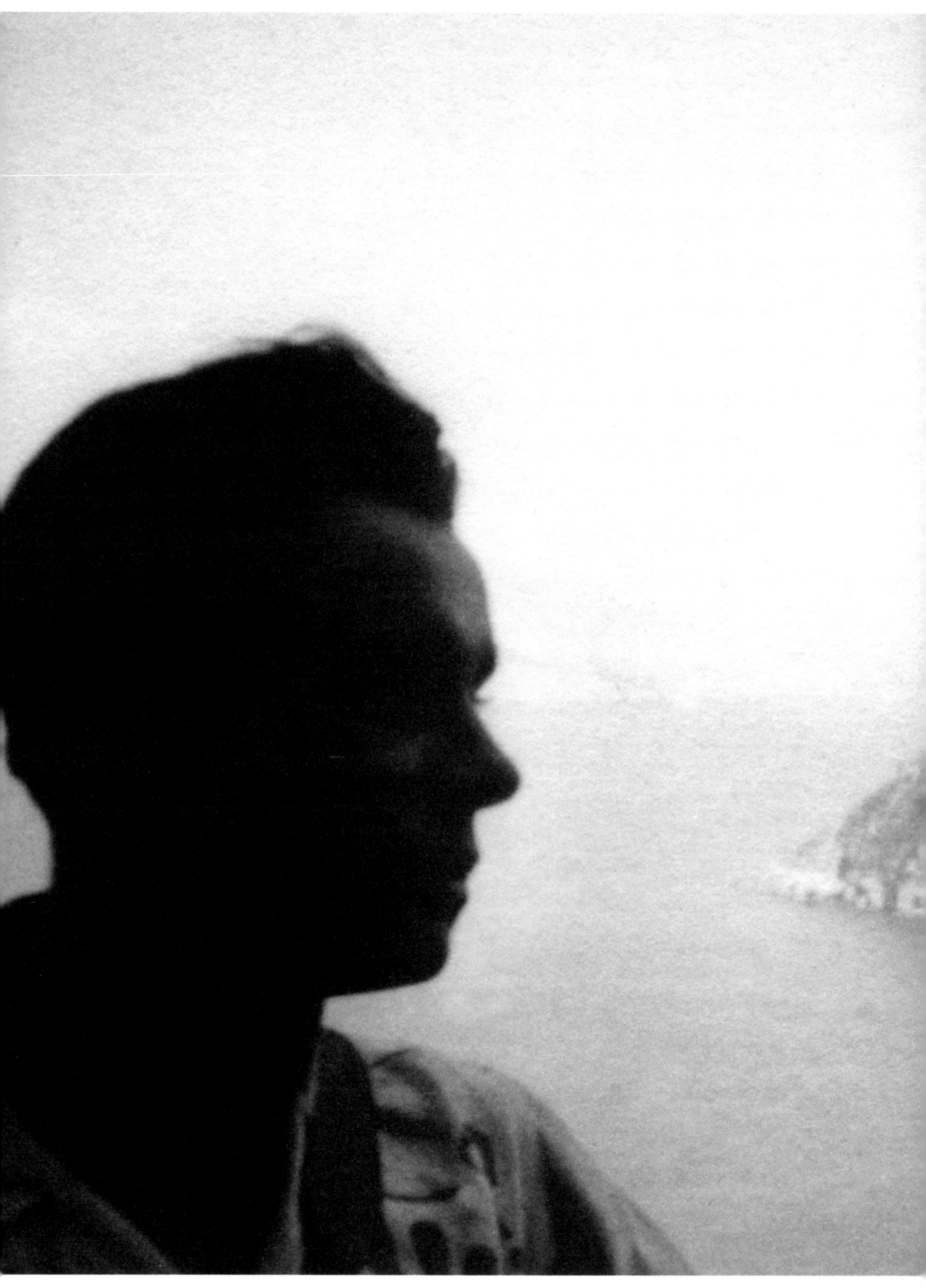

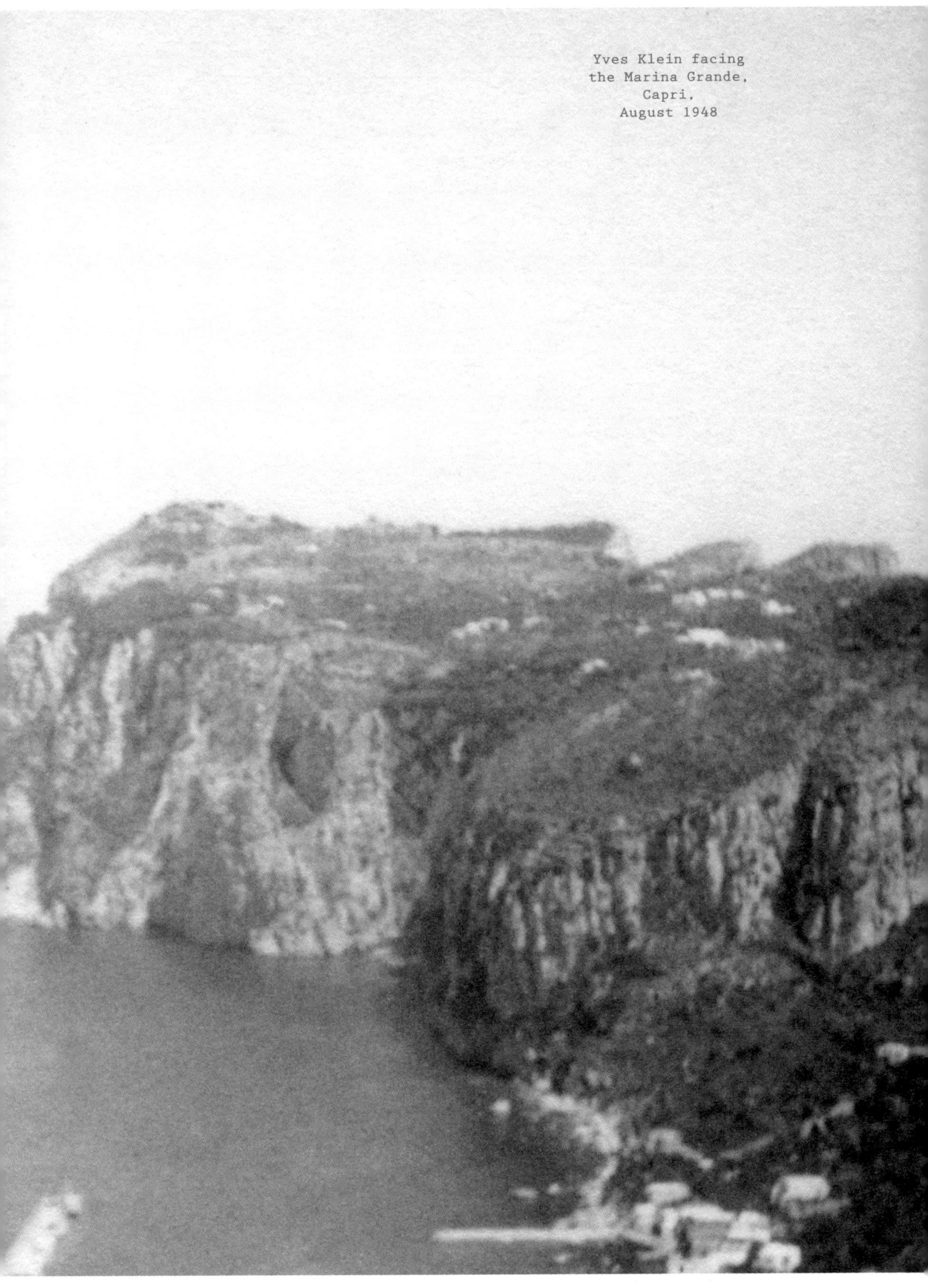

Yves Klein facing
the Marina Grande,
Capri,
August 1948

"BLU BLU BLU".
YVES KLEIN AND ITALY

Cecilia Braschi

On 2 January 1957, with the opening of the exhibition *Yves Klein. Proposte monocrome, epoca Blu* [Yves Klein. Monochrome Propositions, Blue Period] at the Apollinaire Gallery in Milan, Yves Klein officially inaugurated his "Blue Period". By signing himself "Yves le Monochrome" for the first time, he literally became one with his work, forever associating it with the ultramarine-blue pigment he had developed the previous year, and which he would henceforth call IKB – International Klein Blue. For Pierre Restany, the critic and friend who had been closely following the artist's career, this had now entered "another dimension":[1] it was well and truly launched, and never lost momentum – as demonstrated by the exhibitions in Brussels, Paris, Düsseldorf, London, Milan, and Rome that came in quick succession before the end of the year. A turning point for the artist, who had an international career in his sights, this Italian exhibition, which lasted just ten days, was to have decisive and lasting consequences; it catalysed the synergies of a generation of artists, not only French and Italian, but more widely European, who, between the end of the 1950s and the beginning of the 1960s, were in the process of revolutionising the languages and perspectives of art.
The fact that such an important stage in Klein's career took place in Italy is far from incidental, given that his many and constant links with this country had a symptomatic impact on several facets of his art and his character. It was in Italy that Klein discovered an experimental avant-garde scene that offered an alternative to the French and was fully in line with his own research, but also the traces of an ancient artistic heritage, one which he fully embraced when he unabashedly declared himself to be "a classic"[2] – that, and the sources of a religious tradition that was both ancient and rooted in popular culture, and which in many ways nourished his intellectual approach.

In fact, Klein's first familiarity with the peninsula came in 1948, well before he established himself as an artist. He had dropped out of school two years earlier and was earning his living working in the small bookshop that his aunt Rose Raymond had set up for him in her Philips shop in Nice, while looking for a way ahead in his varied interests: judo, philosophy, and, above all, travels. The first trip he made on his own, before Great Britain, Spain, and then Japan, was to Italy, where he mostly hitchhiked

1. Pierre Restany, "Milan 2 January 1957: The Start of the Blue Period", in Pierre Restany, *Yves Klein* (Paris: Éditions du Chêne, 1982), 38. Unless otherwise noted, all translations are our own. Text reproduced in this book pp. 54–55.
2. Yves Klein, "Le dépassement de la problématique de l'art", in *Le Dépassement de la problématique de l'art et autres écrits*, ed. Marie-Anne Sichère and Didier Semin, Écrits d'artistes (Paris: École Nationale Supérieure des Beaux-Arts, 2003), 113.

around the country. The reasons were simple: from Nice, Italy was an easily accessible destination for the twenty-year-old, as well as being cheap and easy to get around on a shoestring.

When Klein crossed the border at Ventimiglia on 3 August 1948, it was barely eight months after Italy had narrowly ratified its constitution, confirming the aspiration to democracy and national unity after more than twenty years of dictatorship. The results of the referendum of 2 June 1946 had been in favour of the Republic and, for the first time, women were granted the right to vote. The opening up of democratic dialogue and of borders meant that people and ideas could circulate more freely.

Despite the still-visible traces of the bombings during the Second World War and the continuing issue of serious poverty, Klein perceived Italy as a country of art and culture where everything seemed "harmonious and fine".[3] In the account he wrote to his parents (pp. 213–215 of this book), the artists Fred Klein and Marie Raymond, he enthusiastically recounted his trip as a series of dazzling experiences: a visit to the Palazzo Pitti in Florence, where he discovered Titian's *La Bella* (also known as *Portrait of a Noblewoman*, 1536–1538), then Pisa and its famous tower, and finally Rome, with its Temple of Saturn, the Forum, the cloister of Saint Paul Outside the Walls, and the Via Ostiensis. A little further south, he visited the Casa del Fauno [House of the Faun] on the archaeological site of Pompeii, which he described as "the most fantastic evocation of the glorious Latin past."[4] Klein would vividly remember the Byzantine and Primitive paintings from the Sienese and Florentine schools that he had the opportunity to admire in the Vatican Museum: a year and a half later, with the framer Robert Savage in London, he himself learned the gold-leaf technique so consummately mastered by Simone Martini and the Lorenzettis six centuries earlier. The same elaborate textures and irregular surfaces were to shine through in the *Monogolds* Klein produced from 1959 onwards, in which the radiance of the bewitching gold backgrounds inspired by the Sienese painters seems to distance these works from any form of representation of the material world.

For Klein, the Italian physical trip was certainly an extension of the "realistic imaginary journey"[5] begun with his friends from Nice, Claude Pascal and Armand Fernandez (the future Arman), during their almost mystical gatherings. In one of the photos of his journey, we see him in 1948 wearing the shirt he had covered, with those same friends, with handprints and footprints (p. 24). The shirt even made "quite an impression"[6] in this chic resort that is Capri. After all the cultural visits, the island's bars and dance halls brought the young man back to his favourite nighttime pastimes, while the days were taken up with bathing, kayaking, boating, and swimming. Klein responded enthusiastically to the natural beauty of this Parthenopean island. In particular, he was dazzled by the famous Blue Grotto, an ancient Roman nymphaeum – a sanctuary dedicated to the aquatic nymphs of mythology – and by the intense blue that makes

3. Yves Klein, *Journal du voyage en Italie*, September 1948, sheet 3 (recto).
4. Klein, *Journal du voyage en Italie*, September 1948, sheet 5 (recto).
5. Yves Klein, "Manifeste de l'hôtel Chelsea, New York, 1961", in *Le Dépassement de la problématique de l'art*, 310.
6. Klein, *Journal du voyage en Italie*, September 1948, sheet 6 (verso).
7. Ibid.
8. Pierre Restany, "La Minute de vérité", invitation card to the exhibition *Yves, propositions monochromes*, Colette Allendy Gallery, Paris, February–March 1956.

this karst cave so distinctive, as well as the silvery sheen conferred on any object immersed in its waters. What was the origin of this matchless play of colours? "There's no point asking", Klein wrote to his parents, "just contemplate".[7] One could almost see this experience as a harbinger of his IKB pigment, which the artist associated with the calm of the deep, and whose intensity, vivid and captivating, is offered to the viewer for pure, immersive contemplation. Later, Klein would evoke another Italian source for the IKB monochromes: Giotto's frescoes, which he discovered in Assisi in April 1958. From Umbria, he wrote to his gallerist Iris Clert, "Dear Iris, there are monochrome paintings in the Basilica of Saint Francis of Assisi that are entirely Blue! It's incredible to realise the stupidity of art historians who have never noticed this before … That is what I call a Precursor! Long live Giotto!" (p. 91).

On his way back to Nice, Klein made the de rigueur stop in Venice, and we find him posing on Piazza San Marco, delighted by the discovery of new artistic wonders, both pictorial and architectural. Given the opportunity to see more than the city's ancient artistic treasures, he would have discovered an effervescent art scene at the Biennale. Finally reopened after six years of closure during the war, and after twenty years of autarky, the Venice Biennale gave pride of place to foreign art with the opening of new international pavilions featuring historic exhibitions (from the Impressionists to Turner, from Schiele to Kokoschka). While the battle between the proponents of abstraction and figuration dominated the debate, the 1948 edition also brought new ideas for the younger generation of Italian artists: Peggy Guggenheim's collection, on show in the Greek pavilion, included what was the first ever exhibition of Surrealist and Dada works in Italy, as well as six paintings by Jackson Pollock, while Lucio Fontana exhibited a ceramic *Scultura spaziale* [Spatial Sculpture] in the Italian pavilion. Like an agglomerate of primordial matter forming a circle around an empty central space, this work seems to evoke an atomic imagination that the then-recent tragedies of Hiroshima and Nagasaki make particularly present and concrete. It was directly in the wake of these experiments that Gianni Bertini exhibited his first works made using the dripping technique in Florence, and that Enrico Baj and Sergio Dangelo launched the Arte Nucleare movement shortly afterwards in 1951 in Milan.

Klein's next trip to Italy with his aunt Rose was coincidentally in 1951 but far from focused on this artistic scene. Together they visited Venice, Lake Garda, and Verona. The local contemporary art was however still not of interest to him. Even when he moved to Paris in October, Klein initially remained aloof from the new art scene shaping up in the capital. His passion for judo continued to take most of his energy. The real turning point came in 1955, the year Klein, who was just beginning his artistic career, met Pierre Restany, who would be the main advocate and promoter of his work in the years to come. Intrigued by the monochrome paintings Klein showed in October at the Club des Solitaires in Paris – the private salon of the Lacoste publishing house – the young critic agreed to organise a solo exhibition for him at the Colette Allendy Gallery. It opened in February 1956 and was accompanied by Restany's famous text "La Minute de verité",[8] in which the critic first used the expression "monochrome propositions", transforming Klein's works forever, from simple paintings into radiant focal points capable of filling the viewer with pure sensitivity. In the summer of 1956, Klein's approach became more radical: in order to intensify the public's contemplative experience of his monochromes, they would all be in the same colour. The natural choice was blue, a colour that "suggests at most the sea and sky, and they, after all, are in actual, visible nature, what is most abstract."[9]

It was through Restany that Klein met Gianni Bertini in 1955. A native of Pisa who had been living in Paris for several years, this independent, experimental artist was a protagonist of the Milanese avant-garde, with which Klein would soon associate. Since 1949, Bertini had been exhibiting at the Salto Gallery in Milan, the headquarters of the Movimento Arte Concreta (MAC) [Concrete Art Movement], of which he was one of the first supporters. This movement, with its innovative, multidisciplinary spirit, quickly became a laboratory for many non-figurative artists. Among its members was the Piedmontese painter Adriano Parisot, whom Klein met in Paris in 1956. Founder of the magazine
I 4 Soli [The 4 Suns], an important forum for contemporary Italian art and criticism, Parisot published one of the first articles on Klein in Italy. Klein stayed with Parisot in Turin in September 1956 and was introduced to the dynamic art scene there. At the same time, Pinot Gallizio, Asger Jorn, and Piero Simondo founded the Mouvement International pour un Bauhaus Imaginiste (MIBI) [International Movement for an Imaginist Bauhaus], while Michel Tapié set up in 1960 the International Center of Aesthetic Research (ICAR), the venue for a number of international events never before seen in Europe – including the first exhibition of the Japanese Gutai group. The Italian painter and playwright Beniamino Joppolo was also part of this group of "Italians in Paris" that Klein began to frequent. An intellectual of Sicilian origin, an anti-fascist and army deserter, Joppolo wrote for Italian daily newspapers and wrote plays, including *I Carabinieri*, later adapted for the cinema by Jean-Luc Godard. In Paris, Joppolo attended the "Lundis de Marie Raymond" – meetings that Klein's mother organised every Monday with the artists and critics in her circle. It was certainly at one of these get-togethers that Klein first heard about Spatialism, a movement founded in Milan in 1947 by Lucio Fontana, whose first manifesto was signed by Joppolo. The writer's philosophical take on Spatialism, advocating a positive vision of a visionary, future-oriented creativity, as well as the movement's ambition to go beyond traditional artistic media, was bound to captivate Klein, then a young, self-taught artist. Convinced that "artists anticipate scientific actions [and that] scientific actions always provoke artistic actions",[10] the Spatialists argued for a transdisciplinary mode of creativity resolutely adapted to modern times.
All these new friendships brought Klein closer to a Franco-Italian artistic network in which Restany was a leading figure. The young critic, who spoke fluent Italian, was strongly engaged with the particularly dynamic Milanese scene where private galleries were backing the initiatives of the groups of artists who had been highly active since the end of the war. As in Turin, the art market was also encouraged by the involvement of new patrons from the world of business and industry. The Torre Breda (also known as the "Milan skyscraper"), a masterpiece of modern engineering in reinforced concrete, shown on a postcard Klein sent to Restany (p. 66), was emblematic of the Lombard city's powerful economic recovery, which would have a profound impact on the contemporary art market. It was against this promising backdrop that Restany began thinking, as early as 1956, of holding a solo exhibition of Klein's work in Milan – an idea that came to fruition when, thanks to Joppolo, he met Guido Le Noci.

Guido Le Noci, a native of Puglia who had already directed the pioneering Borromini Gallery in Como (opened in 1943, it was immediately closed by the police for exhibiting Jewish artists), decided to resume his activity as a gallerist after the end of the war and opened a new space in Milan in December 1954: the Apollinaire Gallery. By entrusting part of the programming to Restany, Le Noci hoped to make his gallery the benchmark for the European non-figurative avant-garde and to be the first in Italy to exhibit the new generation of international artists. United by a deep friendship and intellectual complicity, Le Noci and Restany were constantly working together. In 1954, Restany became a member of the committee for the Lissone Prize, of which the gallerist was then both secretary and a jury member. Set up on the initiative of Lissonese artists in the eponymous small town north of Milan in an effort to broaden local artistic debate, the prize quickly grew to become an event of international scope, thanks to the support of local entrepreneurs and the participation of international critics and art-world figures invited by Guido Le Noci. Klein himself took part in the Lissone Prize on two occasions, in 1959 and 1961.

Encouraging these international synergies, for his new gallery, Le Noci sought out "young painters freed from any codified cultural influence, young people who would usher in a new era."[11] Restany immediately grabbed the opportunity to promote in this pioneering gallery an artist whose unclassifiable works and radical outlook ("For colour! Against line and drawing!"[12]) were already proving disconcerting. By presenting "Yves the Monochrome" in Italy for the first time, Restany hoped to provide Le Noci with the "sensational exhibition"[13] that the gallerist had been clamouring for.

On 28 December 1956, Klein boarded an overnight train with his then partner, the architect Bernadette Allain, Pierre Restany and his wife Aline Dallier, and their artist friends Gianni Bertini, Lutka Pink, and Claude Bellegarde. They took with them trunks full of monochromes, now all strictly blue. Klein was impatient to test the reaction of the Milanese public, which, according to Le Noci, had a huge appetite for the most nonconformist innovations. At the opening, a crowd of French and Italian friends, as well as numerous artists and art lovers from Milan, squeezed into the fifty square metres of the Apollinaire Gallery. Its large glass door opened onto the famous Via Brera, a stone's throw from the academy of the same name that had made this district the heart of Milan's artistic and bohemian life. Since the beginning of the twentieth century, the street's cafés and bistros had been venues for artistic and literary gatherings, such as the famous Bar Jamaica, just a few steps from the gallery, which since 1911 had been an obligatory port of call for many of the artists, writers,

---

9. Yves Klein, "L'évolution de l'art vers l'immatériel. Conférence à la Sorbonne", in *Le Dépassement de la problématique de l'art*, 138. Translated for the catalogue of Klein's exhibition at Gimpel Fils, London, in 1973, reprinted in *Art in Theory, 1900–1990*, ed. Charles Harrison and Paul Wood (Oxford: Blackwell, 1992), 805.
10. *Primo Manifesto dello Spazialismo* [First Manifesto of Spatialism], Milan, May 1947.
11. Laura Calvi, "'Noi che abbiamo le antenne che captano nuovi spazi spirituali.' Yves Klein, Guido Le Noci e Pierre Restany", in *Klein Fontana. Milano Parigi, 1957–1962*, exh. cat., ed. Silvia Bignami and Giorgio Zanchetti (Milan: Electa), 187. Published in conjunction with the exhibition of the same title, organised and held at Museo del Novecento, Milan, 17 October 2014–15 March 2015.
12. This was the motto Klein chose when he was knighted in the Order of the Archers of Saint Sebastian in March 1956.
13. Letter from Guido Le Noci to Pierre Restany, 31 October 1956 (p. 45).

and intellectuals who had forged Milan's cultural history, from Lucio Fontana and Piero Manzoni to Giuseppe Ungaretti and Nanni Balestrini.

The interior of the gallery was designed by the Brutalist architect Vittoriano Viganò, who also designed other emblematic spaces in the city, such as the Salto bookshop and del Naviglio and San Fedele galleries. Far from the conventional tastes of the bourgeois elite of the time, the architect's aesthetic choices – lots of raw concrete and the utmost simplification of volumes and resources – were totally recognisable. The hanging system designed for the gallery presented the works on aluminium rods at a distance from the concrete wall, and at freely adjustable heights. This unusual system – it was later used at the Schmela Gallery in Düsseldorf in June 1957 – was particularly well suited to Klein's monochromes, which were designed to be presented "off the picture rail", their rounded corners and lack of frames reminding the public that these were not ordinary paintings but "phenomena of pure contemplation".[14] Viewers' contemplative experience was also enhanced by the fact that the eleven monochromes were not only all the same colour, but also the same format (78 × 56 cm). Definitively free of any of the "anecdotal" distractions Klein so feared, his "monochrome propositions" invited visitors to experience that "minute of truth" that Restany emphasised in the exhibition presentation text, translated into Italian by Joppolo.[15] Of course, this idea of a contemplative state did not negate the work's market value. On the contrary, it played a role that was all the more important in that, as the artist pointed out, "the most sensational observation is that of the buyers".[16] Despite the apparent equivalence between the monochromes, each was offered for sale at a different price. In this way, Klein wanted to demonstrate that the quality of "pure pictorial sensibility" that visitors were invited to imbibe was specific to each monochrome. This was a far-sighted intuition that could not have gone unnoticed, especially in the eyes of Lucio Fontana, a dominant figure of the Milanese art scene at the time. Fontana had already put traditional notions of painting and sculpture to the test with his *Concetti spaziali* [Spatial Concepts]. He would soon annihilate the two-dimensionality and finiteness of the painting with his *Buchi* [Holes] and *Tagli* [Cuts] series in which, by physically allowing space to "pierce" the work through incisions in the canvas, he would in turn introduce an "other" and potentially, as with Klein, "infinite" dimension.[17] Fontana, a pioneering artist and an attentive and curious observer of the younger generation, was the first enthusiastic buyer of one of the eleven blue monochromes. From this point on, the two artists forged a bond of friendship and intellectual affinity that was marked by regular meetings in Milan

14. Restany, "La Minute de vérité".

15. Pierre Restany, "L'Epoca blu o il secondo minuto di verità", invitation card for the exhibition *Yves Klein. Proposte monocrome, epoca Blu*, Apollinaire Gallery, Milan, January 1957 (p. 49).

16. Yves Klein, "L'aventure monochrome: l'épopée monochrome", in *Le Dépassement de la problématique de l'art*, 233.

17. Carla Lonzi, *Autoritratto* (Bari: De Donato, 1969), 169.

18. Iris Clert, *Iris-Time. L'artventure* (Paris: Denoël, 2003), 145.

19. Restany, "Milan 2 January 1957".

20. "Che coraggio blu!", *Corriere Lombardo*, January 1957, article reproduced in one of Yves Klein's press book (p. 58).

21. Dino Buzzati, "Une fenomeno alla Galleria Apollinaire", *Corriere d'Informazione*, January 1957 (p. 57).

22. Restany, "Milan 2 January 1957".

23. Quoted in Silvia Bignami and Giorgio Zanchetti, "Universi paralleli. Yves Klein e Lucio Fontana", in *Klein Fontana*, 23.

24. Klein, "L'évolution de l'art vers l'immatériel", 134.

25. Restany, "Milan 2 January 1957".

(where they exhibited at the Apollinaire Gallery) and Paris (where they were "stable mates" at the Iris Clert Gallery[18]), as well as by further acquisitions of Klein's works by the Italian Argentinian artist. After the IKB monochrome of 1957, Fontana acquired a *Sculpture éponge bleue* [Blue Sponge Sculpture], a *Relief éponge bleu* [Blue Sponge Relief], an *Anthropométrie* [Anthropometry], a *Monogold*, a *Peinture de feu* [Fire Painting], and a print of *Le Saut dans le vide* [Leap into the Void] – thereby becoming one of Klein's biggest collectors in Italy.

Although the exhibition's legacy was mixed, Restany was pleased with this "modest"[19] success to which he had contributed significantly. It was he who encouraged Italo Magliano, one of the biggest collectors of the time, to buy one of the monochromes exhibited by Le Noci. Another entered the collection of entrepreneur Peppino Palazzoli, who founded the Blu Gallery just three months later, its blue square logo ironically reminiscent of IKB. Palazzoli, however, did not underestimate the risk involved in making what might be considered a venturesome purchase from an eccentric emerging artist. In the summer of 1959, he became the first purchaser of a *Zone de sensibilité picturale immatérielle* [Zone of Immaterial Pictorial Sensibility], and for such an unusual purchase – the work was invisible and intangible, in short, immaterial – he required a receipt from Klein and his gallerist Iris Clert. The receipt, which resembled a cheque, was finalised a few months later. He was followed by the collector Paride Accetti and by the writer Dino Buzzati, who also acquired a *Zone of Immaterial Pictorial Sensibility*. Buzzati recounted the "ceremony" in a column published in *Corriere della Sera* in February 1962 (p. 194).

Other Milanese collectors, even some of the most discerning at the time, were not as adventurous. Antonio Boschi and Marieda Di Stefano, Marie Raymond's collectors, were not convinced by her son's "monochrome propositions", while Giuseppe Panza di Biumo, who had just begun his prestigious collection of contemporary art, parted with the red monochrome (exhibited in Le Noci's office) he had bought on the evening of the opening (he returned it to the gallerist a few days later).

It is true that to play along with such a radical aesthetic proposition was, at the time, a matter of "courage", as suggested by the title of one of the reviews published the day after the opening, recounting the reaction of visitors to the exhibition who "come in, look around, and are stunned. Then they leave, annoyed, or burst out laughing."[20] Most of the commentators in the press referred to the eccentricity of the character and the surprise of the public, as in the review for the *Corriere d'Informazione*, which described the exhibition as "disconcerting", "out of the ordinary", and "paradoxical", the public as "stunned", and the artist as definitely "extraordinary".[21] This article, which contributed enormously to the show's success (according to Restany, it even ensured a "record attendance"[22]), was signed by Dino Buzzati. This was fortuitous, and certainly fortunate, given that the writer was taking the place, exceptionally on this occasion, of Mario Lepore. Lepore had described Klein as "an abstract artist who is sometimes rather decorative",[23] thereby demonstrating a profound misunderstanding of the artist's intentions, which were to avoid any risk of decorative polychromy by devoting himself to a single colour.[24] This text, which Restany described as the "first objective assessment to appear in the mainstream press",[25] marked the beginning of a lasting relationship between Klein and the Italian writer, who wrote four articles about him between 1957 and 1962.

Three of these, published during the artist's lifetime, were carefully pasted into Klein's press books: twelve albums in which he collected press articles, invitation cards, catalogue pages, and photographs accompanied by captions or handwritten comments. In a way, these press books reflect his mental universe and are an ideal tool for constructing the narrative that accompanies all his work. Klein, for example, included Restany's reply to Marco Valsecchi, the Italian critic who, writing in the daily *Il Giorno*, inveighed against the association made between IKB and the blue skies painted by Giotto in his frescoes in Assisi.[26] No doubt amused by the controversy stirred by his work, Klein was happy to take up this felicitous association. After visiting the Basilica of Saint Francis of Assisi in April 1958, he openly referred to the Tuscan painter as the "real precursor of [his] monochromy".[27] This connection, while confirming the "classical" origin of his inspiration, above all enabled him to reaffirm his distance from Russian Suprematism and Unism – especially Malevich's rationalist programme – which had already resorted to monochromy, albeit in a very different context.[28]

In the end, even the most vehement attacks on Klein's work ended up generating a great deal of interest in the exhibition, and the artist, as usual, knew how to get round an obstacle and turn it into proof of his success: "The rather passionate controversies raised by this exhibition", he wrote, "proved to me the value of the phenomenon and the real depth of the upheaval it caused in people."[29] It is undoubtedly not always relevant to distinguish between legend and reality in Klein's work, insofar as the narrative he constructed was at one with his work and his own mythology. For example, in the press book dedicated to the exhibition at the Apollinaire Gallery, there is also an advertisement for Domenico Modugno's famous song "Volare (Nel blu, dipinto di blu)", which was presented at the San Remo Festival in February 1958 and immediately became an international hit. Klein was suggesting that the IKB monochromes exhibited in Milan a few months earlier had inspired Modugno – an idea that he would take up explicitly in his text "L'aventure monochrome"[30] and that would be reiterated by Pierre Restany and then by Dino Buzzati.[31] It doesn't matter that Modugno later testified that the real source of inspiration for the song was a painting by Marc Chagall. The legend had been created, more vivid and inspiring than any supposedly objective truth.

The January 1957 exhibition gave impetus to a new synergy between the Parisian and Milanese scenes, punctuated by a series of exhibitions in which Klein took part, both in Milan and in Paris: in May 1957, the IKB monochrome acquired by Fontana at the Apollinaire Gallery was part of the exhibition of *18 Works from the Private Collection of Lucio Fontana – 18 Works from the Private Collection of Bruno Munari* at the Blu Gallery in Milan. Klein was thus implicitly included in the lineage of these two essential masters of twentieth-century Italian art, alongside Roberto Crippa, Gianni Dova, Enzo Mari, Piero Dorazio, Enrico Baj, and Sergio Dangelo. The last two exhibited again with Klein, Parisot, and Bertini in June, at the revealingly titled *Ouvertures sur le futur* [Openings on the Future] exhibition organised by Restany at the H. Kamer Gallery in Paris.

Before the end of 1957, it was in Milan that Klein shared the walls of the San Fedele Gallery with these same artists, for the *Arte Nucleare* exhibition. The "nuclear" iconography, inspired by the scientific research of the time, sometimes evoking spiral movements (Enrico Baj), sometimes corpuscles of matter and micro-organic forms (Sergio Dangelo and Gianni Colombo), openly refers to the atomic and nuclear imaginary that haunted people's minds. However, the artists broke with the frightening and destructive connotations of these images and saw them as an eminently poetic revolutionary opportunity. Just as they advocated "bombarding reality with the violence of [their] investigation, in the same way that we are beginning to bombard physical nuclei in atomic experiments",[32] Klein, for his part, invited viewers to become aware that "we are living in the atomic age, where everything material and physical can disappear overnight, to be replaced by all the most abstract things we can imagine",[33] and that "it will not be with rockets, sputniks, or spaceships that Man will conquer space; but by inhabiting it with sensibility."[34] Already linked with the MIBI and with the CoBrA group, the Surrealists gathered around the Belgian Édouard Jaguer, the group of nuclear artists, founded in 1951 by Enrico Baj and Sergio Dangelo, had proved their ability to forge fruitful international relationships. By admitting Klein to the ranks of the nuclear movement, Baj was merely confirming that the same state of mind was shared across borders.

The *Arte Nucleare* exhibition in 1957 represented the first moment of coming together for a whole new generation of artists. Another participant in the exhibition was Piero Manzoni, with whom Klein had signed the manifesto "Contro lo stile" (The End of Style) just a month earlier (along with Restany, Arman, Baj, Bertini, and Dangelo, among others). "De Stijl is dead and buried",[35] declared the signatories, reiterating their rejection of the most rationalist approaches of the avant-garde in favour of an eminently more sensitive, even spiritual, form of creative inspiration. Direct descendants of the nuclear artists and Lucio Fontana, they declared an end to all "stylistic conventions", including the gestural painting that had marked the earlier work of several of them, and henceforth saw the work of art as a pure "modifying presence".[36] The quintessence of this concept, Klein's monochrome proposals were explicitly designated as the last possible alternative to the tabula rasa.

Following on from these artistic exchanges and collaborations, Klein was invited to take part in the first issue of the magazine *Azimuth,* founded by Piero Manzoni and Enrico Castellani in 1959, printed by Antonio Maschera, and designed by Cecco Re. It published texts by intellectuals and critics such as Gillo Dorfles, Guido Ballo, Vincenzo Agnetti, and Bruno Alfieri, and poets such as Edoardo Sanguineti, Nanni Balestrini, and Elio Pagliarani. Basing itself on the "Contro lo stile" manifesto, *Azimuth* embodied the new avant-garde in Milan. In the first issue, published in September 1959 and featuring an entire page coloured IKB, the works of over forty artists were

26. Restany, "L'Epoca blu".
27. Klein, "L'aventure monochrome", 258.
28. Klein, "L'aventure monochrome", 259.
29. Klein, "L'aventure monochrome", 232.
30. Ibid.
31. Dino Buzzati, "Sortilegio a Notre-Dame", *Corriere della Sera*, 4 February 1962 (p. 194).
32. "Premier manifeste de la littérature nucléaire", Milan, 3 February 1952 (original in French).
33. Yves Klein, "Ma position dans le combat entre la ligne et la couleur", in *Le Dépassement de la problématique de l'art*, 51.
34. Klein, "L'évolution de l'art vers l'immatériel", 123.
35. "Contro lo stile. Manifesto Nucleare", Milan, September 1957.
36. Ibid.

reproduced, all of whom shared a reference to Fontana – a common inspiration highlighted by the prominence given to Fontana throughout the issue. It was in the second and final issue of the magazine that this new trend took shape. The second issue of *Azimuth* served as a catalogue for the exhibition *La nuova concezione artistica* [The New Artistic Conception], organised by the Azimut Gallery – almost homonymous except for an *h* – founded by Manzoni and Castellani in a basement in Via Clerici 12 in Milan. While the eight artists on show (Klein, Manzoni, Castellani, as well as the Germans Heinz Mack, Otto Piene, Kilian Breier, and Oskar Holweck, and the Brazilian Almir Mavignier) all sought total creative freedom and shared the same desire for radical simplification, for several of them, the monochrome became the main means of going beyond the materiality of the work.

Without in any way downplaying the specificity of each artist, it has to be admitted that there was a widespread trend that, as Guido Ballo wrote in the first issue of *Azimuth*, was at work "within the international language" and was pushing the limits of modern art "towards a new dimension", that is, "beyond painting".[37] Like the journal of the ZERO Group and the Schmela Gallery in Düsseldorf, *Azimuth* became a meeting place for a network of German, French, Italian, and Dutch artists, one that was even more extensive because it gathered the kinetic (or "programmata") art groups Gruppo T and Gruppo N, and the future Groupe de Recherche d'Art Visuel (GRAV) [Research Group for Visual Art], whose members came together for the first time in the *Motus* exhibition at the Azimut Gallery in April 1960.

In September 1961, all these trends came together again at the twelfth Lissone Prize. Alongside Manzoni, Castellani, and members of Gruppo T and Gruppo N, Roman artists Francesco Lo Savio, Franco Angeli, Tano Festa, Mario Schifano, and even some future members of Arte Povera group, such as Jannis Kounellis and a young Giulio Paolini, were exhibiting works that were already openly conceptual. On this occasion, Klein exhibited a *Fire Painting*, the fruit of his barely begun research into the elements, which anticipated a further affinity with the Italian art scene. The elements such as fire, rain, and vegetation in his *Fire Paintings* and *Cosmogonies* – works exhibited at the La Salita Gallery in Rome in June 1961 – echoed Alberto Burri's research in his *Combustioni* [Combustions] and Piero Manzoni's *Corpi d'aria* [Bodies of Air] and *Fiato d'artista* [Artist's Breaths].

These experiments could have gone even further if Klein's project for the 1960 Milan Triennale had been accepted. Once again, it was Fontana who invited him to take part in this multidisciplinary event, which set out to bring together artists from the worlds of architecture, design, and the applied arts. On this occasion, Klein conceived a new *Architecture de l'air* [Air Architecture] project: a site-specific installation, conceived for the staircase of the Triennale palace, made entirely of air, water, and fire. But this air-architecture project was not only too costly, it also went beyond the very notion of architecture and transposed it into an utopian universe, a term that could not really capture the poetic and visionary scope of the artist, who, at the same time, was also designing his *Rocket pneumatique* [Pneumatic Rocket], a rocket with no engine that was propelled by sucking in and breathing out air. In October 1961, Klein conceived another visionary project to be carried out in Italy. He envisaged jets of fire spouting from the famous fountains in the garden of the Villa d'Este in Tivoli. Despite a letter to the town's mayor from Jean Larcade, director of the Rive Droite Gallery (p. 166), the project went nowhere.

Meanwhile, the alliance between Le Noci and Restany remained strong. When the critic launched the Nouveau Réalisme movement, it was again the Apollinaire Gallery that had the exclusive rights to the group's first exhibition in May 1960. For the occasion, Restany published his manifesto, written at the Hotel Manzoni in Milan, where he stayed during his sojourns in the Lombard capital (the official act of constitution of the group did not take place until October of the same year, in Klein's flat in Paris). The members of the group were subsequently shown again at the Apollinaire Gallery, and Yves Klein had a new solo exhibition opening there in November 1961. Entitled *Le Nouveau Réalisme de la couleur* [The New Realism of Colour], this exhibition was a veritable retrospective. On show were *Reliefs planétaires* [Planetary Reliefs], *Anthropometries*, *Cosmogonies*, *Fire Paintings*, a *Monogold*, a *Sponge Relief*, and a *Sponge Sculpture*. The opening was attended by the friends and artists who had gathered around *Azimuth* some time earlier: Giovanni Anceschi and Gianni Colombo, founders of Gruppo T, Piero Manzoni, Fausto Melotti, and Emilio Scanavino.

For this retrospective at the Apollinaire Gallery, Klein elected to travel once again to Italy, for what would be his last trip, in the company of Rotraut Uecker, the German artist he had met in the summer of 1957 and who became his wife in January 1962. Before travelling to Milan in November 1961 for the opening of the exhibition, the couple first went to Rome to view a footage on the making of the *Anthropometries*, which was to be included in the film *Mondo Cane*. Made by Italian directors Gualtiero Jacopetti, Paolo Cavara, and Franco Prosperi, this movie consists of a series of short sequences on cultural practices and ancestral rites around the world. Alternating real, truncated, and even faked scenes, with the aim of exploiting the viewer's voyeurism, it can be considered a forerunner of "trash cinema" and the origin of the "mondo" genre. The agreements drawn up with the directors in April 1961 stipulated that the script for the sequence, written by Klein, would be strictly adhered to, and guaranteed the artist a say over the final cut (p. 162). These agreements were far from respected. In the final version of the film, Jacopetti completely disregarded Klein's intentions and replaced his *Symphonie monoton-silence* [Monotone-Silence Symphony] with languorous music, while the voice-over presented the artist as a "Czechoslovak painter" and poured scorn on his work and on contemporary art in general. When the film was previewed at the Cannes Film Festival in May 1962, Klein walked out of the screening room, deeply wounded.

A few months earlier, in January 1961, Klein and Rotraut had travelled to Cascia to pay homage at the monastery of Saint Rita. There, they secretly deposited a surprising ex-voto consisting of a transparent box divided into several compartments. The upper part consisted of three tubs filled with IKB pigment, pink pigment, and gold leaf; the lower part contained three gold ingots – the proceeds of the first four sales of the *Zones of Immaterial Pictorial Sensibility* – resting on blue pigment. In the central part of the box was a handwritten text by Yves Klein on accordion-folded paper, an act of thanksgiving to Saint Rita. Klein thanked her "for all the powerful, decisive,

37. Guido Ballo, "Oltre la pittura", *Azimuth*, no. 1, 1959, n.p.

and marvellous help" she had already given him, and placed himself under her protection so that his art would always be of "great beauty".[38] This very special work remained hidden for over twenty years, only to be rediscovered by chance following an earthquake in 1982.

Little did anyone know that, during one of his previous pilgrimages, Klein had already offered the saint an IKB monochrome as a sign of gratitude for the commission of his monumental works by the opera-theatre in Gelsenkirchen, Germany. On this occasion, Klein had asked his aunt Rose to intercede with Saint Rita, of whom she was a devout follower. This IKB monochrome was used for over twenty-five years in the Christmas crib in the church's oratory, where it served as a sky. This pious use kept it from getting soiled, and it was found in perfect condition in 1984.

Dino Buzzati's last article about Klein, written after the artist's death in June 1962, alludes to many other mysterious actions that he may have performed without leaving the slightest trace. Here was one final way of impressing his viewers, between reality and myth, by the man whom Buzzati defined as "one of the most extravagant and disconcerting artists of this century"[39] and who had, in line with his work, just vanished into thin air.

38. Yves Klein, "Prayer to Saint Rita" (1961), in *Le Dépassement de la problématique de l'art*,
(see translation pp. 223-224 of this book)
39. Dino Buzzati, "Addio al folletto", *Corriere della Sera*, 9 June 1962.

TOUR

1948–1951

GRAND
TOUR

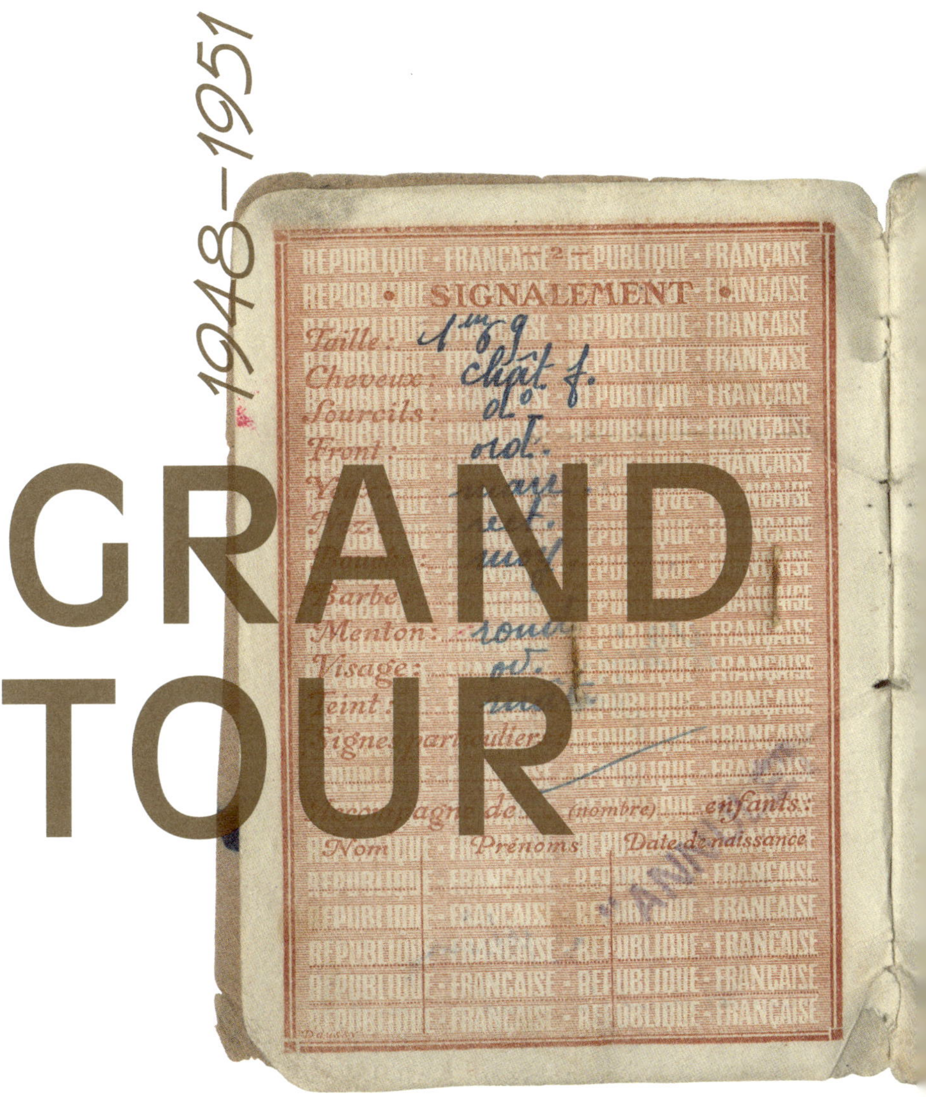

GRAND

Yves Klein's passport,
1948

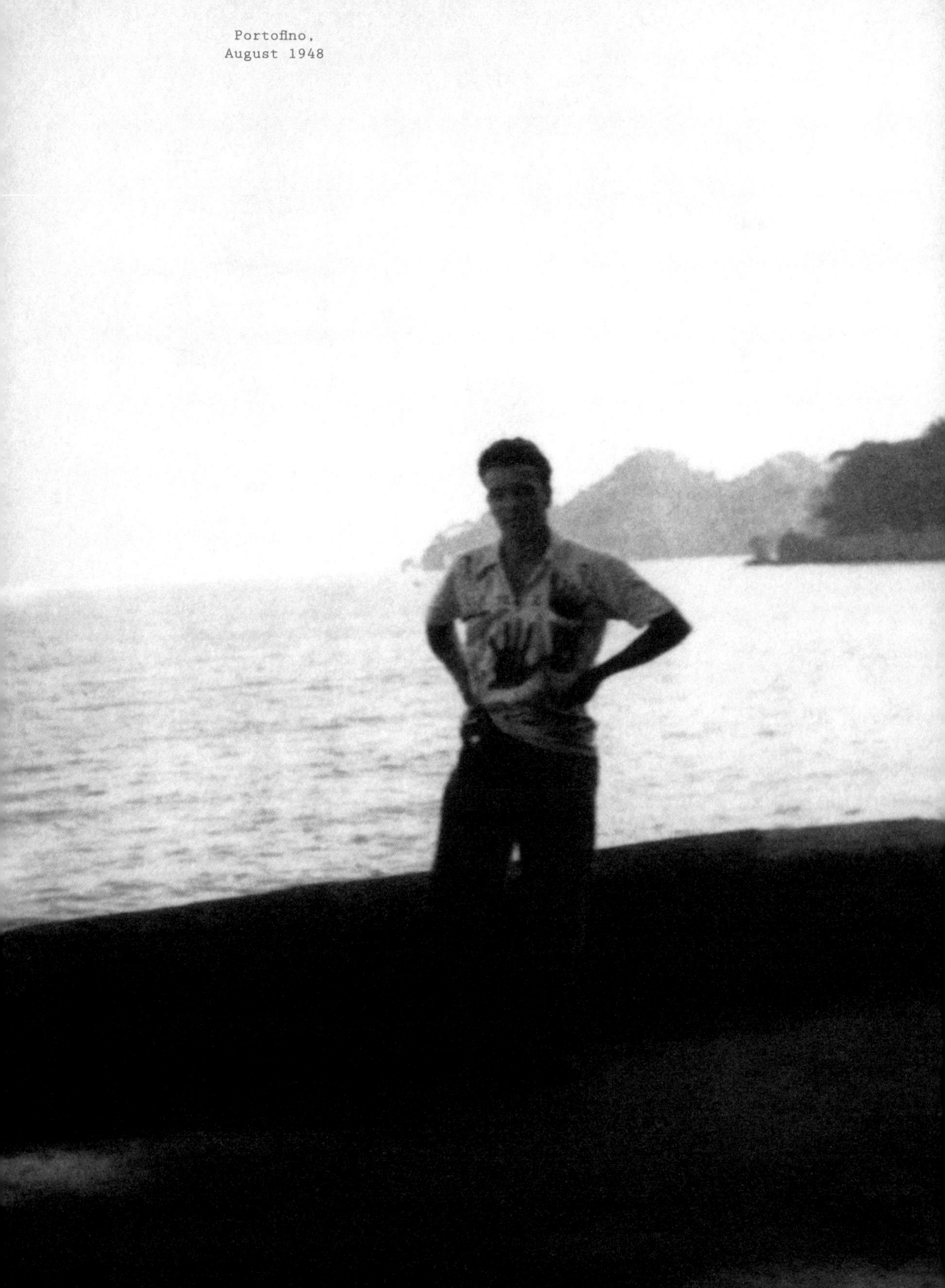
Portofino,
August 1948

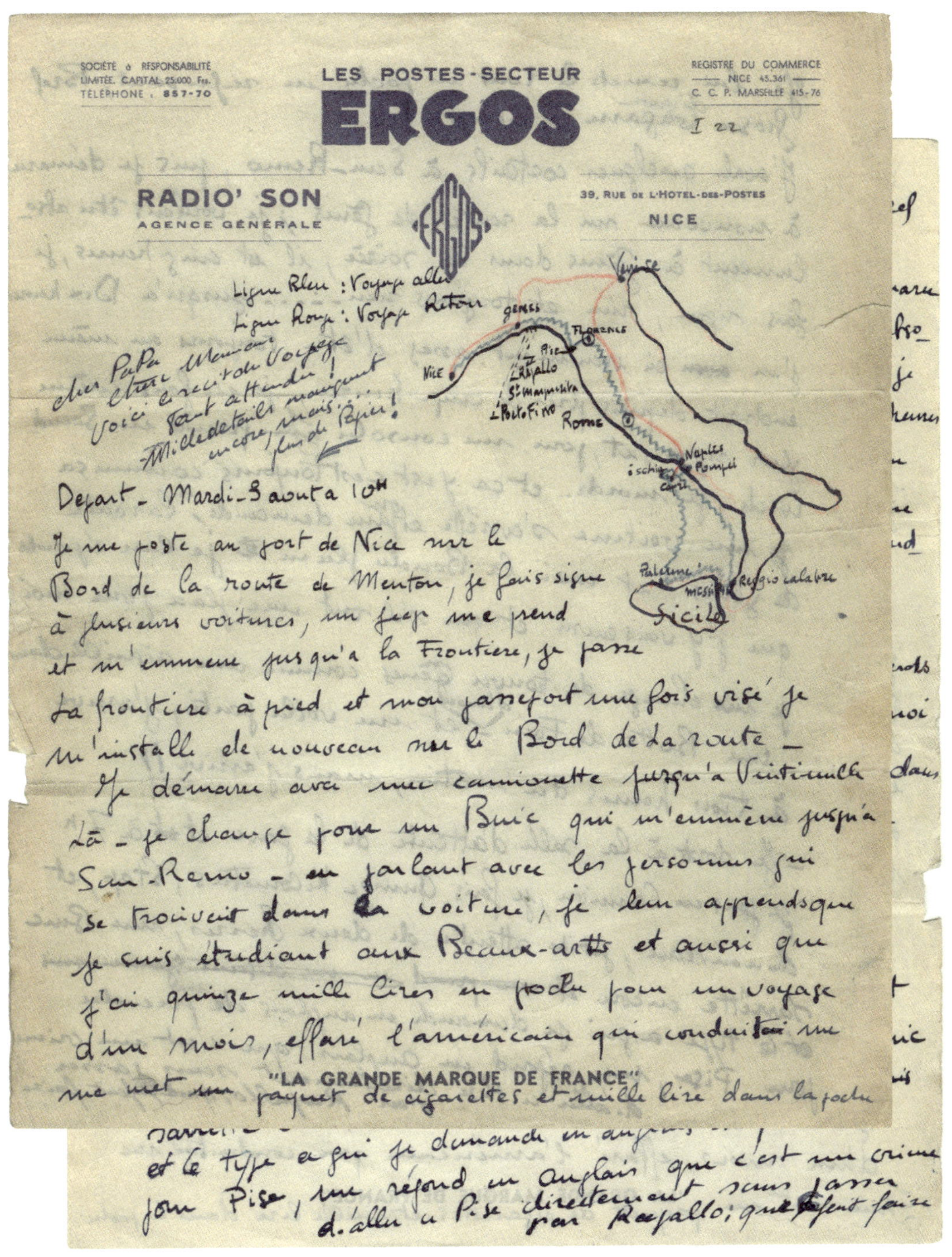

Ligne Bleu : Voyage aller
Ligne Rouge : Voyage Retour

cher Papa
Chère Maman
Voici le récit du Voyage
Il faut attendre
Mille détails manquent
encore, mais ...
fini de Pise!

Départ — Mardi — 3 aout à 10H

Je me poste au port de Nice sur le
Bord de la route de Menton, je fais signe
à plusieurs voitures, un jeep me prend
et m'emmène jusqu'à la Frontière, je passe
la frontière à pied et mon passeport une fois visé je
m'installe de nouveau sur le Bord de la route —
Je démarre avec une camionnette jusqu'à Vintimille
Là — je change pour un Buic qui m'emmène jusqu'à
San-Remo — en parlant avec les personnes qui
se trouvait dans la voiture, je leur apprends que
je suis étudiant aux Beaux-arts et aussi que
j'ai quinze mille Lires en poche pour un voyage
d'un mois, effaré l'américain qui conduisait
me met un paquet de cigarettes et mille lire dans la poche
[...] et le type à qui je demande en anglais ...
pour Pise, me répond en Anglais que c'est un crime
d'aller à Pise directement sans passer
par Rapallo; qu'il faut faire

Journal du voyage en Italie,
sent to the attention of Marie Raymond
and Fred Klein, Yves Klein's parents,
September 1948 (excerpt)
Translation pp. 213-215

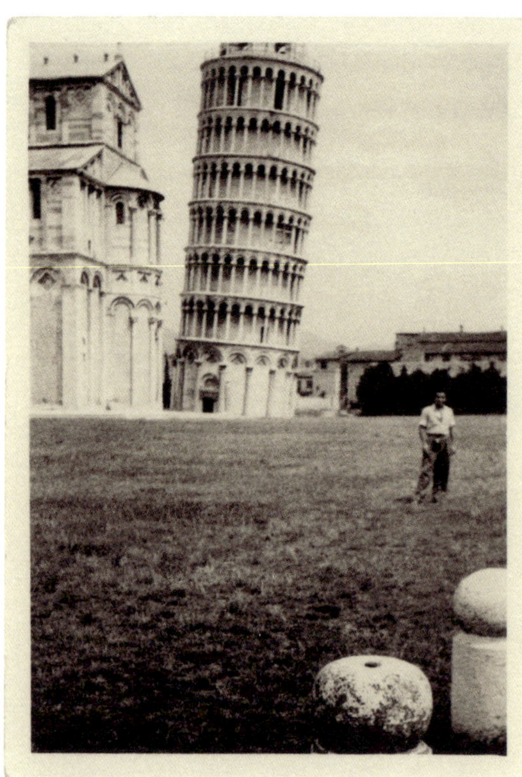

Leaning Tower
of Pisa,
Piazza dei Miracoli,
Pisa

Piazza Santa Croce,
Florence

Yves Klein on the
terrace of a café
in Florence,
August 1948

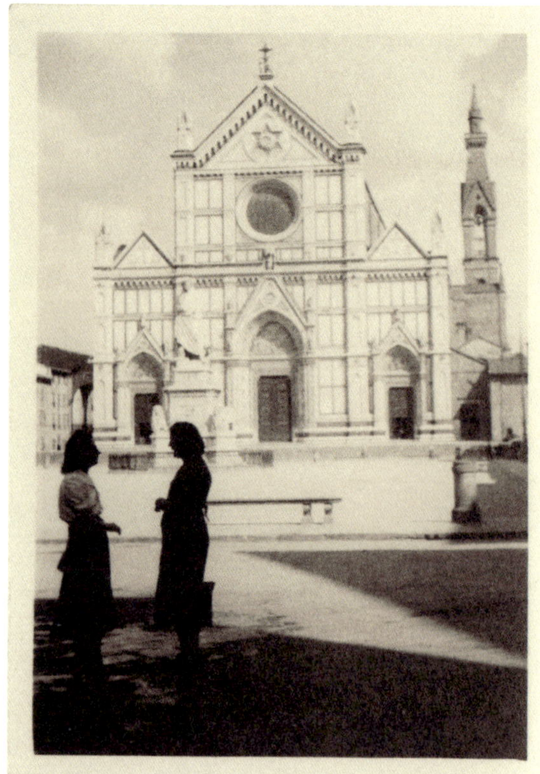

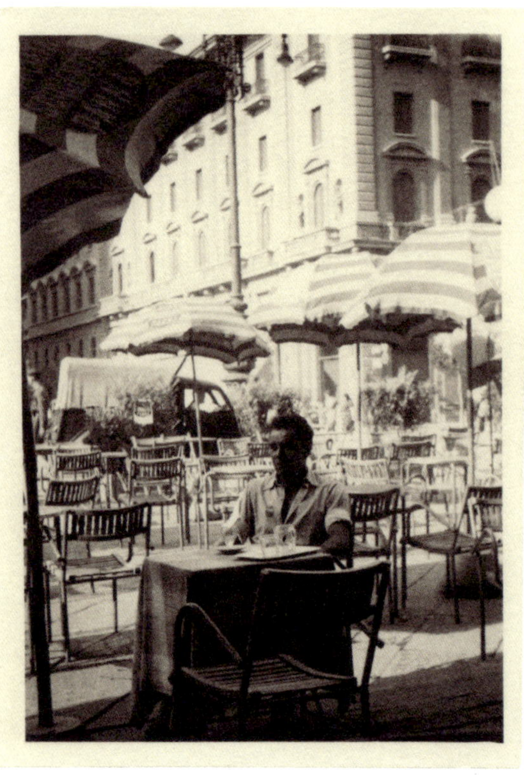

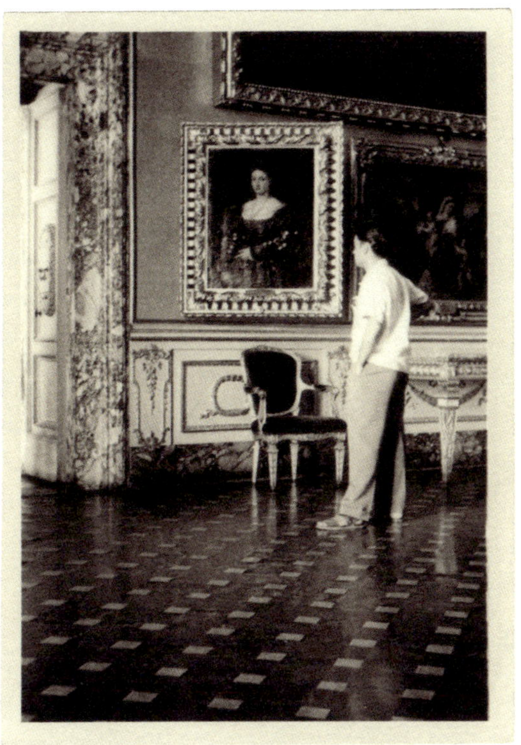

In August 1948, Yves Klein hitchhiked
alone all over Italy. He passed through
Ventimiglia, San Remo, and Genoa,
visited Rapallo, Santa Margherita,
Portofino, Pisa, Florence, Rome, Naples,
Vesuvius, Pompeii, Herculaneum, Amalfi,
Sorrento, and lastly Capri. From there,
he took a boat for Ischia, Reggio Calabria,
Messina, Stromboli, and then back to Capri.
On his route home, he went back through
Naples, Rome, Florence, and Venice,
from which he took the train back
to Nice.

Visit to the
Palazzo Pitti,
Florence. Yves Klein
in front of Titian's
La Bella (1536-1538),
August 1948

Postcard from
Yves Klein, sent from
Rome to his parents,
11 August 1948
Translation p. 215

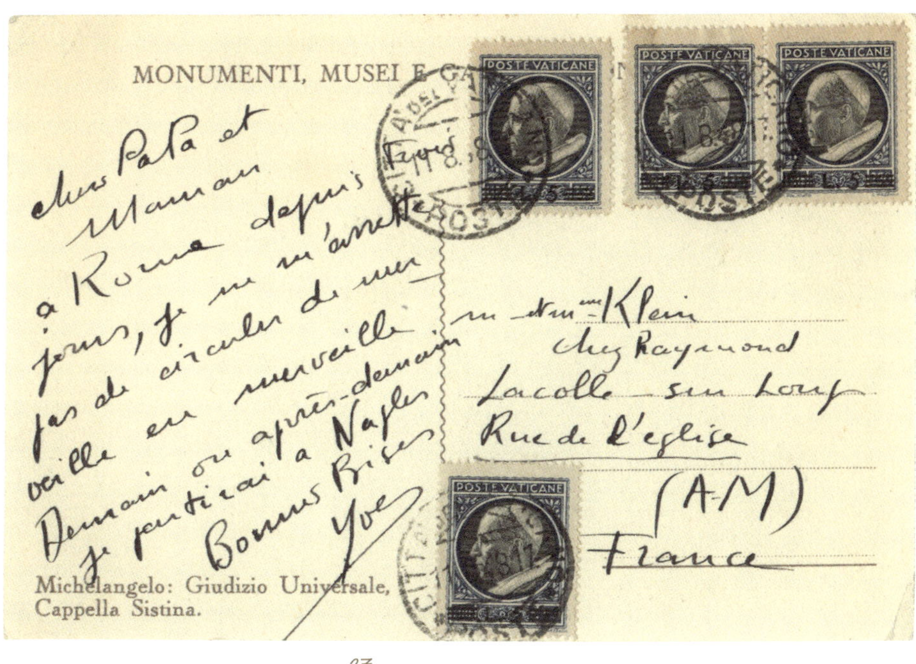

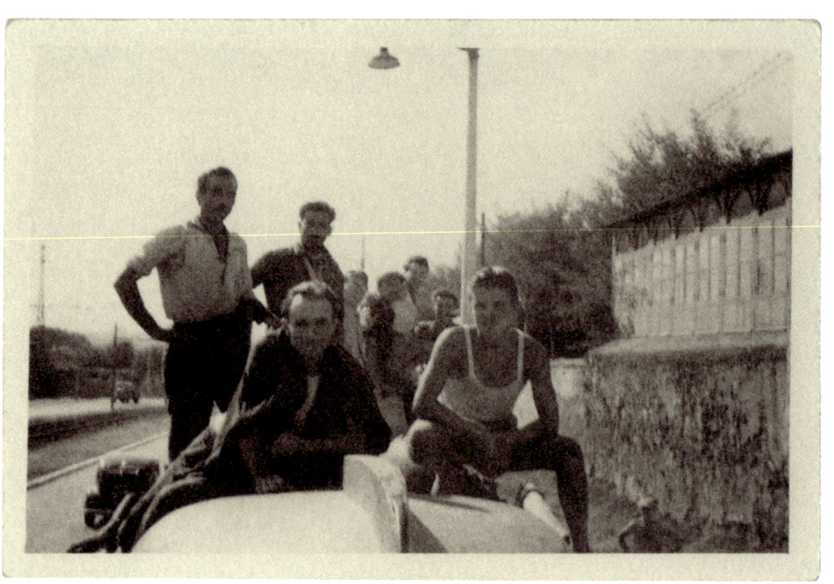

On the road,
in a truck, between
Rome and Naples,
August 1948

Postcard from
Yves Klein, sent from
Pompeii to his parents,
14 August 1948

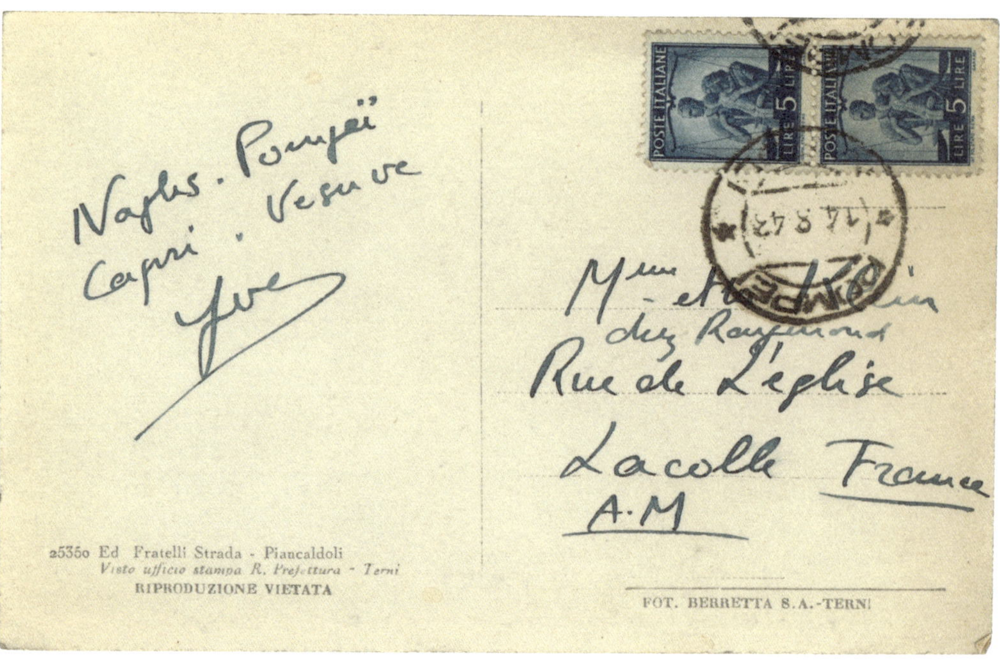

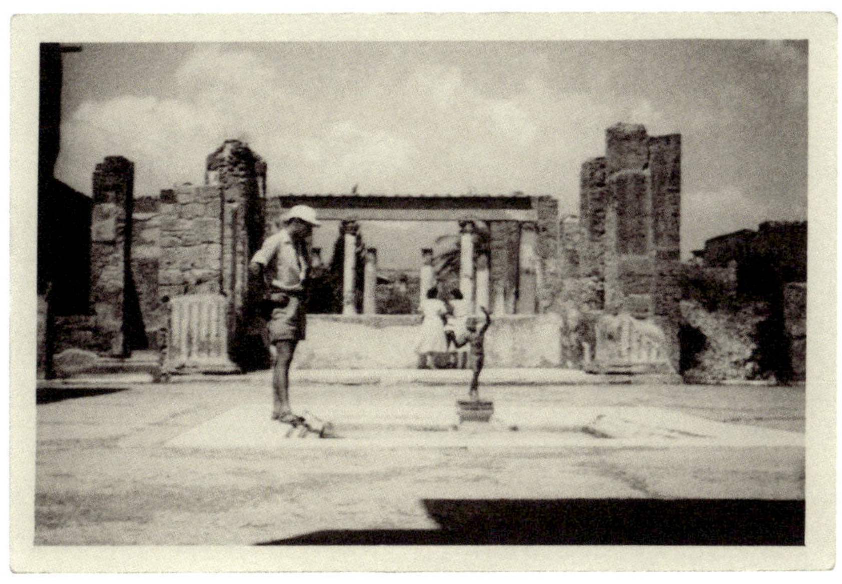

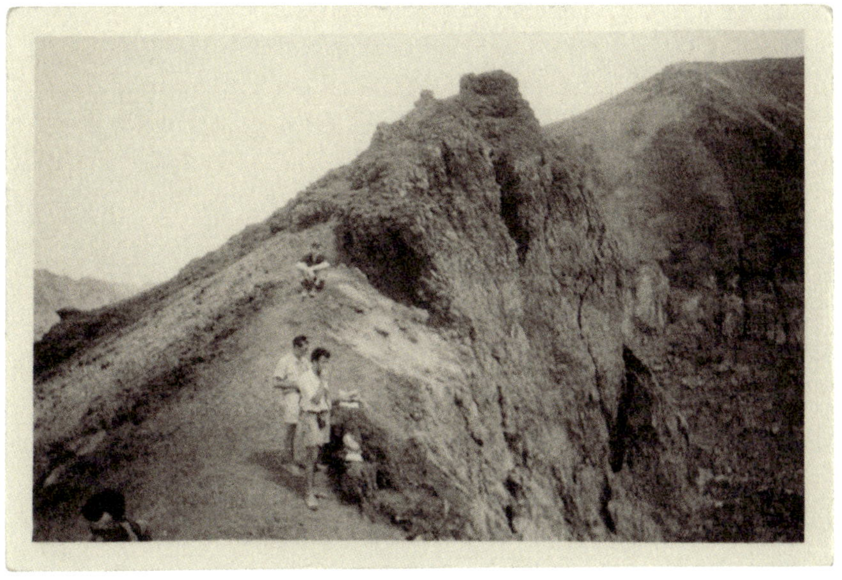

29

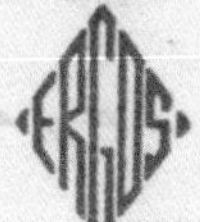

c'est le plus fantastique jeu de couleurs
que je n'ai jamais vu dans toute la nature.
l'impression générale de Capri et d'ailleurs un véritable
éblouissement de couleurs, et, pourtant jamais trop fortes
mais plutôt douces et en toutes toutes agréables —
Capri — Anacapri — grotte Azur — grotte
Merveilleuse etc

a Capri au bout de 7 jours de délices nous rencontrons
par hazard un belge qui a un petit voilier de
huit mètres de long et tout seul s'embête, n'ose pas
affronter la mer, ni faire de grandes randonnées
on le décide et nous partons !!

cette fois c'est un voyage par mer, un jeu plus dur
tout de même en effet, nous sommes toute la journée
cramponnés sur un coté du bateau
pendant que le mat et la voile penche d'un
autre — et ainsi nous voyageons pendant
quatre jours et voyant : Ischia, la cote du golfe

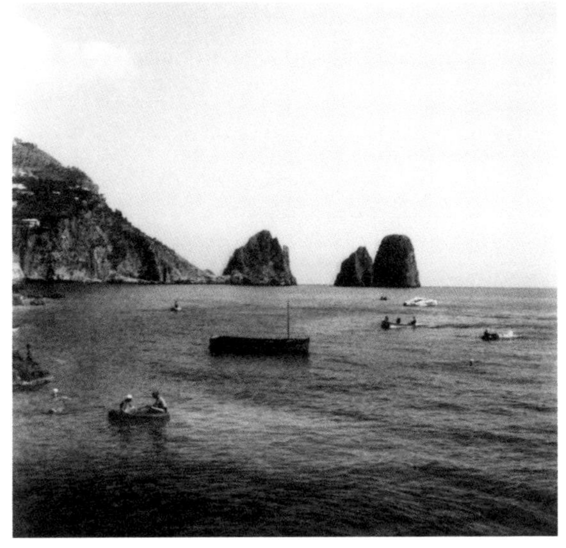

Port of Capri

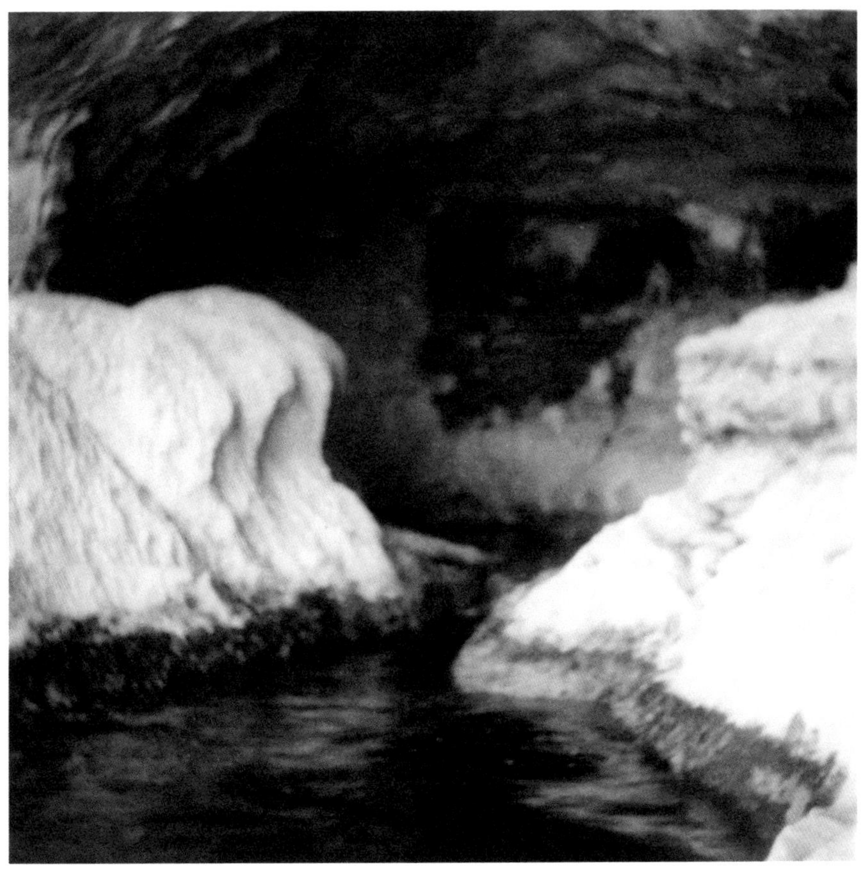

The Blue Grotto
(*grotta azzurra*),
Capri, August 1948

Rose Raymond
on Lake Garda,
September 1951

Yves Klein and his aunt Rose travelled
together in 1951 in Northern Italy.
They visited Lake Garda, Verona, and Venice.
It was Rose who taught Yves Klein
the devotion of Saint Rita, patron saint
of lost causes, a popular cult figure
in Italy and in the southeast of France
who played an important role in his life.

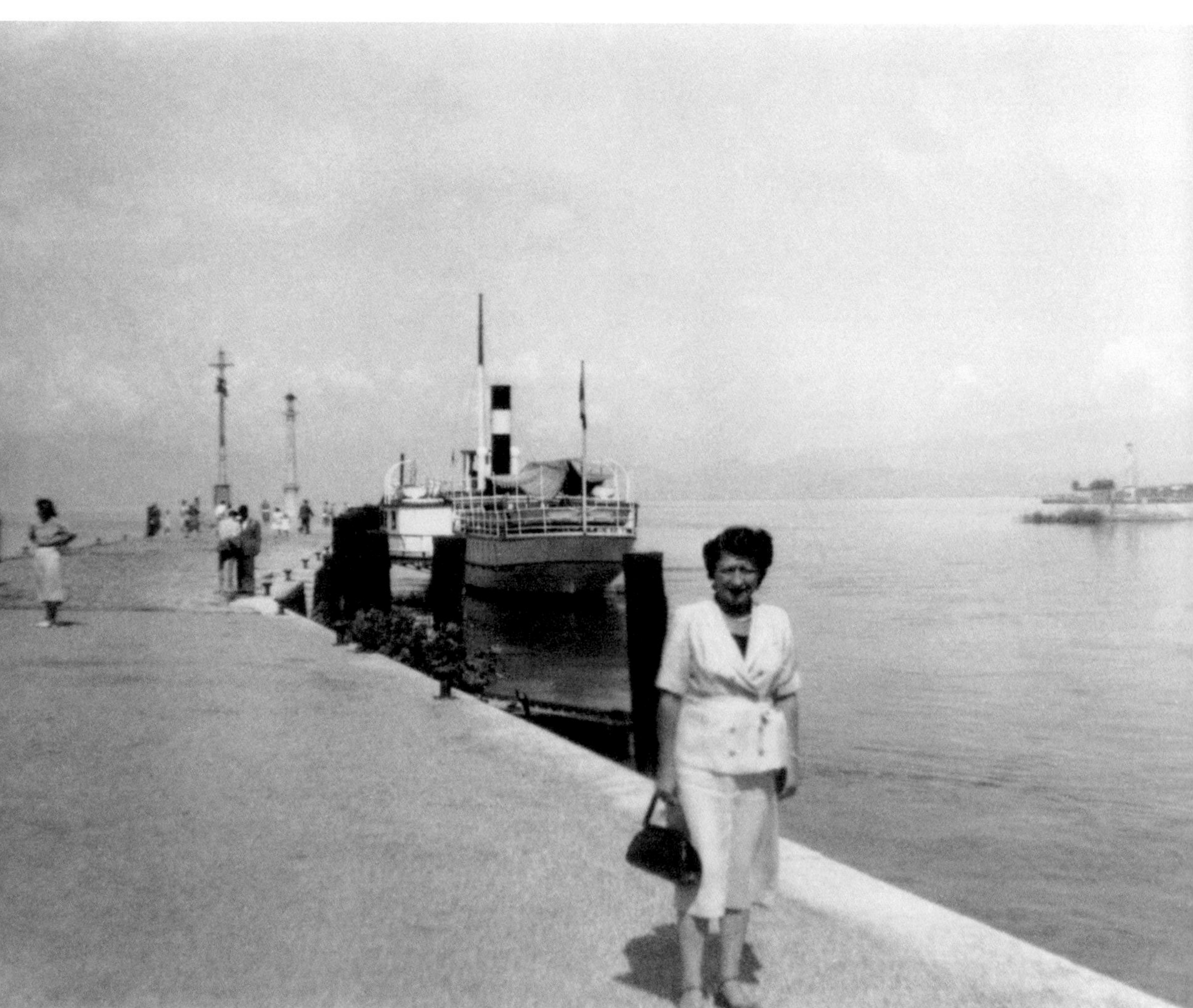

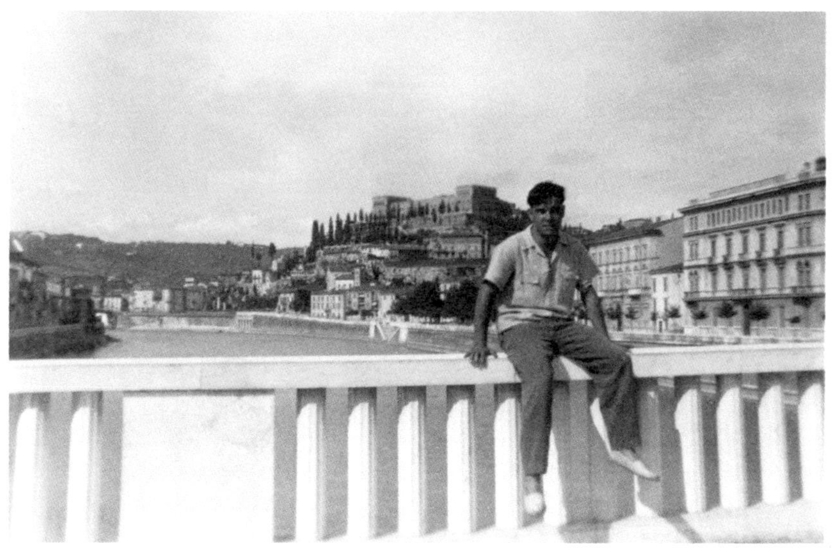

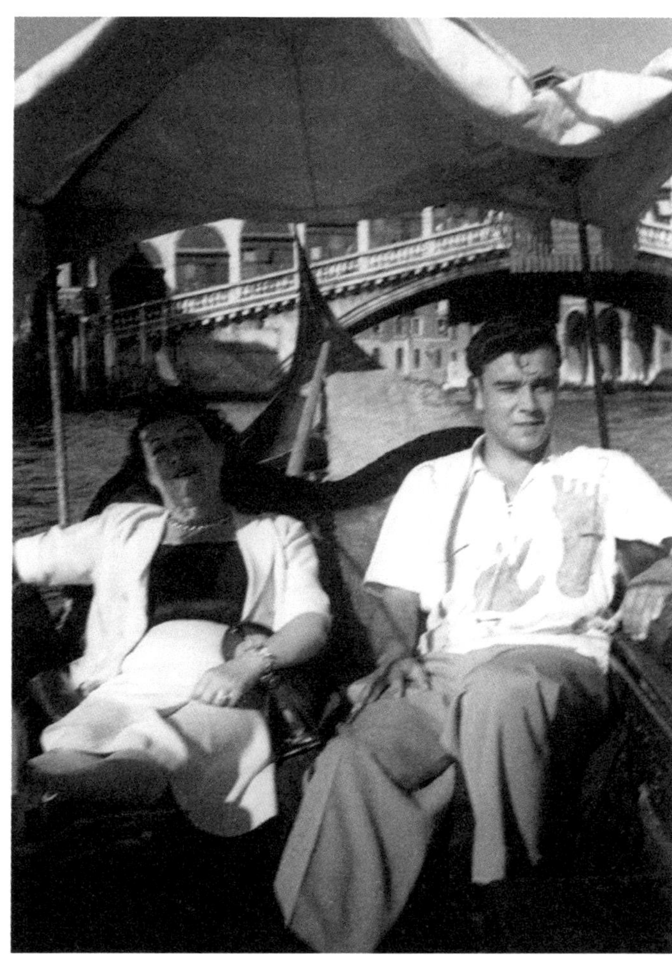

Yves Klein on Ponte
Nuovo del Popolo,
Verona, September 1951

Yves Klein and
Rose Raymond in Venice,
September 1951

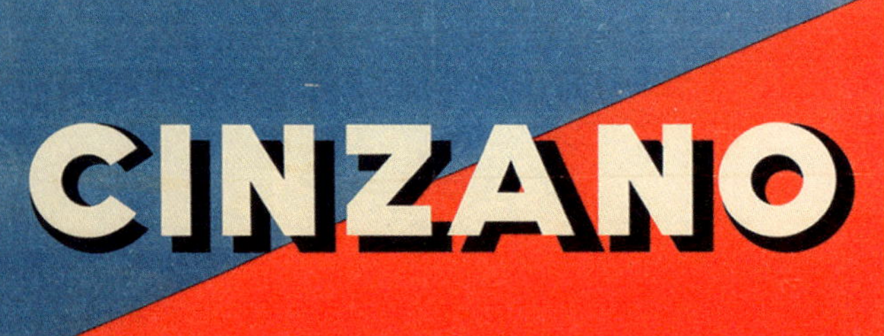

Yves KLEIN
II6, rue d'Assas
Paris 6ème

Paris, le 22 Septembre I95I.

Société CINZANO
Monsieur Ariès
30, Avenue Kléber
Paris

Monsieur le Directeur,

Sur la recommandation de Monsieur Villequey,
employé à votre service publicité, j'ai l'honneur de solliciter de
votre bienveillance, un emploi de Représentant ou Propagandiste.

Je suis Français, agé de 23 ans et célibataire.

Je possède une formation de bachelier qui,
toutefois, n'est pas sanctionnée par le diplôme. Un séjour en
Angleterre et en Espagne m'a permis d'apprendre ces langues que je
parle couramment. Je vous signale également que je suis titulaire
du permis de conduire poids lourds et tourisme.

Restant à votre disposition pour tout rensei-
gnement complémentaire et avec mes remerciements,

Je vous prie d'agréer, Monsieur le Directeur,
mes respectueuses salutations.

Upon his return, Yves Klein sent off
his application for a position representing
the Cinzano company, a Piedmont brand
of aperitifs and sparkling wines famous
for its "Turin vermouth".
Translation p. 215

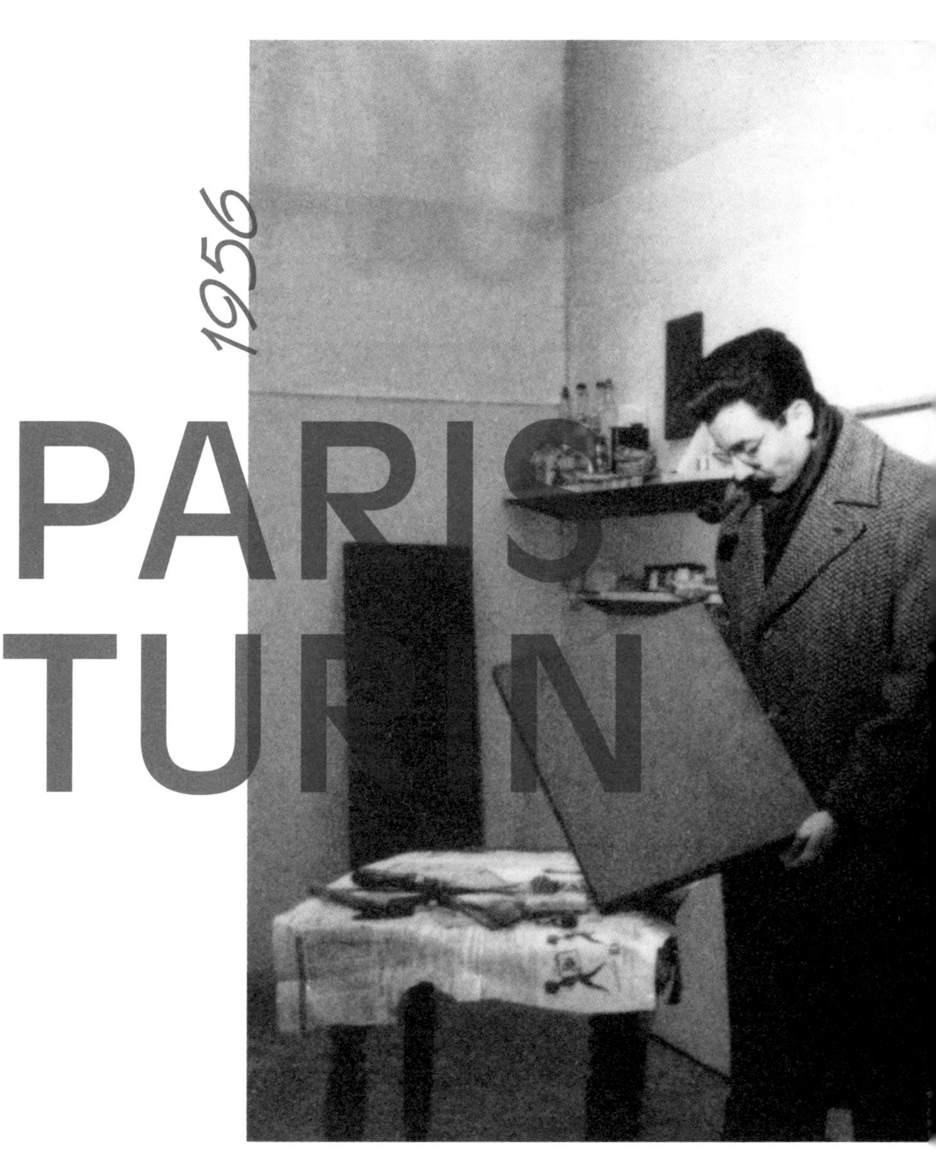

TURIN

1956

PARIS

TURIN

PARIS

Pierre Restany
in Yves Klein's studio,
9 Rue Campagne-Première,
Paris, 1956

Yves Klein
34 boul Raimbaldi (Raimbaldien! comme Restany.)
Nice. A.M.
et ta article "La proportion (illisible) dans (illisible) avec Peugeot?? pour juillet! monochrome...

le 10 Juillet

Ma chère tato et mon
cher Pierre

J'envoie ce jour un mandat de
8.000 Frs en te remerciant infini-
ment mon cher vieux Restany!
Tu es un type énorme!
J'ai fait bon voyage me voila
sur la côte... tous les jours
je me baigne dans mon Époque
bleue — Quel plaisir de
plonger et d'évoluer ainsi dans
ma Couleur!!

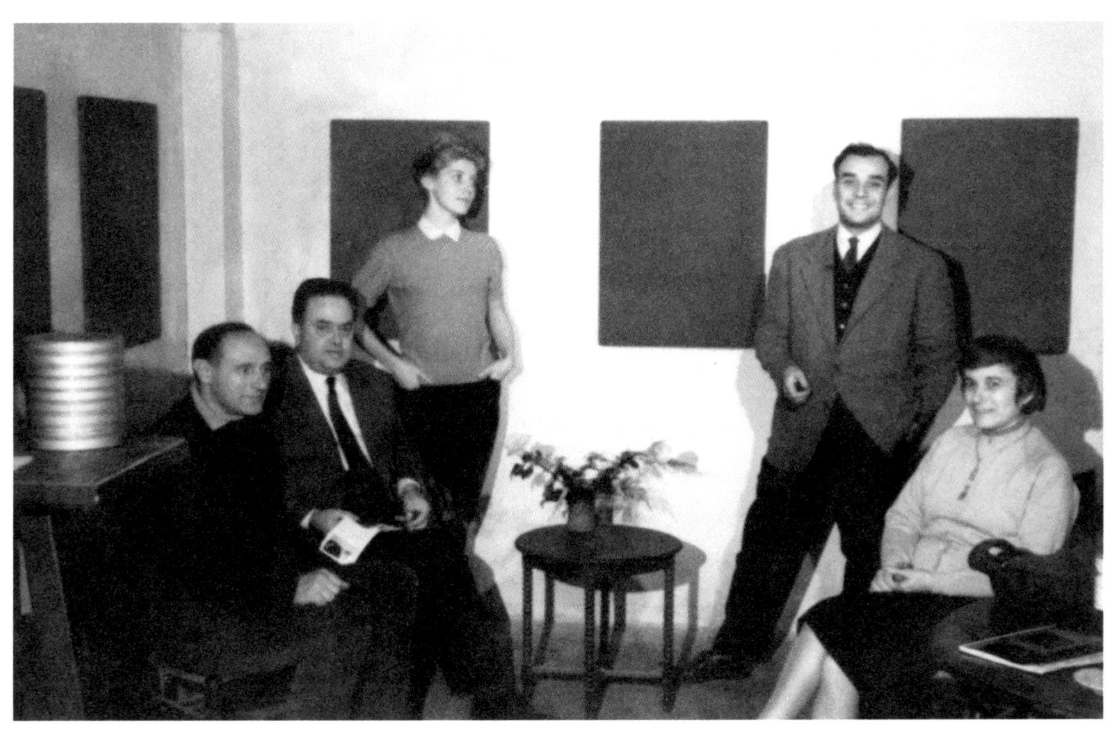

Sculptor Carlo Sergio Signori,
playwright Beniamino Joppolo,
Bernadette Allain (Yves Klein's partner
at that time), and artist Carla Rossi
around Yves Klein at his studio,
9 Rue Campagne-Première, 1956

Yves Klein,
Untitled Blue Monochrome (IKB 259),
1956
A work that
once belonged to
Italian sculptor
Carlo Sergio Signori

Yves Klein's studio,
9 Rue Campagne-
Première, Paris,
1956

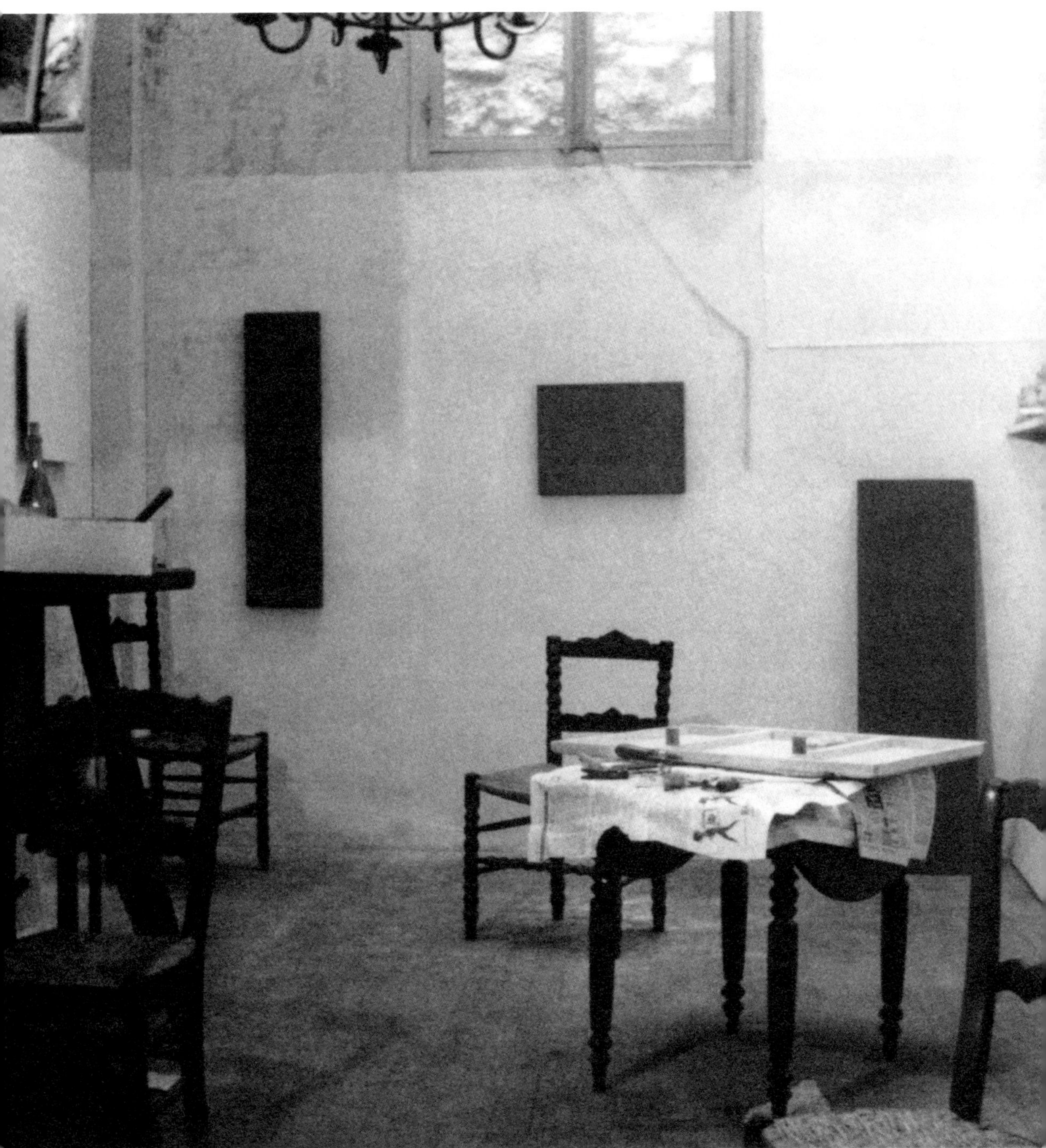

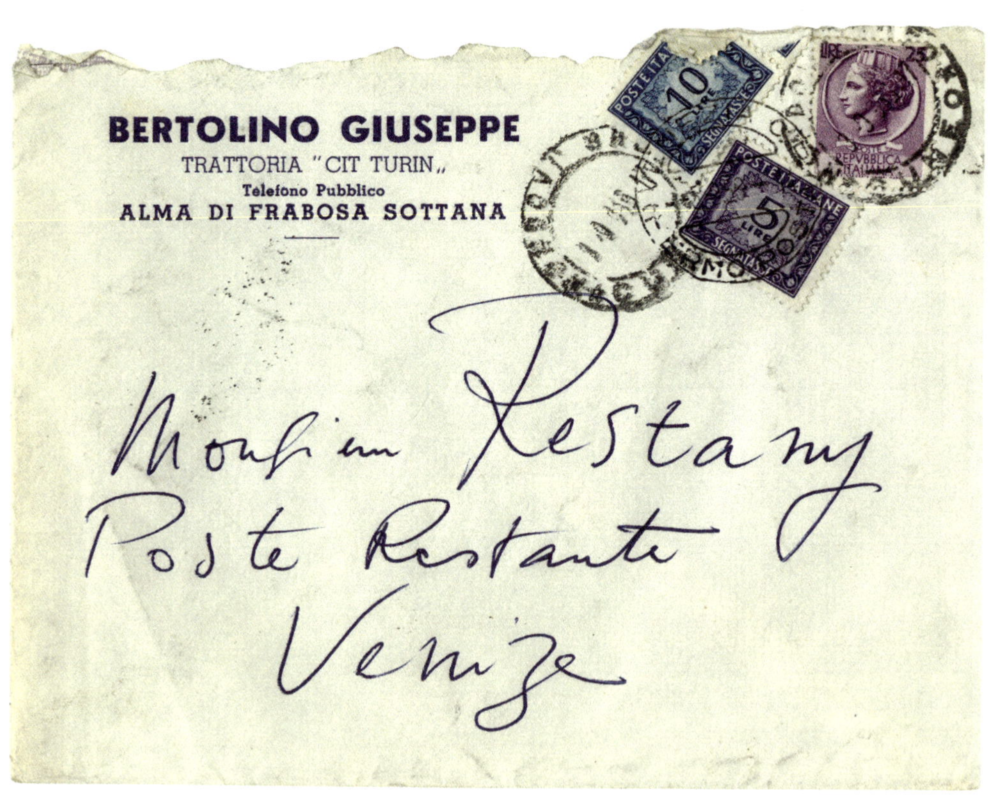

Envelope of a letter sent to Pierre Restany
from Turin, where Yves Klein was staying,
from 2 to 9 September 1956, at the home
of the artist Adriano Parisot, founder
of the *I 4 Soli* magazine

During this stay, Klein and Parisot went
to Alba together to meet Emanuele Micheli,
a surgeon, knowledgeable collector,
and supporter of the magazine.

Traditional Japanese graphic art
has always been a great fascination
of mine: writing, signs, and gestures.
When I see how Klein transformed all that
in his monochrome works, I wonder just
how much his own intuitions were one
with that reality. Combining the practice
of martial arts, his version of "an Asian
ascesis", with his method, I realised how
coherent his choices were, and that
those transformations revealed a new,
absolute ideogram: Y.K.B.

Adriano Parisot

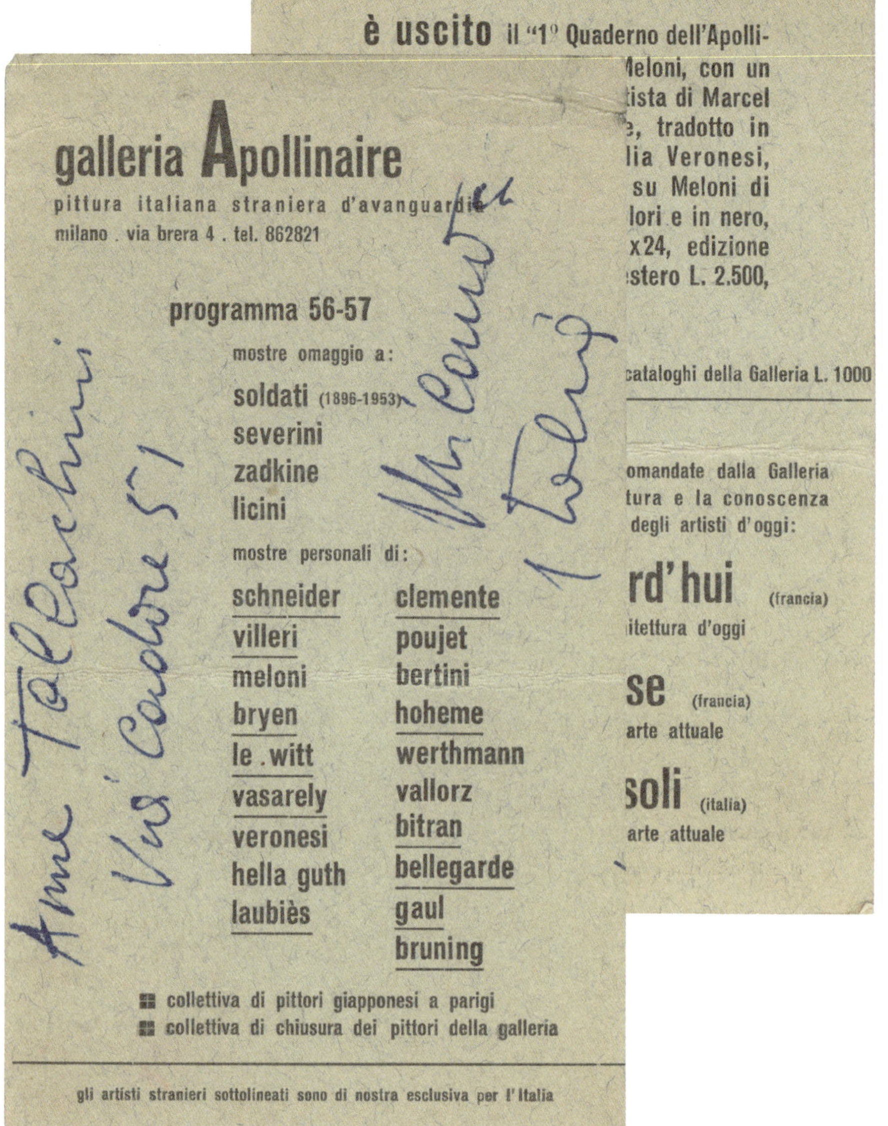

Apollinaire Gallery programme from
1956-1957, probably given by Guido Le Noci
to Yves Klein during his visit to Paris
in October 1956
At this time, Yves Klein's solo exhibition
did not yet feature, since it was only
confirmed by the gallerist in late October.

View of the Apollinaire Gallery,
Via Brera 4, Milan, designed by Brutalist
architect Vittoriano Viganò (1954-1955)

The walls of the gallery are made of exposed
concrete, Viganò's favourite material,
which he considered the perfect backdrop for
the artworks. These were fixed
to aluminium uprights detached from
the wall by fifty centimetres. In this way,
the artworks were almost framed by
their own shadow. This system of hanging
singularly characterised the
Apollinaire Gallery, and Le Noci called
it his "armoury".

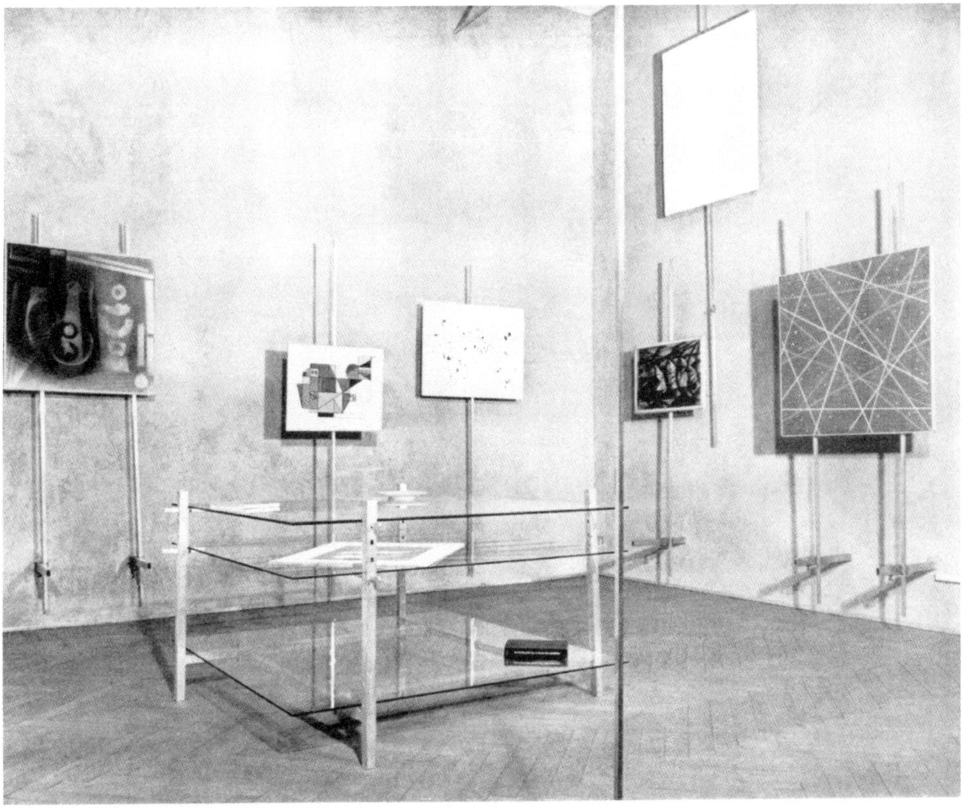

Soluzione particolare: tutte le pareti di muro sono lasciate grezze. Con questa materia ruvida e incolore il muro scompare, e questo è il miglior sfondo, forse, per la pittura. Il muro grezzo non fa superficie, non avvicina, non lega, è come il cemento nelle zone mancanti degli affreschi, e rende più preziosa questa pittura senza cornice.

I quadri sono fissati a montanti di alluminio, sospesi, distaccati dal soffitto e dal pavimento (così la porticina interna è distaccata dal pavimento).

Per queste steli metalliche che la caratterizzano, Le Noci chiama la sua galleria « sala d'armi ».

Pareti di muro grezzo, a intonaco rustico naturale: soffitto bianco, illuminazione a lampade fluorescenti a vista, a 40 cm. dal soffitto. I quadri sono sospesi a montanti in alluminio naturale fissi a muro, distaccati 50 cm. dalla parete.

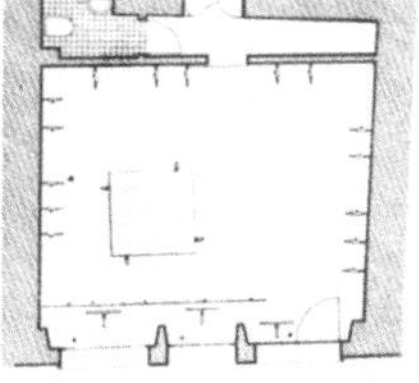

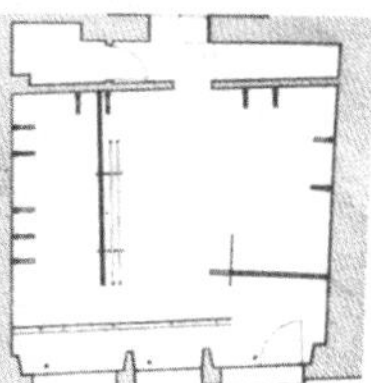

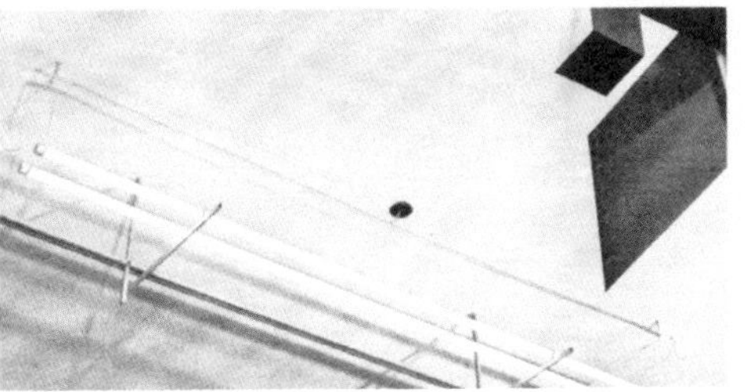

Le Noci has confirmed his agreement:
the exhibition will be held from 2 to
12 January 1957. Just ten days isn't much,
right in the middle of the winter
sports period. It's better than nothing,
Yves thinks, who blindly believes
in his luck and who is preparing a series
of ad-hoc blue propositions:
eleven wooden panels, slightly rounded
at the corners and all in the same format,
seventy-eight centimetres by fifty-six.
At my request, he decided without
hesitation to now sign his artworks
with his name. The Milan catalogue will
therefore include the mention "Yves
Klein, proposte monocrome, epoca blu".
As a kind of commentary, he declared
to me, "That way I have the impression
of entering the great dawning
of monochromy."

Pierre Restany

galleria **A**pollinaire

Mio caro Pierre

Sono completamente d'accordo con te; se tu credi
che è necessario farla quest'anno, la mostra di
Yves, facciamola senz'altro: allora la possiamo
fare dal 2 all'11 gennaio, così cominciamo
il nuovo anno con una mostra _choc_.
Se crederai che sarà necessario fare un'altra
mostra, più in là, di quelle che intendi tu, facciamola.
Più in prudenza, la mia, più che saggezza, in
questo momento, è preoccupazione materiale
per far fronte ai miei impegni e andare
avanti. Ma quando sarò più tranquillo, di
quelle mostre che intendi tu, non una, ma
tre all'anno ne farò.
Ti prego di andare da Bryen e comincia
a preparargli a mettere da parte il materiale
della mostra.
   Ti abbraccio fraternamente assieme a Tato
Combina tu con Yves
                                    tuo Guido

31 ott 56

Letter from
Guido Le Noci
to Pierre Restany,
31 October 1956

The gallerist confirmed Yves Klein's
solo exhibition from 2 to 11 January 1957,
to "begin the year with a sensational
exhibition".
Translation pp. 215-216

Yves Klein, *Untitled
Blue Monochrome*
(IKB 104), 1956
Dedication
on the back: "Yves 56,
to the uncompromising
Guido Le Noci"

Yves Klein at
his studio, 9 Rue
Campagne-Première,
Paris, 1956

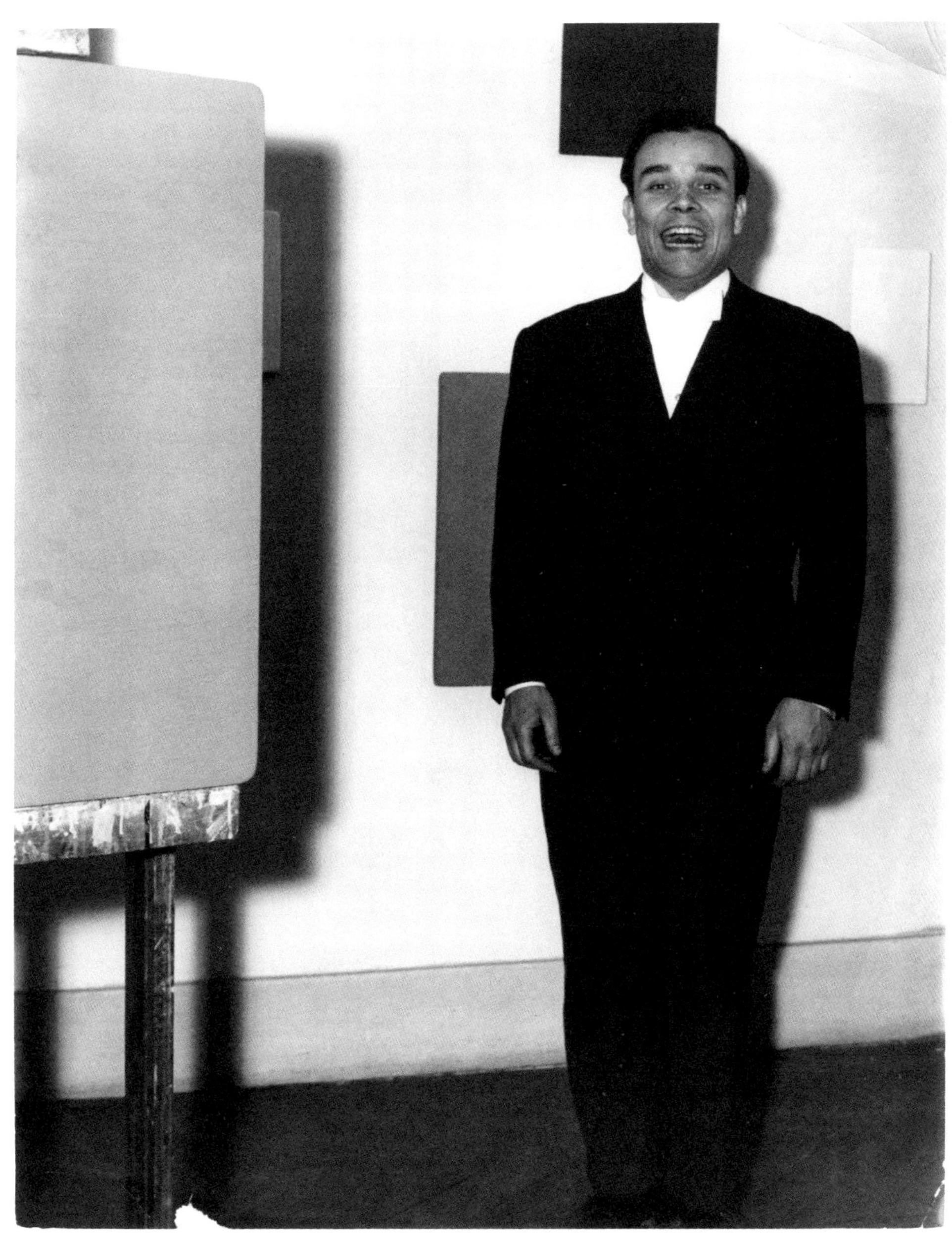

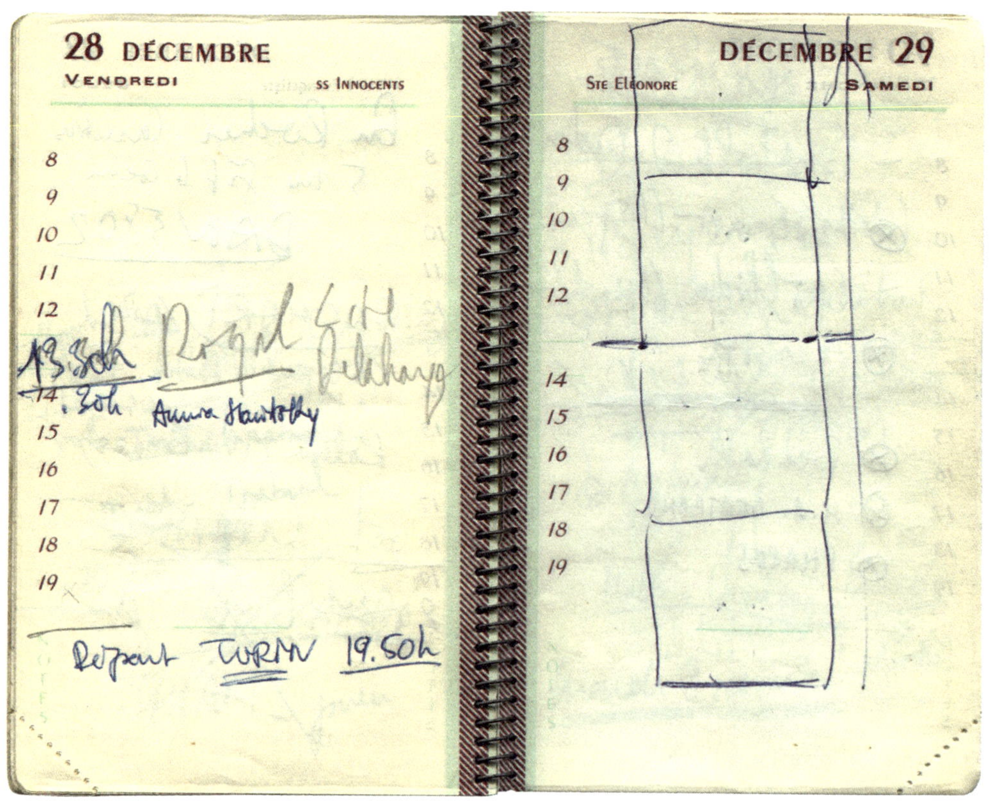

Yves Klein left by train on 28 December 1956, in the company of Bernadette Allain, Pierre Restany and his wife Aline Dallier, and artists Gianni Bertini, Lutka Pink, and Claude Bellegarde. They spent the new year in Turin and arrived in Milan on 1 January 1957, the day before the inauguration of Yves Klein's exhibition at the Apollinaire Gallery.

MILAN

1957

MILAN

pittori della scuola di parigi

Pierre RESTANY presenta

YVES KLEIN

proposte monocrome
epoca Blu

galleria Apollinaire
2 - 12 gennaio 1957

Invitation card
to the *Yves Klein.
Proposte monocrome,
epoca Blu* exhibition,
Apollinaire Gallery,
Milan, 2-12 January
1957

MILAN

Yves Klein,
*Untitled Blue
Monochrome* (IKB 100),
1956
Artwork acquired
by Lucio Fontana,
dedicated on the back:
"* Yves 56 Collection
Lucio Fontana Milan"

Eleven blue monochromes were presented
in the Milanese gallery. One red monochrome
and one yellow monochrome were also hung
in the office of Guido Le Noci.

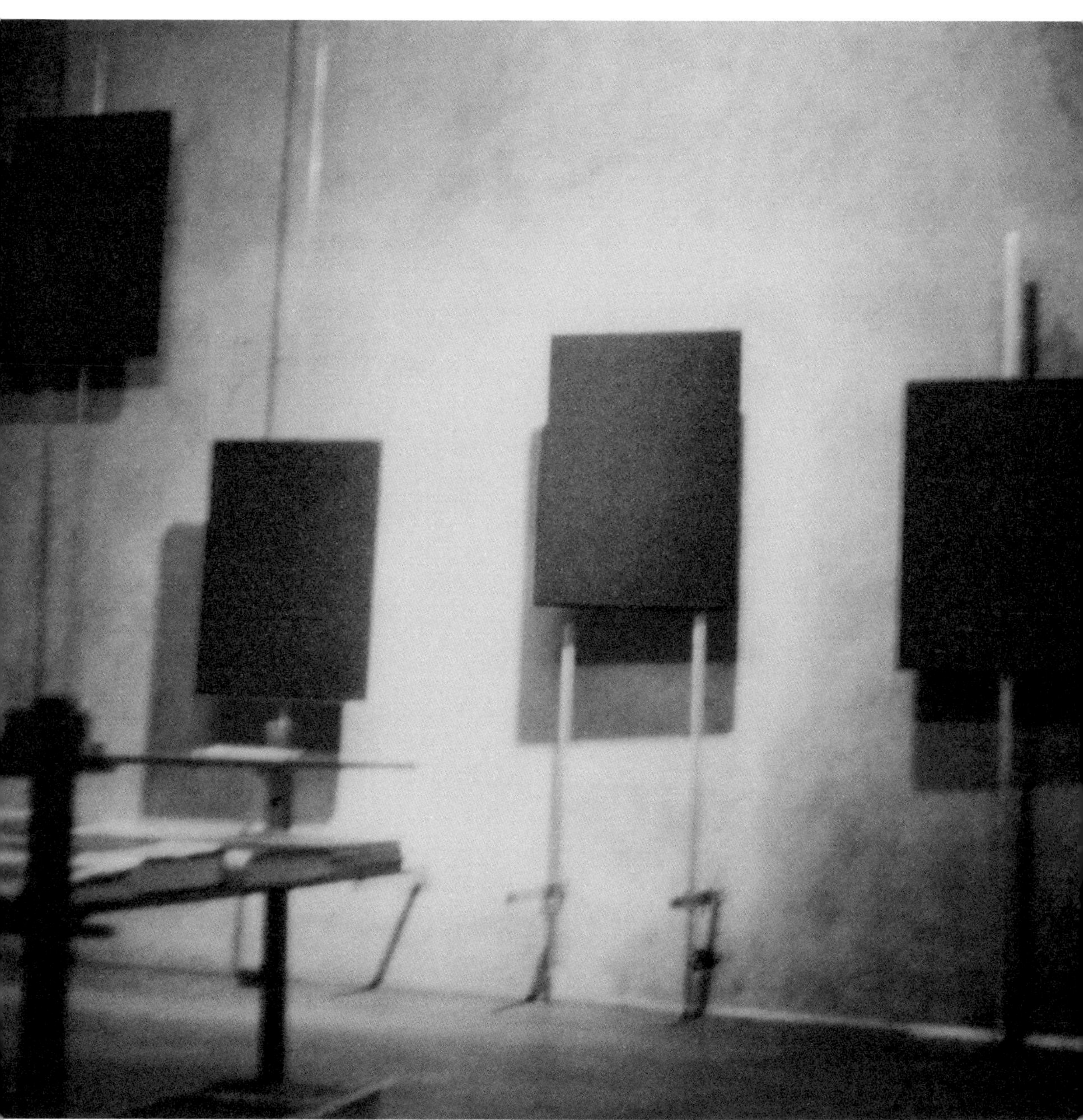

51

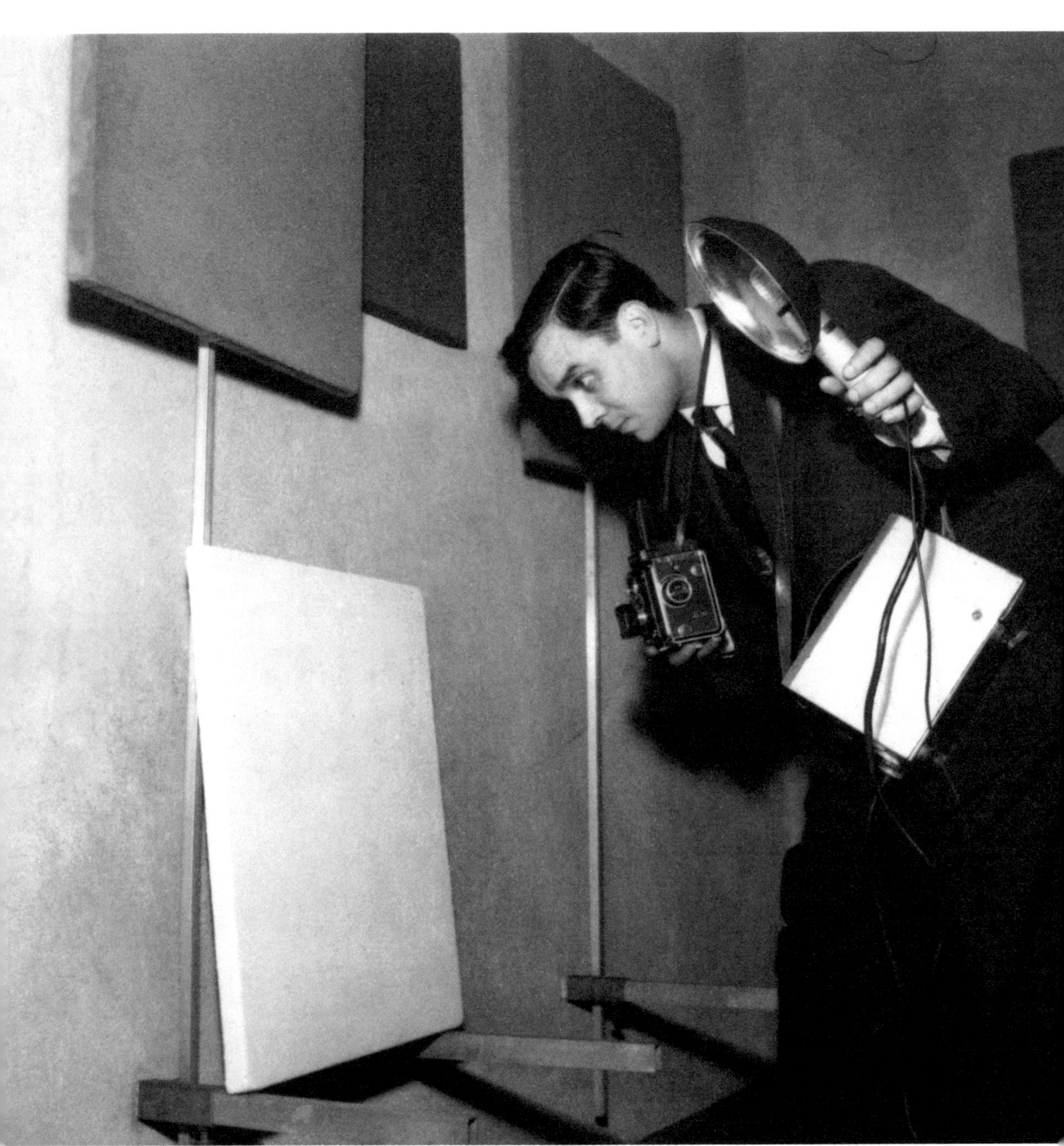

Vernissage of the *Yves Klein. Proposte monocrome, epoca Blu* exhibition, 2 January 1957, Apollinaire Gallery, Milan

Each of these blue propositions,
all similar in appearance, were perceived
by the public as clearly distinct from
each other. The nonprofessionals passed
from one to the next, as was fitting,
penetrating in an instant state
of contemplation the worlds of blue. …
The most sensational observation was
that of the buyers. Each selected from
among the eleven displayed paintings
the one that pleased them the most
and paid its price. The prices, of course,
were all different. This fact demonstrated
that, on the one hand, the pictorial
quality of each painting was perceptible
by something other than the material and
physical appearance and, on the other,
that those who made their choice
recognised that state of things to which
I refer as Pictorial Sensibility.

Yves Klein

Pierre Restany
Milan 2 January 1957: The Start
of the Blue Period

Once hung, the eleven blue panels
literally saturated the space of
the Apollinaire Gallery, which at the time
opened directly onto Milan's famous
Via Brera. It came as quite a jolt to the
unsuspecting Le Noci. It was a revelation,
and from that moment, his enthusiasm
never waned. Apart from the gallery's
loyal collectors, not many people
attended the opening. One of them was
a young artist, an unknown, a follower
of the tachism that was in vogue at the
time. He came back every day for the
duration of the exhibition, irresistibly
attracted by the monochrome idea:
his name was Manzoni, and this was
the illumination that turned his thinking
upside down and changed the course
of his career. In December of the same
year, he produced his first "achrome"
paintings. In my preface to the
exhibition, drawing conclusions from
the previous experience, I emphasised
the total autonomy of colour, further
enhanced by the exclusive choice of
sovereign blue and its symbolic power,
which I compared, taking my argument
to its logical conclusion, to Giotto's blue.
I also reiterated my warning against
equating Klein with Malevich. In vain.
The conformist press was up in arms
against me. In an article in *Il Giorno* dated
8 January 1957, Marco Valsecchi took up
the Suprematist objection by throwing
the false bomb of the "white square on
a white background" at me. Picking up
on my reference to Giotto's blue, the
Giorno columnist concluded with this
peremptory judgement: "It is not even
impudent, it's just plain comical." Le Noci
offered Valsecchi a public debate on
the matter: in vain. I sent the newspaper
editor a clarification, invoking the right
of reply: in vain, as my letter was not
published. But all this noise about the
exhibition attracted people. A last-
minute replacement for the *Corriere
d'Informazione* correspondent, who
couldn't make it, Dino Buzzati was sent

to the Apollinaire Gallery to find out
what it was all about. The eleven blue
paintings caught his imagination and
compelled his respect, so to speak.
In the *Corriere* of 9–10 January, he wrote
"Blu, Blu, Blu", a very witty and deeply
honest article, imbued with the tender
irony that this gentleman of Italian
letters had always shown towards the
maverick characters who intrigued him.
This article secured the exhibition's
success and record attendances.
Buzzati's article was the first objective
assessment to appear in the mainstream
press, and it had a very positive
psychological effect on Klein's morale.
After the scandal, critical success.
To begin with, some modest sales.
Well-known collectors bought
monochromes: Italo Magliano, a regular
visitor to the Apollinaire Gallery; Count
Panza di Biumo, then a fervent follower
of the Paris School, who chose the only
red monochrome exhibited in the
annexe as a reminder of the previous
series (he would part with it some
time later, without having understood
the importance of the message:
he wasn't "ready"); Lucio Fontana,
the master of Spatialism, whose series
of canvases with holes in them (*Buchi*)
was beginning to make him famous,
and whose *Tagli* (lacerated canvases)
would draw their own lessons from the
monochrome. Significant coincidences
then snowballed: the industrialist
Peppino Palazzoli, who had also bought
a monochrome, opened a contemporary
art gallery a few months later and named
it Blu Gallery, with a monochrome IKB
symbol. At the 1957 San Remo Song
Festival, Domenico Modugno triumphed
with the hit of the season: "Nel blu,
dipinto di blu" [In Blue Painted Blue].
Another remarkable coincidence: during
the exhibition, Klein decided to give
a judo demonstration. The director
of the club that welcomed him as guest
of honour was none other than
Bruno Contenotte, the future director
of the metamorphic luminous spaces
that won him international renown.
Among local avant-garde artists,

the most favourable to Klein were Baj
and Dangelo, the driving forces behind
the Nuclear Art movement and the
magazine *Il Gesto*, who invited him
to take part in a group show in October
1957. Together with me, Yves Klein
signed the manifesto of the Nuclear
artists against style. The Milanese echoes
of the blue exhibition were heard here
and there around Europe, particularly
in the German press. When Klein left
Milan in January 1957 to return to Paris,

his career had entered another
dimension: it had been launched and
would never stop.

In Pierre Restany, *Yves Klein* (Paris:
Éditions du Chêne, 1982), 37–38.

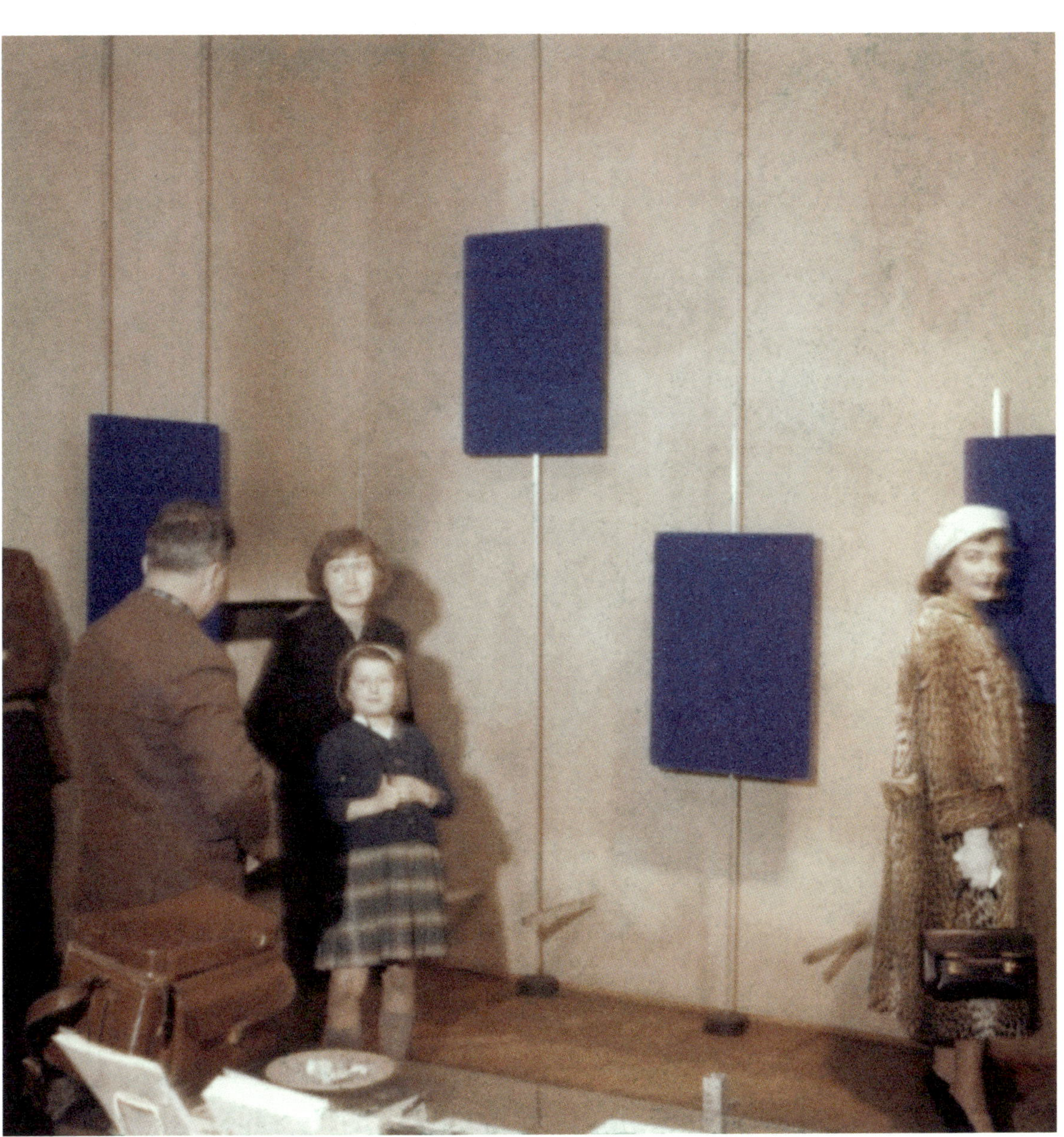

Yves Klein performing a judo hold on artist Claude Bellegarde at the Apollinaire Gallery, Milan, 2 January 1957

A few days after the vernissage, Yves Klein performed a judo demonstration at the Jigorô Kanô Club, Via San Senatore in Milan. The owner of the club was none other than the artist Bruno Contenotte, whom Klein had met at his exhibition opening and who was also passionate about martial arts. He opened the first judo school in Milan in 1956.

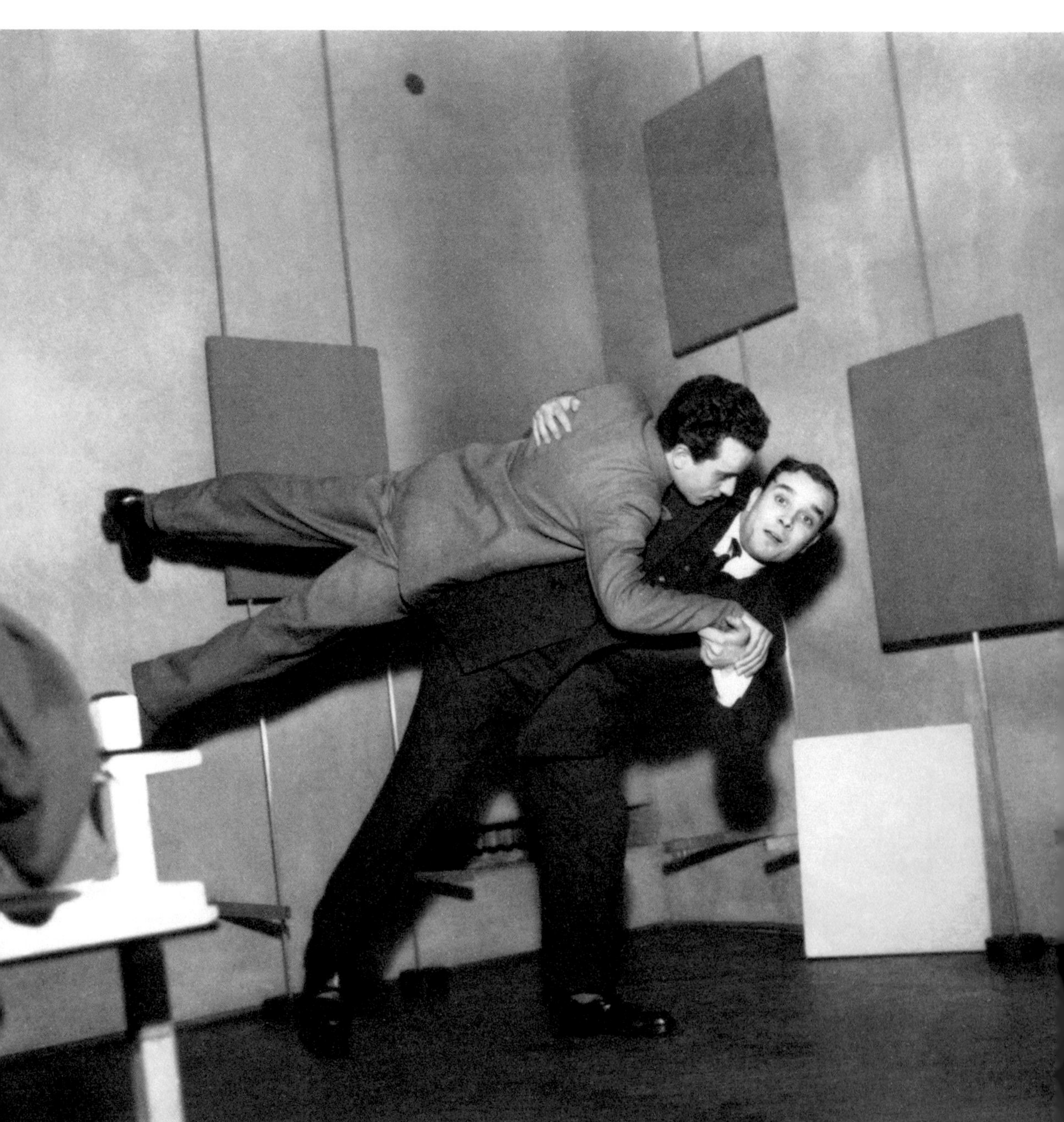

Blu Blu Blu

Yves Klein, campione di lotta giapponese e pittore di superavanguardia, presenta la mostra di pittura più paradossale che si sia mai vista a questo mondo

Per una fortuita indisponibilità del titolare della critica d'arte, il sottoscritto, che critico non è, è stato incaricato di visitare una mostra personale, e di riferire a guisa di cronista.

E poiché il caso ha molta fantasia, si è dato che questa mostra d'arte fosse una delle più singolari, se non la più singolare e sconcertante da quando esiste arte sulla terra. Cosicché il titolare della critica, impossibilitato a intervenire, si dirà: «Ma guarda un po', ogni mese di mostre d'arte ne vedo centinaia che più o meno si assomigliano talmente da risultare una mostra sola, e scriverne è un faticosissimo problema; poi ne viene una fuori del normale, sulla quale ci sarebbero da dire tante cose, e io non posso andarci; e mi sfugge così l'occasione di fare una bellissima figura». (Mentre un semplice cronista, per quanto sia solerte e diligente, come fa a farne, di belle figure?).

La mostra era, ed è aperta, fino al 12 gennaio, alla galleria Apollinaire, in via Brera 4, il covo, mi dissero, dell'avanguardia più oltranzista, la sala più polemica d'Italia, dove passano i fenomeni viventi, i pazzi, gli anarchici, i rivoluzionari, i terroristi, i frenetici della estrema avanscoperta.

E' una piccola sala con una piccola vetrina sulla strada. Poco più in là, per ironia del caso, c'è un'altra bottega d'arte, pure con vetrina, fedele ai più risaputi schemi della pittura benpensante. Cosicché la gente, che viene da piazza della Scala, nel breve spazio di sei sette metri precipita (o s'innalza) da un probo ma oleografico paesaggio da anticamera di dentista all'astrattismo più integrale.

Si penserebbe che il proprietario di tale bottega dovesse essere una specie di mostro mentale, una creatura allucinante, dedita, che so io, all'*haschich* o alla *marijuana*, o un facineroso che passa le notti confezionando macchine infernali, o un cupo fanatico macerato da sotterranee ascesi.

E' rimasto sbalordito

Guido Le Noci è invece l'uomo più mite, cortese e amabile che si possa immaginare. Certo, egli farebbe un sacrificio personale pur di convertire, voi riluttanti, all'arte cosiddetta non figurativa. Ma queste sollecitazioni appassionate, le esercita con una tale discrezione che voi ve ne accorgete soltanto dopo, a cosa fatta. Sia come sia, è indubitabile che nella Galleria Apollinaire si celebrano i riti più inquietanti ed esoterici dell'arte moderna: in questo campo la fede di Le Noci è solida come le piramidi d'Egitto e chiedergli per esempio se lui crede che Mondrian sia veramente un grande artista è come entrare in Vaticano e chiedere al Papa se veramente esiste Dio.

Eppure quest'uomo, rotto, possiamo dire, alle temerità più acrobatiche, capocordata dei sesti gradi superiori del colore, capitano dei «commandos» delle arti belle, anche lui stavolta, di fronte alle opere del pittore francese Yves Klein, è rimasto, diciamolo francamente, sbalordito.

Sbalordito, ma, aggiungiamolo subito, estremamente interessato. E gli ha subito aperto la porta, lo ha fatto accomodare, e ha esposto i suoi quadri alle pareti.

Quante volte, dinanzi alle sfrenatezze dell'arte moderna, si è sentito dire: ormai tutto è stato sovvertito, *più in là di così non può andare*. Eppure più in là si è andati sempre.

Ebbene, nel caso di Yves Klein è impossibile sbagliarsi. In fatto di rinuncia figurativa, di purità formale, di astrattismo, *più in là di così non si potrà andare nei secoli dei secoli*.

Entriamo in merito. Intanto Yves Klein è, come uomo, oltre che come artista, un tipo straordinario. Nato a Nizza ventotto anni fa; studi nautici e di lingue orientali; allenatore di cavalli da corsa; campione di judo nello stesso Giappone, dove ha conquistato il «quarto dan della cintura nera del Kodokan» di Tokio due anni fa; e di lotta giapponese egli appunto offrirà un'esibizione qui a Milano, sabato sera, alle ore 21, presso il Club Jijoro Kano in via San Senatore 5, vicino a via Sant'Eufemia.

Ma più straordinari di tutto sono i suoi quadri. Alla Galleria Apollinaire ne espone 12.

Il primo, rettangolare, base centimetri 56 per centimetri 78 d'altezza, rappresenta... Ah, scusate, al tempo: il cronista, trascinato dall'antica abitudine, stava per fare una spaventosa «gaffe». Parlare di «rappresentazione» alla Galleria Apollinaire è come parlare di corda nella casa dell'impiccato.

Sono tutti senza firma

Dunque, il primo quadro, delle misure che abbiam detto, è costituito da una superficie liscia e uniforme di uniforme colore blù unito, un bel blù per la verità, di tono oltremarino; su questa superficie non c'è un segno, una linea, un punto, una minima macchia o interruzione, soltanto blù tutto uguale, lievemente e regolarmente increspato come la cementite dei nostri appartamenti. Ed ora passiamo al secondo quadro.

Il secondo quadro, rettangolare (base cm. 56 per cm. 78) è costituito da una superficie liscia e uniforme di uniforme colore blu unito, un bel blu, di tono oltremarino, senza un segno, una linea, una macchia, eccetera, vedi come sopra.

Il terzo quadro, idem. Il quarto, idem, e così via. Undici quadri assolutamente identici (almeno nell'apparenza) formati da rettangoli blu senza il più piccolo segno, neanche la firma c'è. Solo il dodicesimo è diverso: invece che rettangolare è quadrato e invece di blu è rosso.

Ma possibile — si chiederà — che fra un quadro e l'altro non ci sia la minima differenza? Si risponde: una differenza c'è e consiste nel fatto che Yves Klein ha eseguito questi quadri *in diversi stati d'animo*. Ma si riconosce in qualche modo nei dipinti questa diversità di stato d'animo creativo? No, assolutamente no. Insomma, volendo fare un paragone letterario, sarebbe come una poesia fatta così:

*Mmmmmmmmm
mmmmmmmmm
mmmmmmmmm
ecc.*

(dato che, con buona pace di Rimbaud, nell'alfabeto il colore blu è rappresentato dall'«m» e non dall'«o», il quale è notoriamente rosso).

Ora conviene dare la parola al presentatore Pierre Restany il quale dice «Attenzione: queste enunciazioni monocrome esigono da te, o lettore, tutto quel patrimonio di disponibilità che occorre per fare le rivoluzioni e debellare i tiranni». E più avanti: «Il Blu domina, vive. Siamo dinanzi al Blu-Signore, padrone assoluto della più definitiva tra le frontiere liberate, il Blu degli affreschi di Assisi: questo vuoto colmo, questo Niente che afferma il Tutto Possibile, questo soprannaturale silenzio astenico del colore, questo X infine che, al di là dell'aneddotico e del pretesto formale, determina la immortale grandezza di Giotto».

La reazione della gente

E la gente? La gente reagisce in tre modi.

La maggioranza sghignazza o protesta che è l'ora di finirla con queste prese in giro e così via.

Una minoranza riconosce che per lo meno la faccenda è estremamente spiritosa.

Una minoranza delle minoranze resta meditabonda, domandandosi se in un futuro lontanissimo uno di questi quadri non sarà per caso appeso al Louvre (in queste cose, dopo tutto quello che si è visto negli ultimi decenni, chi se la sente di giurare?)

A proposito, il prezzo. E' modestissimo; 25.000 lire al quadro. Acquirenti finora due: un noto sarto collezionista d'arte astratta e il pittore-scultore Lucio Fontana, quello dei buchi per intenderci, il quale ha dimostrato, con questa compera, di essere un uomo pieno d'umorismo e sportivissimo.

Dino Buzzati

CORRIERE LOMBARDO

a ★ Milano C

Che coraggio blu!

ARTE o coraggio? Questa è la domanda che ci si pone entrando nella galleria Apollinaire in via Brera 4 dove, in questi giorni, espone il pittore nizzardo Yves Klein. Guardate i quadri, accanto all'artista che li ha dipinti.

Essi sono blu, completamente blu, senza una virgola e senza una macchia d'altro colore. La gente entra, guarda, trasécola. Poi, o esce indispettita o si mette a ridere. Però c'è anche chi li compera, quei quadri, per la somma in fondo modesta di 25 mila lire. E bisogna anche affrettarsi ad acquistarli perchè sembra che, dopo questo «periodo blu», il pittore inizierà un «periodo rosso» e si rischia di rimanere senza la sua «prima maniera».

Yves Klein's press book,
article "Che coraggio blu!", published
in *Corriere Lombardo*, January 1957.
"People walk in, look, are dumbfounded.
Then, they either leave annoyed
or start to laugh."
Translation p. 217

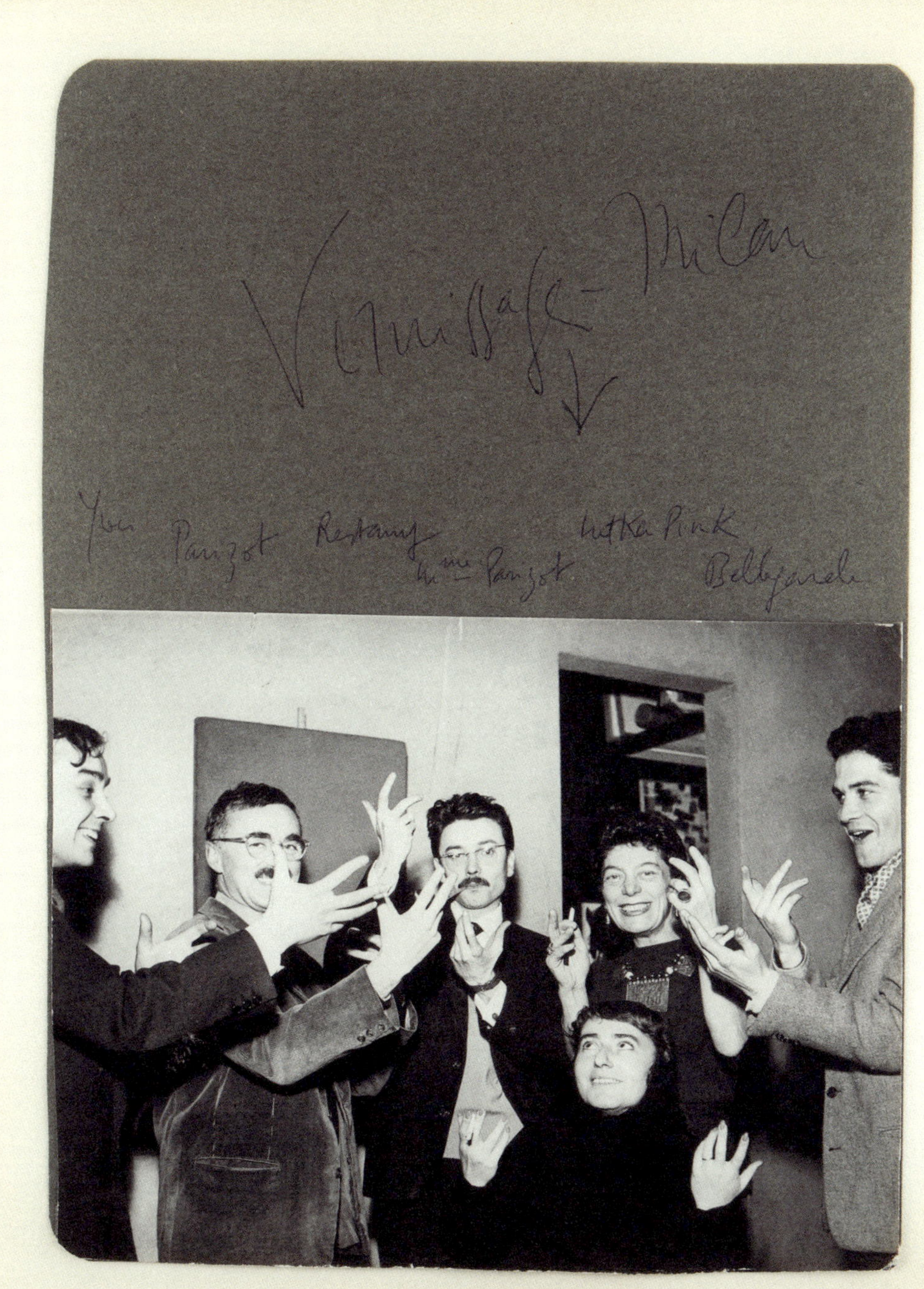

Yves Klein's press book,
photographs from his exhibition opening
at the Apollinaire Gallery
Here, we recognise Yves Klein,
Pierre Restany, Adriano and Ada Parisot,
Lutka Pink, and Claude Bellegarde.

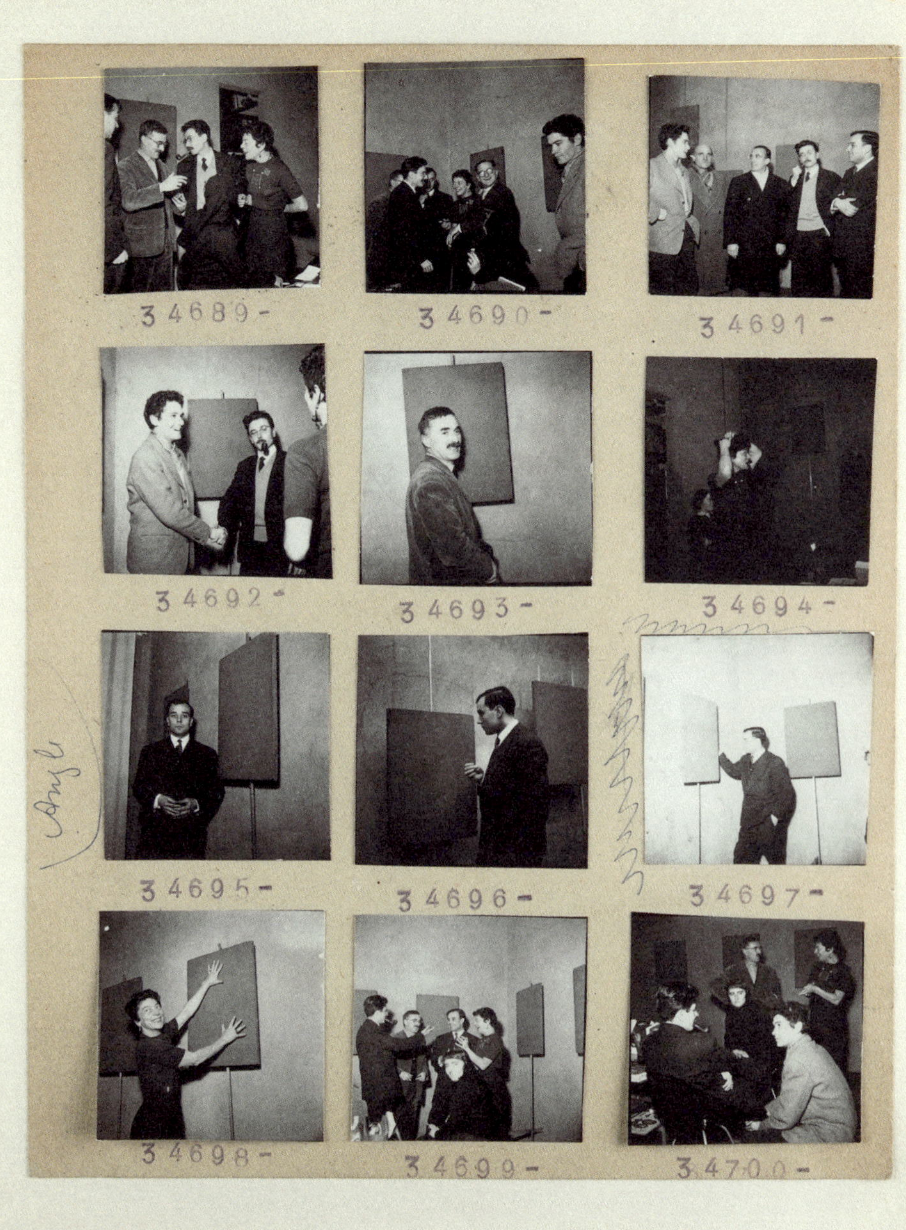

Monsieur le Directeur,

Mis en cause par votre collaborateur M. VALSECCHI dans l'article qu'il a consacré à l'exposition d'Yves KLEIN (numéro d'Il Giorno du Mardi 8 Janvier dernier), je vous serais reconnaissant de bien vouloir publier la mise au point suivante :

— M. VALSECCHI semble user et abuser d'une fort élémentaire psychologie, dont il n'est pas peu fier, au point de se croire tout naturellement autorisé à lire entre les lignes d'une préface toutes les soi-disant arrière-pensées de l'auteur. Une confiance aussi aveugle en ses propres possibilités de jugement, une telle absence de doute méthodique sont de très dangereux états d'âme : M. VALSECCHI devrait s'en inquiéter s'il était toutefois capable de sincérité envers lui-même.

— N'en déplaise à ce dernier, nous ne sommes pas des provocateurs. Cette exposition fait suite à une série de manifestations analogues que j'ai organisé en France, à Paris et à Marseille notamment.

La démarche d'Yves KLEIN est profondément originale et actuelle. Comme je le disais dans ma préface à cette exposition milanaise (ce que M. VALSECCHI s'est bien gardé de citer), aucune confusion n'est ici possible avec Mondrian et Malevitch.

L'évolution de ces deux peintres, et celle de Malevitch notamment ne s'éclaire complètement qu'en fonction de l'idéologie cubiste qui leur était contemporaine. Le très beau geste de Malevitch qui l'a conduit au carré noir sur fond blanc de 1913 et au carré blanc sur fond blanc de 1919,

....../

Monsieur le Directeur d'IL GIORNO
Via Settala 22
MILANO – ITALIE

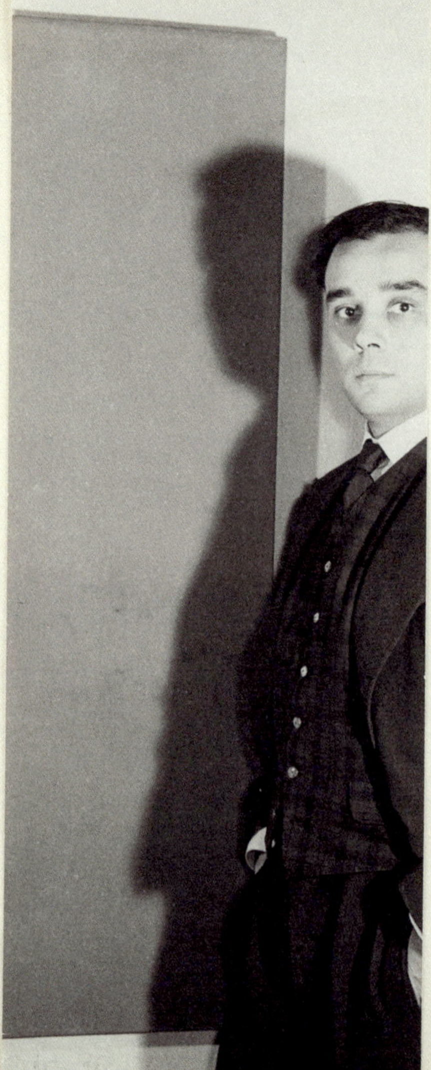

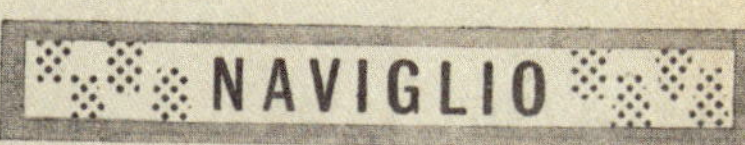

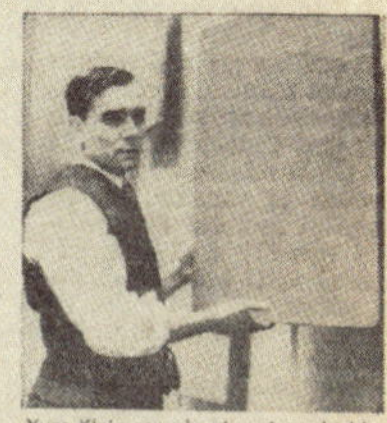

NAVIGLIO

L'avanguardia in tram

di ADELE CAMBRIA

ERANO le nove e un quarto di sera, via Manzoni era deserta, spazzolata dal vento freddo. Il tram numero 16 era quasi vuoto, c'erano tre uomini seduti in fila — uno dietro l'altro — parlavano a voce alta, in francese. Uno di loro era molto giovane, pallido, aveva le tempie magre e i capelli rasati come le guance. Portava una bombetta nera, una redingote nera, antiquata, un ombrello arrotolato alla Chamberlain. Sembrava un orfano travestito da gentleman. I tre discorrevano di Firenze, una meravigliosa città, ma si capiva che pensavano ad altro. Improvvisamente, quello con la bombetta domanda: «Si potrà fare una mostra anche a Roma?». «Certo che si può fare...», risponde l'amico più anziano, e aggiunge: «All'inaugurazione invitiamo un vescovo, Zavattini e De Sica... E' gente che fa sempre la sua figura, ma intanto pensiamo alla mostra milanese...». «Si inaugura lunedì, è vero?», chiede l'altro giovanotto. «Allora — dice — sabato sera potete venire a vedermi in via Senatore... Farò lo judo, ma solo per pochi intimi!».

Il giovanotto che avrebbe fatto lo judo solo per pochi intimi, era anche lui un pittore. Lo si riconosceva subito, alcuni giornali avevano pubblicato le sue fotografie, e aveva parlato anche alla radio. Aveva detto di essere nato a Nizza, e di aver fatto il libraio per un certo periodo, sulla Costa Azzurra. «Allora, la letteratura è un'altra delle sue passioni...?», gli aveva domandato l'incauta radiocronista. «Per carità, signorina, non dica queste cose... — aveva risposto lui — Sono degli anni che io non apro più un libro!». La radiocronista volle vendicarsi. «Ah, capisco... ed è per questo che si è messo a fare l'allevatore di cavalli, in Irlanda!».

Il pittore si chiama Yves Klein, ha trent'anni, ed è «cintura nera» dello judo. Dipinge quadri blu, tutti blu, senza nessun disegno nè alcun altro colore che affiori sulla tela. Come è logico, questi dipinti appartengono al «periodo blu» dell'artista, ma egli ha anche un «periodo rosso»: ha dipinto cioè dei quadri completamente rossi, esclusivamente rossi. In una galleria del centro, espone ora undici quadri blu e uno rosso.

Lunedì, nella stessa galleria, si inaugura la personale di un altro pittore: quello con la bombetta che è — naturalmente — inglese. Si chiama Ralph Rumney, ha ventitrè anni, è vissuto in Cornovaglia, a Parigi, in Sicilia. Nel 1955 ha pubblicato una rivista d'avanguardia, «Altre voci», alcuni suoi dipinti sono in Giappone.

Ralph Rumney si presenta da sè, in questa mostra milanese. Scrive: «Io cerco di materializzare i feticci dell'età delle macchine. Noi guardiamo avanti, al tempo in cui gli artisti non saranno più legati a uno stile personale. Al tempo in cui — nella anonimità — saremo liberi di lavorare senza l'obbligo di ripetere, o "sviluppare", ciò che è stato raggiunto».

Yves Klein's
press book,
article "L'avanguardia
in tram" by
Adele Cambria,
published in *Il Giorno*,
12 January 1957
Translation p. 218

It is likely that even this "monochrome proposal" by Klein will elicit cries of heresy and scandal, but as we know, to the point of utter boredom, anytime something new happens in the art world, it's like stepping on a bed of snakes. What matters is that painting continues to renew itself just as people renew themselves, as has always happened and will always happen.

Guido Le Noci

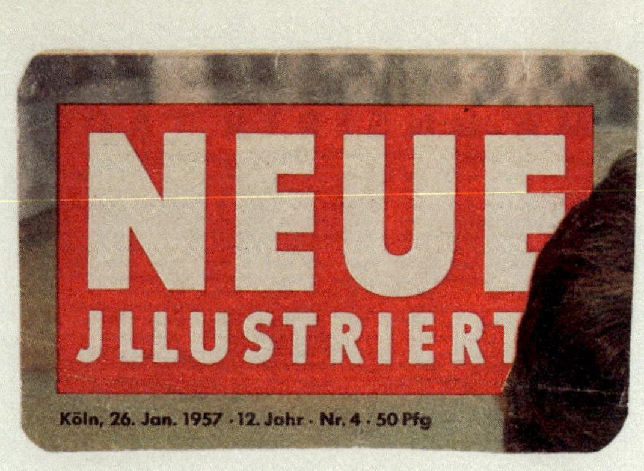

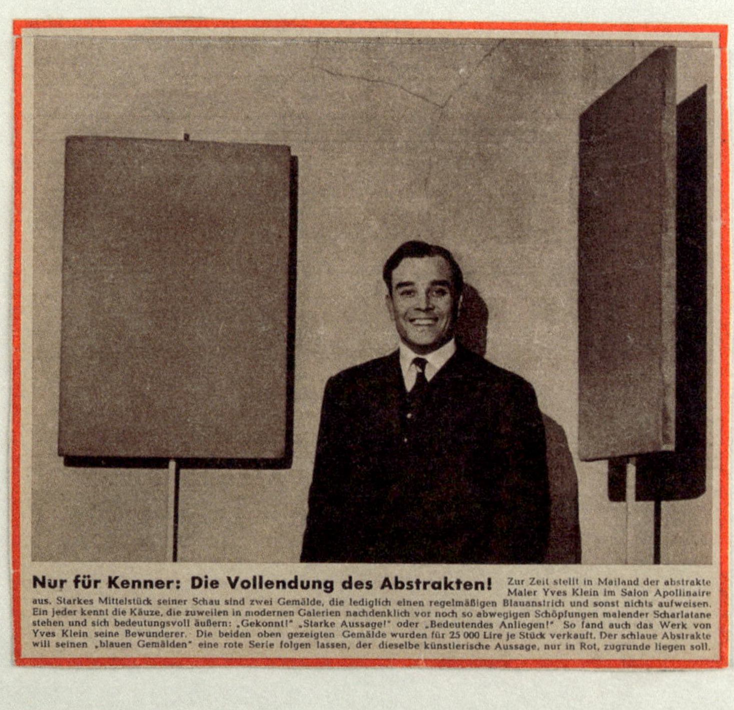

Nur für Kenner: Die Vollendung des Abstrakten! Zur Zeit stellt in Mailand der abstrakte Maler Yves Klein im Salon Apollinaire aus. Starkes Mittelstück seiner Schau sind zwei Gemälde, die lediglich einen regelmäßigen Blauanstrich und sonst nichts aufweisen. Ein jeder kennt die Käuze, die zuweilen in modernen Galerien nachdenklich vor noch so abwegigen Schöpfungen malender Scharlatane stehen und sich bedeutungsvoll äußern: „Gekonnt!" „Starke Aussage!" oder „Bedeutendes Anliegen!" So fand auch das Werk von Yves Klein seine Bewunderer. Die beiden oben gezeigten Gemälde wurden für 25 000 Lire je Stück verkauft. Der schlaue Abstrakte will seinen „blauen Gemälden" eine rote Serie folgen lassen, der dieselbe künstlerische Aussage, nur in Rot, zugrunde liegen soll.

Yves Klein's press book, article published in *Neue Illustrierte* magazine, Cologne, 26 January 1957

Yves Klein,
Untitled Red Monochrome
(M 62), 1956

Artwork acquired
in January 1957 by
Giovanna and Giuseppe
Panza di Biumo, two of
the greatest Italian
collectors of modern
and contemporary art.
Several days later,
they took it back
to the Apollinaire
Gallery, where they
had bought it.

The Milanese exhibition had an
international impact. Yves Klein later
exhibited his blue monochromes in May 1957
at the Iris Clert Gallery in Paris and
Schmela Gallery in Düsseldorf, then in June
of the same year at Gallery One in London.
The press articles of these exhibitions,
like the ones written in reaction to that
of Milan, expressed divergent opinions,
some laudatory, others disparaging.

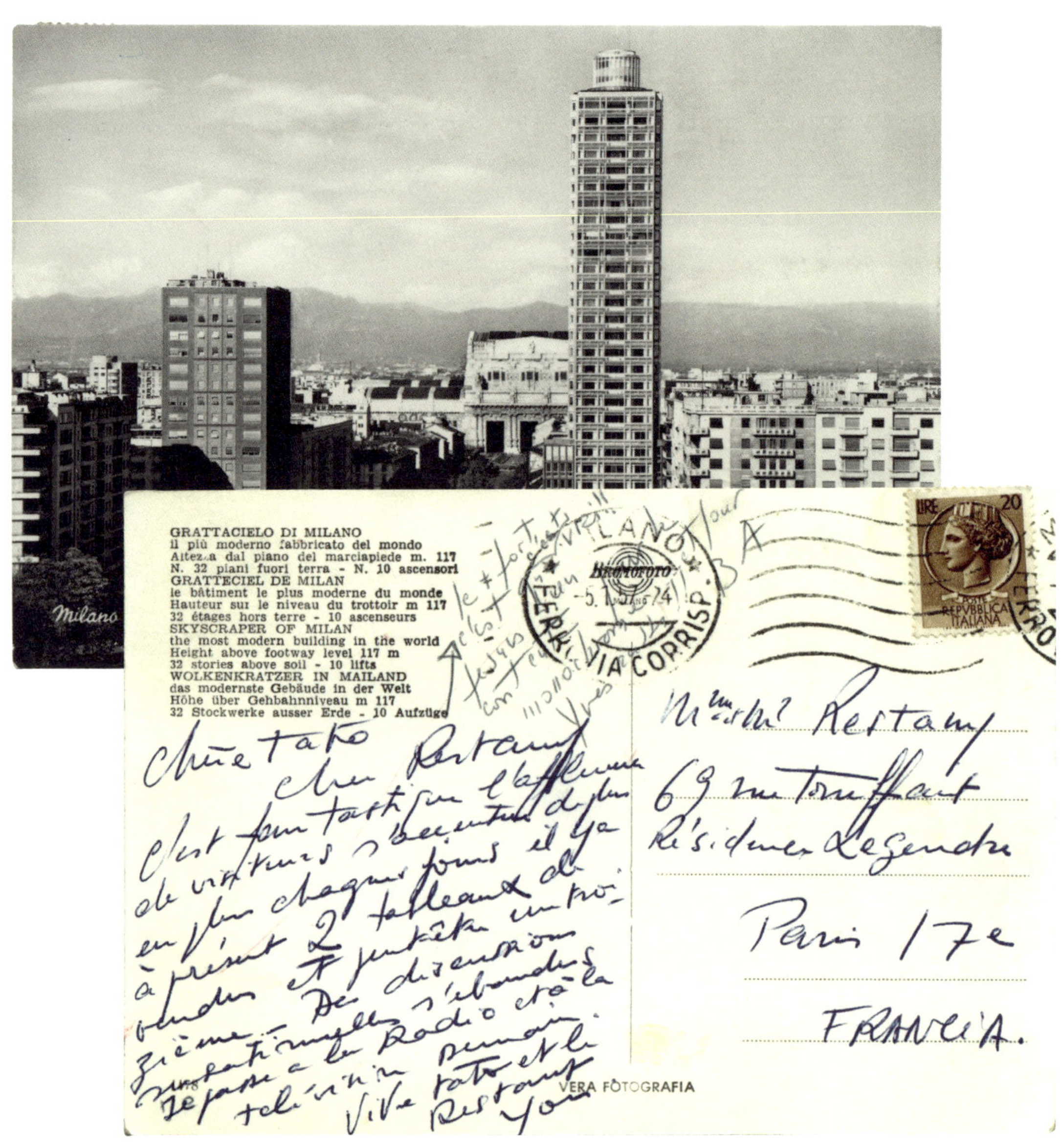

Postcard from Yves Klein and
Bernadette Allain to Pierre Restany,
sent from Milan, 5 January 1957

In it, Yves Klein evokes the affluence
of the visitors to the exhibition as well
as his spots on Italian radio
and television.
Translation p. 218

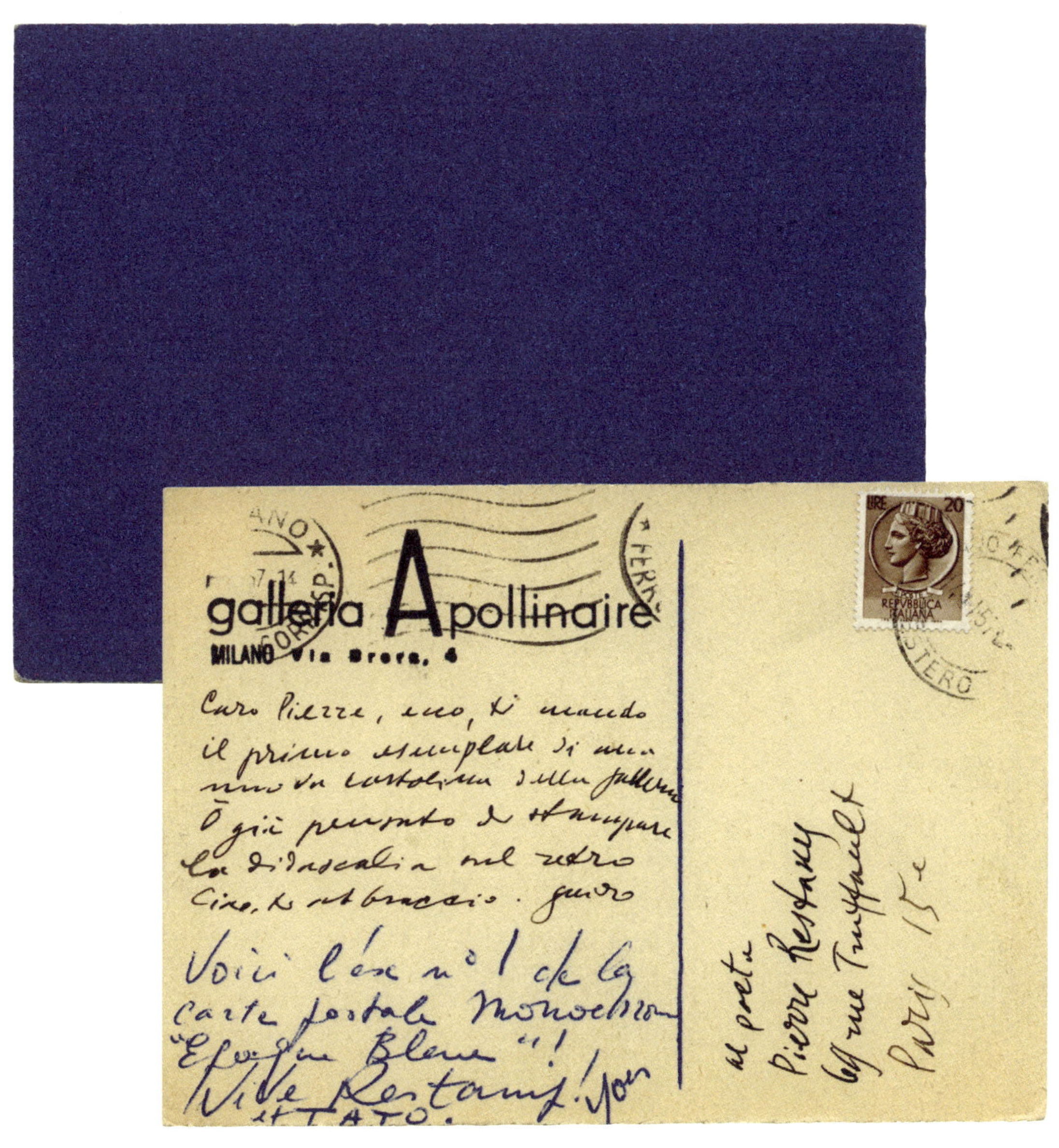

Postcard from Yves Klein and Guido Le Noci
to Pierre Restany, sent from Milan,
14 January 1957

Apollinaire Gallery made a "blue period"
postcard after the exhibition,
with the recto in IKB.
Translation p. 218

i 4 Soli

Segnalazione — gennaio - febbraio 1957

Proposition monochrome

Yves a exposé, au mois de février 1956, chez Colette Allendy, une dizaine de tableaux, de formats divers, peints d'une seule couleur, unie, sans variations ni nuances dans les tons, et fixés à des distances différentes en avant du mur de soutien, projetés en un mot hors de la cimaise.

A la suite des controverses qui se sont élevées autour de cette conception assez neuve de l'expression chromatique, basée sur un véritable acte de foi dans les possibilités de résonance affective de la couleur en soi (1), je crois nécessaire d'approfondir la notion de « proposition monochrome » que j'ai été amené à utiliser dans ma préface à cette exposition.

Pourquoi avoir parlé de « proposition monochromes »? C'est que nous sommes chaque fois ici en présence d'une couleur unie offerte à la contemplation.

A ce niveau la couleur est **proposée**. La proposition est une équation : donc un système équilibré, à partir d'une certaine notion zéro, représentée justement par le foyer théorique d'un champ visuel optimum, qu'elle-même détermine. Une « proposition monochrome » se réduit à l'équilibre d'un système **format-couleur**. Ceci dans l'abstrait de la création personnelle de l'artiste. Mais, cet équilibre une fois atteint, la proposition doit naturellement former un tout, une **entité** et doit être considerée come tel avec ses **exigences spatiales** — elle engendre une « aura » de développement, et alors se pose un problème de situation, situation du lecteur par rapport à l'oeuvre.

Le problème que nous abordons est celui de la couleur en situation, qui implique d'ailleurs une radicale exclusivité (de même que deux situations s'excluent dans le drame).

On peut concevoir que pour le peintre lui-même, la recherche s'arrête à cette mise en situation. Mais il apparaît incontestablement, à partir de là, un faisceau de complexes développements qui sont la manifestation d'une existence seconde. L'architecture intervient désormais et son rôle est de prévoir les possibles aménagements de cette survie, sa canalisation vers la coexistence, la détermination du lieu géométrique des « degrés zéro » dont nous parlions tout à l'heure.

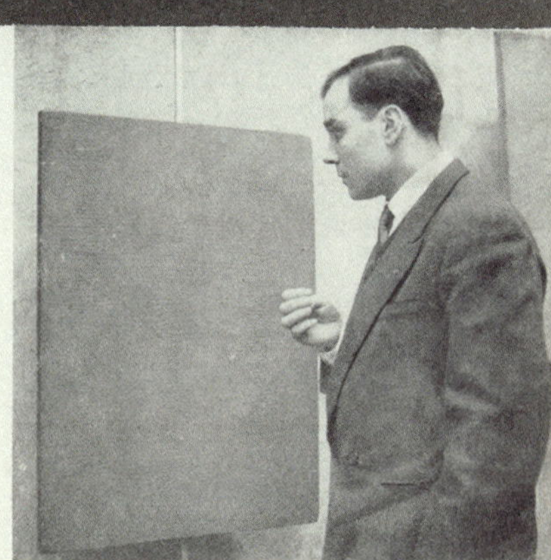

Yves Klein -: mostra galleria Apollinaire

A la limite nous en arrivons — par opposition aux prétentions synthétiques de la polychromie architecturale — à une conception rigoureusement analytique de la monochromie. La couleur ainsi proposée devient le diapason rythmique d'un ensemble conçu en fonction d'elle, raison élémentaire d'être, et non plus prétexte à l'utilisation du support.

Ce n'est que dans cette perspective que la monochromie peut éviter les impitoyables revanches de la matière, les incompréhensions nées de la terrible contamination « objective » de notre sens visuel, et surtout l'échec définitif, la désintégration du champ coloré dans l'espace ambiant qui se traduit par la sensation d'un rapport direct (générateur de « valeurs » synthétiques) entre l'oeuvre et le support, la toile et la cimaise.

P. Restany

Yves Klein's press book,
article "Proposition monochrome"
by Pierre Restany about Klein's solo
exhibition in Milan, published in
I 4 Soli magazine, January-February 1957
Translation pp. 218-219

Vernissage of the *Yves Klein.
Proposte monocrome, epoca Blu* exhibition,
2 January 1957, Apollinaire Gallery,
Milan

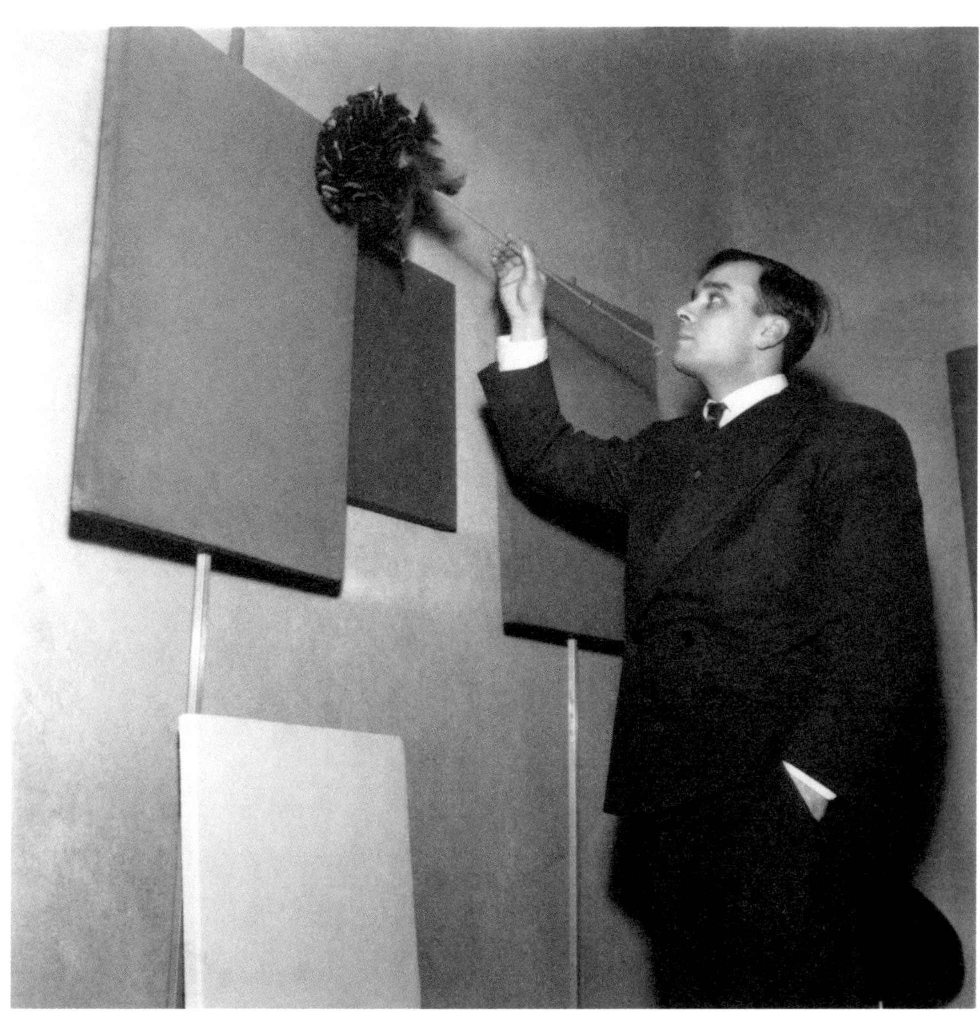

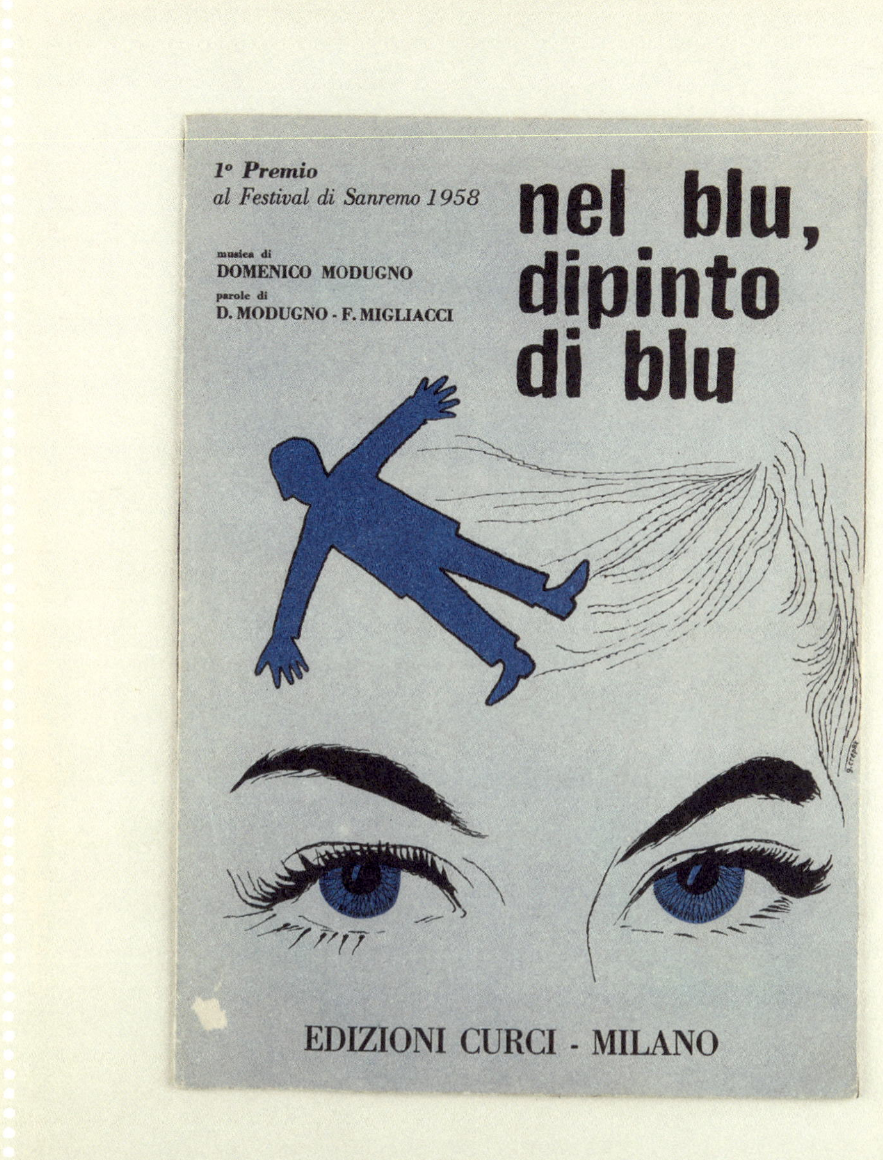

Yves Klein's press book, advertisement
for the "Nel blu, dipinto di blu" song,
written by Franco Migliacci and
Domenico Modugno, 1957

In "L'aventure monochrome", Yves Klein
highlights "the extraordinary success of the
song … [that he had inspired in] Modugno,
"Nel blu, dipinto di blu", by exhibiting
a blue period in Milan in 1957", meaning his
exhibition at the Apollinaire Gallery.
By attributing the inspiration for this song
to himself, Yves Klein demonstrated his
desire to extend his pictorial revolution
of the "blue period" to all components
of the culture of his day.

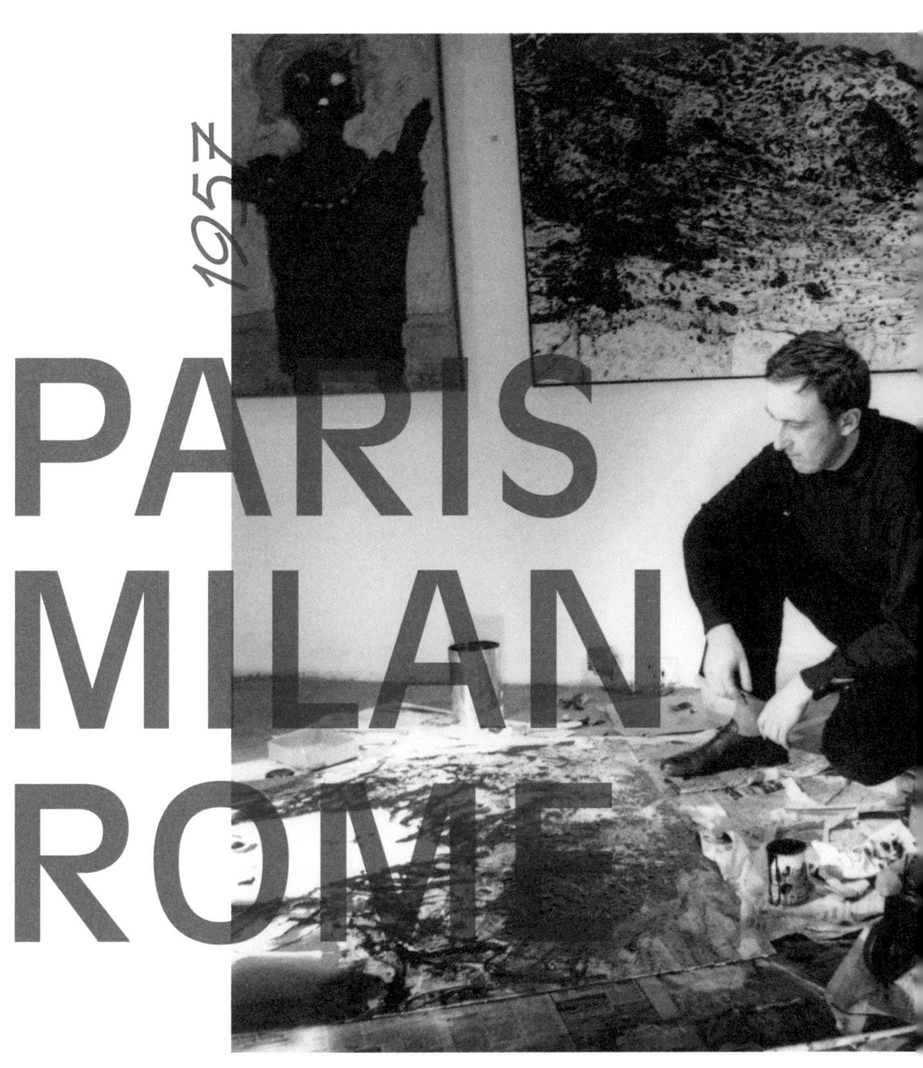

Artist Enrico Baj
in his studio,
Via Teulié,
Milan, 1957

Invitation card sent to Lucio Fontana
for the double exhibition *Yves Klein.
Propositions monochromes* held at
the Iris Clert Gallery in Paris from
10 to 25 May and at the Colette Allendy
Gallery, from 14 to 23 May 1957
Translation p. 219

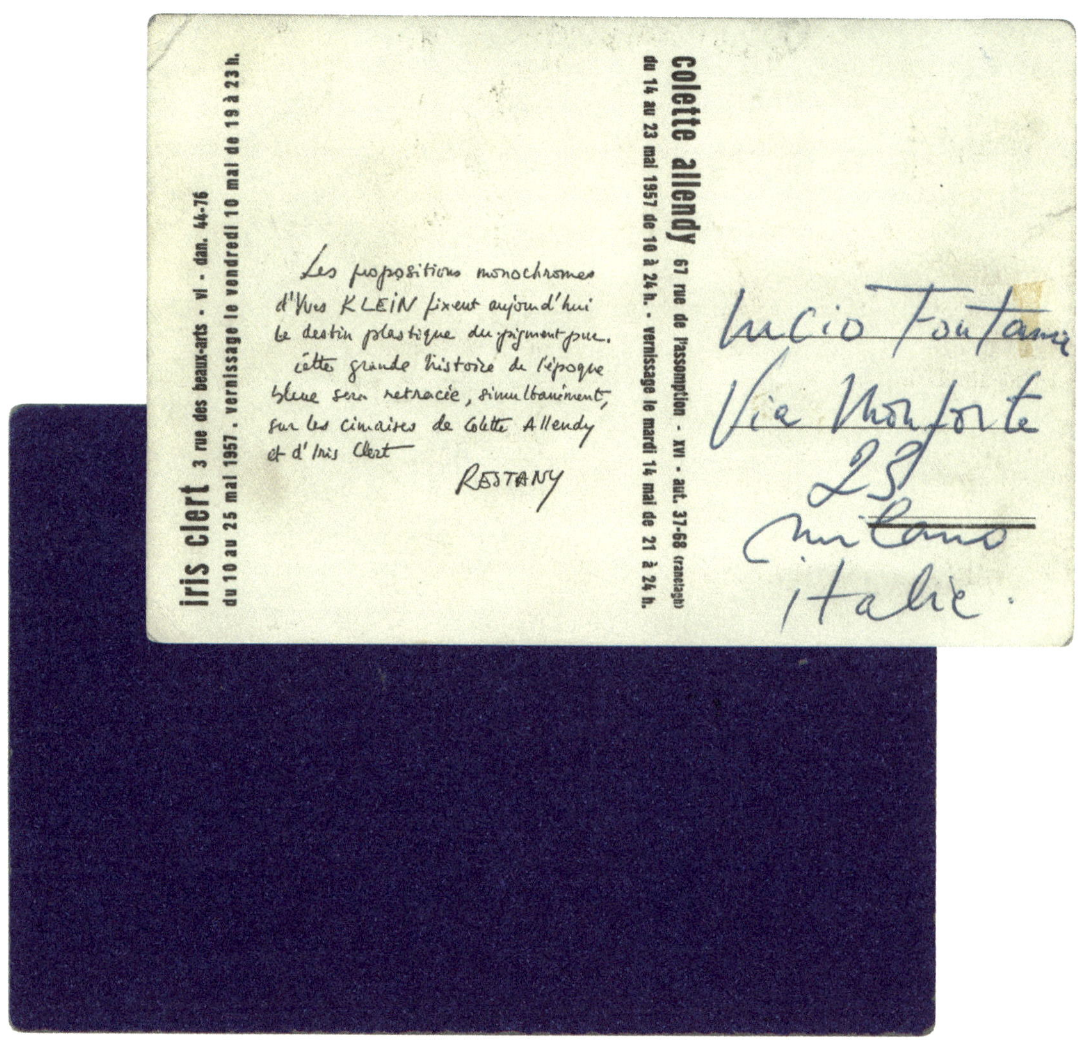

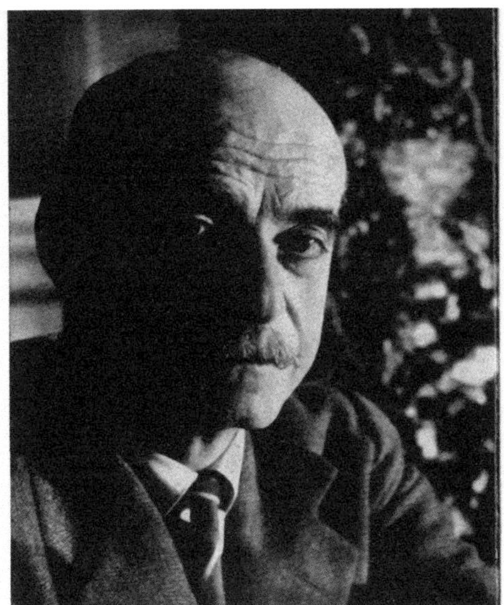

18 opere della collezione privata di
BRUNO MUNARI

ARP	MELANI
BALLA	MESCIULAM
DORAZIO	MUNARI
DONATI	PRAMPOLINI
HUBER	SCHAWINSKY
KANDINSKY	SOLDATI
KRAMPEN	SOTTSASS
MAGNELLI	TINGUELY
MARI	VERONESI

18 opere della collezione privata di
LUCIO FONTANA

BAJ	DANGELO
BURRI	DE LUIGI
BERGOLLI	DOVA
BELLEGARDE	KLEIN
BEMPORAD	LICINI
CALDER	NANDO
CERCHIARI	PEVERELLI
CAPOGROSSI	SCANAVINO
CRIPPA	ZAGNI

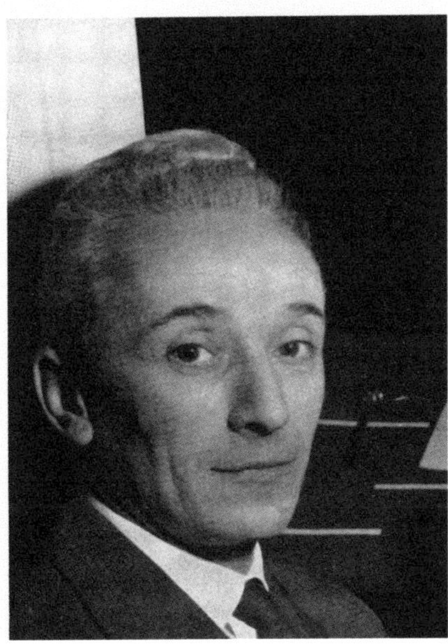

On Wednesday 15 May 1957, the exhibition
*18 Works from the Private Collection of
Lucio Fontana - 18 Works from the Private
Collection of Bruno Munari* was inaugurated
at the Blu Gallery in Milan, the high temple
of encounters and discussions dedicated
to the contemporary avant-garde.
Among the artworks presented in this
exhibition was Yves Klein's blue monochrome
that Lucio Fontana had acquired from
the Apollinaire Gallery in January
that same year.

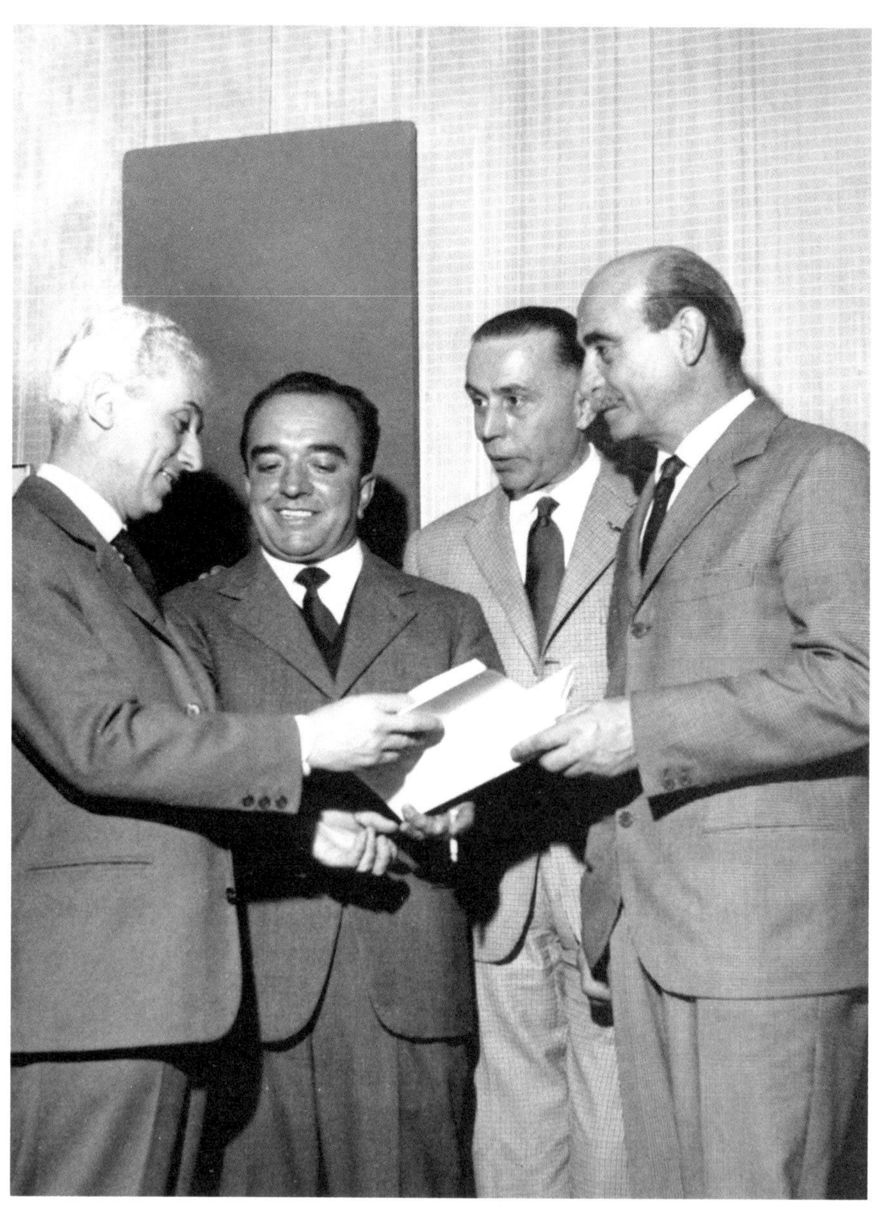

Vernissage, 15 May 1957
Among others, we see Bruno Munari,
Lucio Fontana, and Peppino Palazzoli,
Italian collector, patron, and founder
of the Blu Gallery, in front of Yves
Klein's monochrome (IKB 100).

Anno I - n. 15

il Micro-Salon
di Iris Clert di Parigi
in esclusività per l'Italia
alla Galleria Apollinaire
di Milano

Giugno 1957 - Edizione italiana

ouverture
sur le futur

arnal

baj

barré

bellegarde

benrath

bertini

bertrand (h.-a).

boïlle

brüning

bryen

dangelo

halpern

hundertwasser

jaffe

koenig

parisot

pink

rainer

staritsky

tsingos

van haardt

sculptures de : delahaye — kricke — signori

peinture cinétique de tinguély

composition monochrome d'yves klein

h. kamer
90, boulevard raspail
paris   bab. 00-97

Invitation card for the group exhibition
Ouvertures sur le futur, organised
by Pierre Restany at the H. Kamer Gallery
in Paris, vernissage on 25 June 1957

Enrico Baj, Sergio Dangelo, Gianni Bertini,
Adriano Parisot, and Yves Klein
(with a *Monochrome Composition*) participated
in this exhibition.

Letter from Yves Klein to Enrico Baj,
5 June 1957 (excerpt)

At Enrico Baj's request, Yves Klein made
a list of art critics he could put him
in touch with. Since Charles Estienne
did not reply, he gave him other names:
Pierre Restany, Michel Ragon,
Julien Alvard, and Louis-Paul Favre.
Translation p. 219

Yves Klein, *Untitled*
Blue Monochrome,
1957
Artwork once belonging
to Enrico Baj

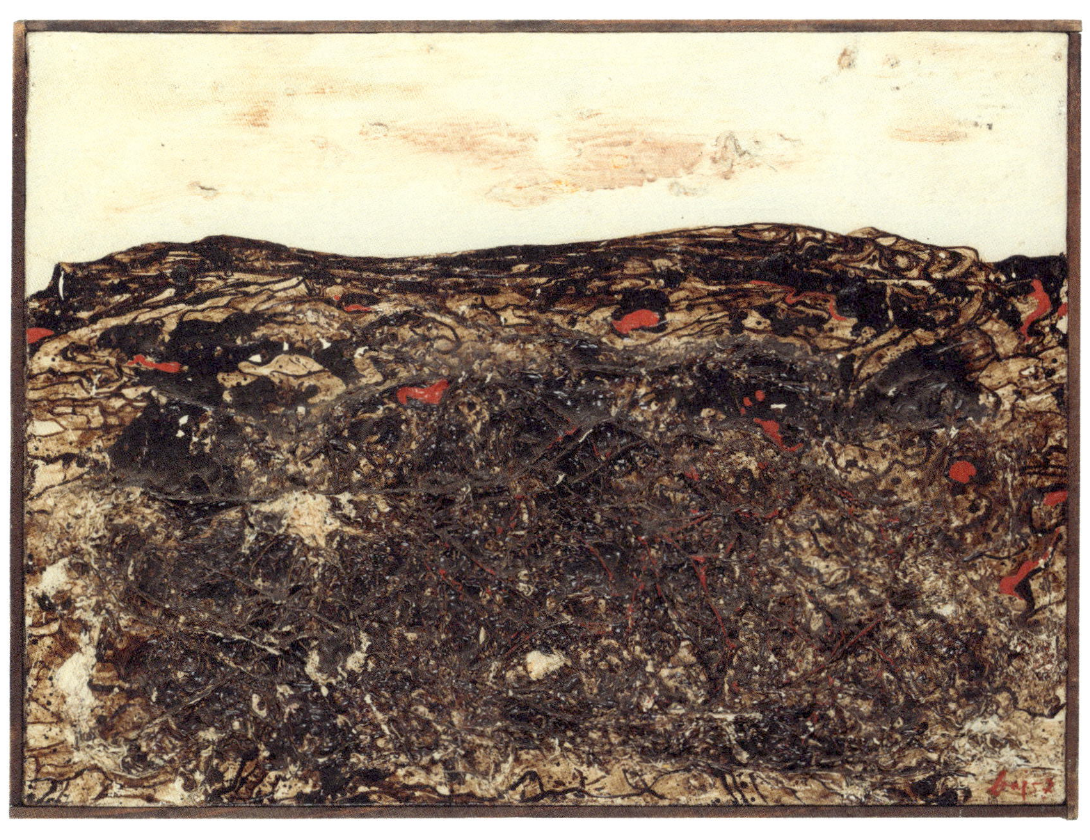

Enrico Baj,
Untitled, 1957
Artwork once belonging
to Yves Klein

Yves Klein and Enrico Baj met in
January 1957 on the occasion of the Yves
Klein exhibition at the Apollinaire Gallery.
They became friends and Baj invited Klein
to join the Arte Nucleare movement that
he had created with Sergio Dangelo
and Gianni Colombo.

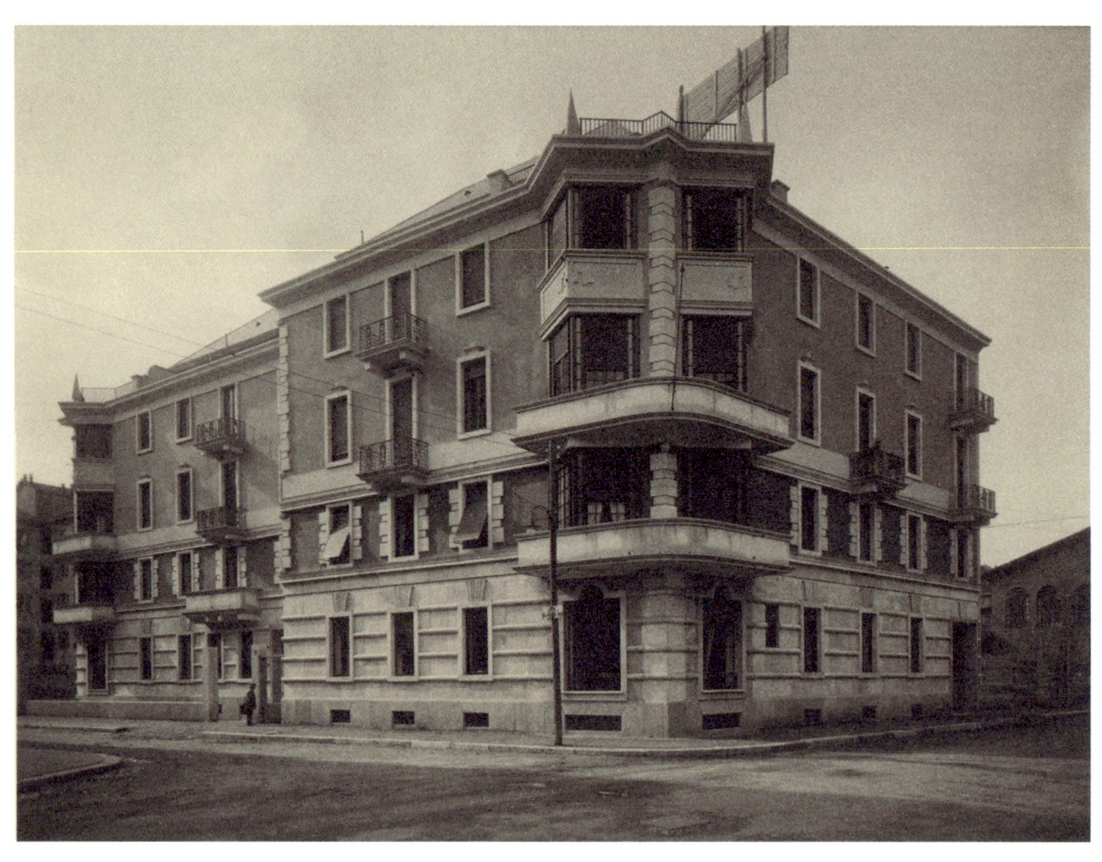

Building designed by architect
Piero Portaluppi, Via Aldrovandi 3 /
Via Jan 15 in Milan, where the famous couple
Antonio Boschi and Marieda Di Stefano,
collectors of Marie Raymond's artworks,
lived on the second floor

From 1931 onwards, they devoted their time
to forming a collection that assembled over
two thousand artworks, and their apartment
became a social hub for the Milanese
art scene. The artworks were everywhere,
from floor to ceiling, piled one on top
of the other without interruption,
including over the doors, according to
a very personal logic and combinations.
In July 1957, Yves Klein delivered
two artworks on paper to them by
his mother, Marie Raymond.

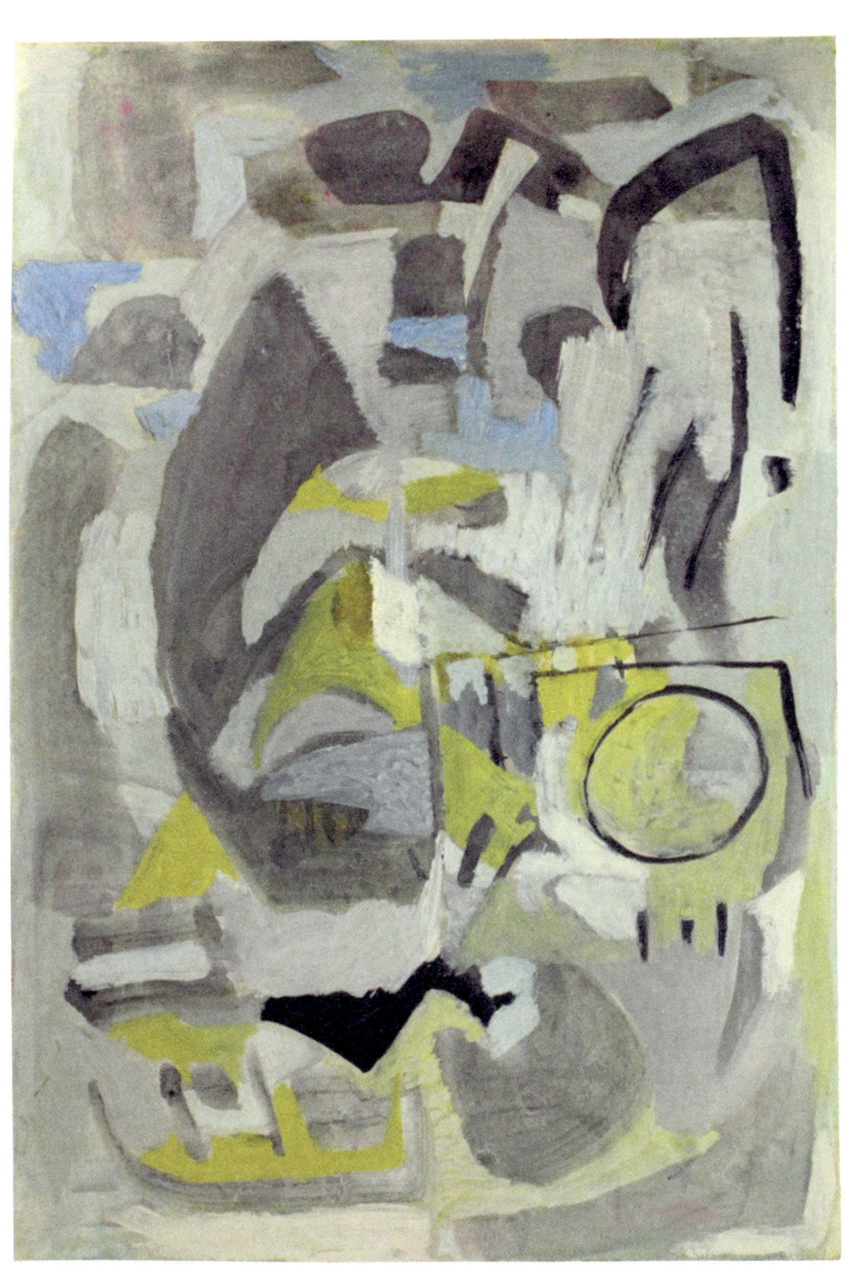

Marie Raymond, *Composition*, 1957
Dedication on the back from Yves Klein:
"To Madame Marieda / Boschi on /
behalf of my mother / Yves Klein /
Paris, 7 July / 1957"

CONTRO LO STILE

CONTRE LE STYLE

THE END OF STYLE

J'aime les assertions que l'artiste prend sur lui d'assumer au-delà de la sclérose des exercises de style.

Amo le proposte che l'artista sa gettare oltre lo sclerotico esercizio di stile.

Gianni Bertini

Movimento Arte Nucleare   Milano   via Teullié 1

CONTRO LO S[TILE]

NEL FEBBRAIO 1952 IL PRIMO […]
MAVA LA NOSTRA VOLONT[À …]
CONCESSIONE A QUALUN[QUE …]
COSI' SI ESPRIMEVA LA NOS[TRA …]
NIO DELL'ANGOLO RETTO […]
MACCHINA, CONTRO LA […]
METRICA.

DA ALLORA ABBIAMO PRO[…]
ZIONE DI OGNI POSSIBILE […]
MATISMO «TACHISTE» O […]
TIVO, AL GRAFISMO, ALLA […]
AL CALLIGRAFISMO, ALLE […]
MATERISMO, SINO ALLE A[…]
BERTINI (1957).

ALLE SPERIMENTAZIONI TE[…]
PER VICENDEVOLI SUGGEST[…]
SPAZI IMMAGINARI (CFR. P[…]
MATERIA» DEL 1951 (BAJ E […]
RAZIONI» DEL 1953 (BAJ […]
NI) ALLE «NUOVE FLORE[…]
ANIMALI E FAVOLE» (BAJ […]
«SITUAZIONI ATOMIZZATE […]

MA OGNI INVENZIONE RISC[…]
DI RIPETIZIONI STEREOTIP[…]
TILE: E' QUINDI URGENTE I[…]
AZIONE ANTISTILISTICA P[…]
«AUTRE» (CRF. MICHEL TA[…]

«DE STIJL» E' MORTO E SEP[…]
— L'ANTISTILE — CHE […]
ULTIME BARRIERE DELLA […]
COMUNE, LE ULTIME CHE L[…]
ANCORA OPPORRE ALLA […]
L'ARTE.

GIA' L'IMPRESSIONISMO L[…]
GETTI CONVENZIONALI; CU[…]
VOLTA TOLSERO L'IMPERAT[…]
TIVA E VENNE POI L'ASTI[…]
RESIDUA OMBRA DI UNA ILL[…]
SENTAZIONE. L'ULTIMO AN[…]
PER ESSERE OGGI DISTRUTT[…]
OGGI L'ULTIMA DELLE CON[…]

NOI AMMETTIAMO COME U[…]
LIZZAZIONE LE «PROPOSI[…]
KLEIN (1956-1957): DOPO DI […]
BULA RASA» O I ROTOLI D[…]

TAPPEZZIERI O PITTORI: B[…]
UNA VISIONE SEMPRE NUOV[…]
LA TELA E' OGNI VOLTA LA […]
PREVEDIBILE «COMMED[IA …]

NOI AFFERMIAMO L'IRREPETIBILITA' DELL'OPERA D'ARTE: E CHE L'ESSENZA DELLA STESSA SI PONGA COME «PRESENZA MODIFICANTE» IN UN MONDO CHE NON NECESSITA PIU' DI RAPPRESENTAZIONI CELEBRATIVE MA DI PRESENZE.

Milano, Settembre 1957.

Firmatari: Armand, Enrico Baj, Bemporad, Gianni Bertini, Jaques Colonne, Stanley Chapmans, Mario Colucci, Dangelo, Enrico De Miceli, Reinhout D'Haese, Wout Hoeboer, Hundertwasser, Yves Klein, Théodore Koenig, Piero Manzoni, Nando, Joseph Noiret, Arnaldo Pomodoro, Gio Pomodoro, Pierre Restany, Saura, Ettore Sordini, Serge Vandercam, Angelo Verga.

The last stylistic works that we recognize
are the "monochromes" of Yves Klein
(1956–1957); only the bare boards
– or Capogrossi's rolls of textile –
can follow them.

Manifesto "The End of Style"

"The End of Style" manifesto was written
in Milan in September 1957 and signed
by Arman, Enrico Baj, Gianni Bertini,
Sergio Dangelo, Yves Klein, Piero Manzoni,
Arnaldo and Giò Pomodoro,
and Pierre Restany, among others.

"Once upon a time impressionism
helped painting get rid of conventional
subject-matter; cubism and futurism later
got rid of the need for the realistic
reproduction of objects; and abstraction
finally removed the last traces of
representational illusion. A new
– and final – link today completes this
chain: we, nuclear painters, denounce,
in order to destroy, the final convention,
s t y l e."
Transcription pp. 219-220

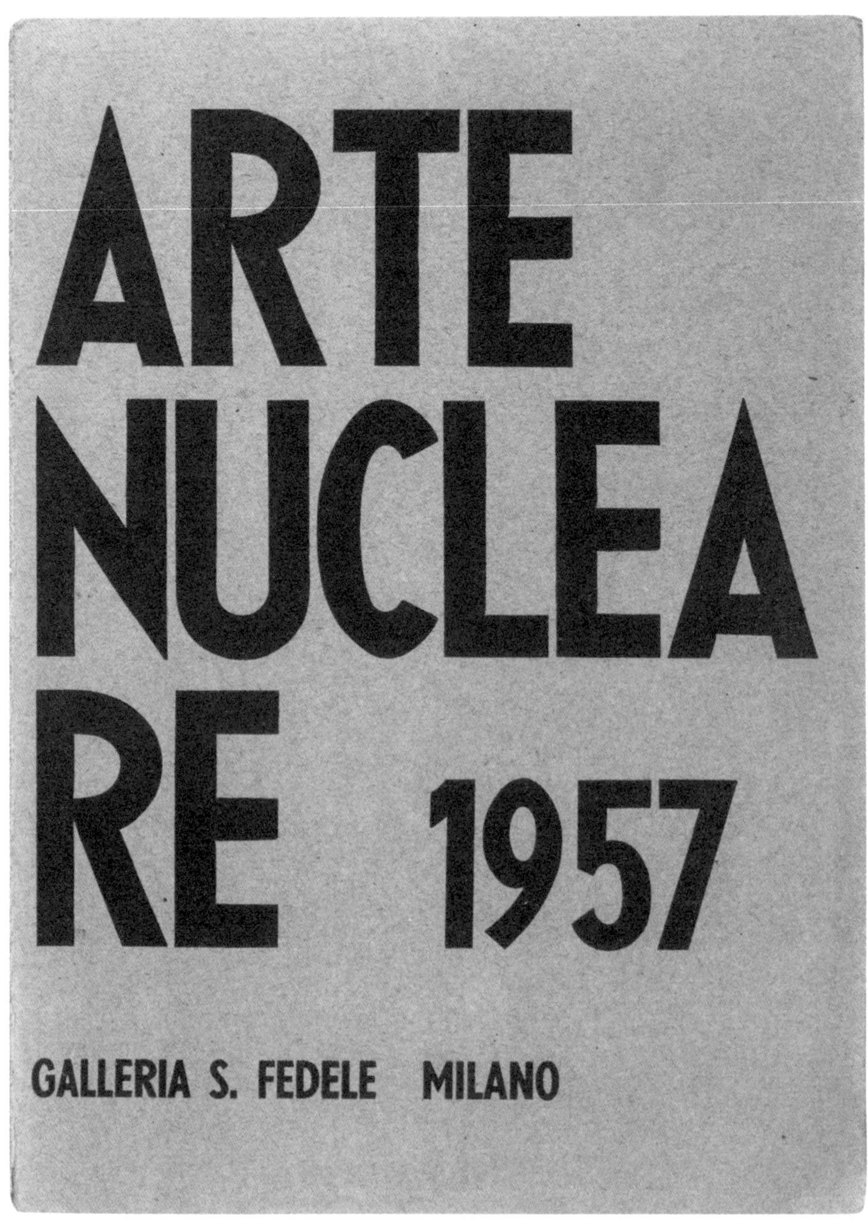

Cover of the
Arte Nucleare
exhibition catalogue,
San Fedele Gallery,
Milan, 12-30 October
1957

San Fedele Gallery was promoted
by Jesuit fathers who initiated a series
of first-rate exhibitions in the 1950s.
In October 1957, they organised
Arte Nucleare, with the participation of
Enrico Baj, Franco Bemporad, Gianni Bertini,
Sergio Dangelo, Yves Klein, Piero Manzoni,
Arnaldo and Giò Pomodoro, Mario Rossello,
Ettore Sordini, Angelo Verga, Asger Jorn,
and Serge Vandercam.

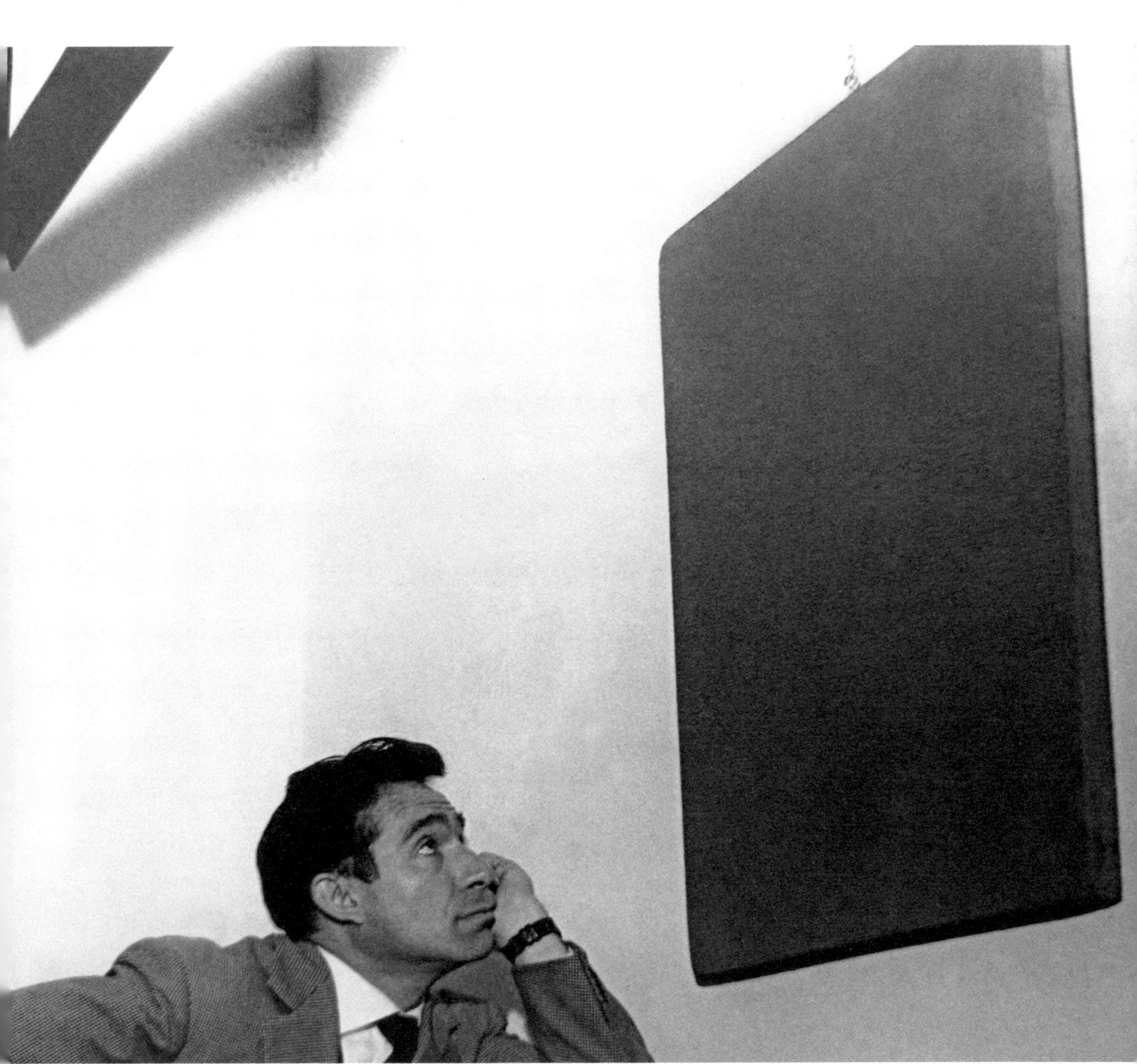

The actor, stage director, and writer
Ugo Tognazzi, in front of a blue monochrome
by Yves Klein at San Fedele Gallery
in Milan, on the occasion of the vernissage
of the *Arte Nucleare* exhibition,
12 October 1957

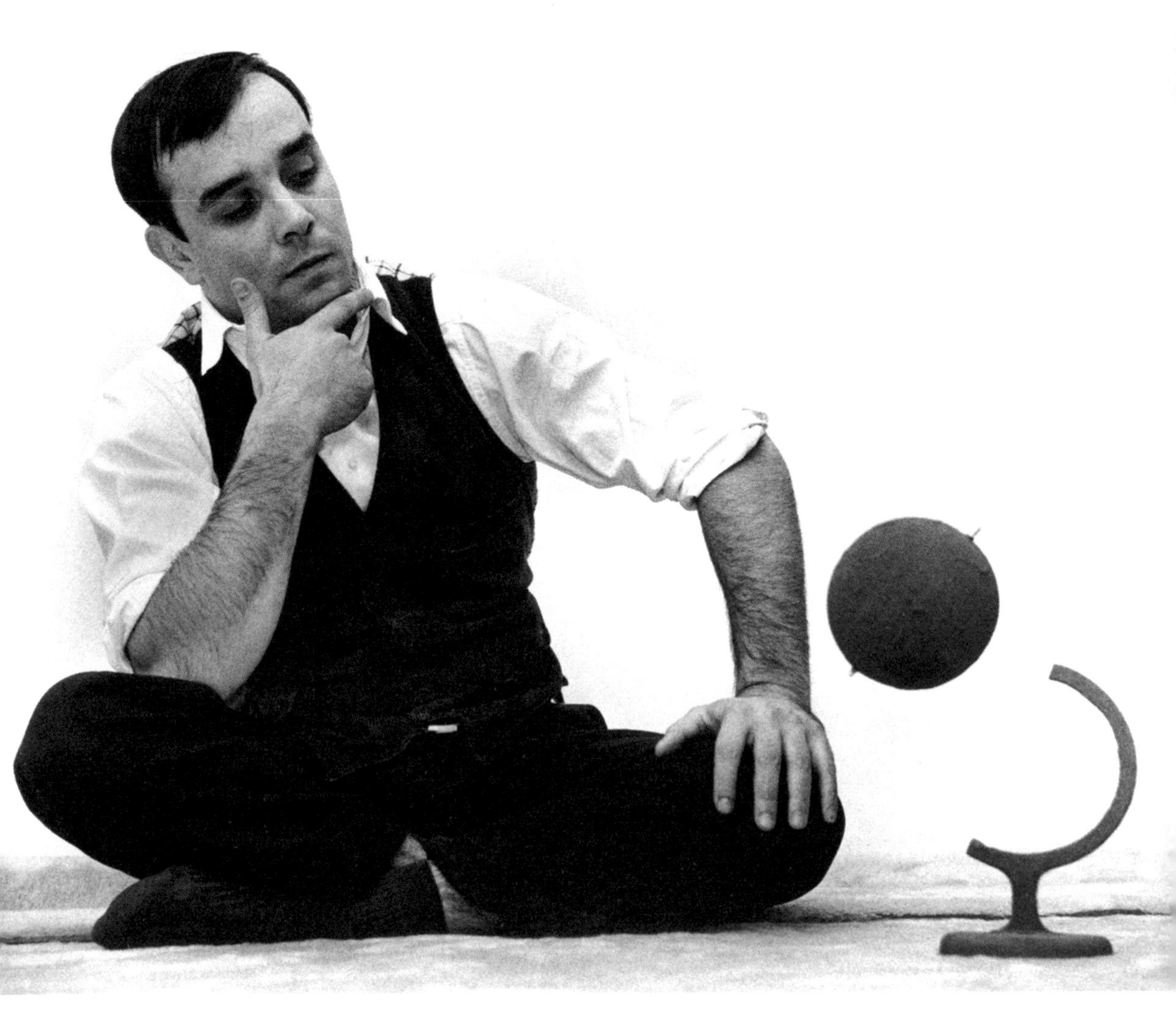

In 1957, Yves Klein declared that the whole
world is blue. He created a globe on this
occasion (*Globe terrestre bleu* [Blue Earth
Globe] [RP 7], 1957). Four years later,
in April 1961, the astronaut Gagarin
declared: "The Earth is an intense and
deep blue."

Italian art magazine *L'Esperienza moderna*, nos. 3-4, December 1957, with a double page dedicated to the era of space exploration, from Yves Klein's book collection

Founded by the artists Gastone Novelli and Achille Perilli, *L'Esperienza moderna* magazine was published between 1957 and 1959. In just four issues, to which European artists, poets and critics contributed, it became a primordial source for the avant-garde trends.

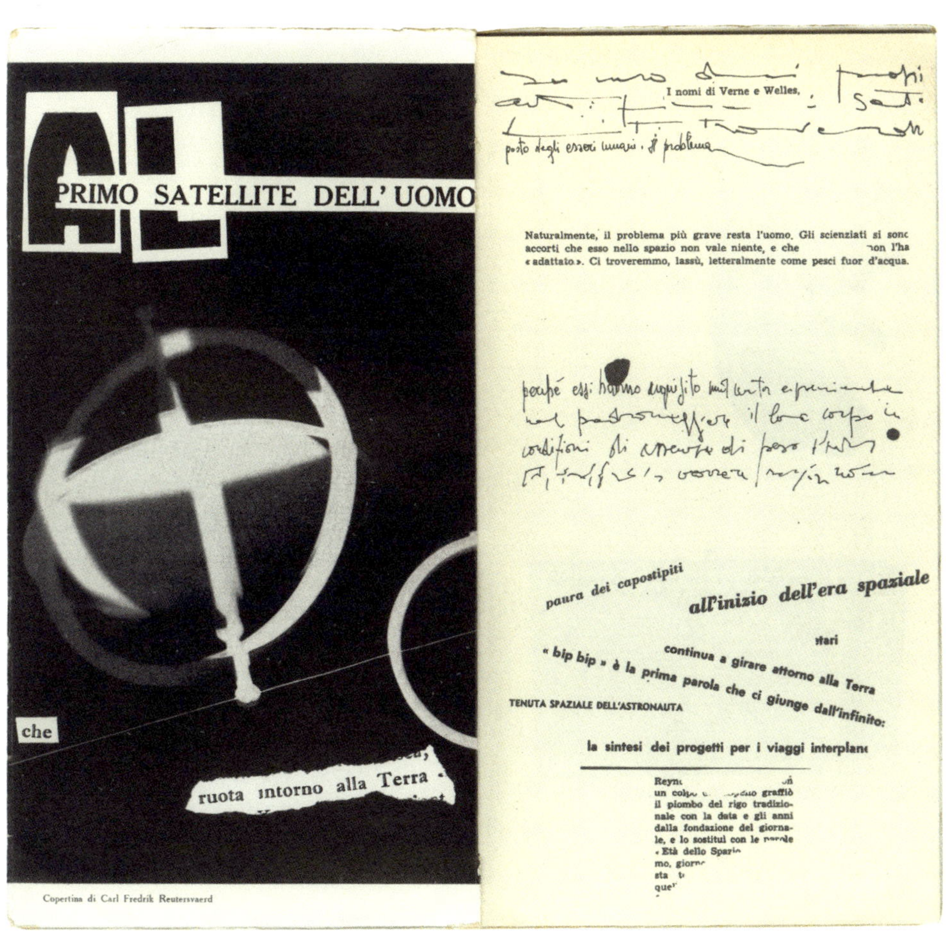

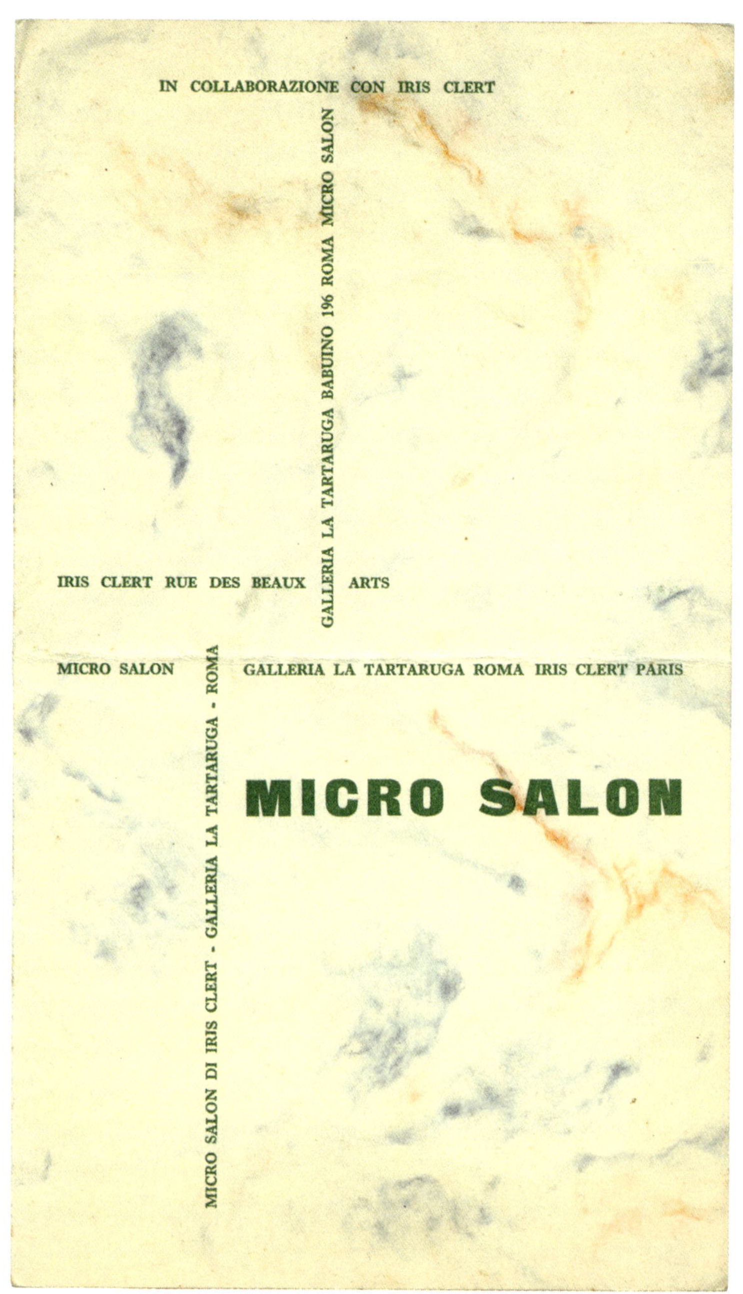

Invitation card to the *Micro-Salon* group
exhibition held at La Tartaruga
Gallery, Rome

After an exhibition co-produced
by Iris Clert Gallery at Apollinaire Gallery
in June 1957, the *Micro-Salon* exhibition
opened in Rome at La Tartaruga Gallery
on 18 December of the same year. Among the
artworks exhibited was a small monochrome
by Yves Klein.

Founded in Rome in February 1954 by
Plinio De Martiis and co-ordinated with the
help of his wife Maria Antonietta Pirandello
(aka Ninni), as soon as it opened,
La Tartaruga became a privileged site
of encounters between Italian and foreign
artists, critics, gallerists,
and intellectuals.

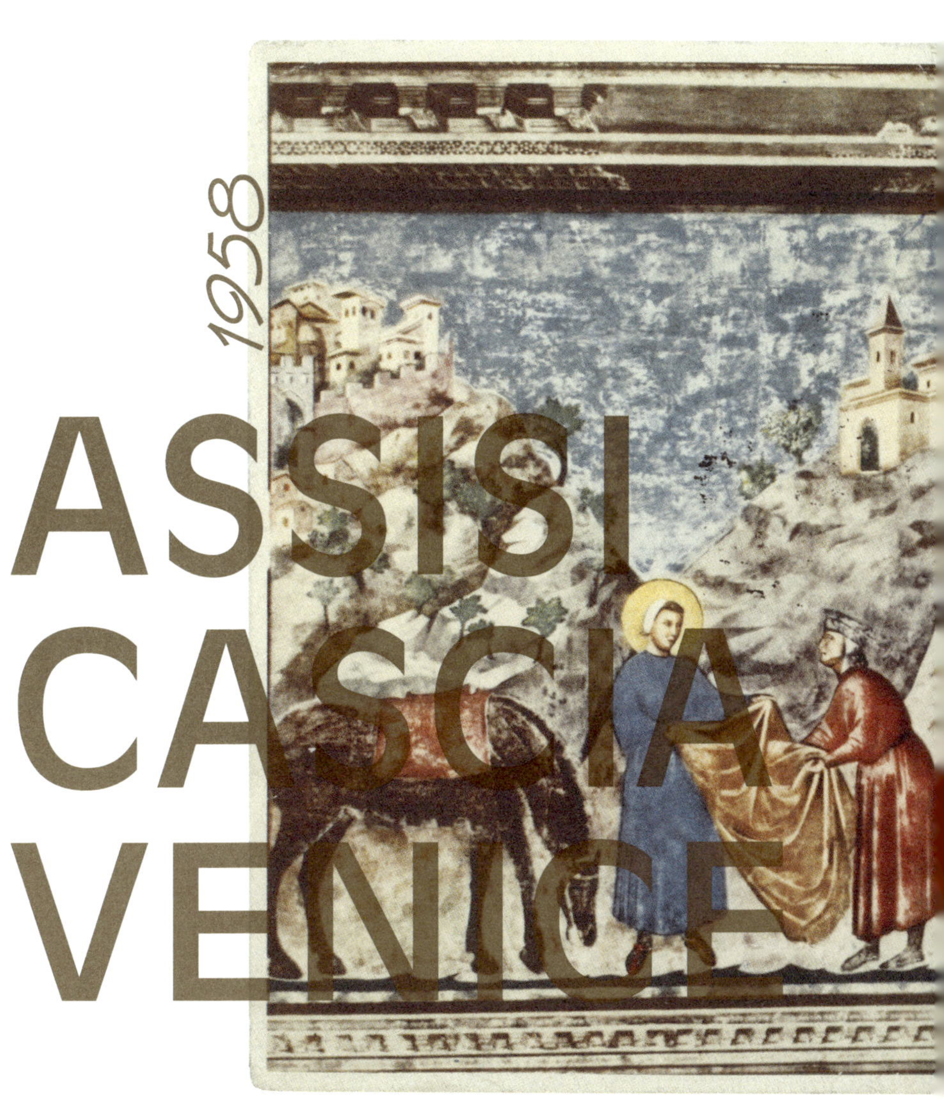

Postcard sent from Assisi to Iris Clert
on 7 April 1958, "Francis gives his tunic
to a beggar", reproduction of a scene
from the frescoes of the life
of Saint Francis by Giotto

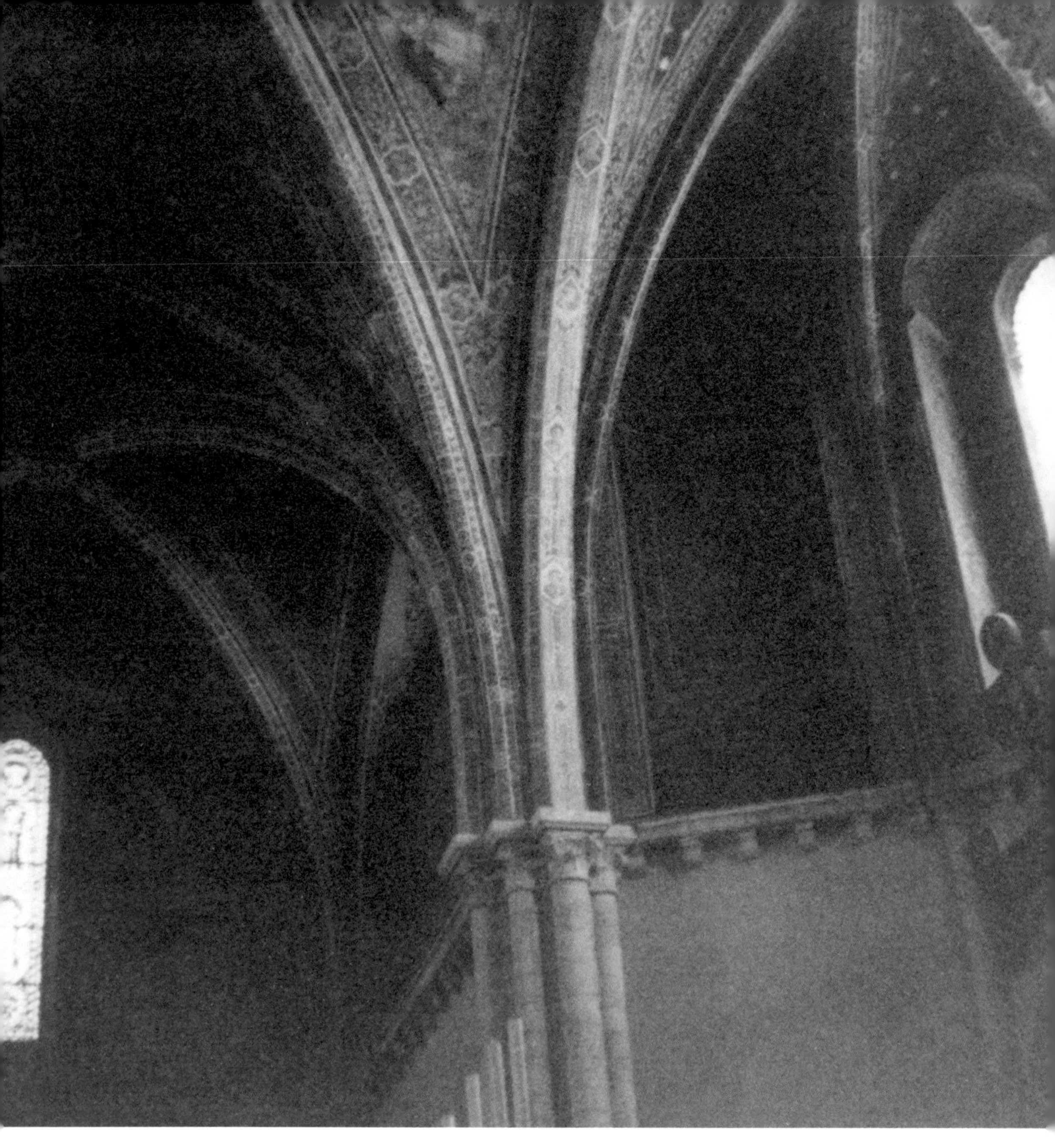

Photo of the nave of
the Basilica of Saint
Francis in Assisi,
by Yves Klein

For his thirtieth birthday, Yves Klein
travelled to Assisi and visited the Basilica
of Saint Francis. There he discovered,
in the nave of the upper church, the azure
panels painted by Giotto that serve as
a background to the scenes from the life
of Saint Francis and thus declared Giotto
his true predecessor in monochromy.

Yves Klein photographed
by his aunt Rose in
front of the Basilica
of Saint Francis,
Assisi, April 1958

Back of the postcard
sent from Assisi
to Iris Clert
on 7 April 1958

Yves Klein evokes
the "entirely blue
monochrome paintings"
by Giotto.
Translation p. 220

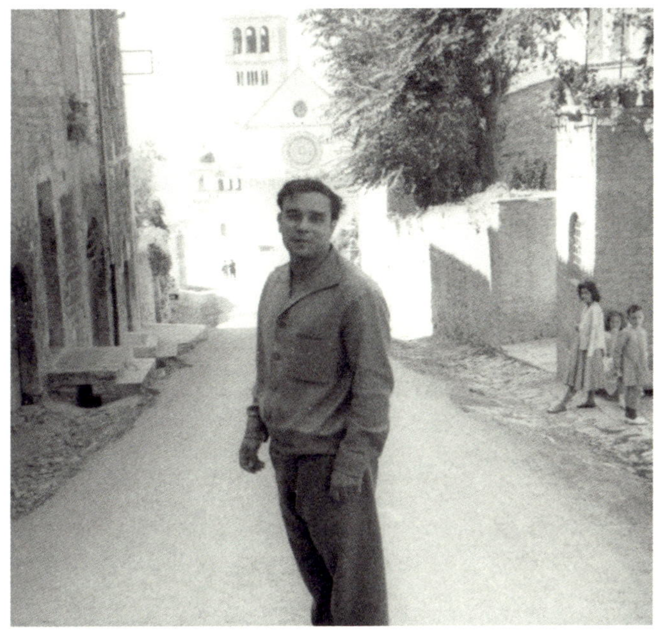

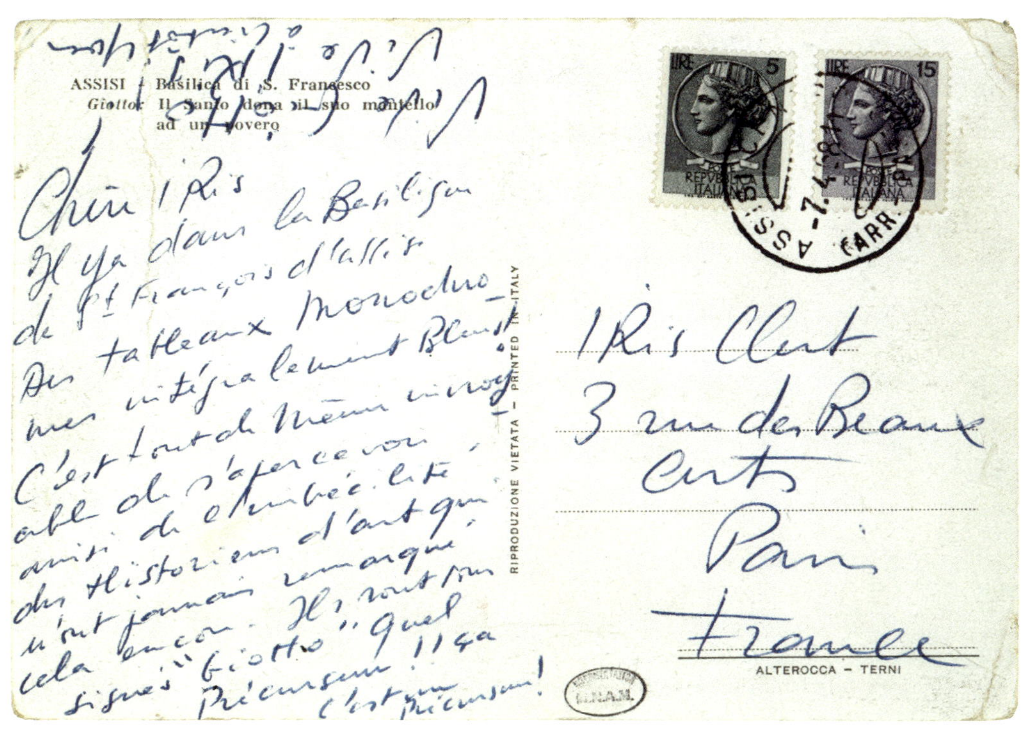

Ma chère Miramau,

Tantine et moi avons décidé de faire un petit voyage ensemble en Italie du 1er septembre au 15 — Voilà !

Il n'y a pas de possibilités de... avant — si tu viens, viens donc...

Letter from Yves Klein and Rose Raymond
to Marie Raymond in which they evoke
their journey in Italy from 1 to
15 September 1958.
A blue stamp is pasted on the letter,
which Yves Klein had created on the occasion
of his double exhibition at the Iris Clert
Gallery and the Colette Allendy Gallery
in Paris in May 1957.
Translation p. 220

Yves Klein, *Untitled Blue Monochrome*, 1958
Dedication on the back from Yves Klein:
"In Recognition of Saint Rita / 15 September
1958 / Yves Klein aka The Monochrome";
and from Rose Raymond: "From Paris /
thanks to Saint RITA / Rose-Marie Raymond"

In September 1958, Yves Klein and his aunt
Rose travelled together once again in Italy
and went to Cascia in the province
of Perugia to visit the Saint Rita Basilica
and Monastery. On this occasion,
they gave a blue monochrome to the monastery
as a sign of gratitude to Saint Rita
for the commission of monumental blue
monochromes and blue sponge reliefs
by the Musiktheater im Revier
in Gelsenkirchen, Germany.

Yves Klein in front
of the Saint Rita
Basilica of Cascia,
15 September 1958

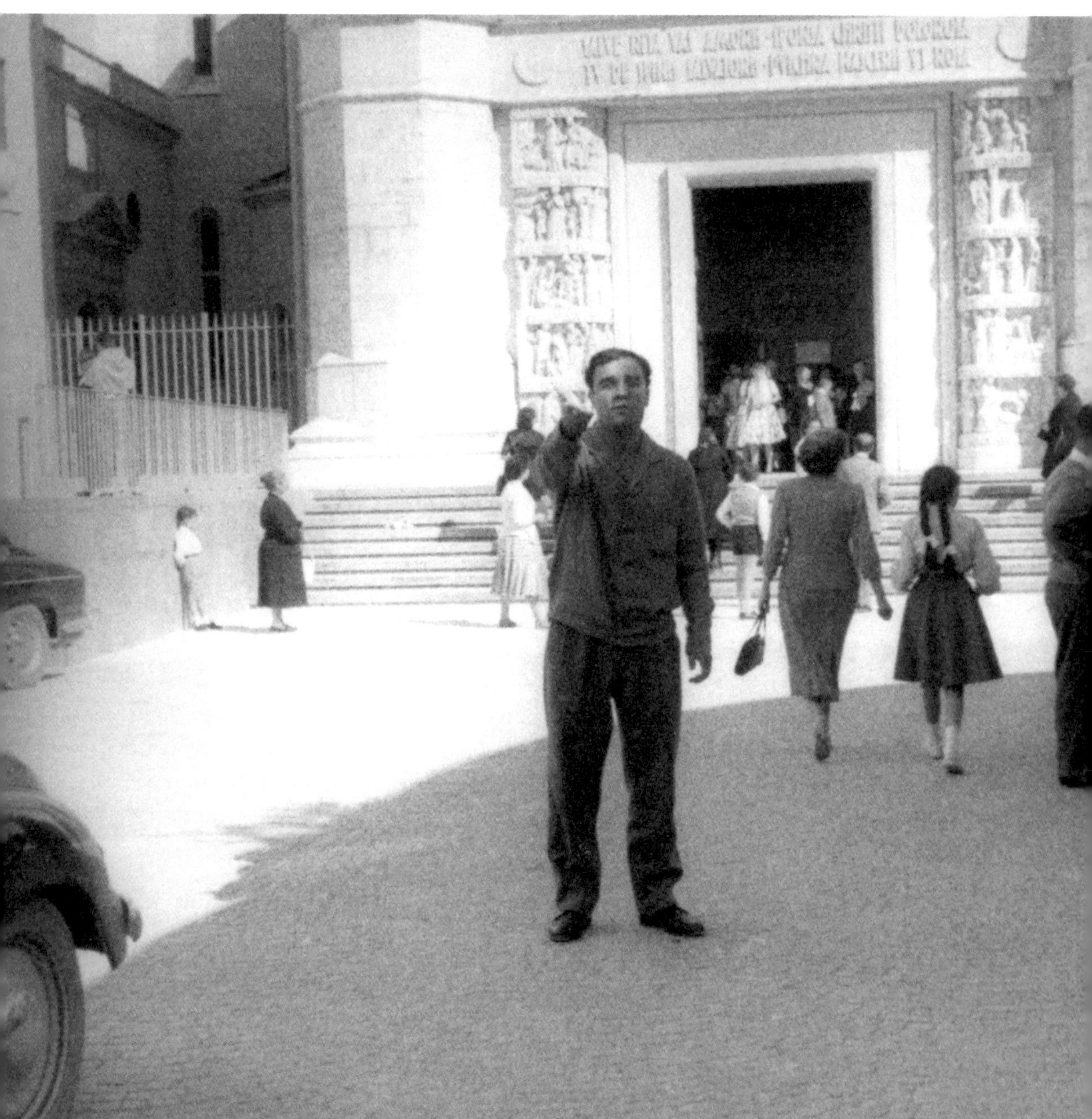

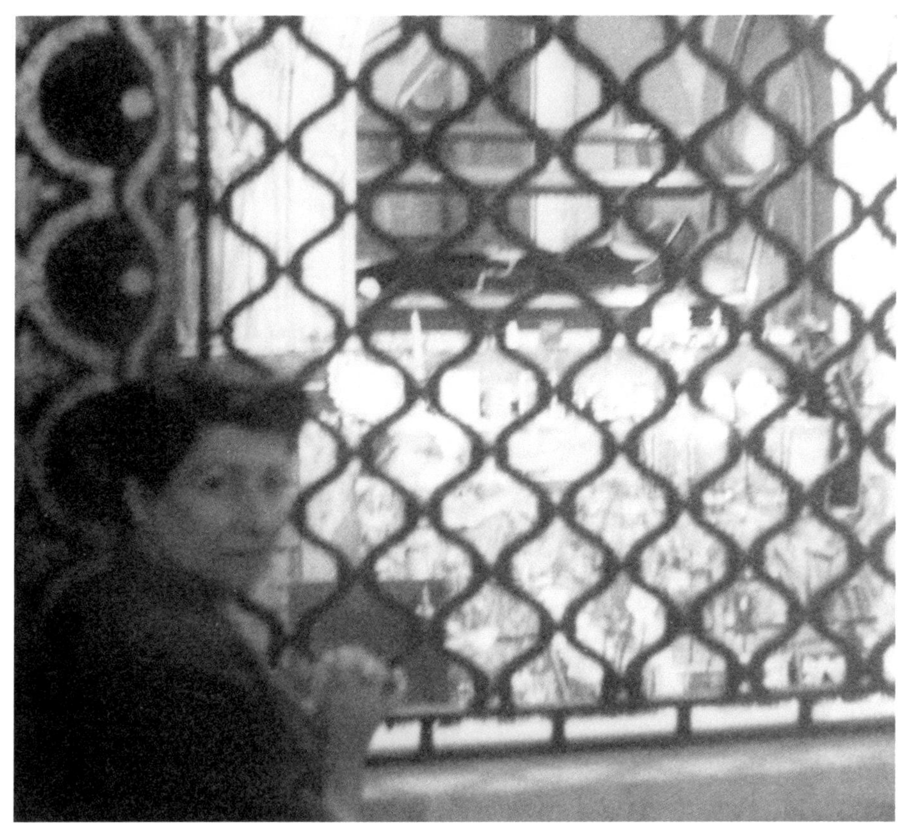

Rose Raymond,
15 September 1958,
inside the apse where
the Saint Rita Chapel
had been installed,
surrounded by a
wrought-iron fence.
The body of the saint
is located in
a display case, which
is itself placed inside
a glass sarcophagus.

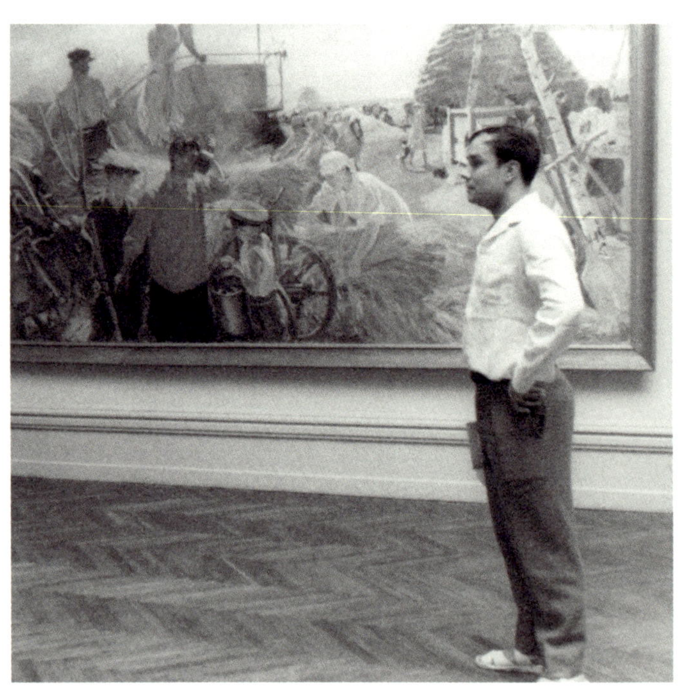

Yves Klein in front of
an artwork by Russian
artist Arkady Plastov,
at the Soviet Pavilion
of the twenty-ninth
Venice Biennale,
September 1958

Advertisement for
the Paradiso restaurant
of the Venice Biennale,
1958, with handwritten
annotations by
Yves Klein

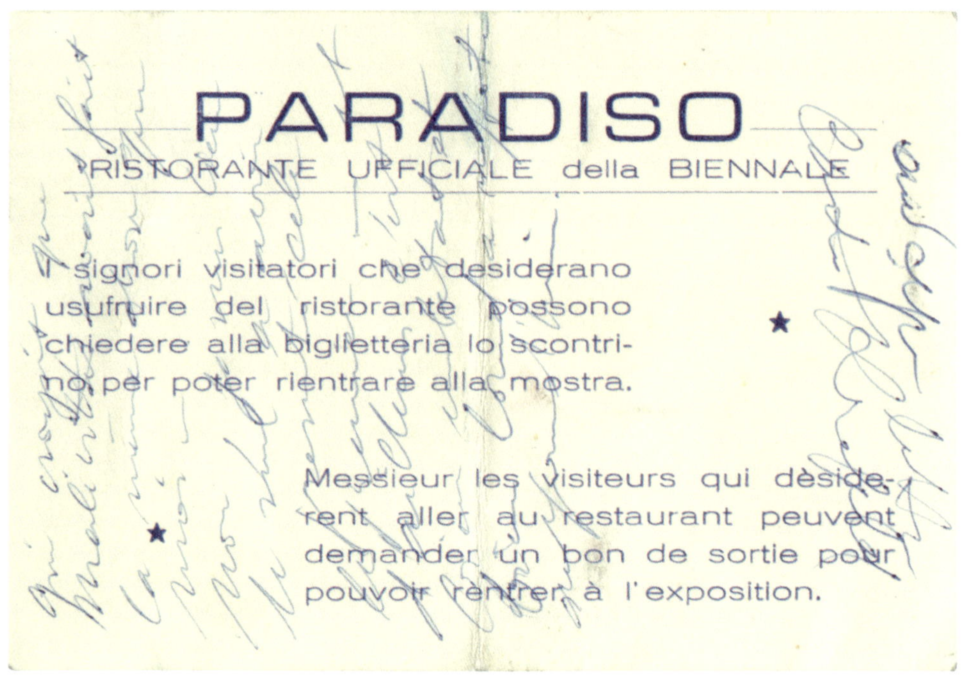

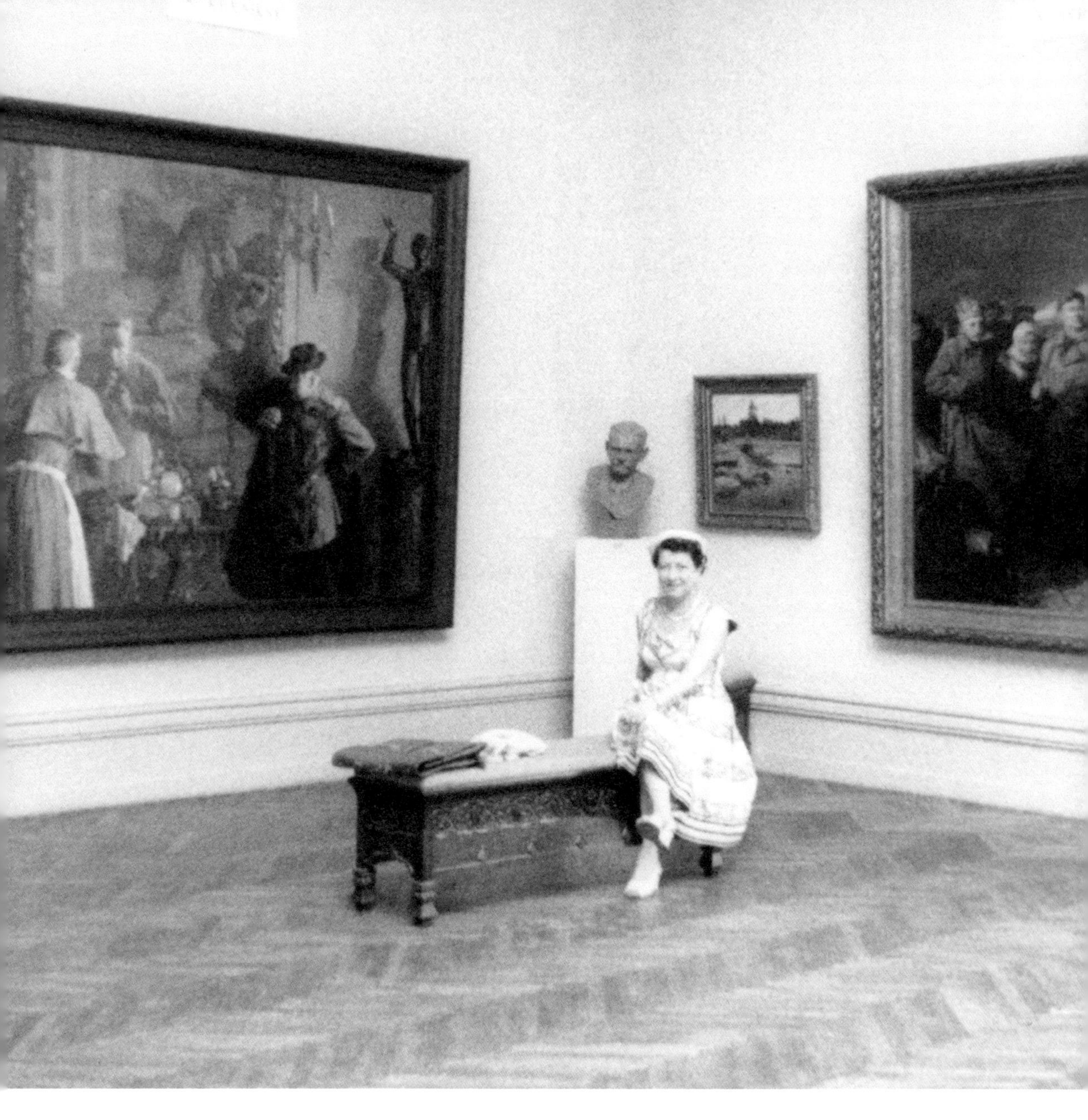

<table>
<tr>
<td>

Rose Raymond at
the twenty-ninth Venice
Biennale, September
1958

</td>
<td>

On their return voyage, Yves and Rose
spent a few days in Venice. They stayed
at the Hotel Monaco and visited
the Biennale.

</td>
</tr>
</table>

Postcard sent from
Venice to Rotraut
Uecker, German artist
and Klein's
future wife,
in September 1958

Yves Klein evokes, among others, Elena
Palumbo, a young Italian woman he met at his
friend Arman's place in Nice and who would
later become one of his models for the
creation of the *Anthropometries*.
Translation p. 220

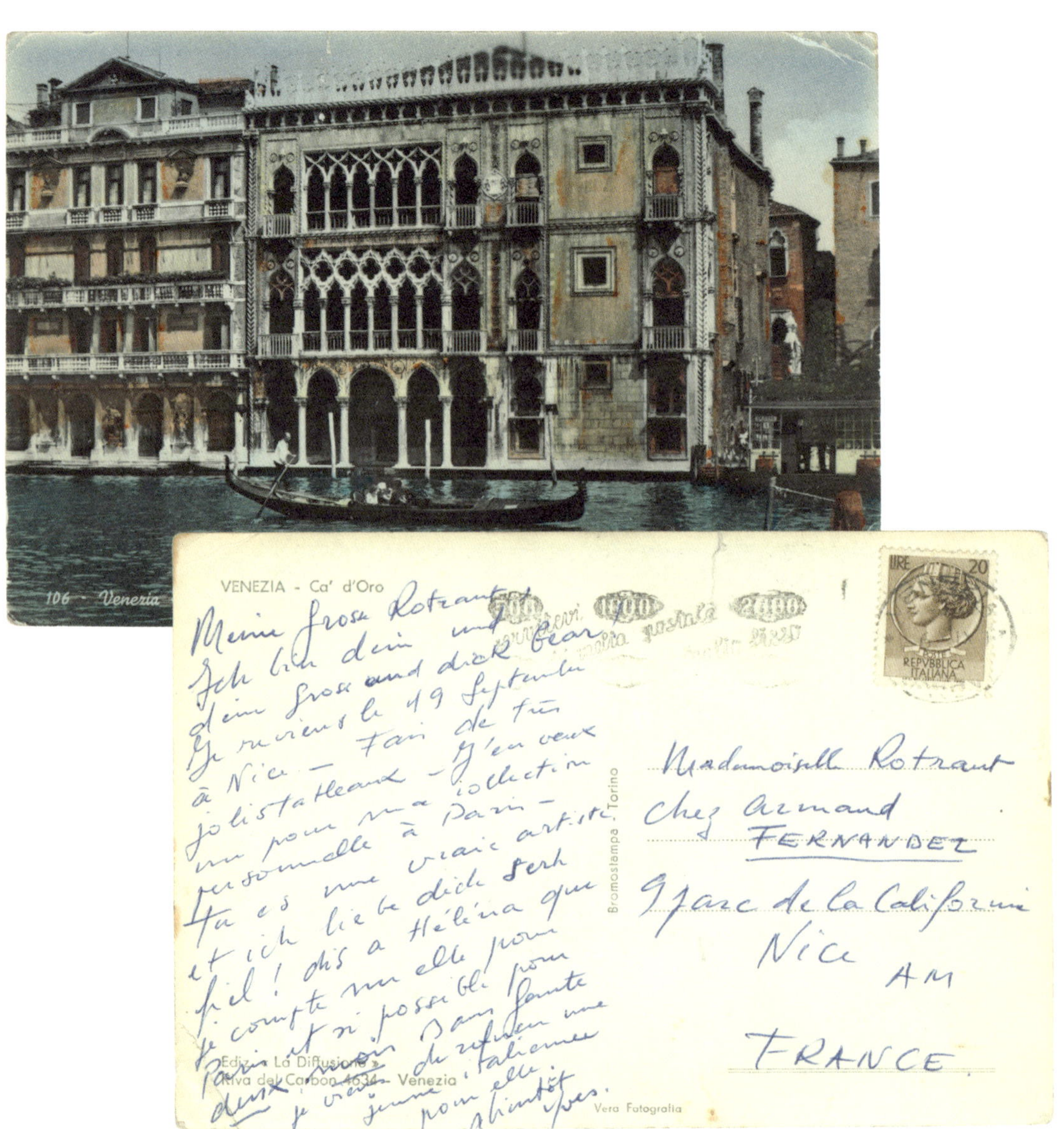

MILAN

1959-1960

PARIS
LISSONE
MILAN

Interior page of *Azimuth* magazine,
issue no. 1, founded by
Piero Manzoni and Enrico Castellani,
September 1959

Yves Klein is represented in it with
one entirely blue page.

PARIS

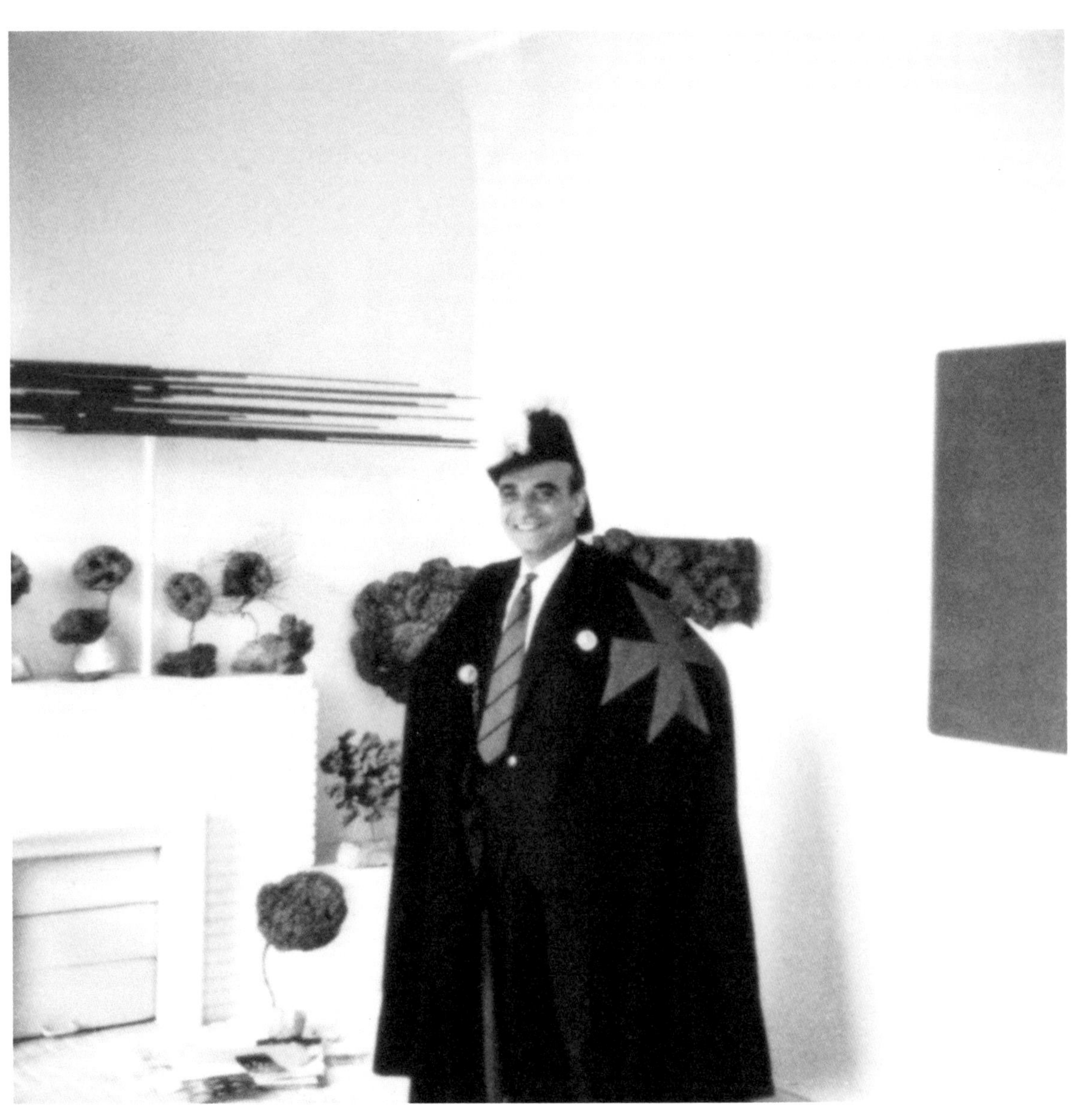

Lucio Fontana at Yves Klein's apartment,
14 Rue Campagne-Première, Paris,
10 April 1959
He wears the uniform of the knights
of the Order of Saint Sebastian, of which
Yves Klein was a member.

Milán 2-5-59

Caro Klein –
    El material que les pedí serría para la Triennale
de Milán, que yo creo Ust. conosca, es una manifesta=
ción internacional de Arte y Architectura – La Co=
mición me ha llamado para darles ideas y orga=
anisar espeftaculos al aire libre entro el Parque
de la Triennale – Jueves, ya tuve una reunión
esepliqué a la Comición qual eron su concepts
y del arch. Werner Ruhan, juntos con otros artistas
mas, nosotros podriamos hacer una demostración
de Arte nueva – En via de mascima la Comi-
sión está de acuerdo, solo me pidieron ideas=
mas concretas, seria necesario vernos y hablar,
precisar en lo posible la forma de realisación,
los gastos, enfin un programa mas concreto y
presentarlo a la Comición, yo estoy seguro que
seria una cosa formidáble para la prosima
Triennale que se inaugura en junio de el
prosimo año 1960 – Si Ust. está de acuerdo
escribame, y mas adelante lo mejor seria
que ustedes se venieran a Milán –
    Hasta pronto y muchos saludos de
                            Fontana

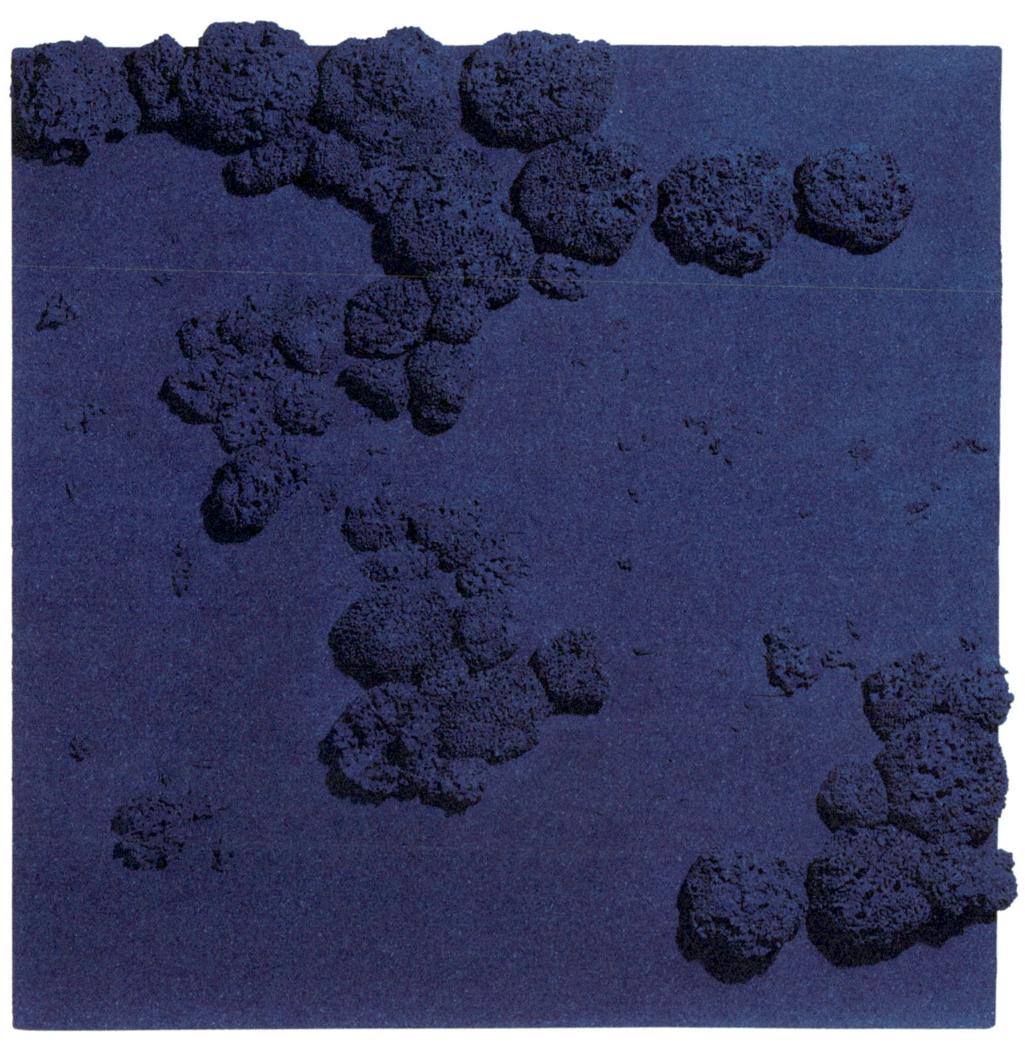

Yves Klein,
*Untitled Blue Sponge
Relief* (RE 51), 1959
Artwork once belonging
to Lucio Fontana

Yves Klein,
*Untitled Blue Sponge
Sculpture* (SE 203),
1959
Artwork once belonging
to Lucio Fontana

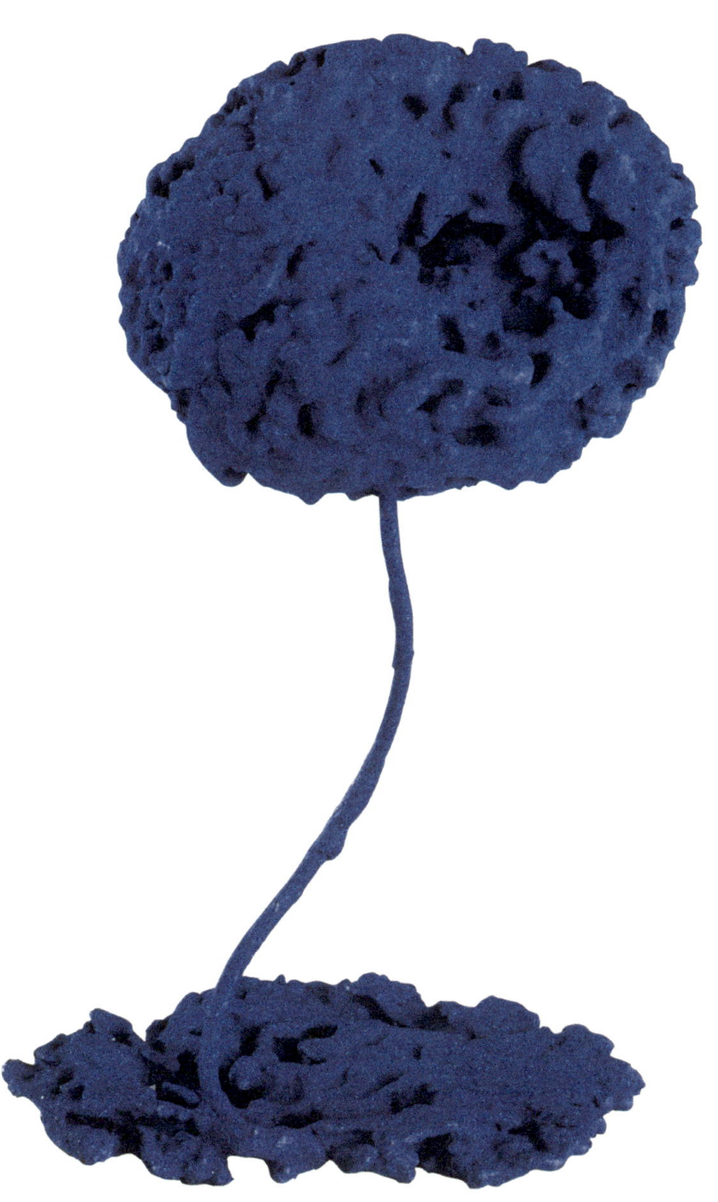

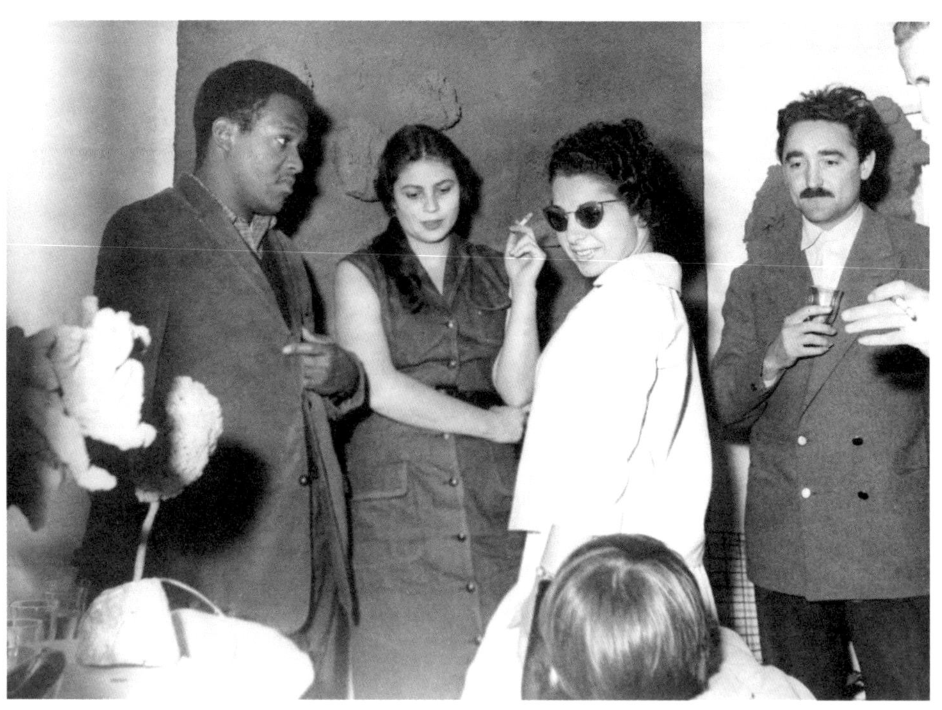

Elena Palumbo was born in Turin.
At the age of twenty-three, she moved
to Nice, working as a *fille au pair*
(live-in nanny) at the home of artist Arman
and musician Éliane Radigue. She quickly
became friends with Yves Klein, who often
visited them. In 1957, she left the Côte
d'Azur and started her interpreter studies
in Paris, which she funded by working
at cabarets in Pigalle as a dancer. She was
passionate about jazz and rubbed shoulders
with great figures such as James Baldwin.
Between 1960 and 1962, Klein and Palumbo
collaborated on the creation of
the *Anthropometries*.

Elena Palumbo during
a cockroach race
organised by
Yves Klein, Iris Clert
Gallery, Paris, 1959

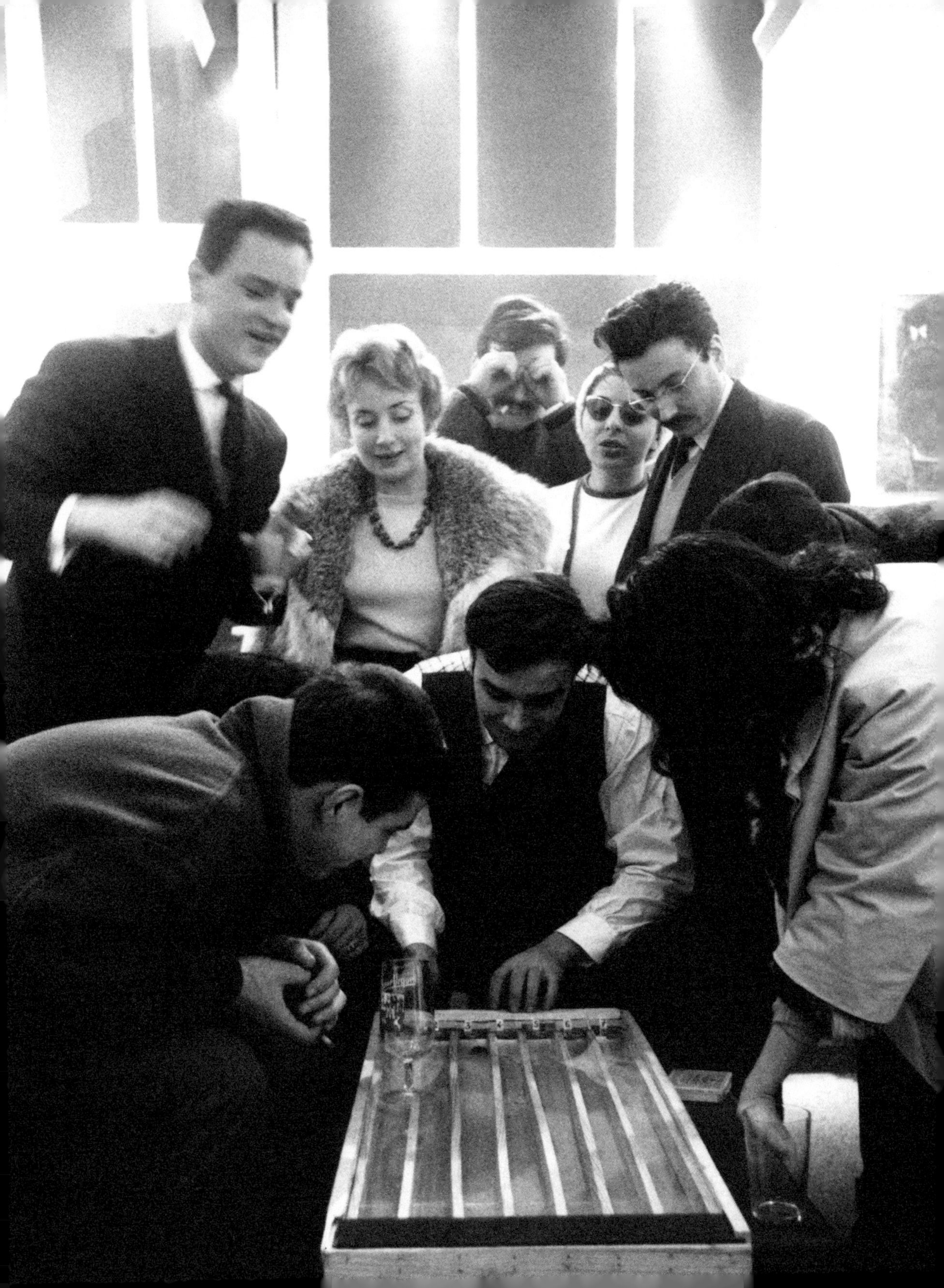

XI
Premio Lissone
internazionale per la pittura

Il Segretario Generale

Segreteria
Milano
via Brera 4
tel. 862821

Galerie Iris Clert
3 Rue des Beaux Arts
PARIS 6

Madame Iris Clert,

j'ai le plaisir de vous communiquer que dans la liste des
artistes invités à figurer au XI Prix Lissone il y a un
peintre qui appartient à votre Galerie; Yves Klein
        Comme vous le savez bien, notre Prix est dedié à la pein_
ture internationale d'avangarde; et l'Ecole de Paris, comme
d'habitude, sera presente avec les meilleurs noms.
        Tandis que je me reserve de faire l'invitation officiel_
le à l'artiste, je vous prie de me donner son adresse per_
sonnelle.
        Je vous joins le Reglement et je vous donne l'adresse de
notre expéditeur charge de ramasser et d'expédier les oeuvres
qui est Mr. Henri Walbaum — 49 Rue Marx Dormoy- Paris 18
Tel. Bot. 6870
        En outre, je vous prie de me faire parvenir, avant la fin
de juillet, la documentation de l'artiste, suivant l'article
7 du Reglement.
        Dans l'attente d'une prompte réponse, je vous présente,
chère Madame, mes salutations bien cordiales.

                                Guido Le Noci

17 Juin 1959

Letter from
Guido Le Noci
to Iris Clert,
17 June 1959

Guido Le Noci contacted Yves Klein through
his gallerist Iris Clert to invite him
to participate in the eleventh International
Painting Prize, Premio Lissone, in Lombardy.
Yves Klein replied directly to accept the
invitation. He presented a blue monochrome.
Translation pp. 220-221

M.
Yves Klein
14, rue Campagne Première
P a r i s   14 (Francia)

13 juillet 1959
Segr/TF/ms

3581

Le sculpteur Lucio Fontana - que depuis de longtemps nous a en-
tretenu sur vos géniales initiatives - et le sculpteur Agenore
Fabbri (membre du Comité Technique Exécutif de cet Institut) nous
ont informé de ce que vous pourriez présenter à l'occasion de la
Douzième Triennale.

Il serait vraiment intéressant de connaitre et d'avoir directement de votre côté des informations détaillées puisque nous désirons que notre Comité Technique Exécutif juge définitivement
au sujet de vos présentations.

Nous serons bien heureux de pouvoir discuter directement avec
vous pour en venir à réaliser ce que les amis mêmes Fontana et
Fabbri nous ont décrit.

Pourtant, nous désirons savoir quels sont les frais que nous de-
vrons supporter.

Dans l'attente de vous lire et de vous rencontrer éventuellement,
veuillez agréer l'expression de nos sentiments les meilleurs.

                              Il Segretario dell'Ente

                              T.Ferraris

Yves Kleiñ was invited to participate
in the 1960 Triennale di Milano thanks
to the support of Lucio Fontana and sculptor
Agenore Fabbri. Since its creation in 1923,
the Triennale aimed to foster interaction
between industry, art, and society at large.
For the 1960 edition, the theme was
"Home and School: International Exposition
of Modern Industrial and Decorative Arts
and Modern Architecture".
Translation p. 221

We propose that the great staircase
be protected by a roof of climatised air;
coloured water jets will fall vertically
over this layer of horizontal air and will
continually be violently projected,
outwards at right angles, which will present
a rather unprecedented spectacle of
a downpour arrested mid-flight above the
visitors' heads as they climb these stairs
at the entrance. In front of these stairs,
there is a kind of paved terrace in red sand,
on the ground, very rigorously flat and
uniform. To the left, a large blue block of
plastic measuring 3 m × 3 m, continually
emitting a monotone symphony.
Opposite the stairs, at the back of this area
of red sand, a wall of fire running on city
gas and, to the left, an animated wall …

Yves Klein

Le 6 Novembre, 1959
Segr/TF/mb
4479

Monsieur
Yves Klein
14 rue Campagne Première
P a r i s 14 (France)

Je regrette de vous avoir répondu en retard et de vous infor_
mer que les membres du Comité technique exécutif de la Douzième Triennale, je compris, ne peuvent achever l'initiative
proposée par les sculpteurs Fabbri et Fontana.

L'engagement financier est si haut que nous ne pouvons pas
même penser à une présentation partielle.seulement.

En vous exprimant nouvellement le regret de ma côté et de cô_
té de mes amis, je vous prie de bien vouloir agréer l'assurance de mes sentiments les meilleurs.

                                    Il Segretario dell'Ente

                                    T.Ferraris

Letter from
Tommaso Ferraris
to Yves Klein,
6 November 1959

Camaiore,IO Settembre 1959

Dear Klein,

     I write you in English,because my French is very poor:
anyhow I hope you may understand English.
I have a magazine of art and poetry,Direzioni,and I am
interested with your works,even if I don't agree with
your position.
Anyhow I think that what you have done and what you
are doing now is at least very important:for this reason I beg you to send me quelques reproductions,or
something you have written.
Which I would like to reproduct dans ma revue.
I expect a letter from you;yours sincerely

Fabrizio Mondadori,Via Locatelli,I Milano.

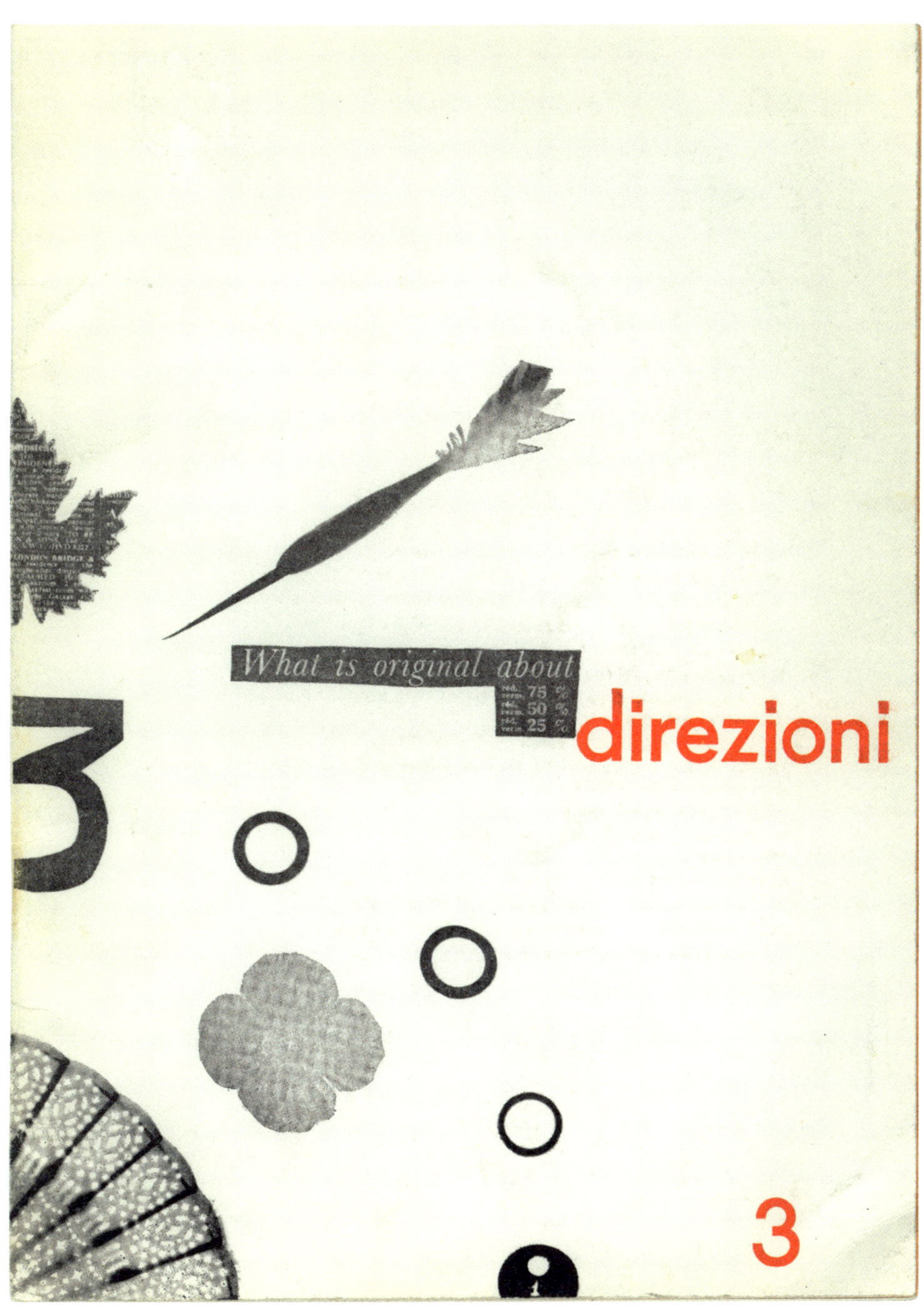

What is original about
direzioni
3

Cher Yves

je t'ai ecrit mais je n'ai pas encore reçu une reponse.

Maintenant donc il l'y aurait a faire une exposition

a Anverse.

Dans cette esposition il l' y aurait Vanderbraun,

Verejen , Fontana , et Moi.   (tous a peu près de la même tendence)

L'organisateur de ça c'est Verheyen; on espère d'avoir ta

partecipation avec deux ou trois pieces. Veux tu

ecrire a Verheyen a ce sujet? On voudrait aussi exposer

l'allemand dont tu m 'as parle et qui est a peu près il

aussi de notre tendence . Veux tu lui ecrire et donner son

adress a Verheyen et a Moi?

apres Anverse ,on pourrat transporter l'exposition a Milan:

je pourrai faire ça dans une petite galerie; mais tu m'a dit

que pour toi c'est facil d'arranger ça chez LE Noci? :

veux tu faire ça? comme ça serait beaucoup mieux.

L'exposition a Anverse c'est en fevier et serait l'exposition

d'ouverture d'une nouvelle gallerie.

A u revoir bientot alors et arrange tout ça le plus vite

possible

Piero Manzoni

Piero Manzoni   via Cernaia 4 Milano

Jef Verheyen   rue Rubens 14 Anverse Belgique.

Piero Manzoni,
Heinz Mack,
and Enrico Castellani
at the inauguration
of the exhibition
*Mack. Rilievi luminosi
e pittura* [Mack:
Light Reliefs and
Paintings], Azimut
Gallery, Milan,
11 March 1960

Azimuth gives us an idea of the network that was built by German, French, Italian, and Dutch artists between 1957 and 1967. The various artists' collectives, including ZERO and Azimuth, placed their own studios at the disposal of artists with similar inspirations. The partner galleries helped to expand the network through numerous experimental exhibitions.

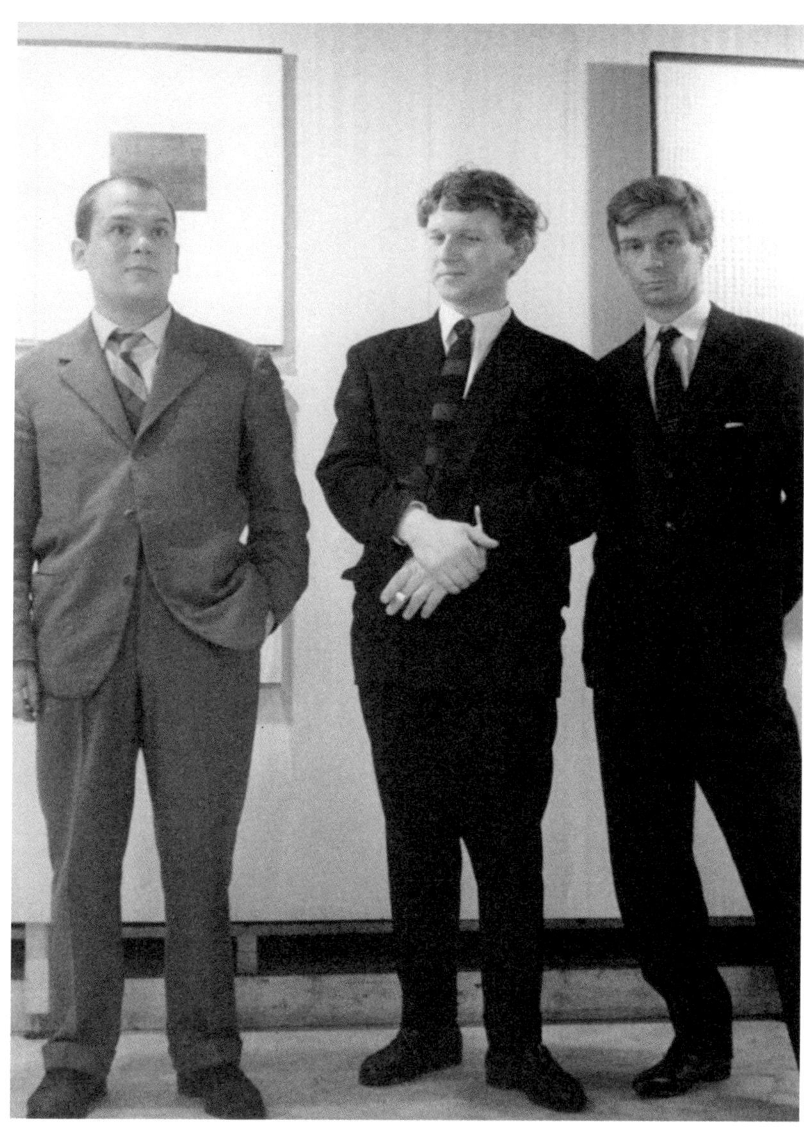

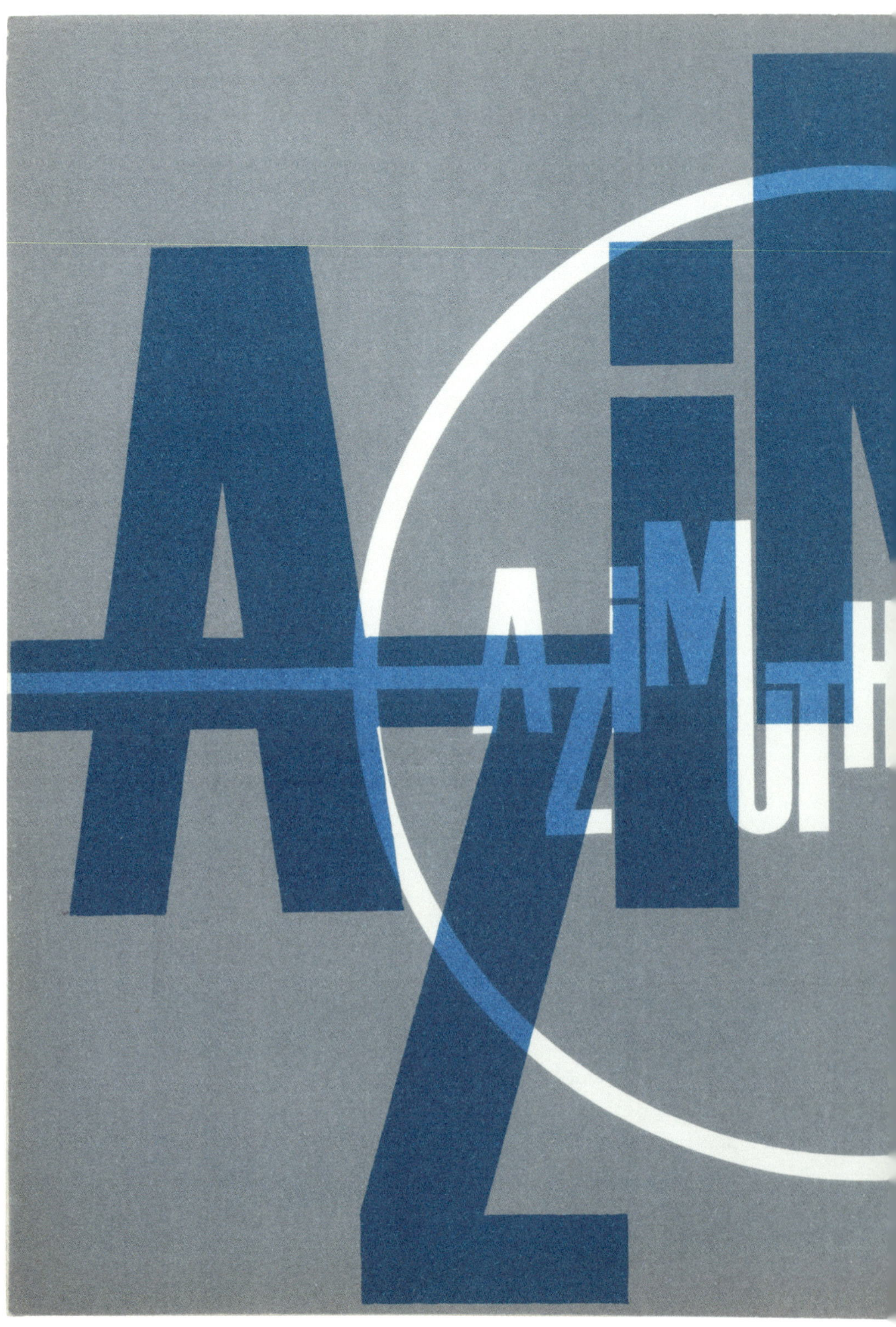

Cover of *Azimuth*
magazine, no. 1,
September 1959

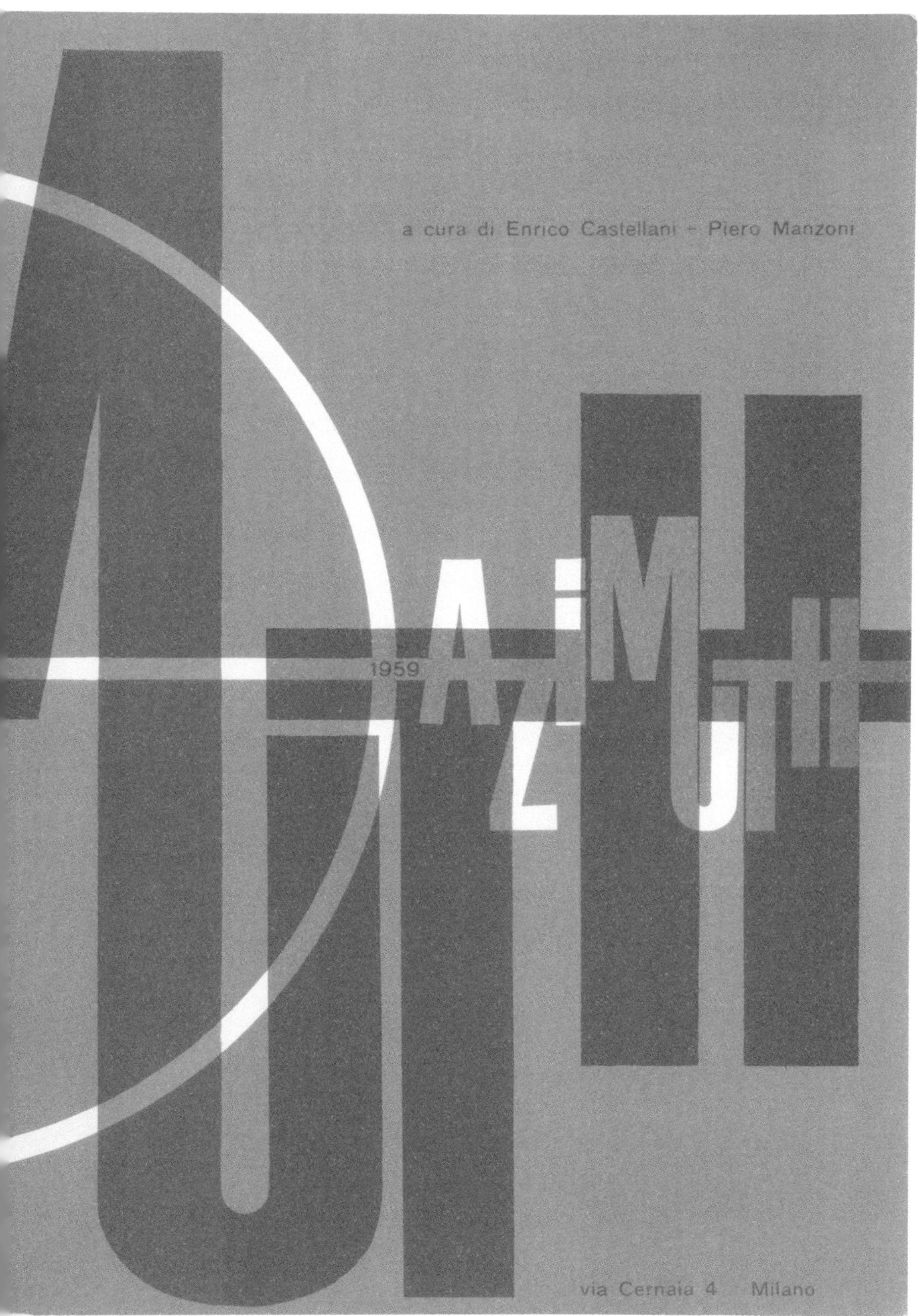

On 3 September 1959, the *Azimuth* magazine
was launched, edited by Piero Manzoni
and Enrico Castellani. It united critics,
artists, and poets from the new avant-garde.

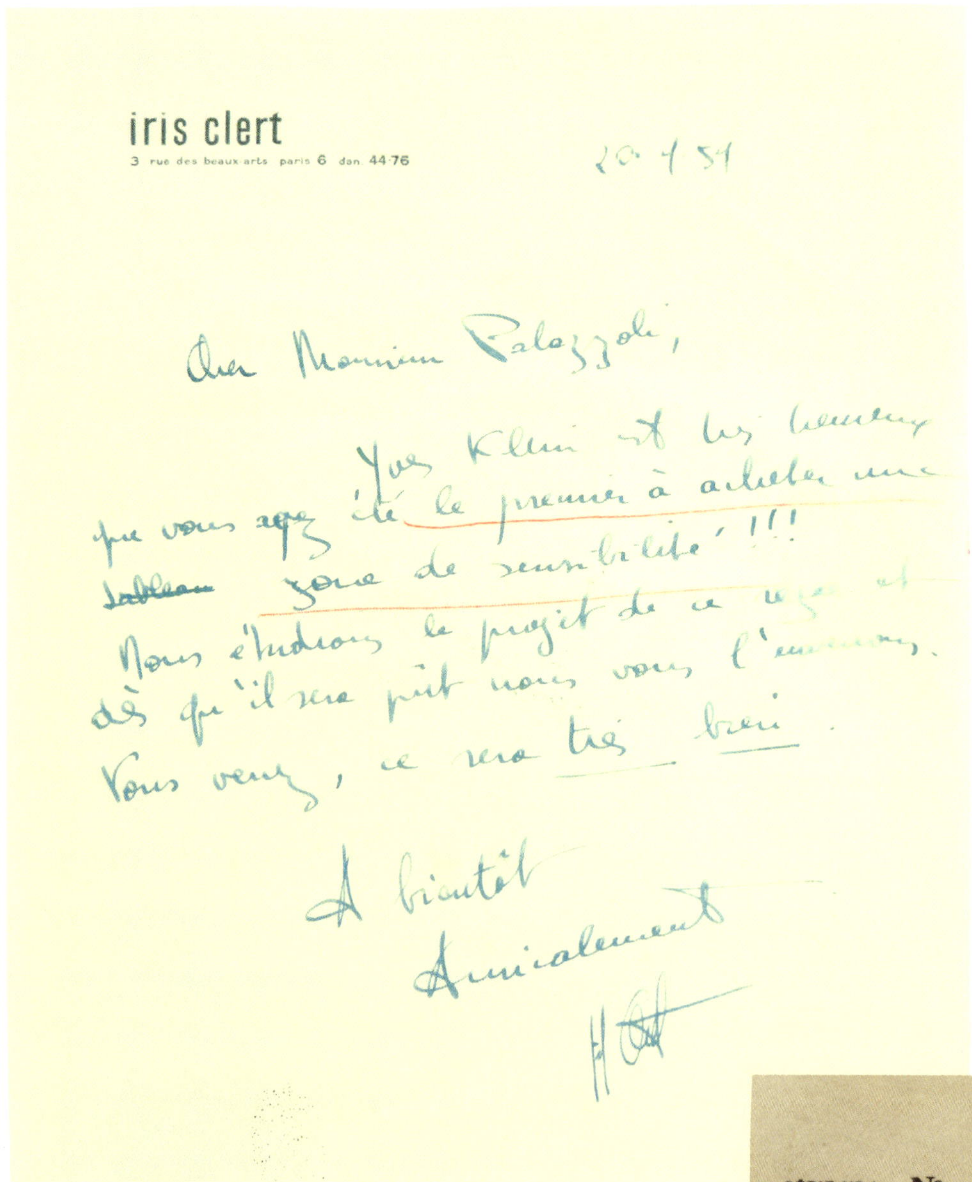

Letter from Iris Clert on 20 September 1959
to Peppino Palazzoli regarding the first
Zone de sensibilité picturale immatérielle
[Zone of Immaterial Pictorial Sensibility]
by Yves Klein, an immaterial work
that he had just acquired that August,
in exchange for a receipt signed
by the artist
Klein and Iris Clert devised a receipt
that was finalised a few months later
and sent to the Milanese gallerist
on 18 November 1959.
Translation p. 222

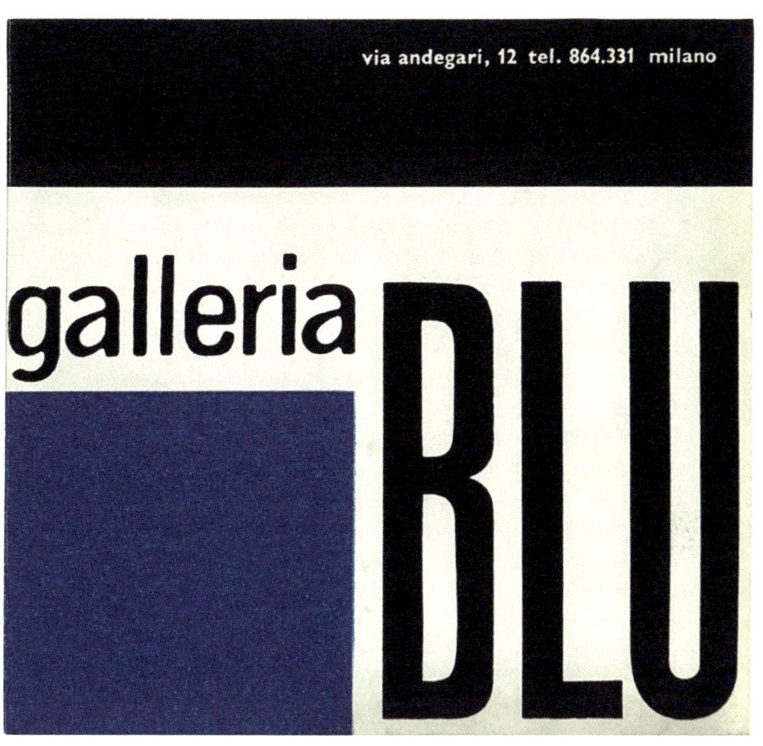

Invitation card for the Blu Gallery,
Milan, 1959
The logo comprised an ultramarine blue
square in IKB by Yves Klein.

Yves Klein, *Zone of Immaterial Pictorial
Sensibility, series no. 1, receipt no. 1,*
18 November 1959
Signed on the back: "Zone transferred
to Mr Peppino Palazzoli of Milan
on 18 Nov 1959 Yves Klein"

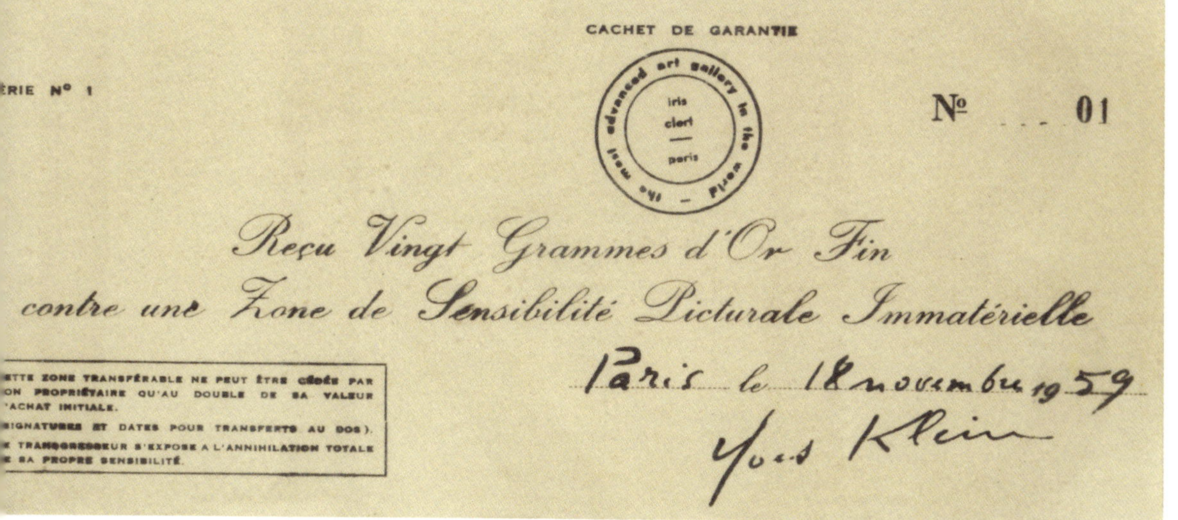

iris clert
3 rue des beaux-arts paris 6 dan. 44-76

le, 24-9-59

M. Paulo Aceti
[...] Monte de [...]
[...]

Cher Monsieur,

Bravo pour votre décision
d'acheter une "zone de sensibilité".
Nous sommes en train de mettre au
point le reçu qui sera un petit chef-
d'œuvre et dès qu'il sera prêt, je vous
le ferai savoir.

M. Palazzoli en a déjà acheté
un et attend son reçu aussi.

À bientôt j'espère
Amicalement

Reçu Vingt Grammes d'Or Fin
contre une Zone de Sensibilité Picturale Immatérielle

Paris le 7 12 1959

Yves Klein

Letter from Iris Clert on 21 September 1959
to collector Paride Accetti regarding
the *Zone of Immaterial Pictorial
Sensibility* he had acquired
She evokes the gallerist Peppino Palazzoli,
who was also awaiting his receipt.
Translation p. 222

Invitation card for
*La nuova concezione
artistica* exhibition,
Azimut Gallery,
Milan,
4 January–1 February
1960

In it, Yves Klein
presented
a red monochrome
(16 × 24 cm) and
a blue monochrome
(78 × 56 cm),
both from 1957.

Yves Klein, *Zone of
Immaterial Pictorial
Sensibility,*
series no. 1,
receipt no. 3,
7 December 1959
Receipt for the
immaterial artwork
acquired by
Paride Accetti

Piero Manzoni suggests Yves Klein
participate in an exhibition at Azimut
Gallery, newly inaugurated in Milan. He also
evokes the publication of the second issue
of the *Azimuth* magazine.

Letter from
Piero Manzoni to
Yves Klein,
ca. May 1960
Translation p. 222

Cover of *Azimuth*
magazine, no. 2,
ca. 15 May 1960

Cher Yves

exscuse moi si je t'ècris suelment maintenant , mais
je n'avais pas ton adresse ; je l'ai eu seulement dèpuis quelque jour.

Donc, tu sais que nous avon ouvert un petit centre- galerie
qui a eu beaucoup de suxcess: on voudrait avoir là une manifestation
de toi.   Est - ce possible? mintenant l'affire"monochrome" sommence
marcher a Milan.

Dans quelque jours sortira le numero 2 de Azimuth, avec
comme toujour , une page bleu!

A bientot et bon travail

Piero Manzoni
via Cernaia 4 Milano

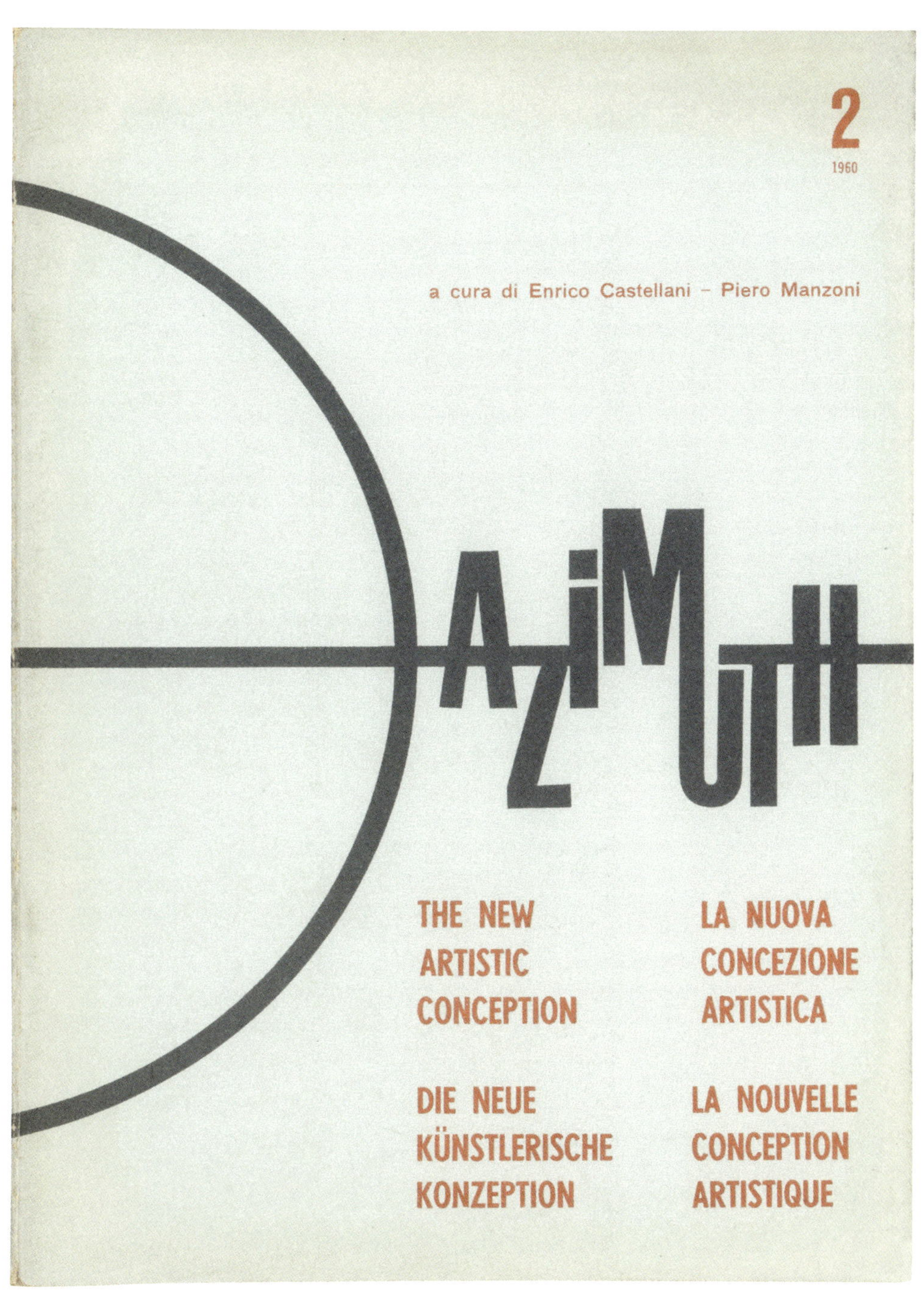

The second and last issue of *Azimuth* magazine, published around 15 May 1960, although the month of January is inscribed on the magazine, served as an exhibition catalogue for *La nuova concezione artistica* exhibition at Azimut Gallery.

The editorial team indicates in the preface, "What we are proposing is an entirely new artistic concept: perhaps other artists are now working based on this new tendency, but those who appear here are its most significant advocates and protagonists."

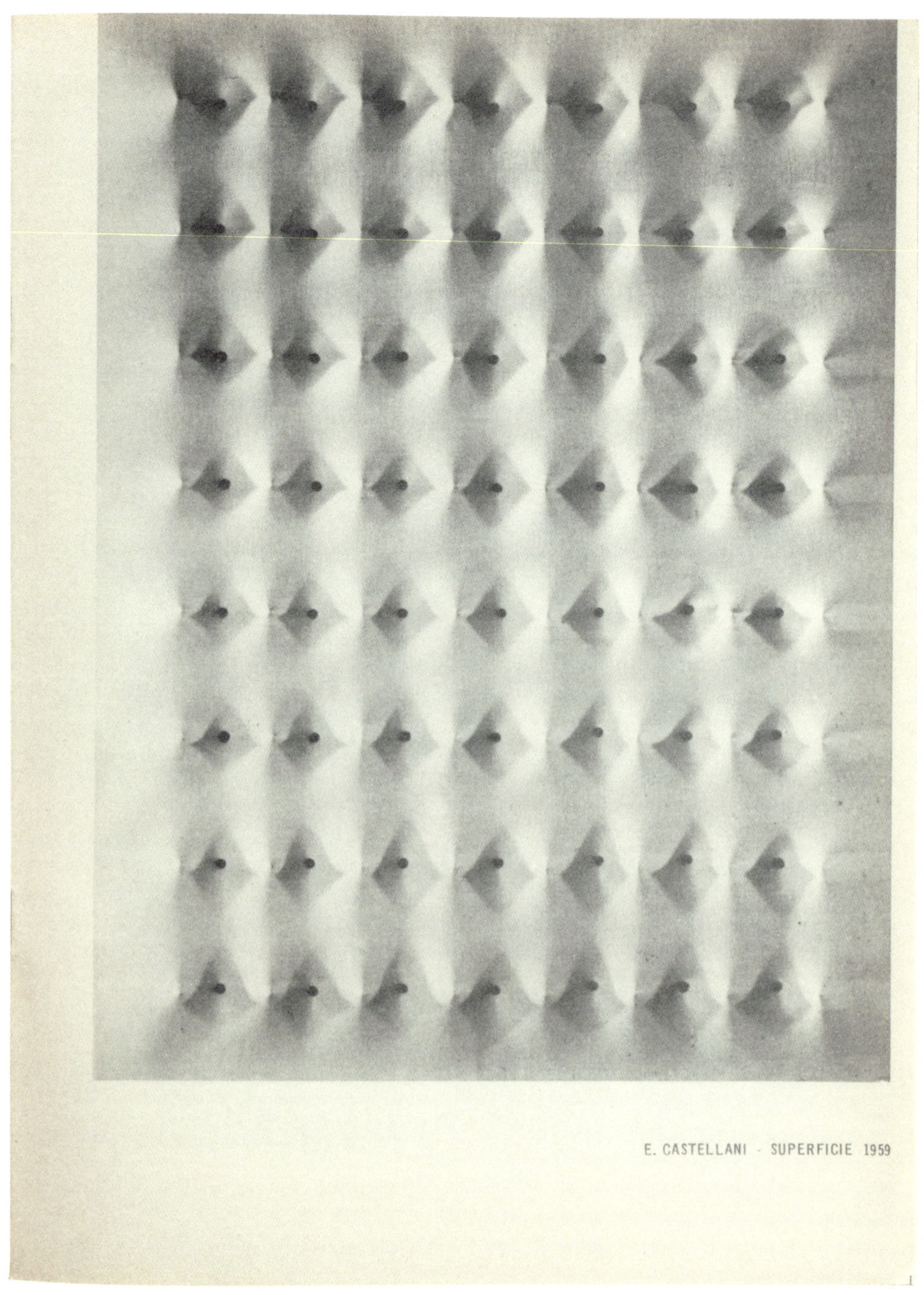

<table>
<tr><td>

Interior pages
of *Azimuth* magazine,
no. 2, 1960

</td><td>

On the left, a page dedicated
to Enrico Castellani. On the right,
to Yves Klein, with the representation
of a blue monochrome.

</td></tr>
</table>

préformés s'eloigne de l'homme, mais seulement pour le retrouver d'une autre manière. Car l'homme fait décidemment partie de cette forme nouvelle de peinture, étant donné que sa collaboration active dans le fait de regarder les tableaux est prémisse pour leur effet. Le tachiste réalise seulement une moitié de l'exécution psychique, il réalise le tableau au moyen d'un procédé formatif, semblable à un bal, mais l'observateur reste passif. La nouvelle peinture se base en effet sur une action réciproque du tableau et de l'organisme humain, et cette action réciproque a comme thème le rapport entre la matière mobile dans le sens de formes faites, et l'homme mobile

dans le sens d'un mouvement émotionnel et en même temps physique. La dynamique qui pouvait déja devenir thème d'un tableau, mais seulement dans quelques points fondamentaux, est devenu maintenant la forme elle-même du tableau.

Il ne faut pas cependant ignorer quelques-uns des mouvements préparatoires dans la peinture de ce demi-siècle, rappelons seulement le futurisme, les visions picturales poussées très avant d'un Malévitch, et encore la libération de la couleur dans les tableaux de la maturité d'un Delaunnay. Mais tout autant peuvent-être regardées la peinture néo-plasti-

Yves
Tinguely
Fontana
Mack
Manzoni:
Castellani
Bury
Mavignier
Uecker
Piene.

Excerpt from a letter by Otto Piene
to Yves Klein, from 31 July 1960, in which
he compiles the list of artists he wants
to invite to participate in *ZERO* magazine,
no. 3
It features Piero Manzoni,
Enrico Castellani, and Lucio Fontana,
among others.

ZERO began as the name of an art magazine
founded in 1958 in Düsseldorf by Heinz Mack
and Otto Piene, before referring to
the group. An international constellation
of artists, the ZERO group gave a particular
meaning that was positive and hopeful
to the movement and elements (fire, air,
and light) associated with the optimism
of "the space age", as the raw materials
of a new kind of art.

PARIS

1960

PARIS

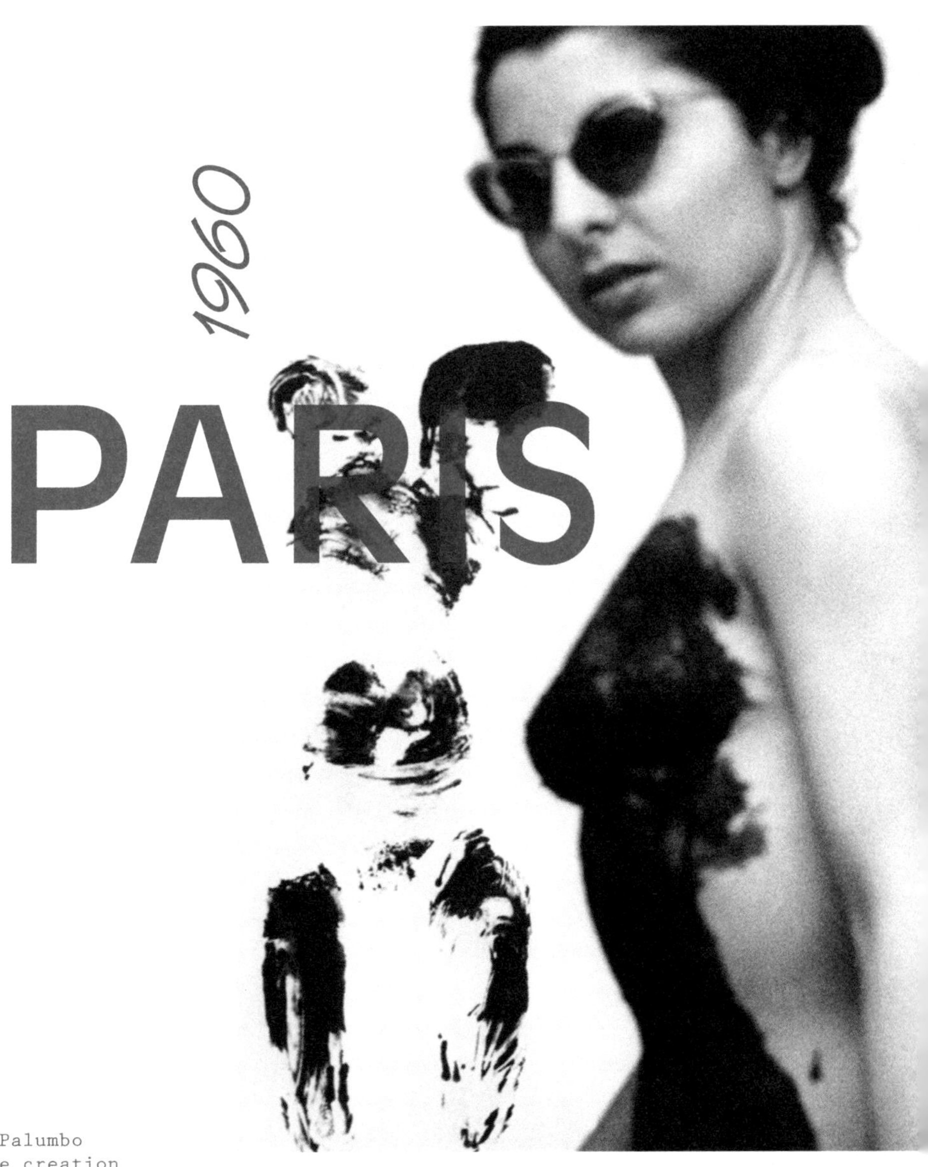

Elena Palumbo
during the creation
of an *Anthropometry*
(ANT 133)
at Yves Klein's
apartment, 14 Rue
Campagne-Première,
Paris, 1960

PARIS

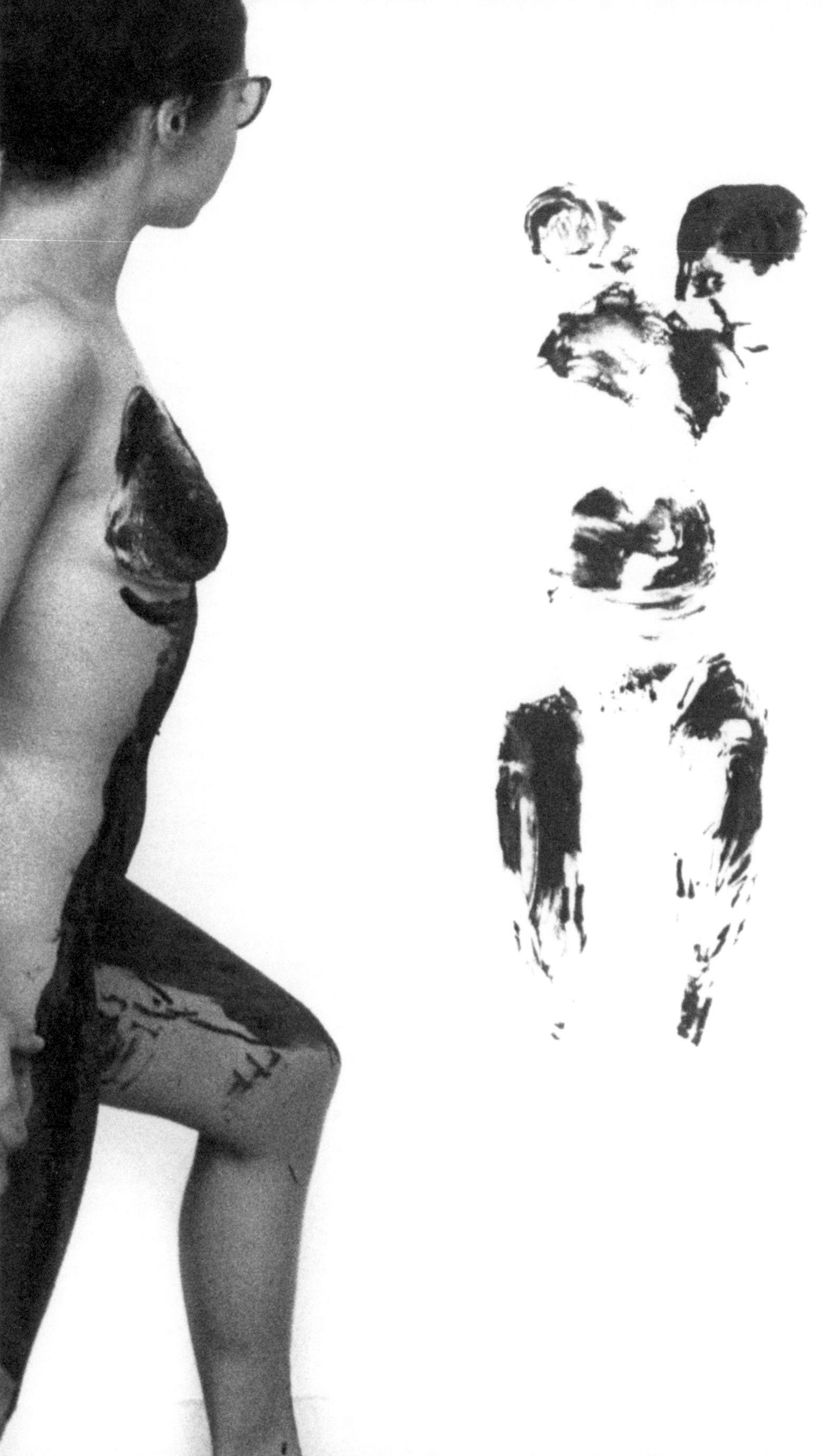

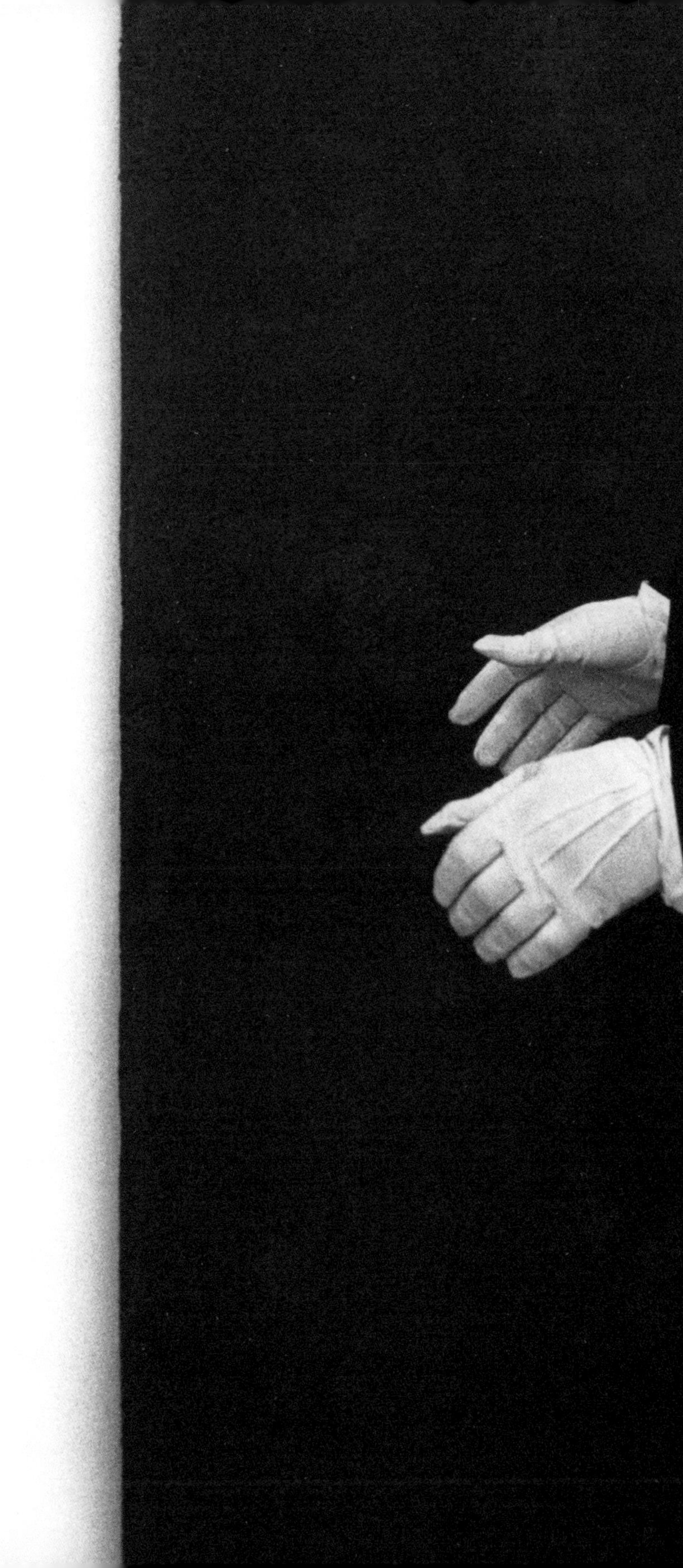

Yves Klein,
Untitled Anthropometry
(ANT 133), 1960

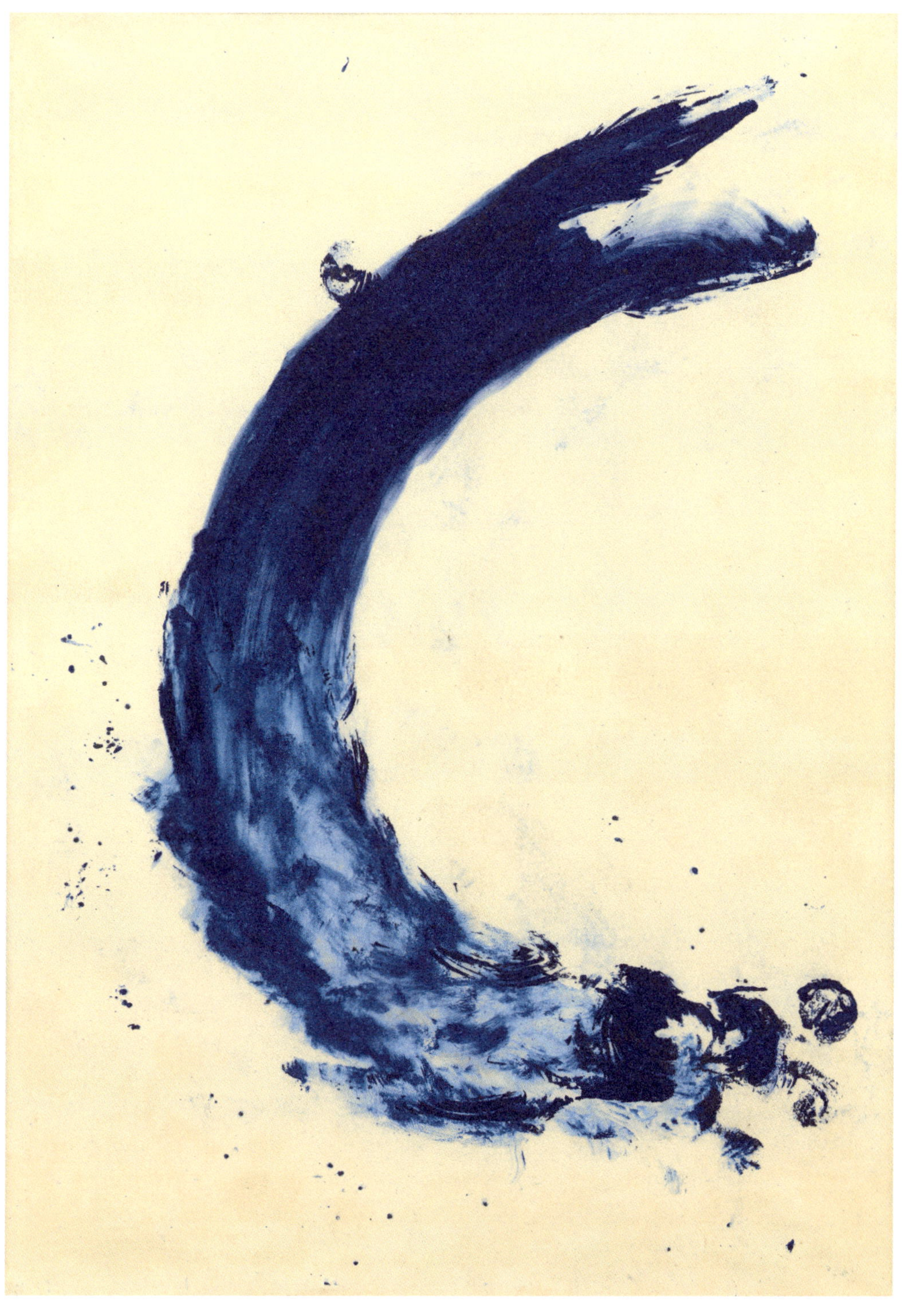

Yves Klein,
Héléna (ANT 111),
1960

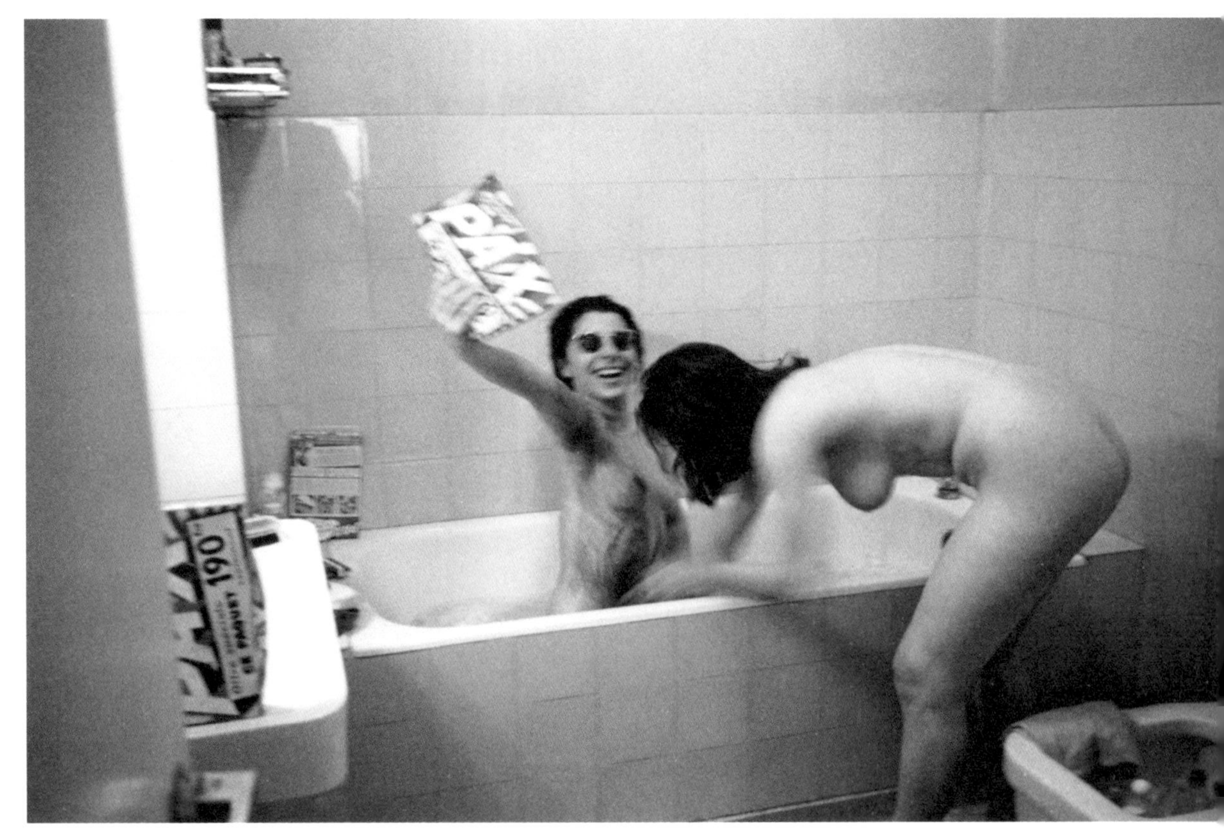

Elena Palumbo
(in the bathtub)
and another model
after a production
session of
Anthropometries,
14 Rue
Campagne-Première,
Paris, 1960

130

I grew up in Italy, a few kilometres from the French border, first not far from
Courmayeur, and then in Bordighera. France was right there in front of me, and I used
to love looking at it through my father's telescopic spectacles. To want to leave my
native province and go and live there was perfectly natural. There was an advert in
Nice-Matin for a job as an au pair, and a few days later, I was on my way to the French
Riviera on my father's moped to meet Éliane Radigue and Arman. A fantastic couple,
three adorable children and immediate immersion in the world of experimental music,
art, and cinema. I was crazy about jazz and poetry. I was twenty-three and had an
irrepressible urge to discover and try everything. I met Yves Klein at their place,
and we became friends straight off, real comrades.
I remember arriving in Paris a few months later. I met Yves in Rue Campagne-Première,
and he took me straight to La Coupole. I can still see myself on Boulevard
Montparnasse, the young girl from Turin who had no idea how things worked,
who hadn't seen anything, or hardly. And there I was, in the heart of the Parisian night,
in this sparkling, free, and undisciplined city. I was amazed.

Yves thought of me for his *Anthropometries* because I had great control over my body
and a lot of discipline: I was a champion fancy diver, skier, skater, and dancer; above all,
I was very enthusiastic and daring, curious about everything and a bit casual too.
A perfect companion for this project. Right from the start, there was a kind of
telepathy between us. Yves spoke very little; he gave me precise instructions and
I knew exactly how to carry them out. It took a lot of precision and concentration,
not pressing your body with too much energy but not too little either. A veritable
choreography was created there, Rue Campagne-Première. It's easy to see that in all
the *Anthropometries* we made together, the shapes of the bodies are always clear
and limpid, just like our collaboration. I never had the feeling that I was simply
a "living paintbrush", as Pierre Restany put it. On the contrary, my body was the active
interpreter of Yves's vision, and I knew precisely how to translate and therefore
transmit his creative thought through a bodily experience that I embraced
and invested with meaning.
Although at the time I didn't understand the full conceptual implications of Yves's
thinking, I did feel that together we were achieving something that no one had
ever done before. The creation of the *Anthropometries* seemed to me like an initiation
ritual. With gestures reminiscent of an ancient priest, Yves showed me how to apply
the IKB, and this application took place in silence, in a very intense atmosphere.
Steeped in blue, I could feel my body transmitting the immaterial cosmic energy
that Yves so often talked about.

Once the session was over, I'd jump in the bath to get rid of the pigment that was
beginning to suffocate me. We played at making fake adverts for PAX detergent
– we laughed a lot. After the solemnity of the performance, we immediately reverted
to our good-natured spirit of frank camaraderie. With Rotraut and Yves, and
sometimes Arman, Jean Tinguely, or Pierre Restany too, we'd spend the evening
in the Rue Campagne-Première flat, sitting on the floor and eating, sharing our plates
and our stories like any group of friends. Not yet fully aware of the incredible scope
of these works, but absolutely certain of their power.

Elena Palumbo Mosca
May 2023

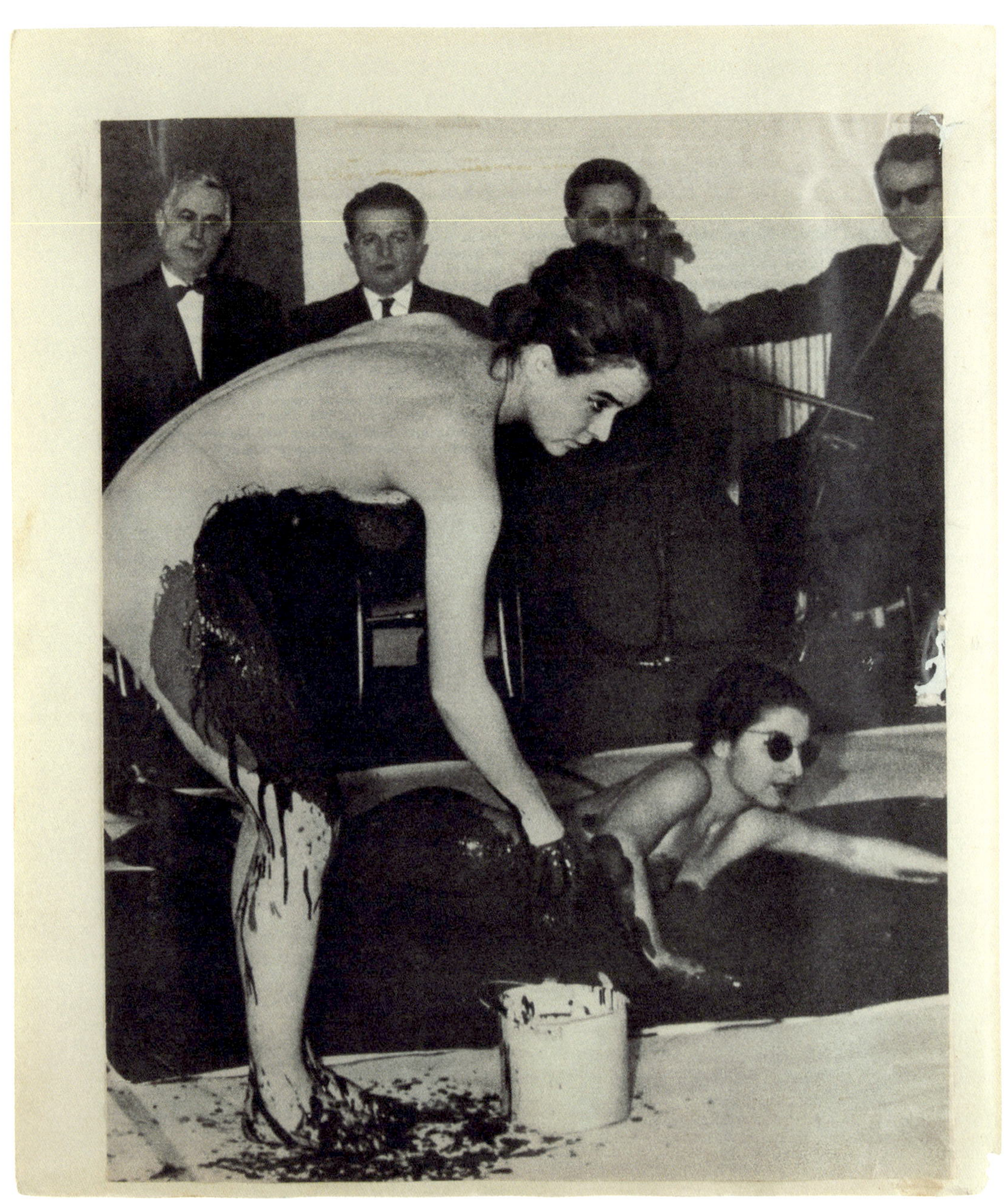

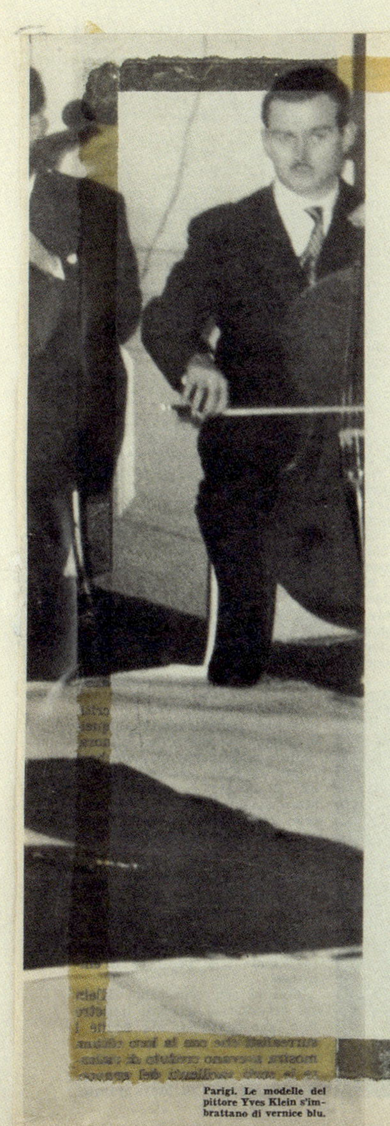

Klein dipinge strusciando le modelle contro il muro

IL NUDO SENZA OBBIEZIONI

di MANLIO CANCOGNI

PARIGI. Gli invitati erano in numero ristretto: qualche pittore, alcuni scrittori, industriali amatori d'arte, collezionisti, signore eleganti, non più di quaranta persone. Tutti in abito da sera. L'ospite, il pittore Yves Klein, che faceva gli onori di casa, cioè della Galerie d'art contemporaine di rue du Faubourg Saint Honoré, li riceveva freddo e gentile, pregandoli d'accomodarsi fra le poltrone schierate, come in una sala cinematografica, davanti a una parete nuda e bianca. Egli restava in piedi, un poco in disparte.

La luce s'abbassò leggermente, quel tanto sufficiente a segnare l'inizio dello spettacolo, un disco cominciò a suonare. Era una musica concreta, vale a dire prodotta non dai soliti e impersonali strumenti, come violini, viole, trombe e contrabbassi, ma da oggetti veri, barattoli, teglie, piatti, pezzi di legno, o da esseri viventi, cani, rane, cornacchie e anche uomini. Nessuno mostrò meraviglia: segno della ''classe'' di quel pubblico. Come la pittura astratta, o l'architettura organica, o i film della nouvelle vague, infatti la musica concreta fa parte del patrimonio di chiunque si tenga al corrente delle cose del mondo e non provoca né stupori né

Yves Klein's press book, 1960, article "Il nudo senza obbiezioni" by Manlio Cancogni, published on the subject of Yves Klein's performance *Anthropométries de l'époque bleue* [Blue Period Anthropometries] presented at the Galerie Internationale d'art contemporain, Rue Saint-Honoré in Paris, on 9 March 1960. Elena Palumbo participated in this performance. Translation pp. 222-223

133

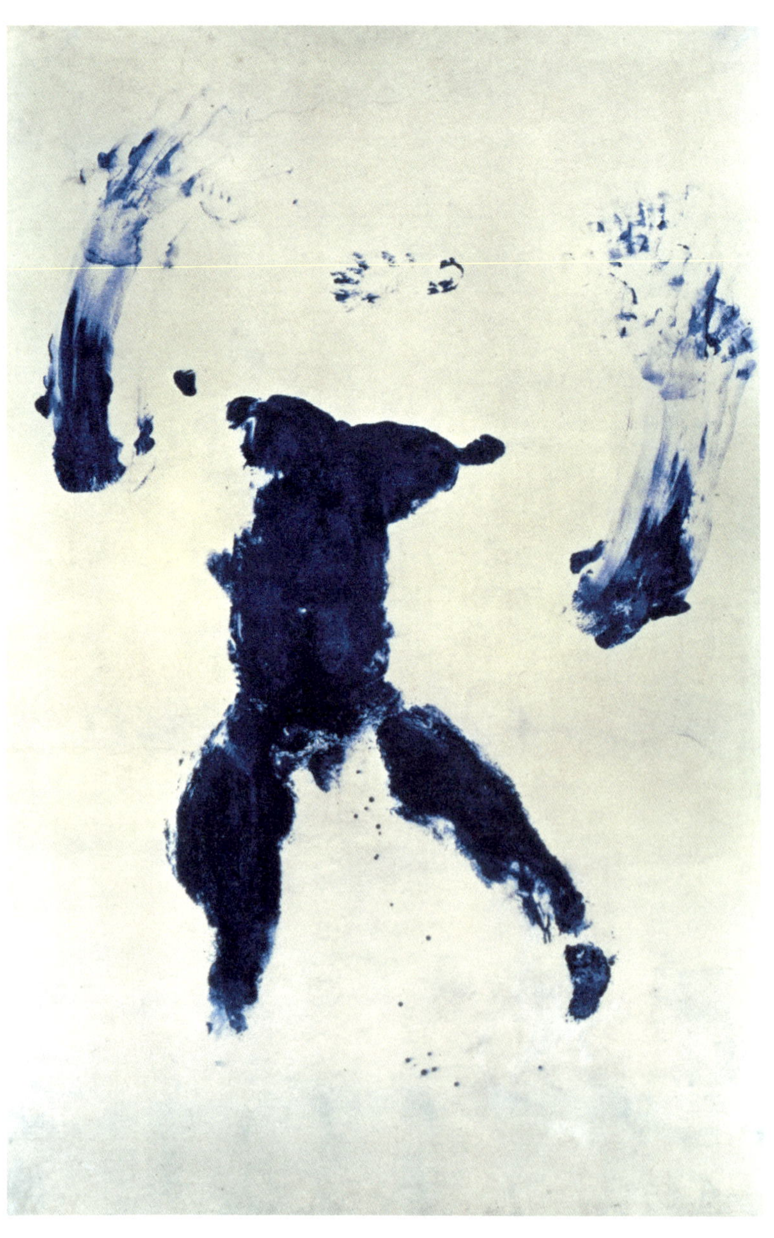

Yves Klein,
L'Exilé d'Ischia
[Ischia's Exile]
(ANT 122), 1960

One of the rare *Anthropometries*
with the imprint of Yves Klein's body.
The title *Ischia's Exile* probably refers
to the exile of the Titan Iapetus, son of
Uranus and Gaia, to the island of Ischia,
as a punishment for turning against Zeus.
Yves Klein visited Ischia island on his
travel in Italy in August 1948.

Yves Klein,
Untitled Anthropometry
(ANT 175),
February 1960
Dedicated below on
the left: "To Guido
Le Noci with all
the esteem and true
friendship of
Yves Klein, Paris,
February 1960"

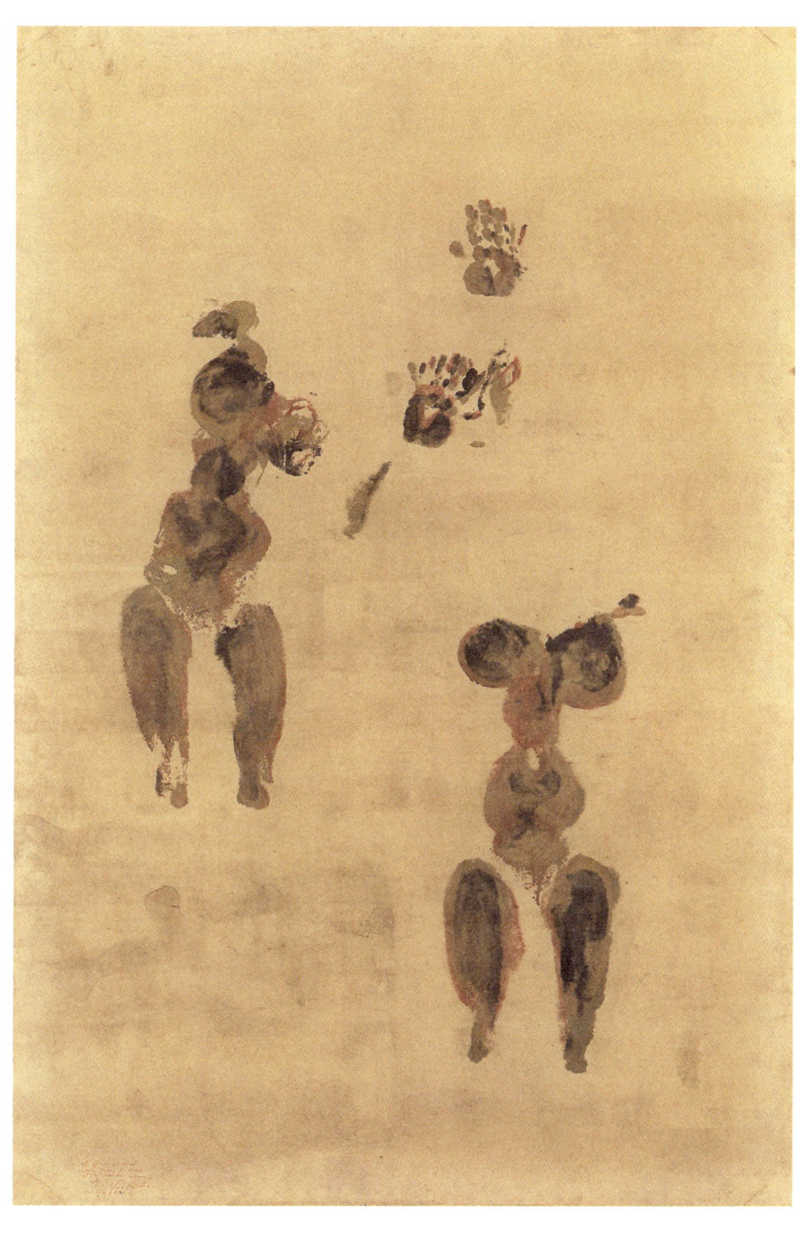

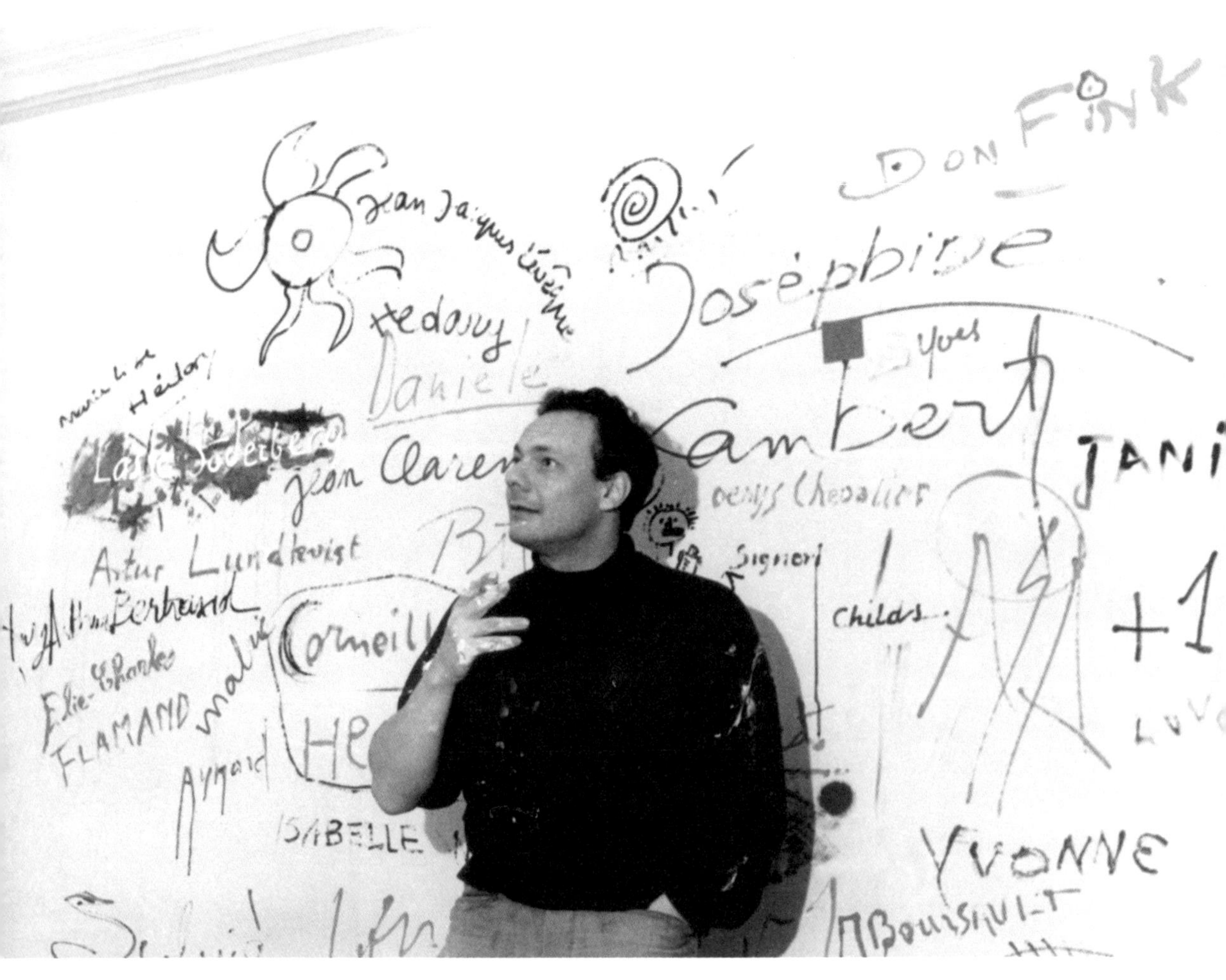

Artist Gianni Bertini in front of the wall
of signatures at his studio,
Rue du Château-d'Eau, Paris,
ca. 1960

Bertini was in the habit of having
every artist and friend who visited his
studio sign the wall, especially during
the many parties he organised. Among the
signatures are those of Piero Manzoni,
Fabrizio Mondadori, Mimmo Rotella,
Valerio Adami, Peppino Palazzoli,
Enrico Baj, Mario Rossello,
Ulrico Schettini, Giorgio Marconi,
Gastone Novelli, Edoardo Franceschini,
and Lucio Fontana. We recognise the
signature "Yves" of Yves Klein at
the top right, accompanied by a little
IKB blue square and another gold one.

Yves Klein and Gianni Bertini
at the vernissage of the exhibition *Bertini.
Le pays réel*, J. Gallery, Paris,
24 January 1962

The two artists met around 1955
through Pierre Restany and immediately
became friends.

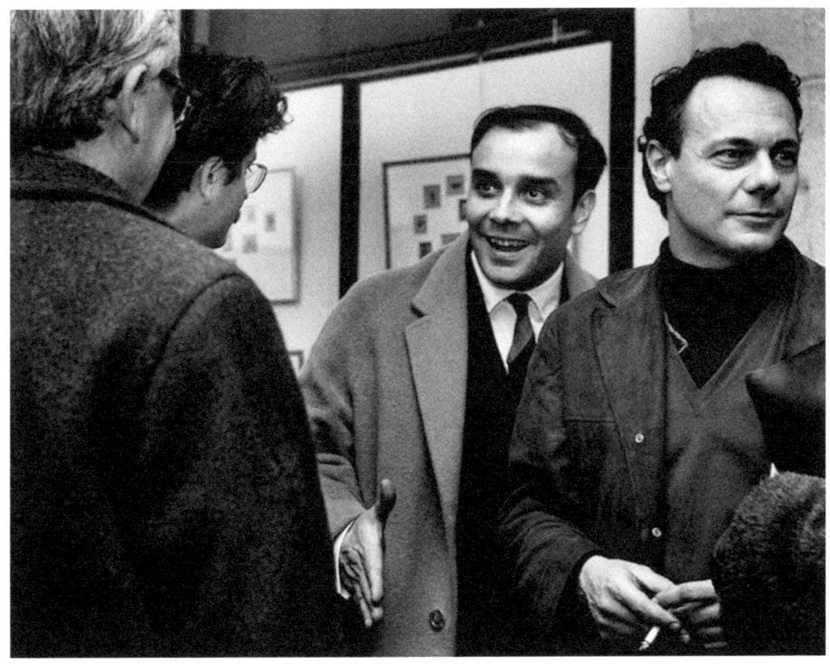

Yves Klein, *Untitled
Blue Monochrome*
(IKB 271), 1960
Dedicated on
the back:
"to Bertini with the
friendship of Yves
Klein 1960"

VENICE

1960

MILAN

PARIS

VENICE

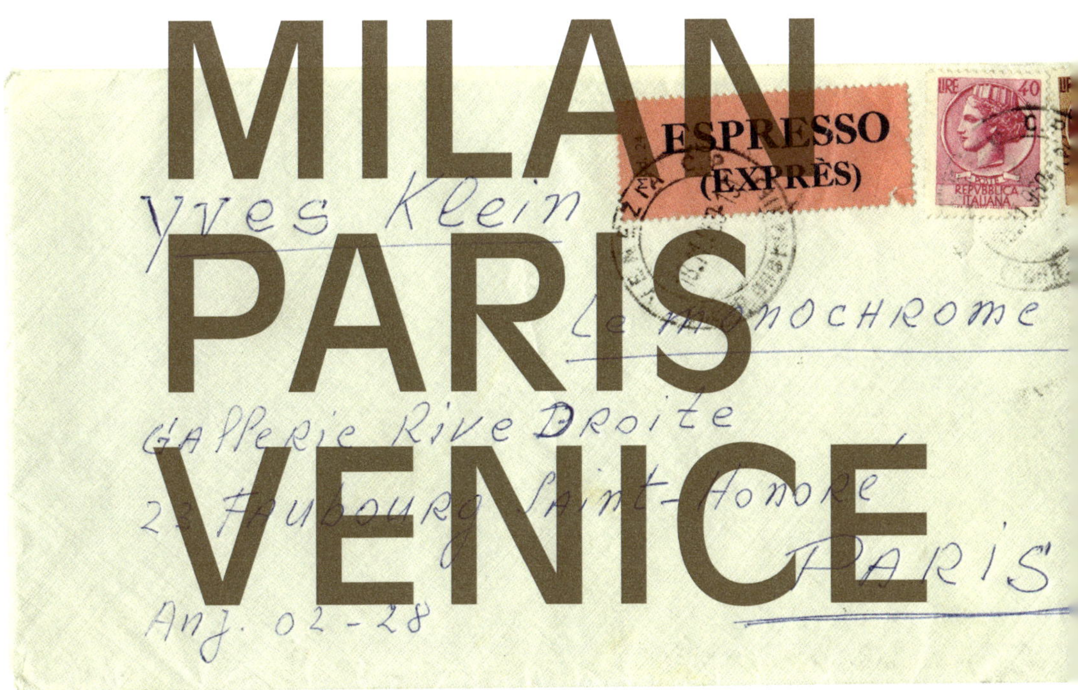

Envelope from
the letter sent by
Venetian gallerist
Giovanni Camuffo
to Yves Klein,
18 November 1960

MILAN

arman
chains
du frêne
yves
le mono
chrome
villeglé
tinguely

arman
chains
du frêne
yves
le mono
chrome
villeglé
tinguely

Cover and inside pages of the first manifesto
of the Nouveaux Réalistes, written by
Pierre Restany in April 1960
The manifesto was published during the
exhibition *Les Nouveaux Réalistes*, held at
Apollinaire Gallery in May 1960.

The copy of the catalogue sent to Yves Klein
features handwritten annotations from
Pierre Restany, Guido Le Noci, and Arman.
Concerning the book of receipts for the
Zones of Immaterial Pictorial Sensibility
presented in the exhibition, Pierre Restany
wrote, "No cheques in circulation yet
but that will come. The immaterial is
on its feet, anthropologically speaking",
and Arman rather facetiously notes,
"Your *zone immatérielle* is very impressive,
we feel its heft and truth."

        Dans le cas de la série n° 4 confiée à M. Lenoci,
pour l'Exposition de Groupe organisée par M. Pierre Restany
à la Galerie Apollinaire, à Milan, en Mai 1960, tenir compte
du fait que la zone n° 1 de cette série n° 4 est déjà réservée
et vendue; donc n'exposer que la zone n° 2 de cette série
n° 4.

        Merci.

        Yves Klein.

Receipt book for the *Zones of Immaterial Pictorial Sensibility, series no. 5,* 1959

In 1959, Yves Klein had these counterfoil receipt books printed in order to carry out the sales of *Zones of Immaterial Pictorial Sensibility*. The blue, on the outside, announces the more substantial presence of the immaterial placed within. At the time of purchase, the name of the buyer was noted on the receipt and on the stub of the receipt book. On the receipt, a framed section specifies the conditions imposed by the artist for the resale of a zone acquired: "This transferable zone can only be sold by its owner for twice its initial value."

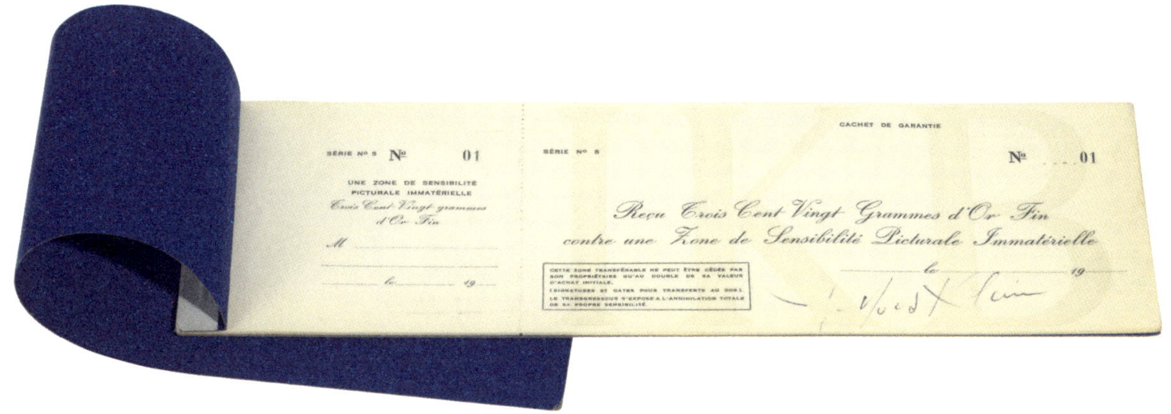

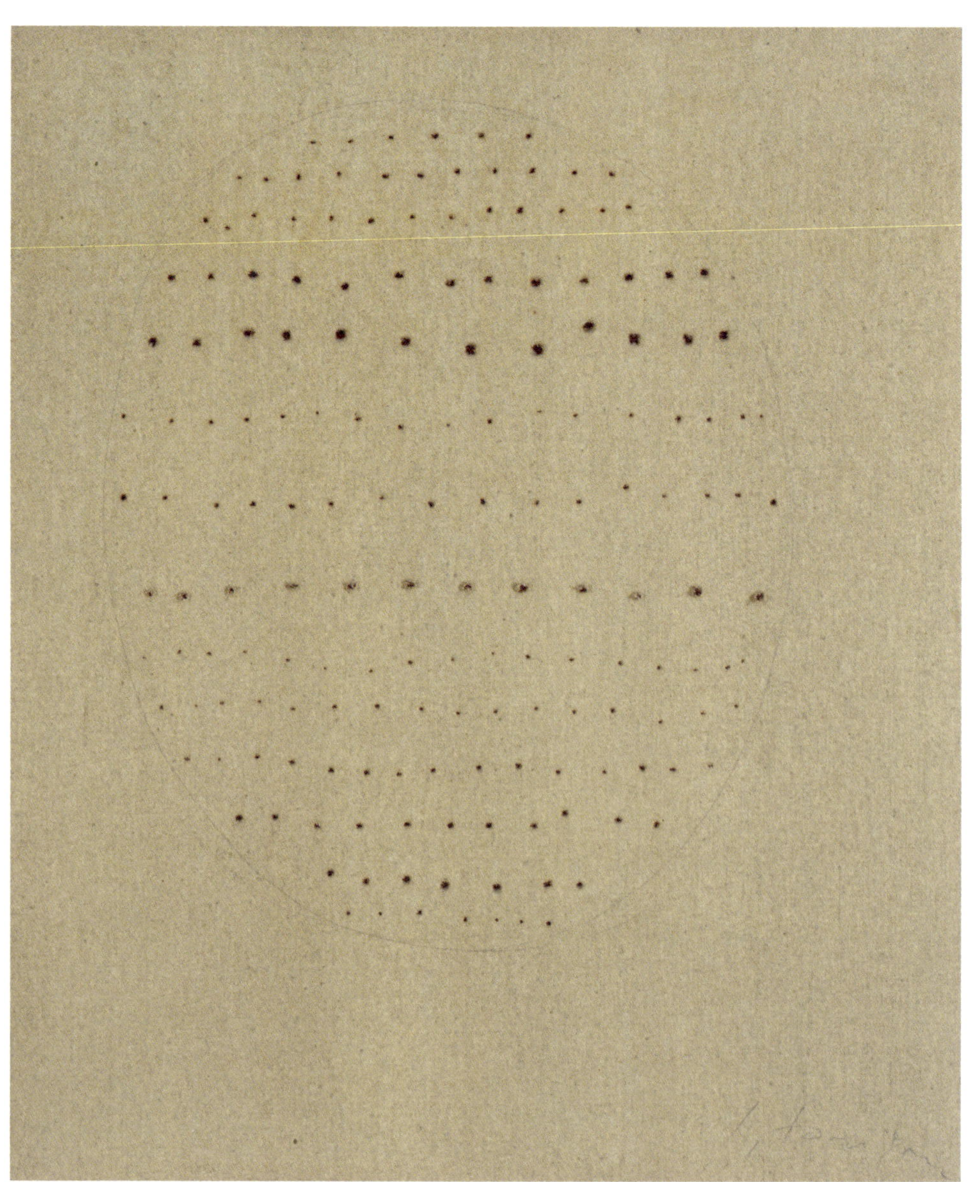

Lucio Fontana,
Concetto spaziale
[Spatial Concept],
1960
Signed and dedicated
on the back: "al amigo
Yves Klein"

Yves Klein,
Monogold "Âge d'or"
["Golden-Age"
Monogold] (MG 42),
1960
Signed and dedicated
on the back:
"to Fontana a
golden-age monogold
1960 Yves Klein"

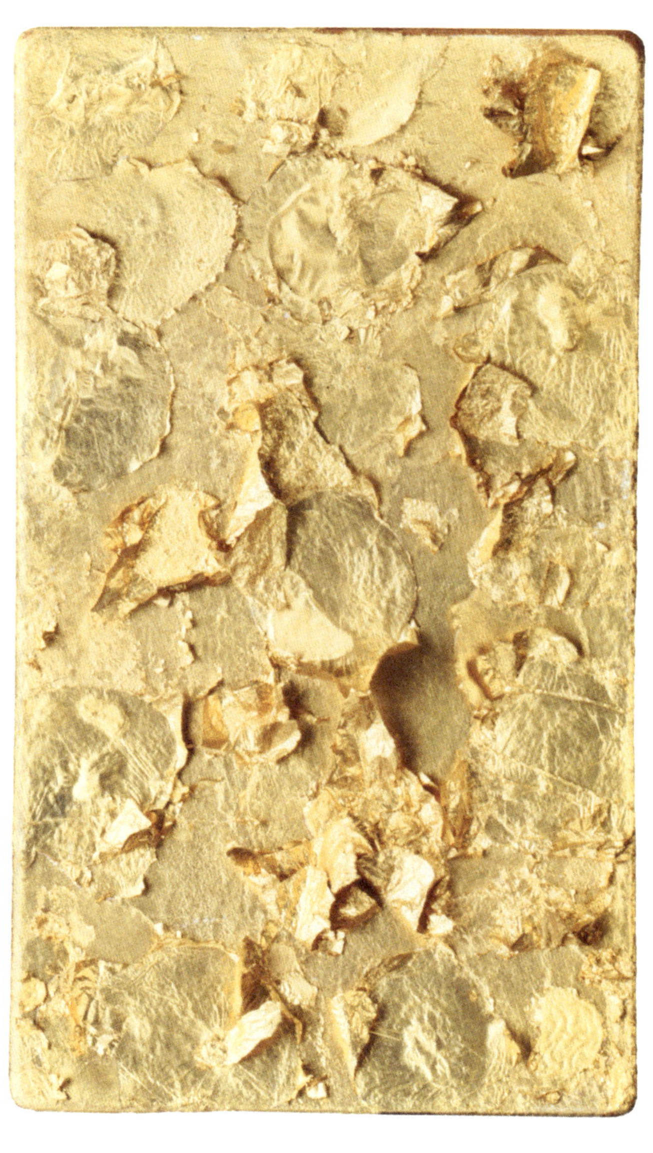

Yves Klein represented the new spirit.
Different from other expressionist
painters such as Rothko, who is
concerned with the luminous vibration
of space, or Pollock, who wants to
destroy space, to explode it, to smash
the picture. Different from myself,
who seeks another kind of space.
He was in the infinite.

Lucio Fontana

Yves Klein
and Lucio Fontana
at the vernissage of
the *Yves le Monochrome*
exhibition,
Rive Droite Gallery,
Paris, 11 October
1960

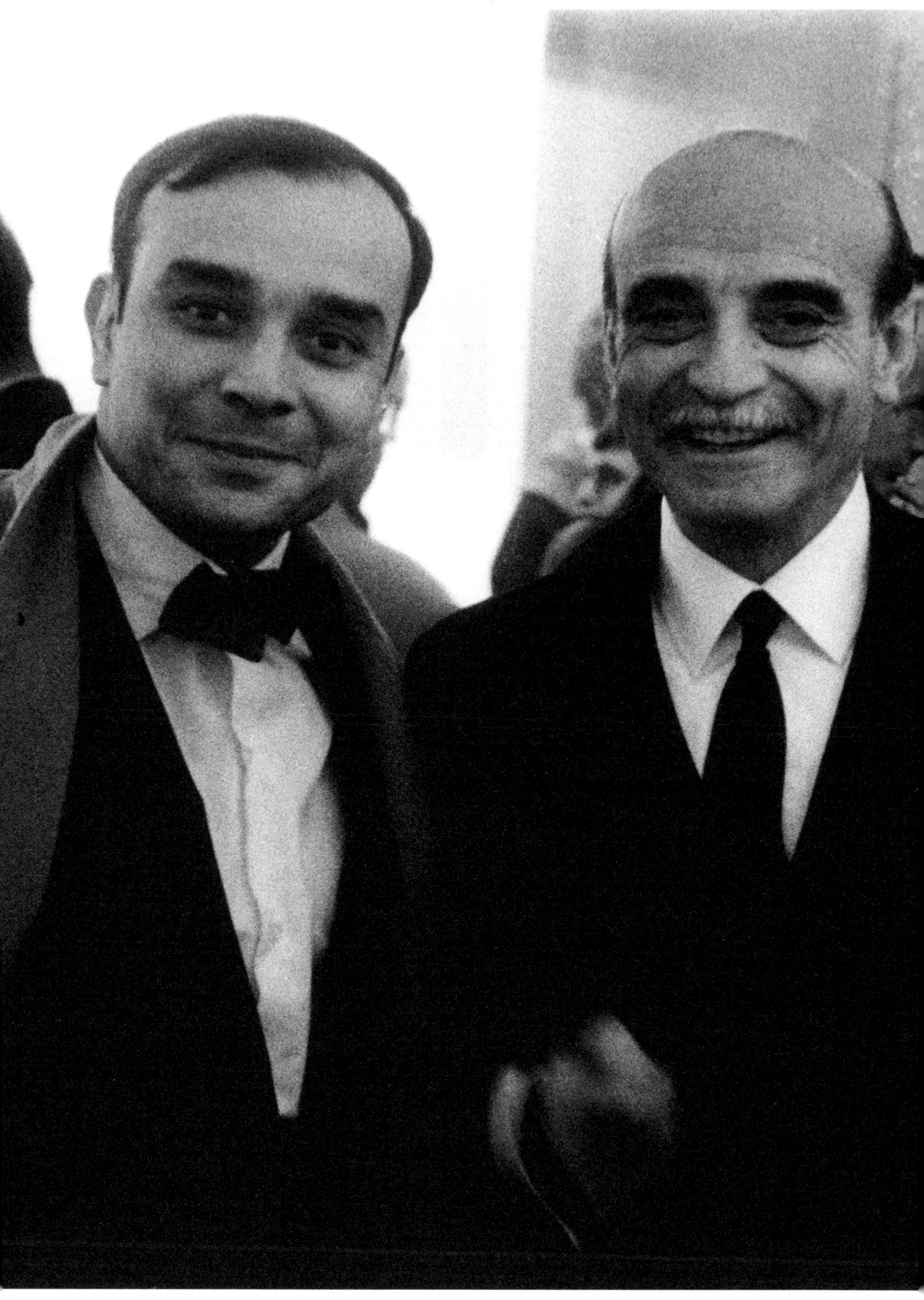

Camuffo Giovanni
Castello 3579
Venezia

Yves Klein
Parigi

Yves Klein

yves mi devi salvare!
Ho sacrificato tanto
per avere una tua opera.
Sono un impiegato.
Hai visto questa maledetta
alta marea
a Venezia
cosa ha fatto al tuo quadro!
Salvami!

La mia casa era diventata
mobile suggestiva:

Letter sent
by Venetian gallerist
Giovanni Camuffo
to Yves Klein,
18 November 1960

tutto era sensibilizzato
dal cromatismo
del tuo quadro.

Io ero felice.
Io ero orgoglioso.
Io ero.

Aiutami, restauraami
il quadro o cambiamelo
Ti prego.

Io credo nella tua
pittura.
Tu sei il nuovo.
Tu sarai il più primitivo
di questa nuova
pittura

In it, Giovanni Camuffo requests assistance
in restoring an artwork that had been
damaged by the *acqua alta* that occurred
in Venice on 15 October 1960. Shortly prior
to this event, Giovanni Camuffo had founded
Galleria del Leone with Attilio Codognato,
just next to Piazza San Marco.
He was the first to exhibit Pop Art and
Nouveau Réalisme artists in Venice.
Translation p. 223

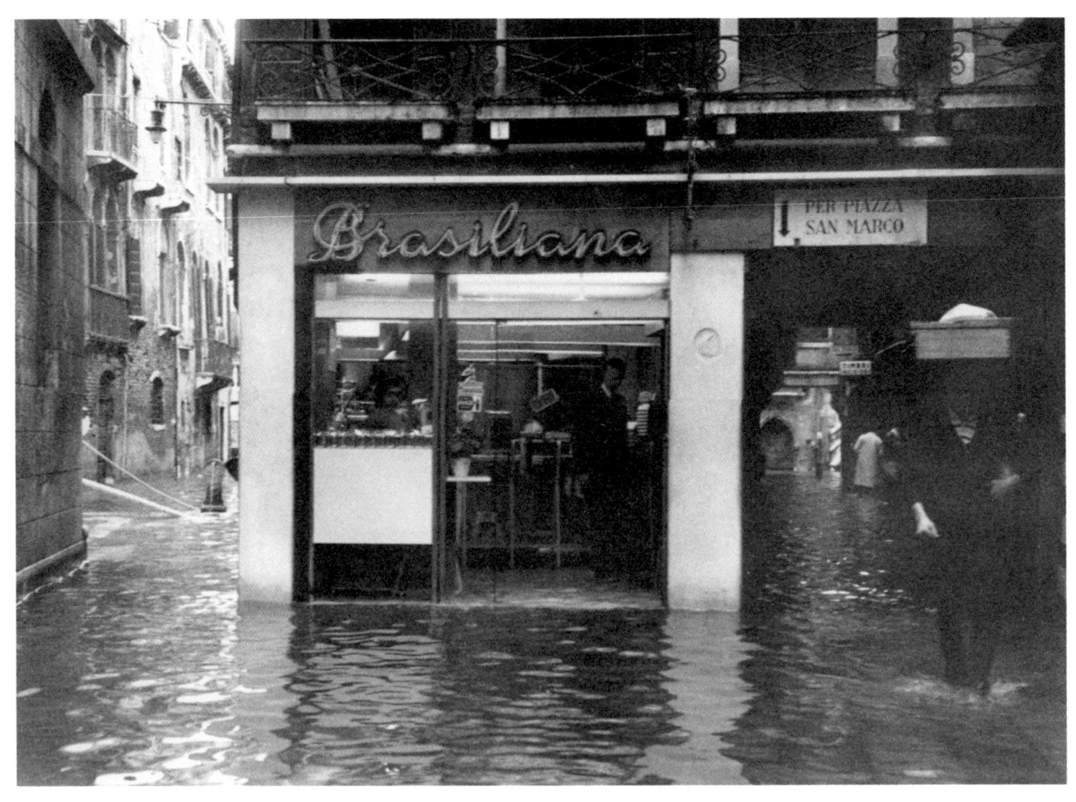

Acqua alta in
Venice, photo sent
by Giovanni Camuffo
to Yves Klein,
18 November 1960

1961

CASCIA

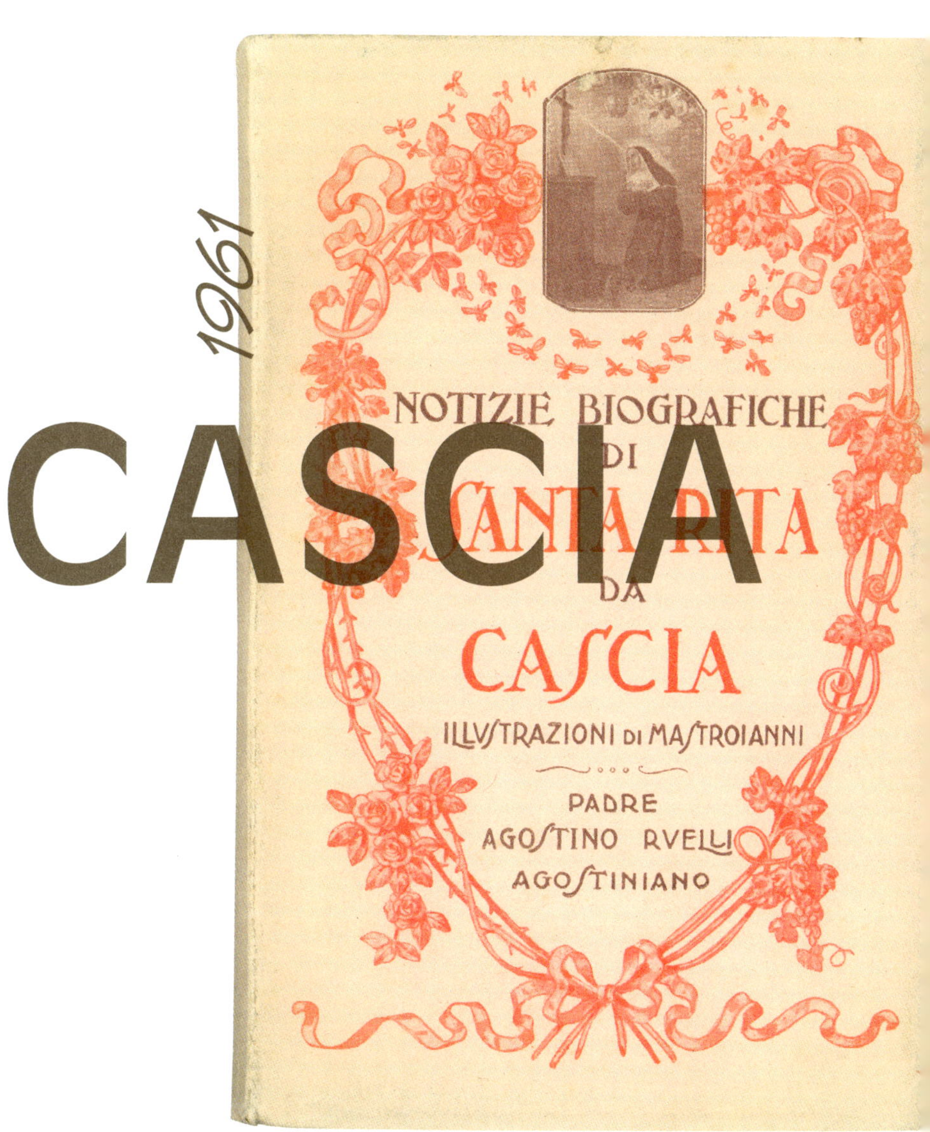

Biographical book
on Saint Rita
of Cascia, published
by Saint Rita
Monastery, Cascia,
1943, from Yves
Klein's book
collection

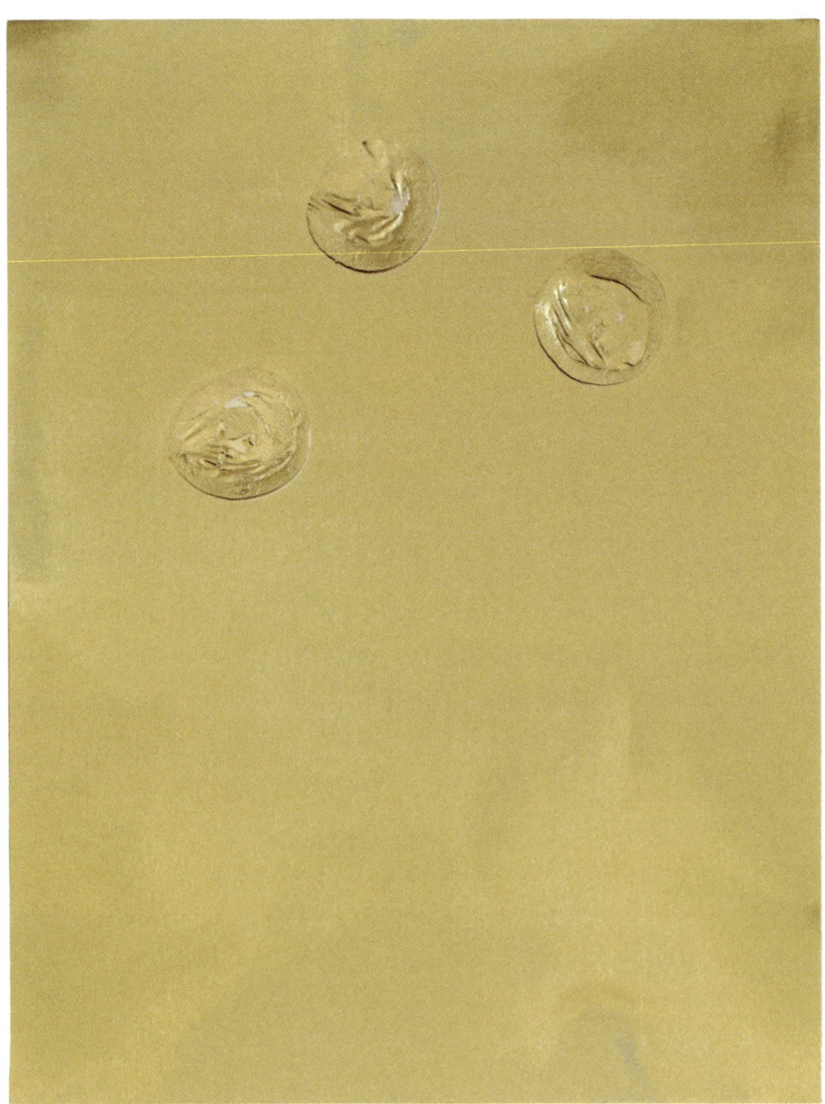

In January 1961, Yves Klein once again
travelled to Saint Rita Monastery with his
partner Rotraut. The goal of this journey
was to bring an ex-voto there, destined
for the patron saint of lost causes and that
he would give - incognito - to the sister
in charge of external relations, at the gate
of the cloister at the convent.
Along with the ex-voto, Yves Klein left
at the monastery a catalogue from his solo
exhibition *Monochrome und Feuer* held at
the Haus Lange Museum in Krefeld, Germany,
from 14 January to 26 February 1961.
In the catalogue was a *Triptyque de Krefeld*
[Krefeld Triptych] composed of three
plates in blue, pink, and gold.

The inside cover of the exhibition
catalogue for *Yves Klein: Monochrome
und Feuer*, Haus Lange Museum,
Krefeld, January 1961, dedicated by
Yves Klein "to Saint Rita of Cascia,
Yves Klein the Monochrome, 1961"

A Sainte Rita
de Cascia

Yves Klein
le monochrome

1961

Yves and I set off from Krefeld by car. It was the middle of January and bitterly cold.
I remember the winter light, the landscapes that flew by and changed as the
kilometres passed. The plains of the Ruhr, the Swiss mountains, the simple,
unique beauty of the Italian countryside. The journey was endless but magnificent.
We were so happy to be leaving together, far from all the tumult.
It was just after the opening of his retrospective at the Haus Lange Museum in
Krefeld in 1961, his first exhibition in a museum, where he had just shown his blue,
gold, and pink trilogy, the immaterial, his air-architecture project, a large fountain
and a wall of fire, which were made there for the first time. Yves was really galvanised
by this show. During the preparations, he secretly built an ex-voto to Saint Rita,
the champion of "impossible and desperate causes", to whom he turned for help
and protection at every important stage of his career. Yves was Catholic and miracles
were always an important part of his life. I think it was a mixture of deep devotion
and mischievous wonder, tinged with magic.

The road to Cascia is long and winding, and it takes hours to get there. As we followed
the bends, the journey became a real pilgrimage, and I could feel this special energy
enveloping Yves. We arrived towards the end of the afternoon. We headed straight for
the monastery of Saint Rita and Yves handed over his offering and a catalogue of his
exhibition to the nun who was on duty. He did not say who he was. The nun
accepted the gift, closed the door almost immediately, and we left just as naturally.
Yves never mentioned this ex-voto again. I never mentioned it to anyone either,
even after his death. I would never have allowed myself to interfere with that gesture.
And so, it was kept secret for almost twenty years.
I sometimes thought about this work. Even though it was hidden hundreds of miles
away, I could feel its presence. Yves had put all his sensitivity into that little box.
Curiously, it was an earthquake that allowed this work to resurface. It had been kept
by the sisters in a room used as a depository for offerings. They took it to the painter
Armando Marocco, who was looking for gold leaf to restore the stained-glass windows.
Luckily, Armando knew about Yves's work and his attachment to Saint Rita, and he
immediately called Guido Le Noci and then Pierre Restany.

The reappearance of the ex-voto was like discovering a real treasure. Everyone was
captivated by this object that, despite its small size, seemed to encompass all Yves's
ideas and work. The handwritten prayer it contains is very moving. He prays to
become a better artist, so that everything he creates will always be of "great beauty",
and that his works will become "invulnerable".
I sometimes wonder if the fact of rediscovering this work has taken away some
of its mystery. But life and art work like a miracle. Everything is interconnected,
like a river digging its own bed. Shortly afterwards, we found the blue monochrome
that Yves had given to the monastery in Cascia in 1958. The sisters used it every year
as the sky in their Christmas crib.
Yves believed in Immaterial Sensibility, in that energy that permeates life, and with
the rediscovery of these two artworks, it suddenly became visible to all.

Rotraut Klein-Moquay
May 2023

Sister Andreina
and Yves Klein's
ex-voto, Saint Rita
Monastery, Cascia,
1999

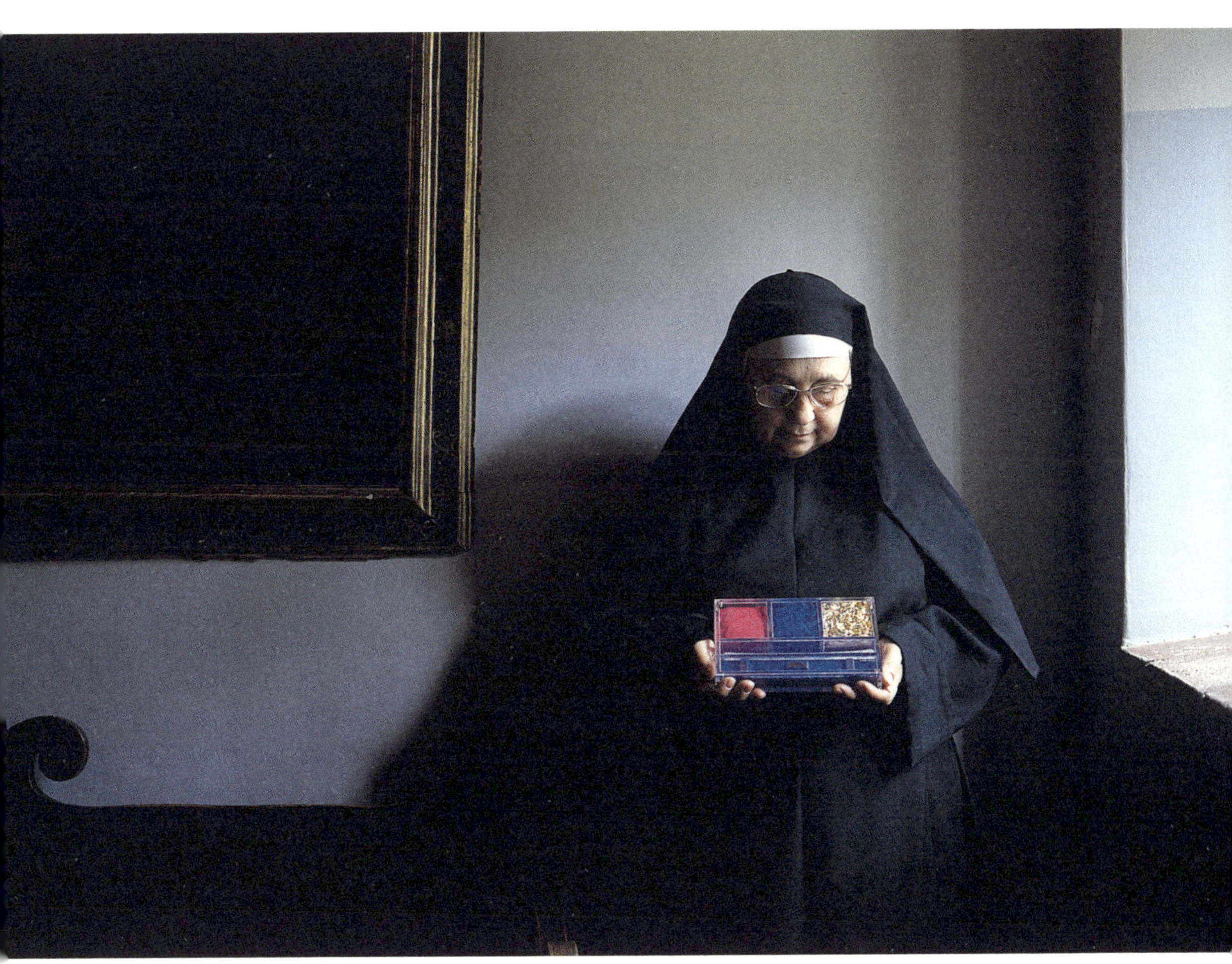

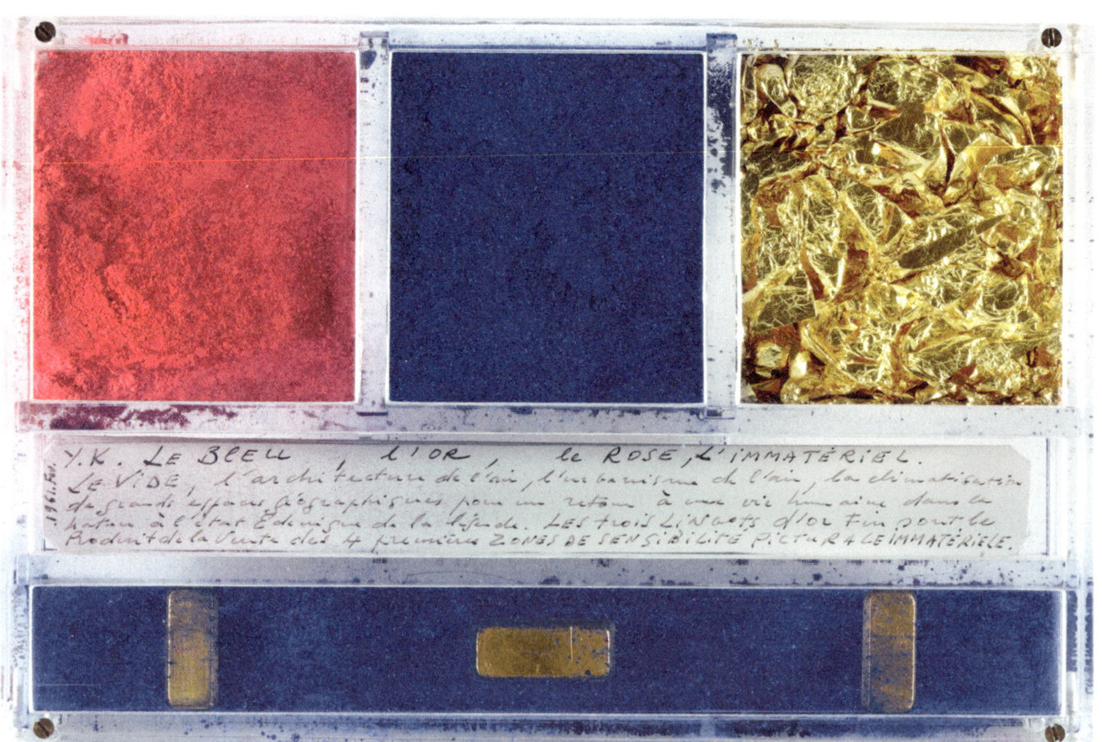

Y.K. LE BLEU, L'OR, le ROSE, L'IMMATÉRIEL.
LE VIDE, l'architecture de l'air, l'urbanisme de l'air, la climatisation
des grands espaces géographiques pour un retour à une vie humaine dans la
nature à l'état Edenique de la légende. LES trois LINGOTS d'or fin sont le
Produit de la vente des 4 premières ZONES DE SENSIBILITÉ PICTURAL IMMATÉRIELE.
1961.Fev.

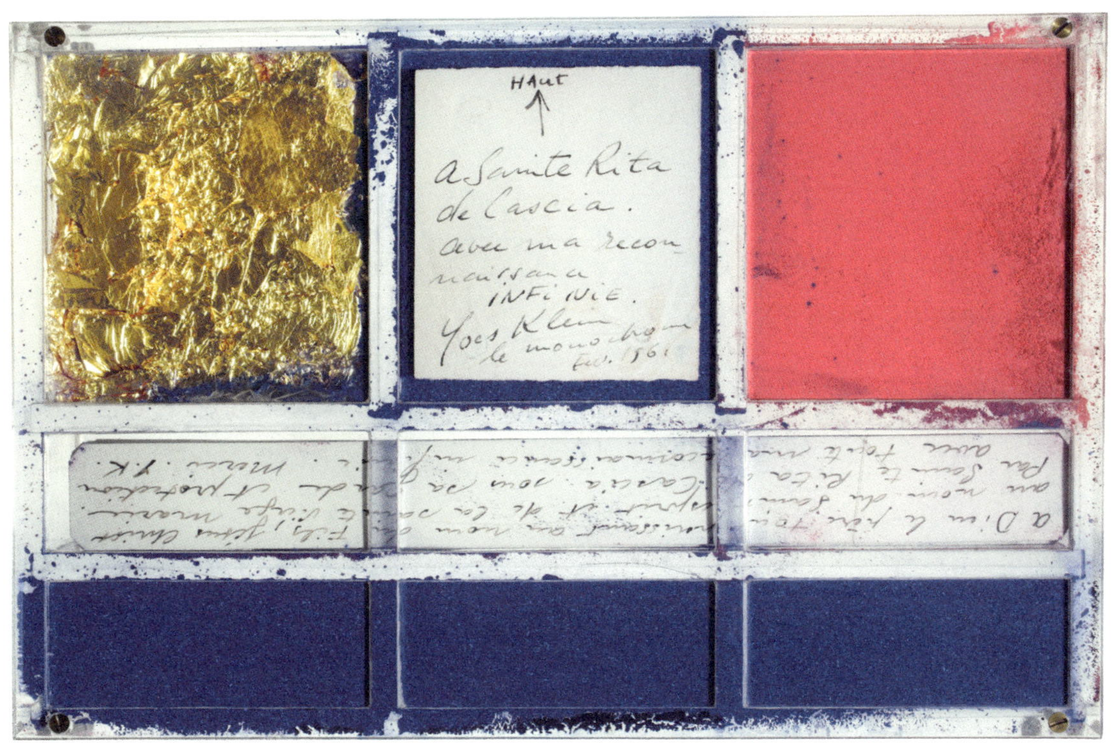

Yves Klein,
*Ex-voto dédié
à sainte Rita
de Cascia* [Ex-voto
dedicated to Saint
Rita of Cascia],
1961 (recto and
verso)
Translation
of the prayer:
pp. 223-224

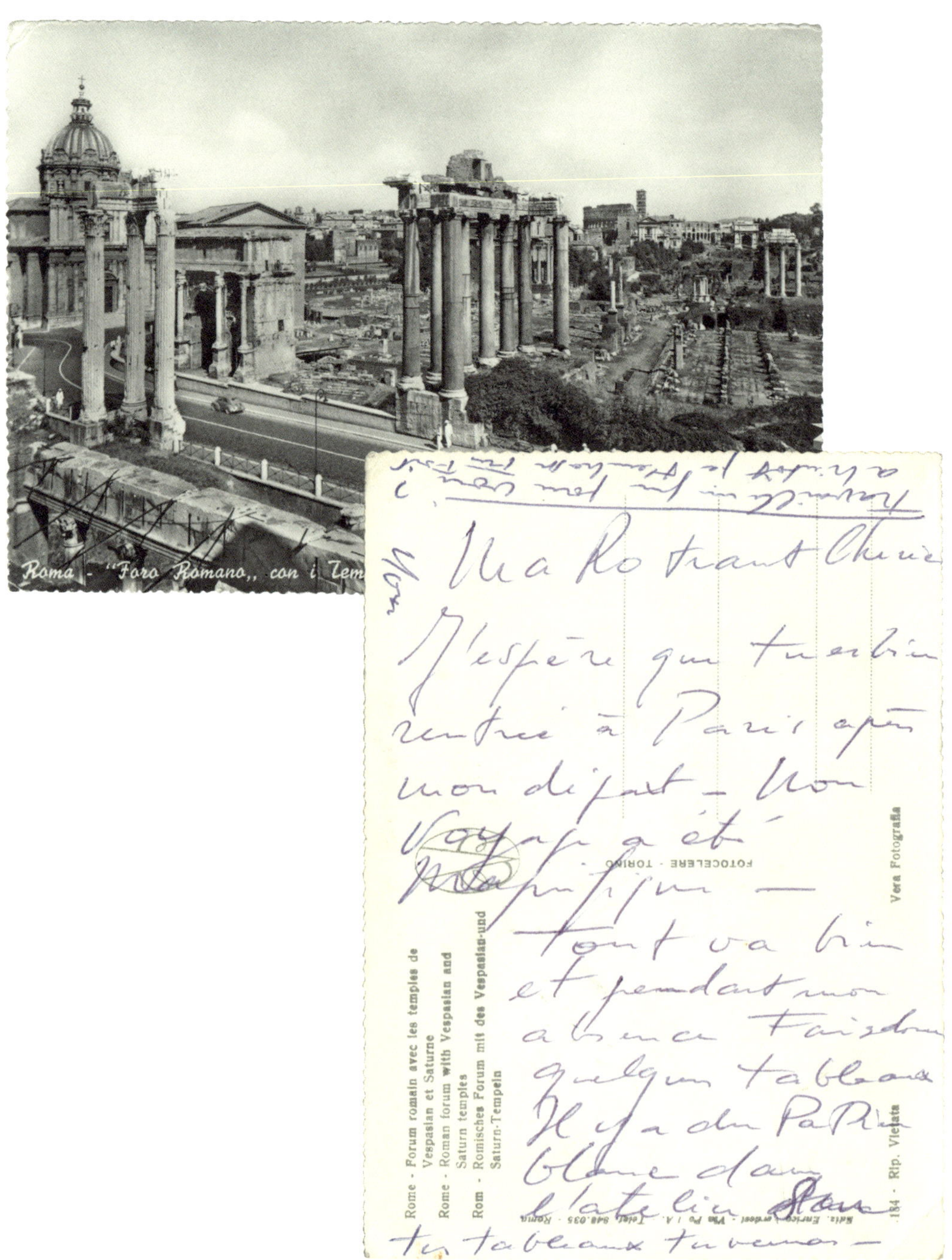

Postcard from
Yves Klein to
Rotraut, sent from
Rome, February 1961
Translation p. 224

ROME

1961

PARIS
ROME

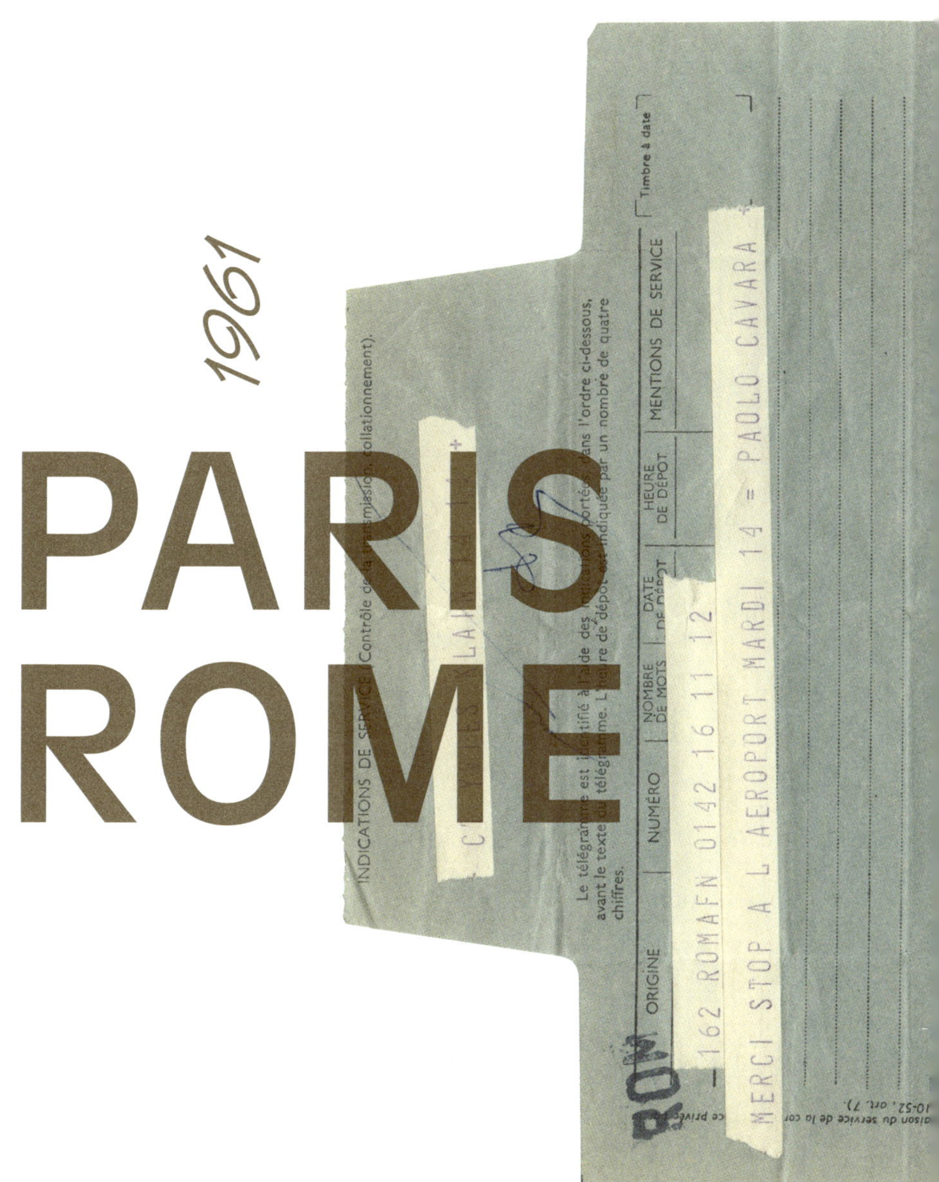

Telegram from director Paolo Cavara
confirming Yves Klein and Rotraut's trip
to Rome in November 1961 to see the edit
of the documentary *Mondo Cane*

PARIS
PARIS

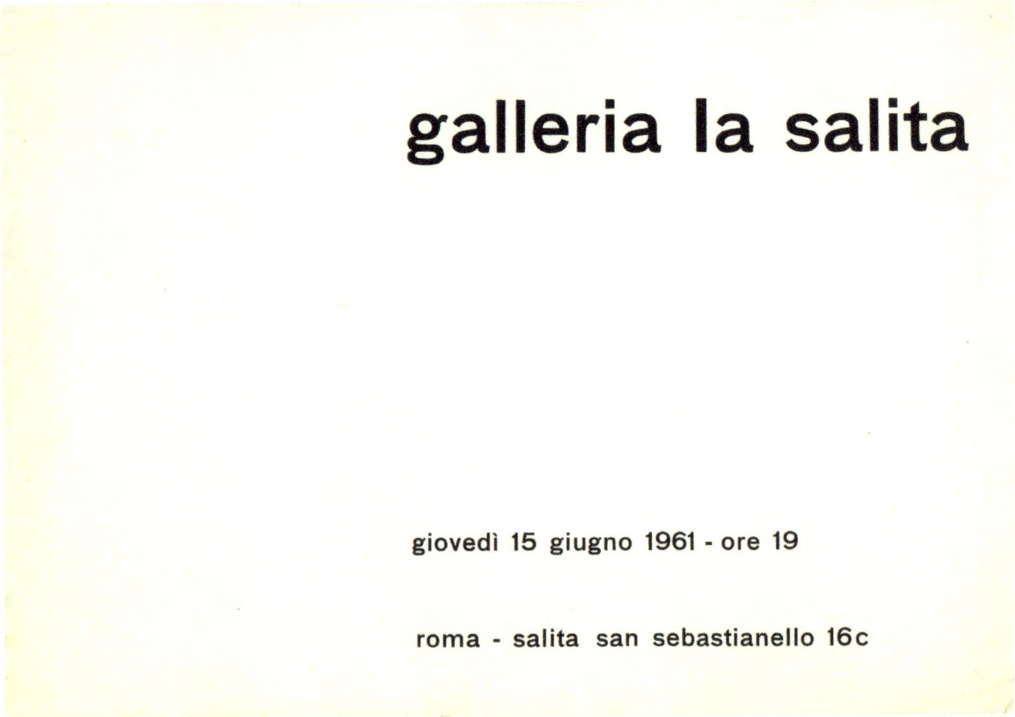

galleria la salita

giovedì 15 giugno 1961 - ore 19

roma - salita san sebastianello 16c

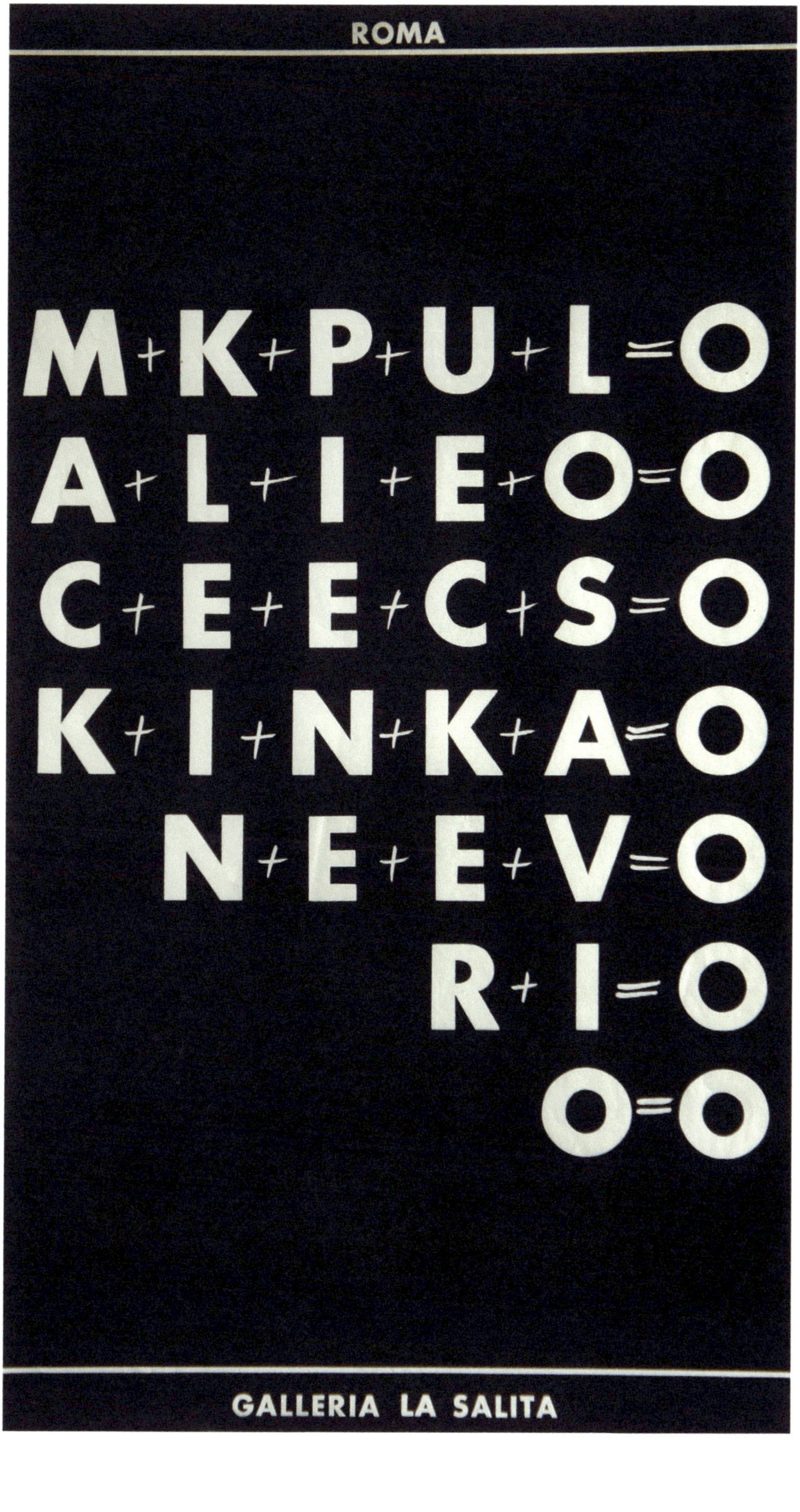

M+K+P+U+L=O
A+L+I+E+O=O
C+E+E+C+S=O
K+I+N+K+A=O
N+E+E+V=O
R+I=O
O=O

<u>AGREEMENT</u>

Mr. Paolo CAVARA, of the Cie CINERIZ, Viale Castrense, 9, ROMA(Italy) formally agrees to adhere to the following scenario written by Mr. Yves KLEIN.

SCENARIO:

<u>PREMIERE SCENE</u>

Décor: Un grand atelier.

a) Aux murs sont accrochés, au début seulement:
       – un grand monochrome bleu
       – un grand relief bleu

b) Au sol, une grande surface de papier blanc qui est au centre (4 m x 2m 80). – Sur cette surface blanche sont allongées les filles (modèles nus). Elles posent.

c) A côté, une sorte de piscine de bleu liquide –profondeur 3 cm. (2m 50 x 1m 20) – l'idée: Une seule palette, une seule couleur.

d) Un chevalet avec une toile blanche (60 Fig.)

e) Au sol, à côté du chevalet: deux toiles 60 Fig.

f) A côté de la piscine:
       – Un gros pinceau
       – Un grand rouleau
       – Une grosse éponge
       – Une éponge moyenne

Action:

a) Yves peint le monochrome au chevalet avec le gros pinceau (Regards sur le poignet)

b) Yves peint le 2ème monochrome au sol avec le rouleau.

c) Yves peint le 3ème monochrome avec les deux éponges – (Effet: empreintes de mains effacées de suite furieusement)

d) Chaque fois, pour peindre ses monochromes, il trempe successivement le gros pinceau, le rouleau et les éponges dans le bleu de la piscine. – Palette !

– Pendant qu'il peint, au début, la camera ne filme que le monochrome accroché au mur, dans le champs de l'action.

– Yves regarde de temps à autres les modèles et aussi le monochrome au mur.

– A la fin, Yves, après avoir fini son dernier monochrome avec les éponges, regarde les éponges toutes bleues, hésite et les pose sur le dernier monochrome tout frais.

......

Contract between the Rive Droite Gallery, Yves Klein, and Paolo Cavara, 12 July 1961

In April 1961, Italian directors Gualtiero Jacopetti, Paolo Cavara, and Franco Prosperi contacted Yves Klein to shoot a session of the *Anthropometries* as part of the documentary *Mondo Cane*, produced by Cineriz. The contract included a script written by Yves Klein, which had to be respected, and the artist reserved a right of inspection with respect to the editing.
Translation pp. 224-225

Still from
the film *Mondo Cane*

On 17 and 18 July 1961, Paolo Cavara
shot a long production sequence of
Anthropometries at the Rive Droite Gallery
in Paris. The *Symphonie monoton-silence*
[Monotone-Silence Symphony] was played
by an orchestra.

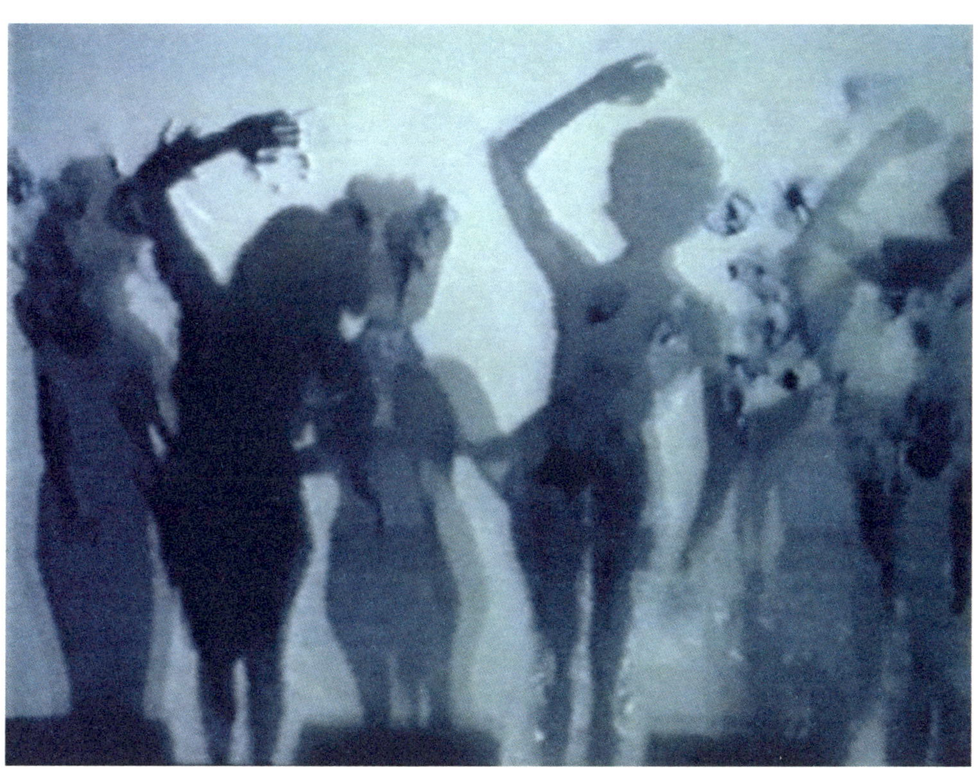

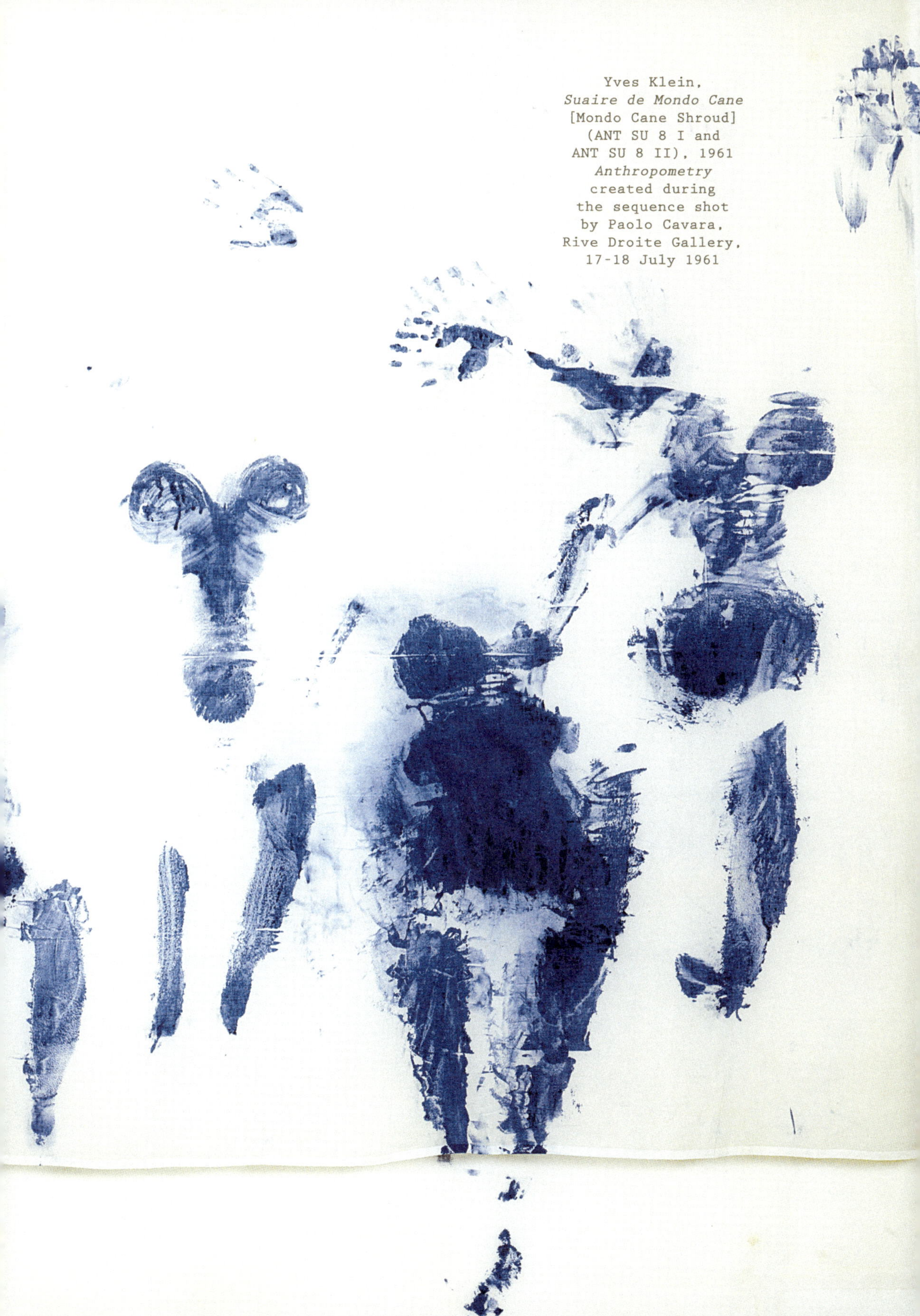

Yves Klein,
Suaire de Mondo Cane
[Mondo Cane Shroud]
(ANT SU 8 I and
ANT SU 8 II), 1961
Anthropometry
created during
the sequence shot
by Paolo Cavara,
Rive Droite Gallery,
17-18 July 1961

PARIS, le 17 Octobre 1961

Monsieur le Maire

de TIVOLI

Italie

Monsieur le Maire,

J'ai l'avantage de soumttre à votre haute
autorité le projet suivant:

- Inclure des jets de feu dans les cascatelles et dans les
  jardins de TIVOLI, au moment de la grande saison d'été.-

Ces arrangements seraiet faits par Yves
KLEIN , le Monochrome, qui a déjà construit des Fontaines de Feu
au Musée de KREFELD (Allemagne) lors de son exposition rétrospec-
tive au début de 1961. Cet artiste a présenté également ces Fontaines de Feu devant le théatre de Werner HUNAU sur la grande
Place de GELSENKIRCHEN (Allemagne) et il a fait quelques autres
manifestations aux Etats-Unis.

Je vous adresse ci-joint un plan des cascatelles
et fontaines avec les jets de feu, afin de vous donner une idée du
projet grandiose que pourrait présenter cet ensemble de feu et d'eaux
à TIVOLI.

A titre d'exemple également, je vous envoie les
plans pour les fontaines du Trocadero qui ont été préparés par Yves
KLEIN.

Espérant que ces projets pourraient retenir votre
attention, je vous prie de croire, Monsieur le Maire, à l'expression
de ma haute considération.

Jean LARCADE

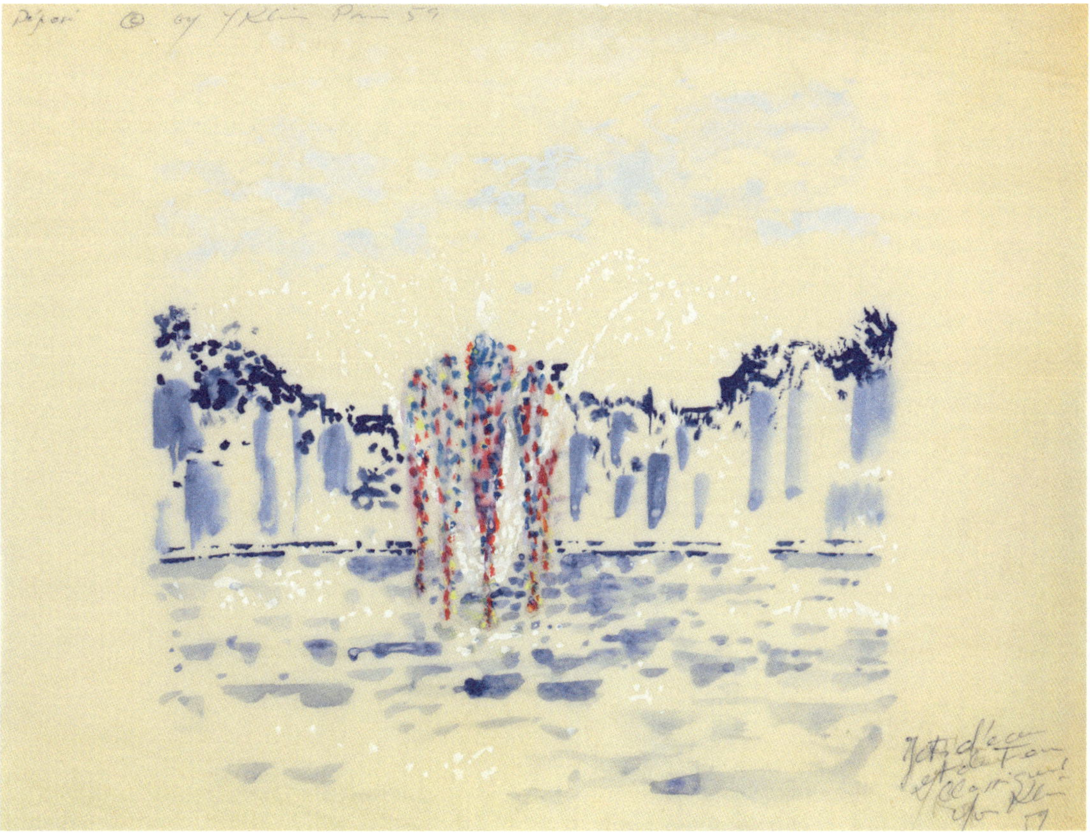

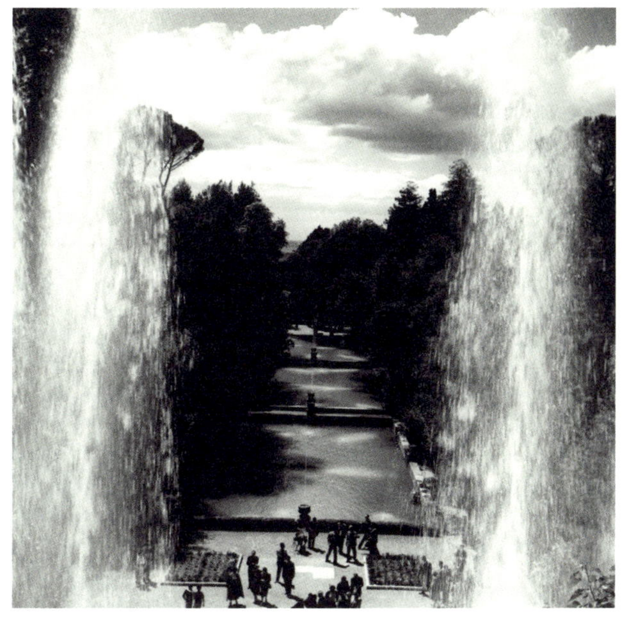

Yves Klein,
Jets d'eau et de feu
[Water and Fire
Fountains]
(D 92), 1959

Photograph
of the fountains
of the Villa d'Este,
bought by
Yves Klein, ca. 1959

Invitation card
for the
double exhibition
*"Concetti spaziali"
de Fontana*,
Iris Clert Gallery
and Rive Droite
Gallery, Paris,
November 1961

Sculptures
by Lucio Fontana
installed at the
Iris Clert Gallery,
November 1961

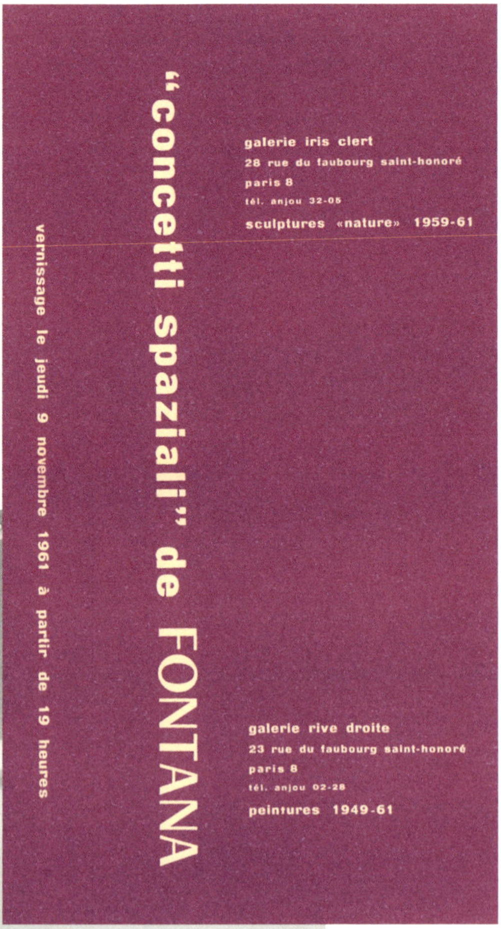

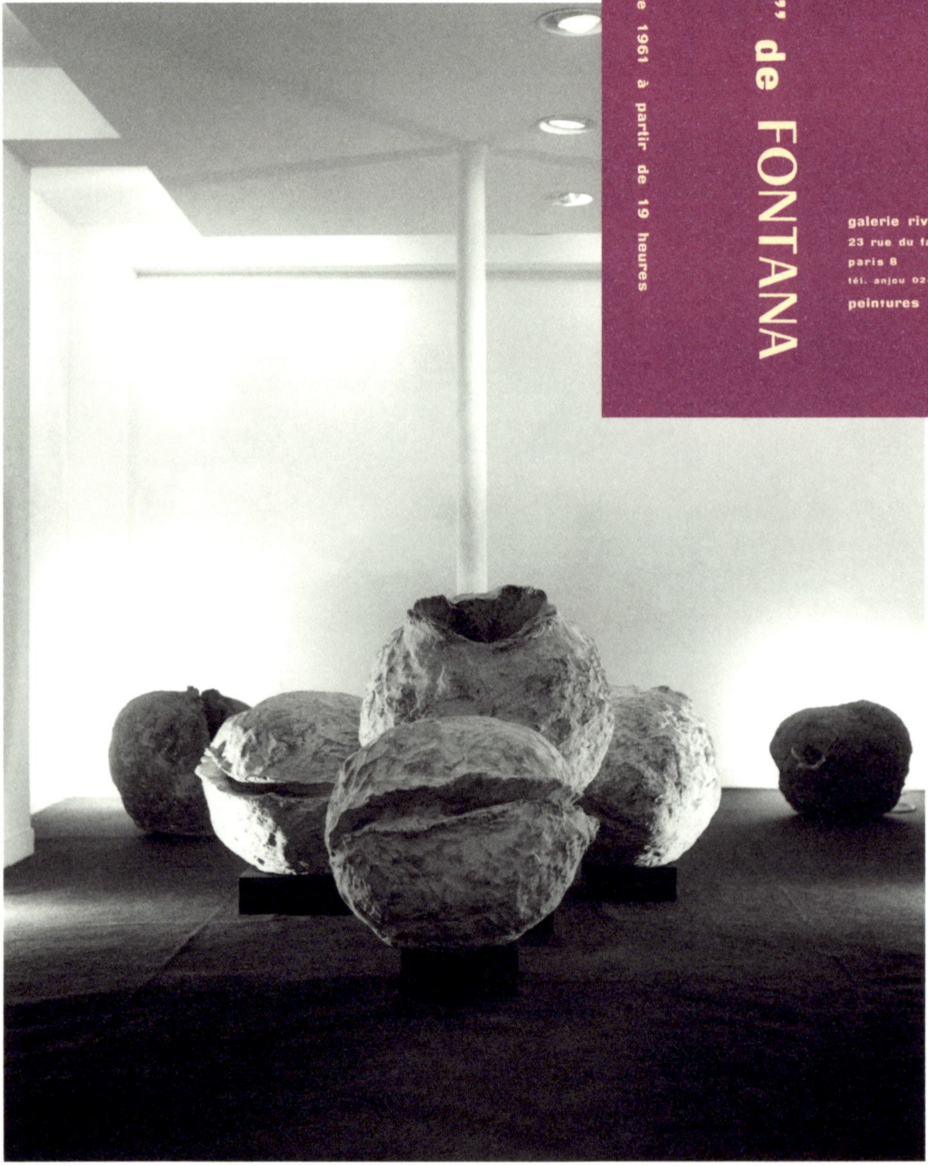

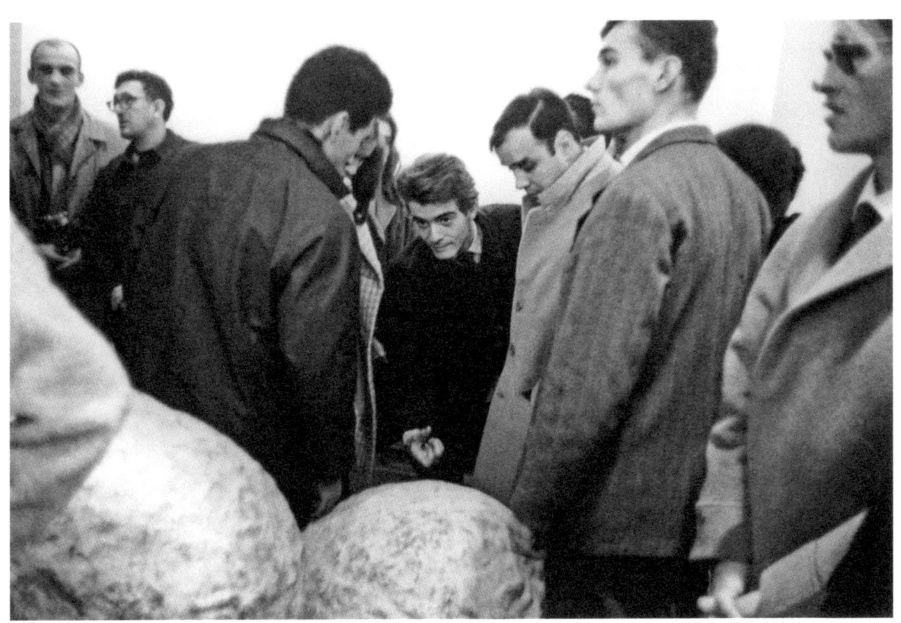

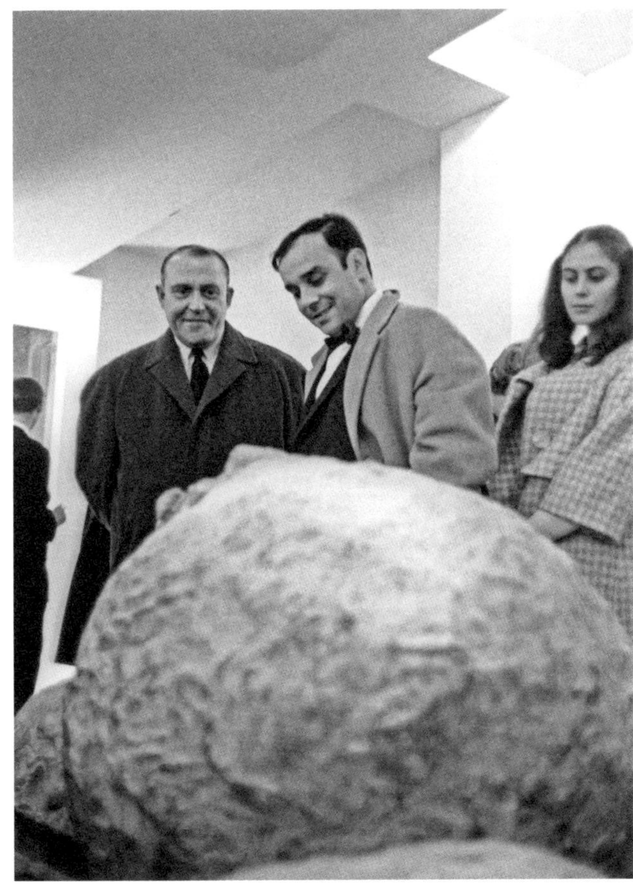

Yves Klein at
the vernissage,
Iris Clert Gallery,
Paris, 9 November
1961

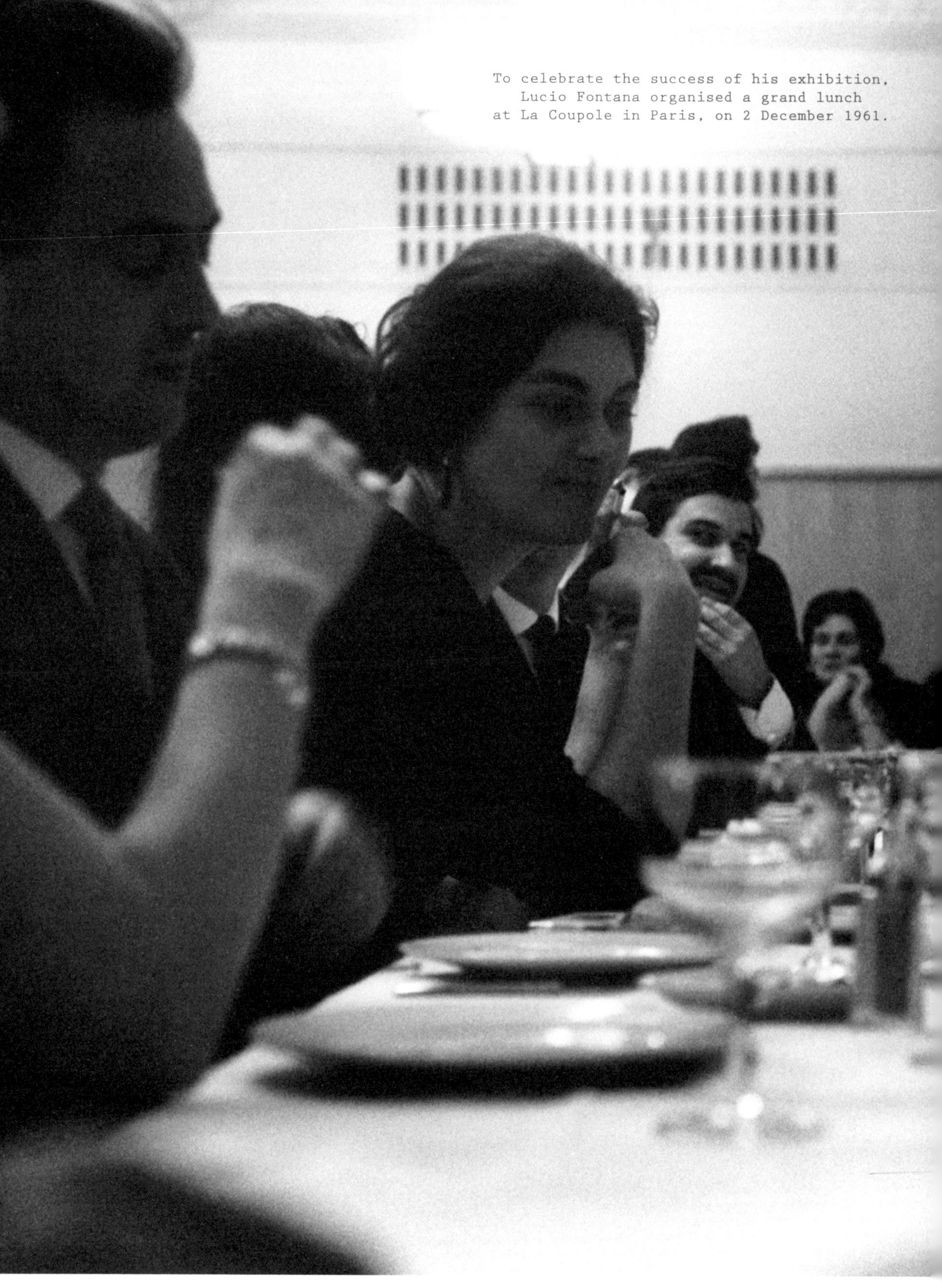

To celebrate the success of his exhibition,
Lucio Fontana organised a grand lunch
at La Coupole in Paris, on 2 December 1961.

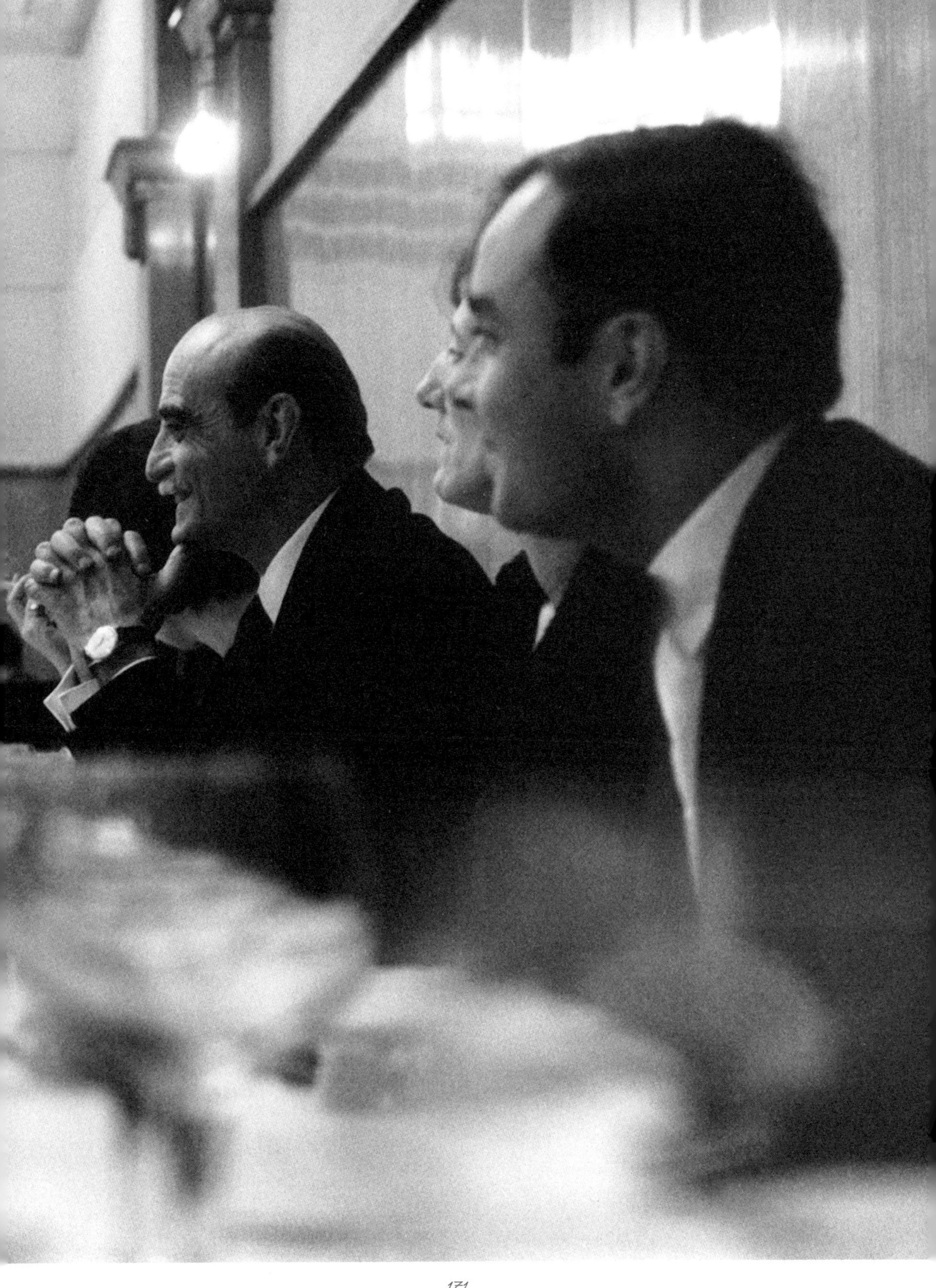

Postcard sent by Guido Le Noci
to Yves Klein to Rome, November 1961

He informs him he has delivered the
invitations for his solo show to
the Milan-Rome train conductor and asks
Klein to be ready on the platform,
holding a piece of blue paper to
identify himself.
Translation p. 225

Postcard from Yves Klein sent on
14 November 1961 from Rome to Paul Wember,
director of the Haus Lange Museum
in Krefeld, where Klein held an exhibition
in January

He evokes his solo exhibition at
Apollinaire Gallery in Milan, which will
be inaugurated on 20 November.
Translation p. 225

ROMA - Il Colosseo e il Tempio di Venere
ROME - Le Colosseum et le Temple de Vénus
ROME - The Colosseum and the Temple of Venus
ROM - Das Kolosseum und der Venus-Tempel

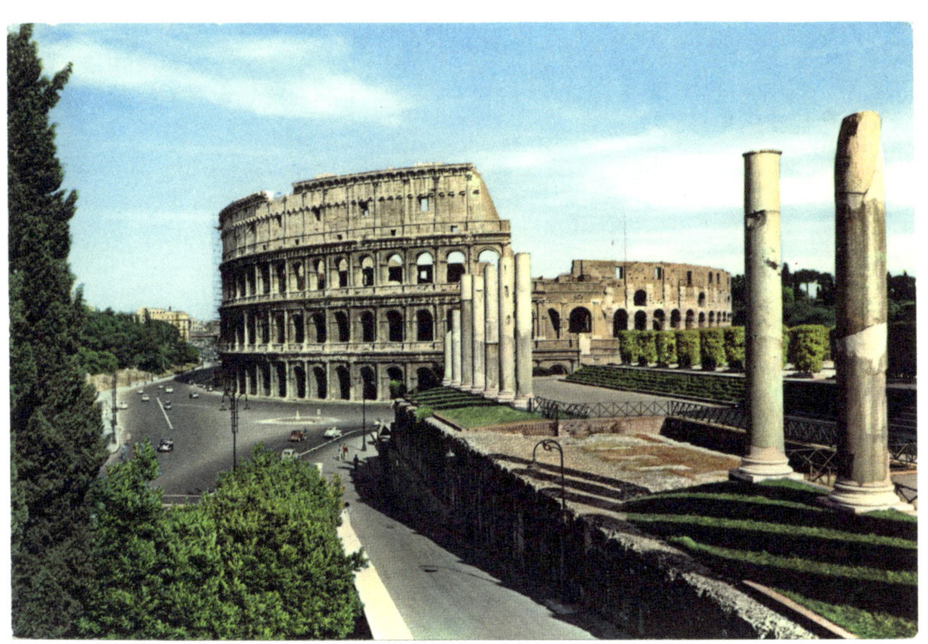

Rome 24 novembre 1961

Cher Monsieur Klein,

je désir encore vous dire le plaisir que j'ai eu de
faire votre connaissance et m'excuser encore une fois
pour l'incident de votre tableau.J'ai beaucoup apprecié
votre gentillesse en vous occupant de la restauration
du même tableau.Il a été consigné pour l'expédition et
j'espére qu'il vous arrivera bientôt.

J'ai écrit à Monsieur Larcade en espérant d'avoir en
suite meilleures et plus vastes occasions de présenter
à Rome vos oeuvres et en lui disant combien je suis dé-
solé pour l'imprévu de douane.L'incompréhension humaine
peut être,quelque fois,plus appréciable que l'enthousia-
sme.

J'espére avoir la possibilité d'aller à Milan pour voir
les tableaux de votre exposition.Je vous écrirai après.

En vous remerciant encore une fois,veuillez,cher Monsieur,
recevoir mes salutations les plus cordiales.

G.T.Liverani

Mr. Yves Klein
14,rue Campagne Première
Paris XIV

Letter from
Gian Tomaso Liverani,
director of
La Salita Gallery,
to Yves Klein,
24 November 1961

They met in Rome in November. Yves Klein
took advantage of his visit to restore one
of his artworks that had been damaged during
the *Mack + Klein + Piene + Uecker + Lo Savio
= 0* exhibition in June. The gallerist
informed him of his desire to present his
artworks in Rome at his gallery.
Translation p. 225

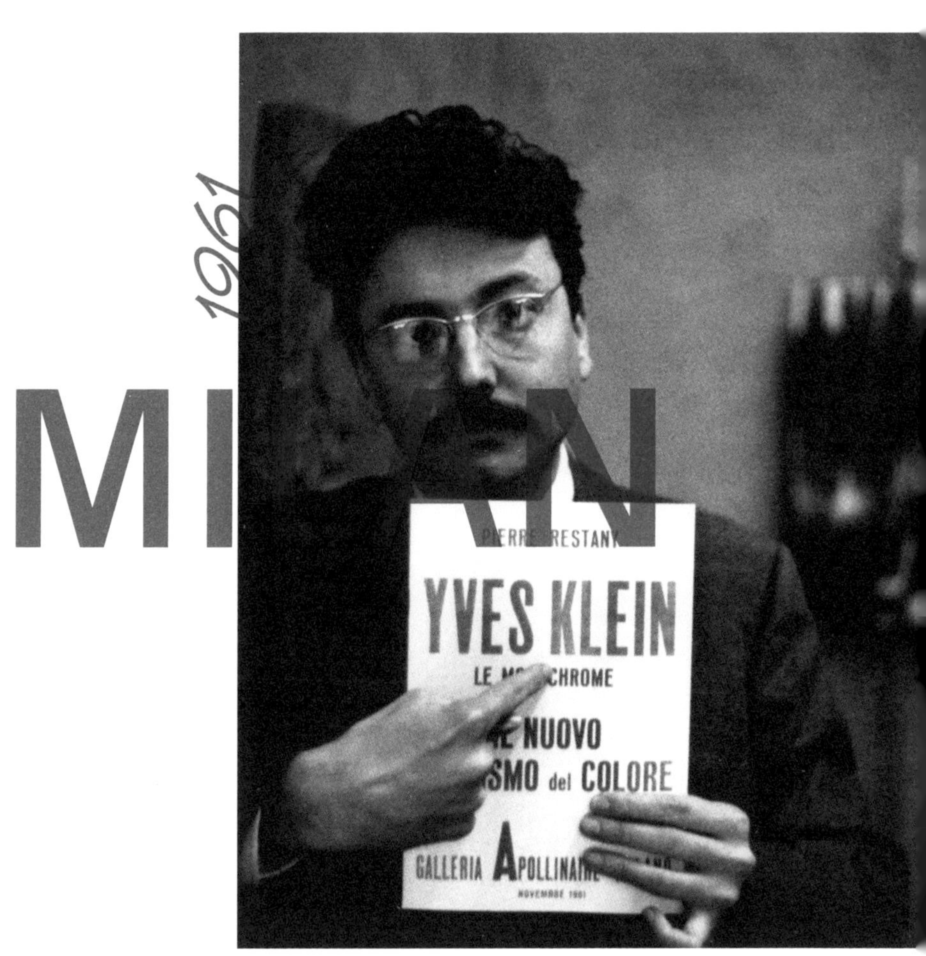

Pierre Restany
at the opening of
the *Yves Klein
le Monochrome.
Il nuovo realismo del
colore* exhibition,
Apollinaire Gallery,
Milan, 20 November
1961

PIERRE RESTANY

YVES KLEIN

LE MONOCHROME

IL NUOVO
REALISMO del COLORE

GALLERIA Apollinaire MILANO

NOVEMRBE 1961

Exhibition catalogue for *Yves Klein le Monochrome. Il nuovo realismo del colore* exhibition, Apollinaire Gallery, Milan, 20 November–30 December 1961

The Klein case is no longer a case.
It is no longer a "strange, absurd joke",
as someone once mumbled in front
of the tabula rasa of his total blue.
It is instead a great spiritual conquest.
A spiritual conquest that has opened
the way for a poetic vision of the physical
world in the space age, towards which,
as I was saying, we are headed,
even without realising it. There is enough
of it to be proud to have tied the gallery's
name to this historic event.

Guido Le Noci

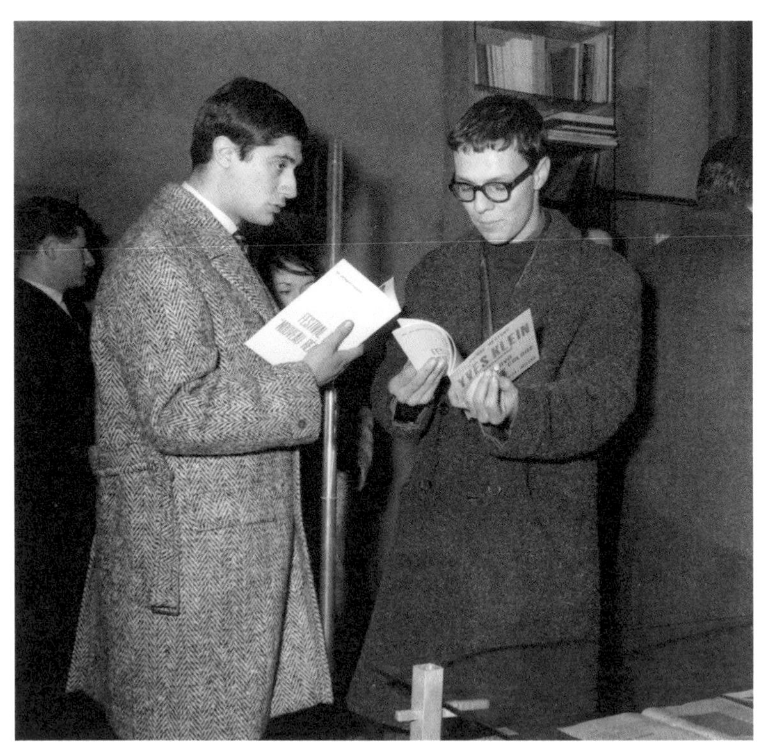

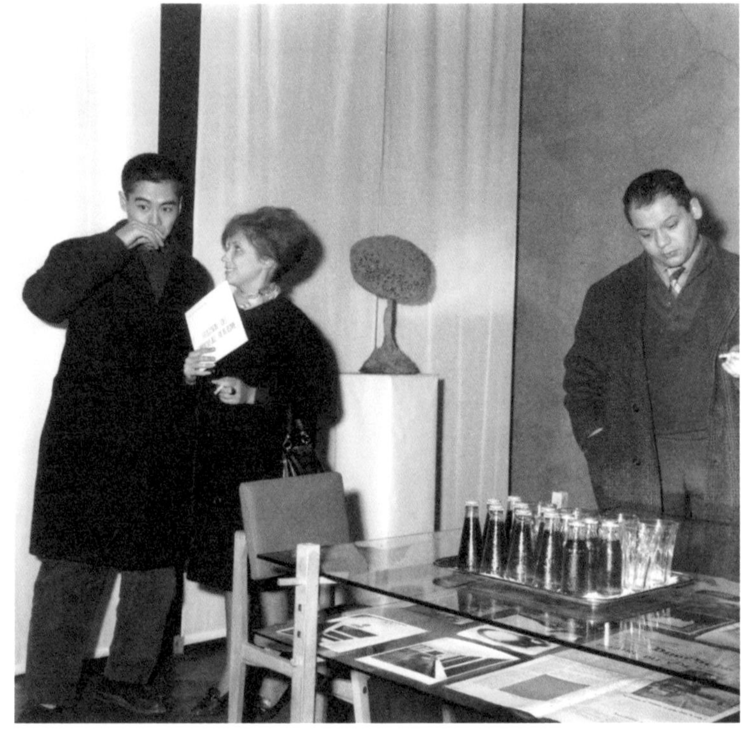

Artists
Gianni Colombo and
Giovanni Anceschi
from Gruppo T

Artists Hsiao Chin,
Pia Pizzo,
and Piero Manzoni

Count
Visconti di Modrone,
Count Giuseppe
and Countess
Giovanna Panza
di Biumo

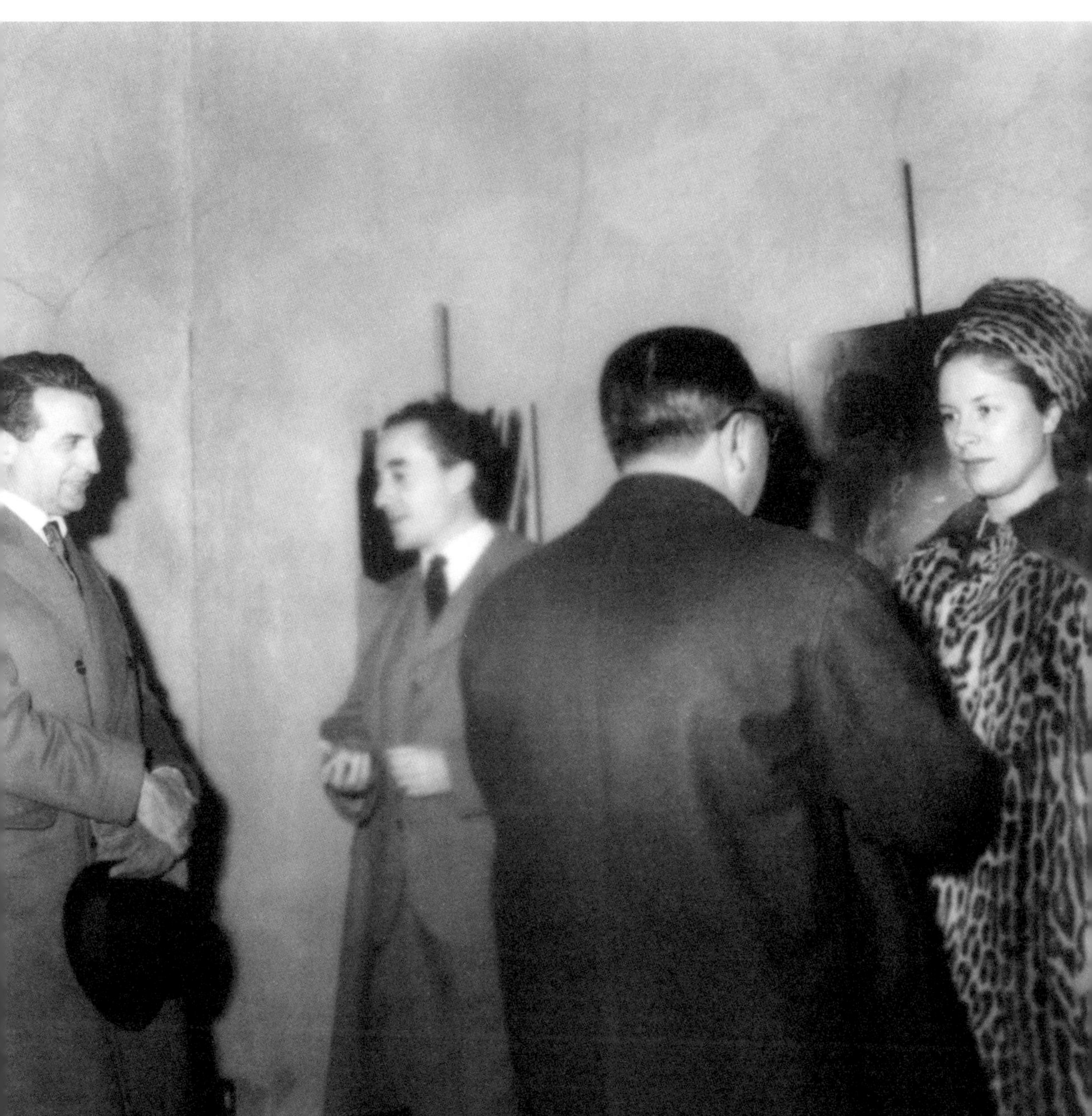

Yves Klein,
Relief planétaire
"Région de Grenoble"
[Planetary Relief
"Grenoble Region"]
(RP 10), 1961

Yves Klein,
Untitled Monogold
(MG 11), 1961

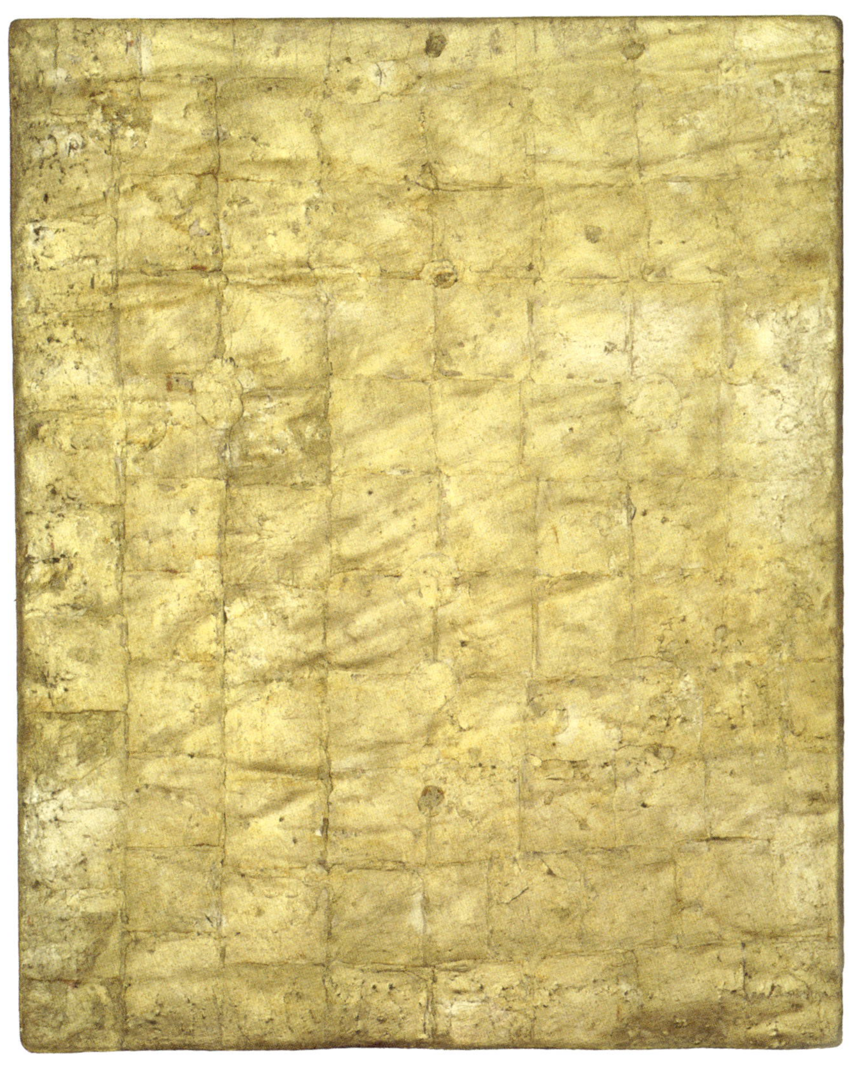

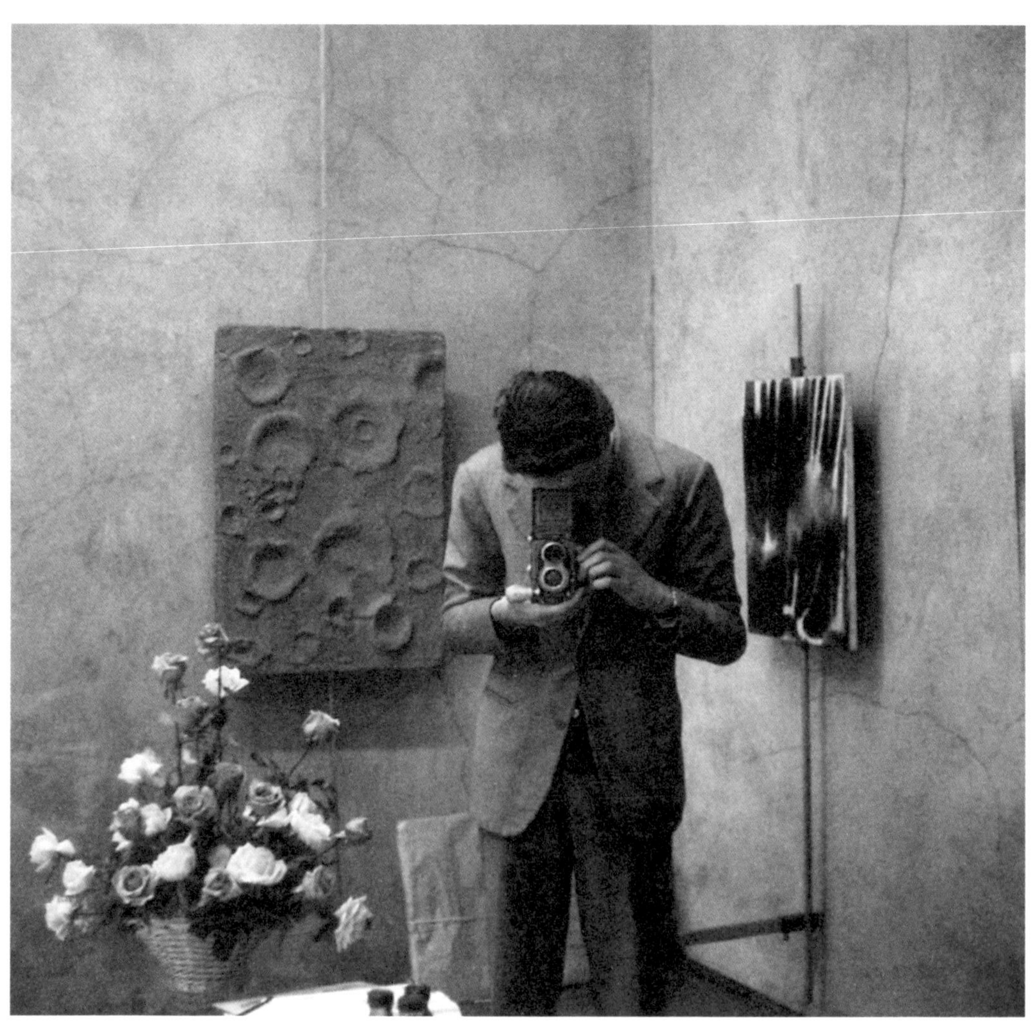

Relief planétaire rose "Lune II"
[Pink Planetary Relief "Moon II"] (RP 21)
and Peinture de feu "Carte de Mars
par l'eau et le feu" [Fire Painting
"Map of Mars by Water and Fire"] (F 83),
Apollinaire Gallery, 20 November 1961

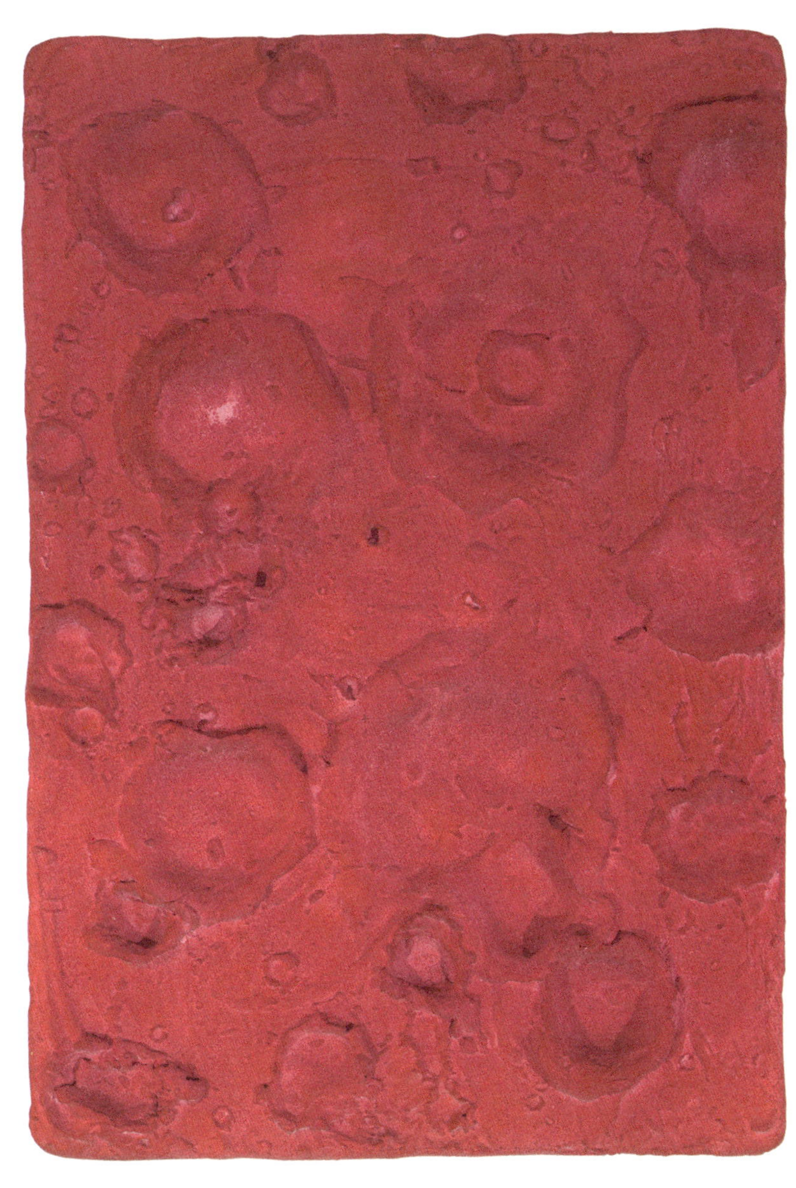

Yves Klein,
Pink Planetary
Relief "Moon II"
(RP 21), 1961

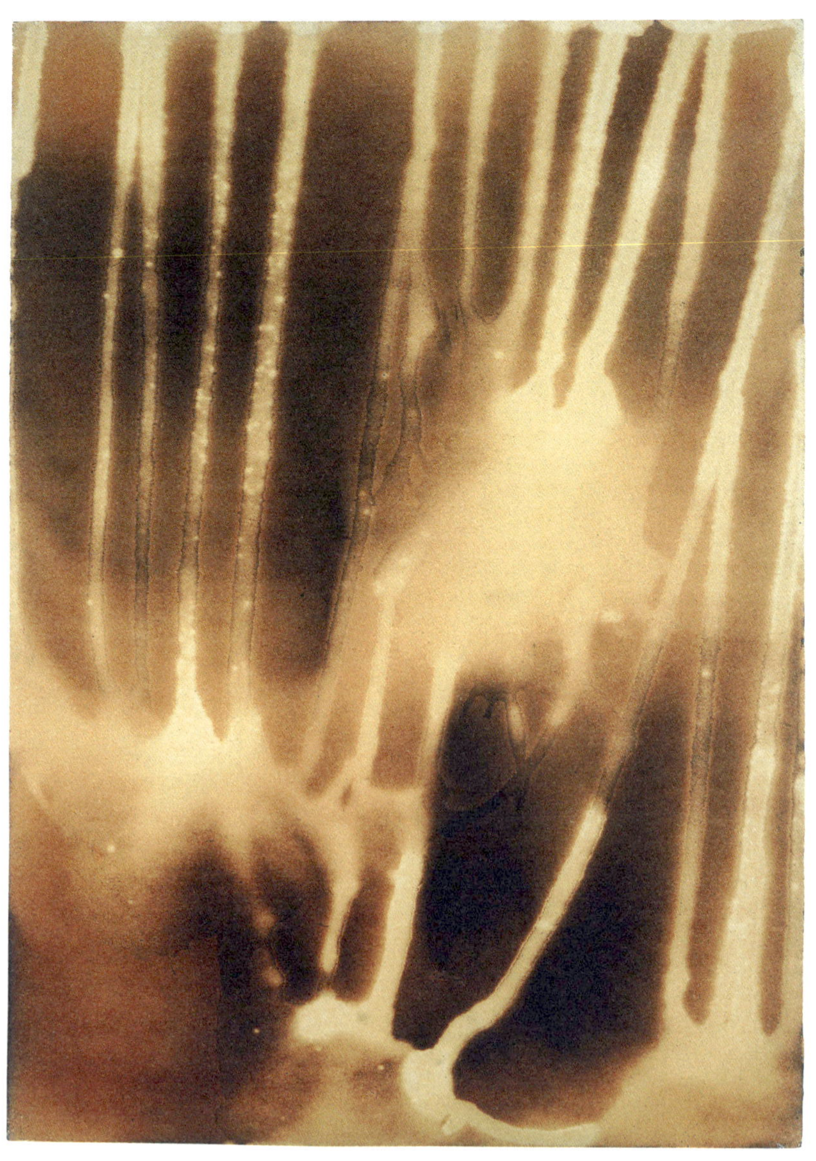

Yves Klein,
Fire Painting
"Map of Mars by
Water and Fire"
(F 83), 1961

Yves Klein,
*Untitled Blue Sponge
Sculpture* (SE 181),
1960

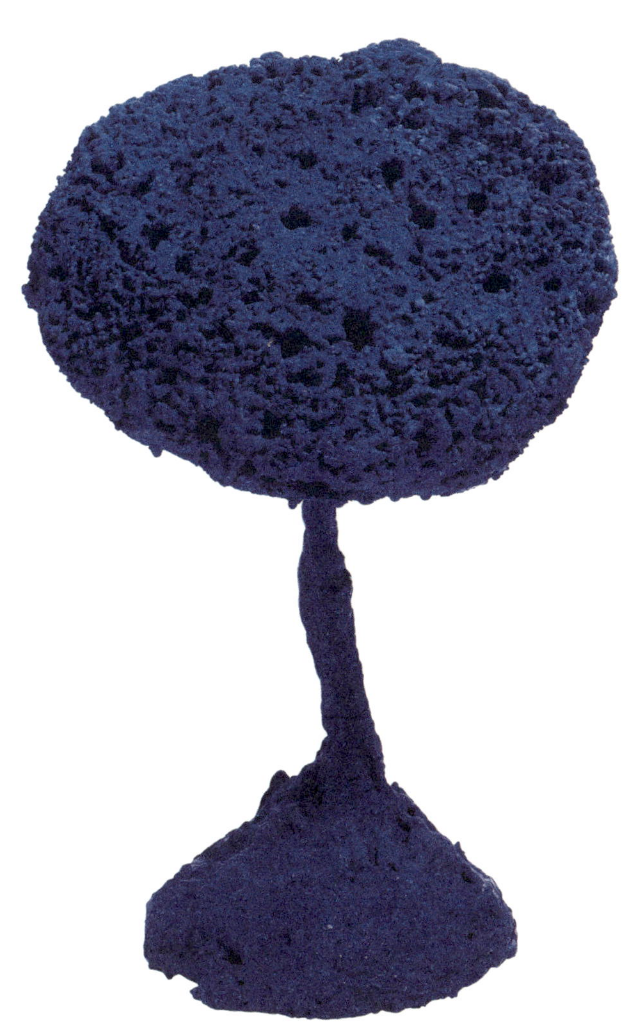

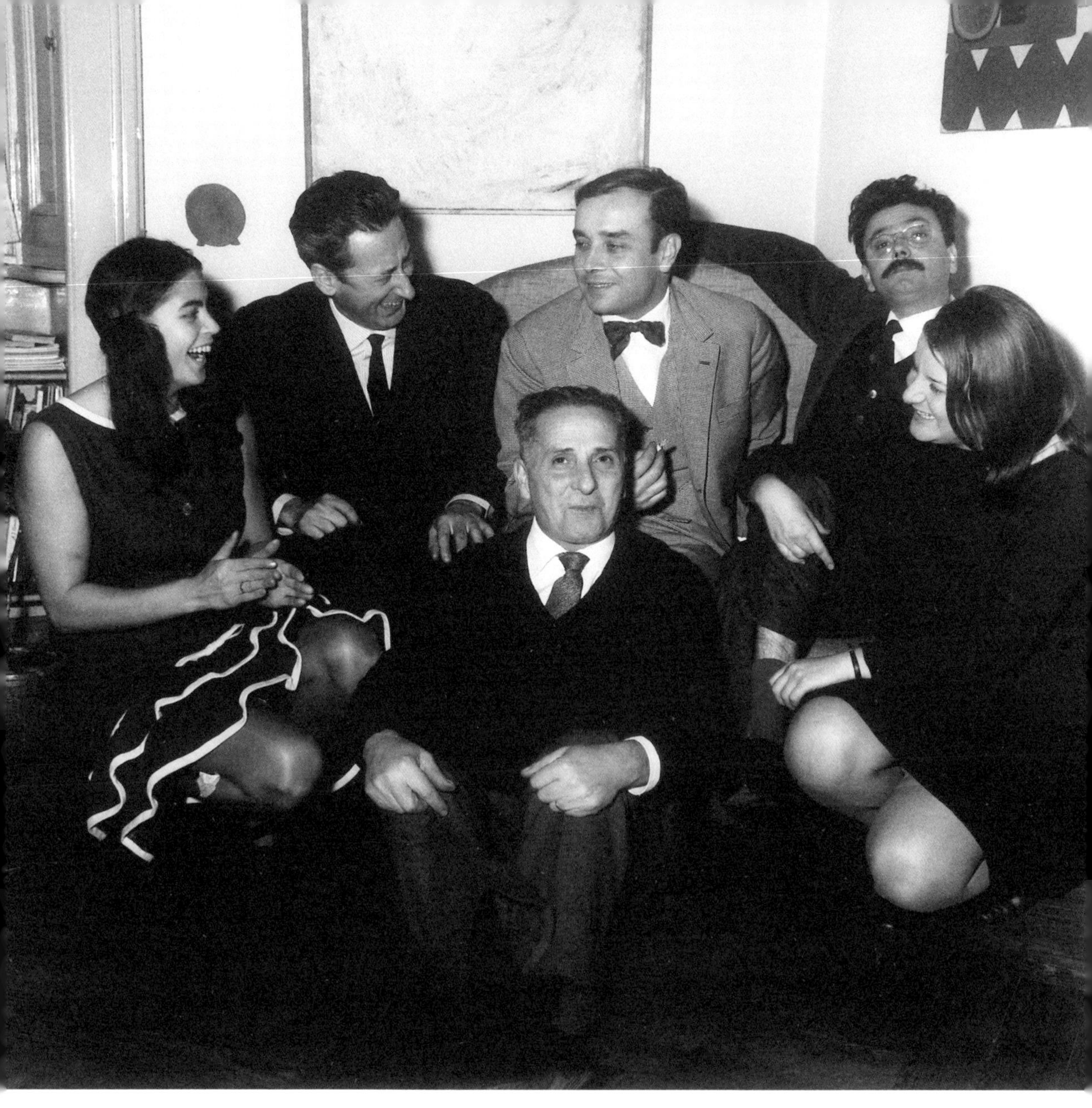

Rotraut,
Jean Larcade,
Yves Klein,
Pierre Restany,
Guido Le Noci,
and Marina Le Noci
at the apartment
of Guido and Eugenia
Le Noci, Milan,
20 November 1961

CANNES

PARIS
CANNES

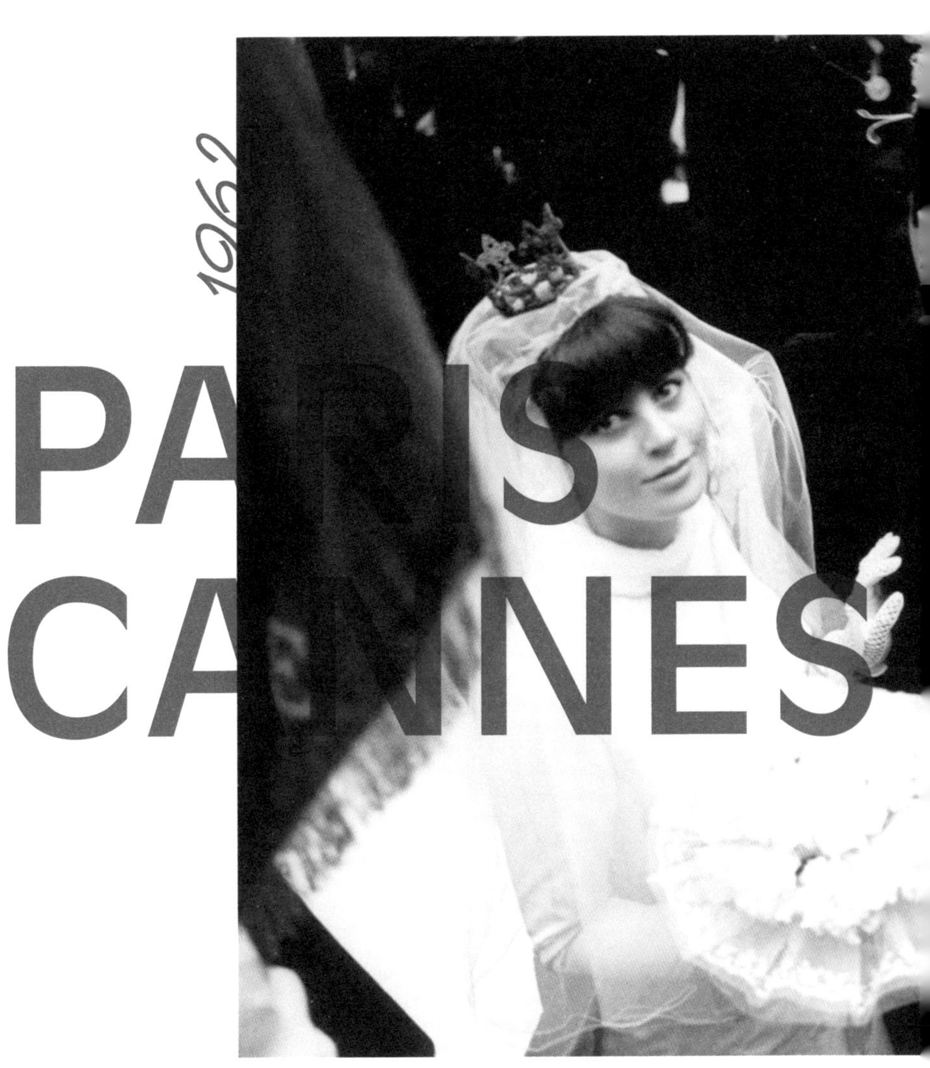

Rotraut leaving the church of Saint-Nicolas-des-Champs, Paris, 21 January 1962

PARIS

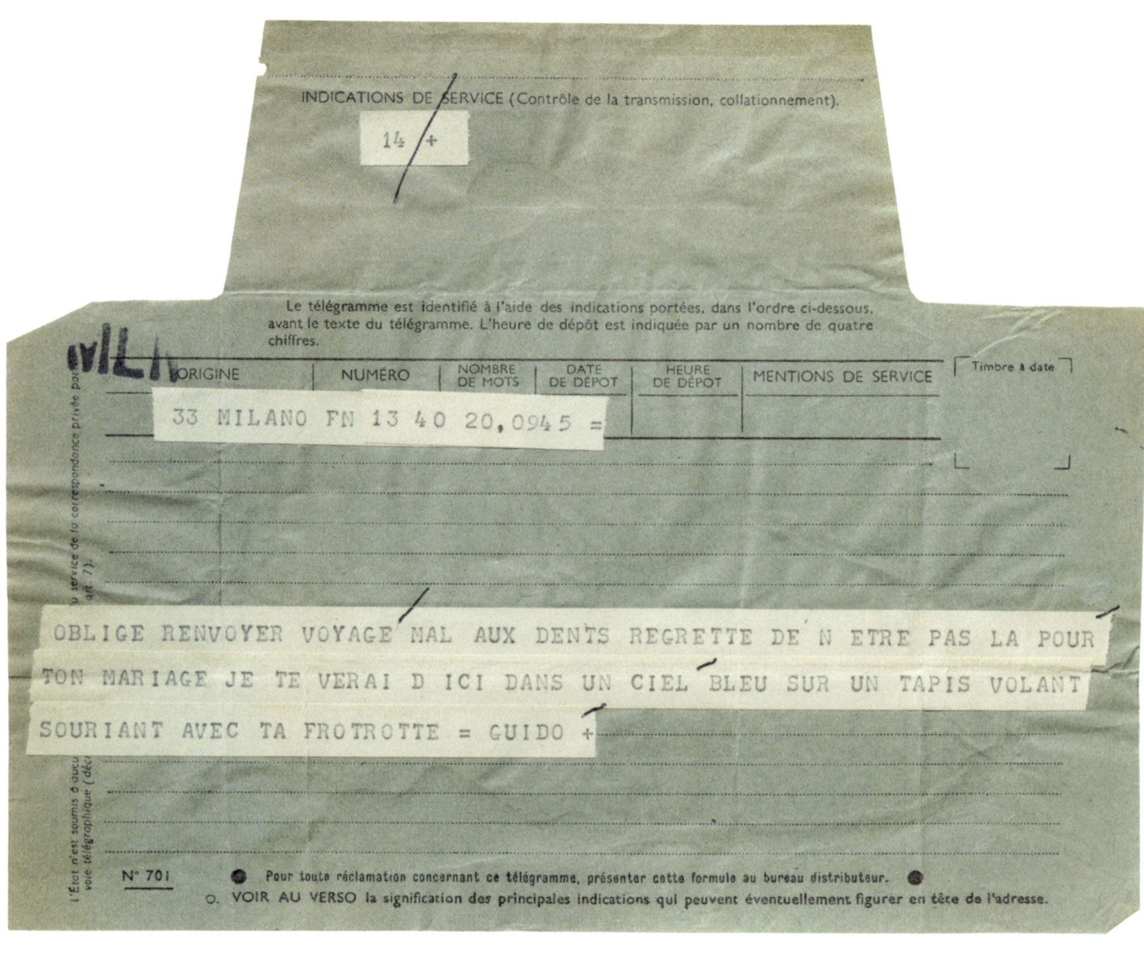

INDICATIONS DE SERVICE (Contrôle de la transmission, collationnement).
14 +
Le télégramme est identifié à l'aide des indications portées, dans l'ordre ci-dessous,
avant le texte du télégramme. L'heure de dépôt est indiquée par un nombre de quatre
chiffres.
ORIGINE | NUMÉRO | NOMBRE DE MOTS | DATE DE DÉPOT | HEURE DE DÉPOT | MENTIONS DE SERVICE | Timbre à date
33 MILANO FN 13 40 20,0945 =
OBLIGE RENVOYER VOYAGE MAL AUX DENTS REGRETTE DE N ETRE PAS LA POUR
TON MARIAGE JE TE VERAI D ICI DANS UN CIEL BLEU SUR UN TAPIS VOLANT
SOURIANT AVEC TA FROTROTTE = GUIDO +
N° 701   Pour toute réclamation concernant ce télégramme, présenter cette formule au bureau distributeur.
O. VOIR AU VERSO la signification des principales indications qui peuvent éventuellement figurer en tête de l'adresse.

Yves Klein's diary, 1962

Friday 26 January at 1 pm, Yves Klein
has an appointment with Dino Buzzati on
the Pont au Double in Paris, to proceed
with the sale of a *Zone of Immaterial
Pictorial Sensibility*.

Jean Larcade, Yves Klein, and Dino Buzzati
on the Pont au Double in Paris during
the sale of the *Zone of Immaterial Pictorial
Sensibility, series no. 1, zone no. 5,*
26 January 1962

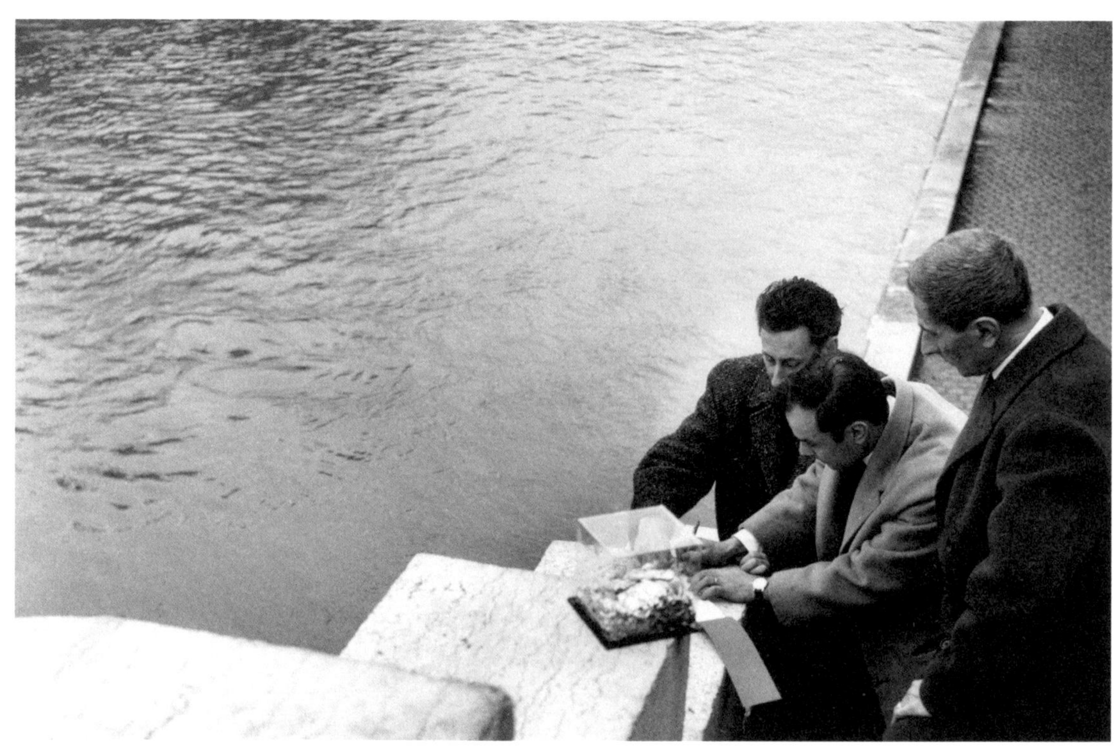

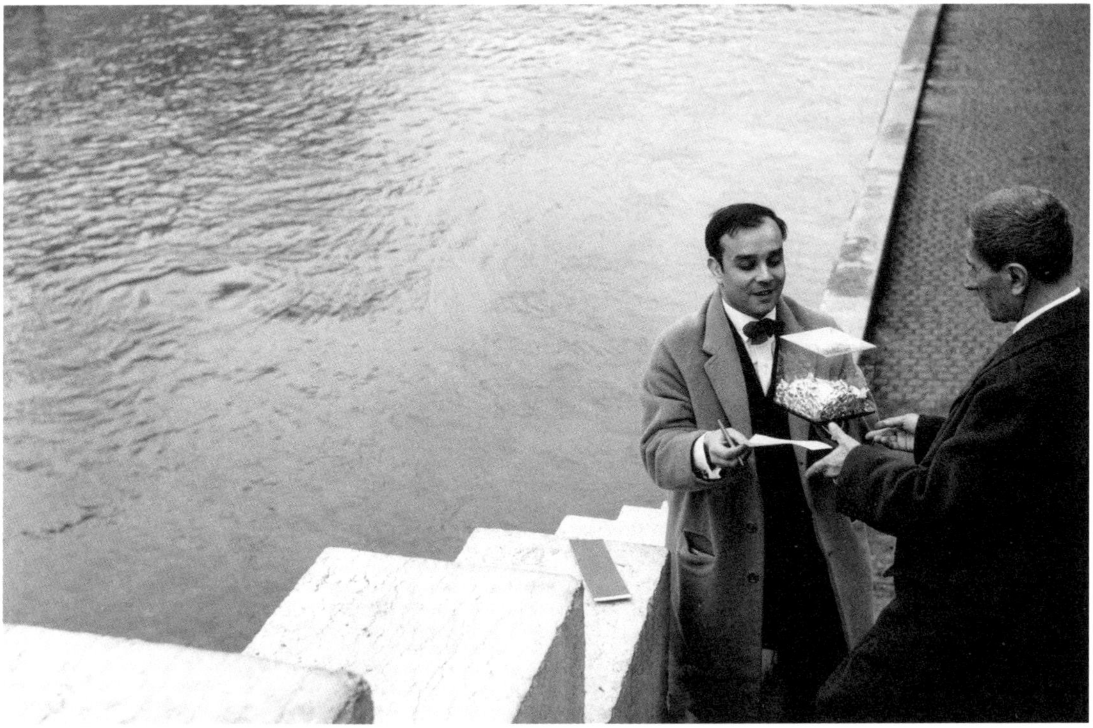

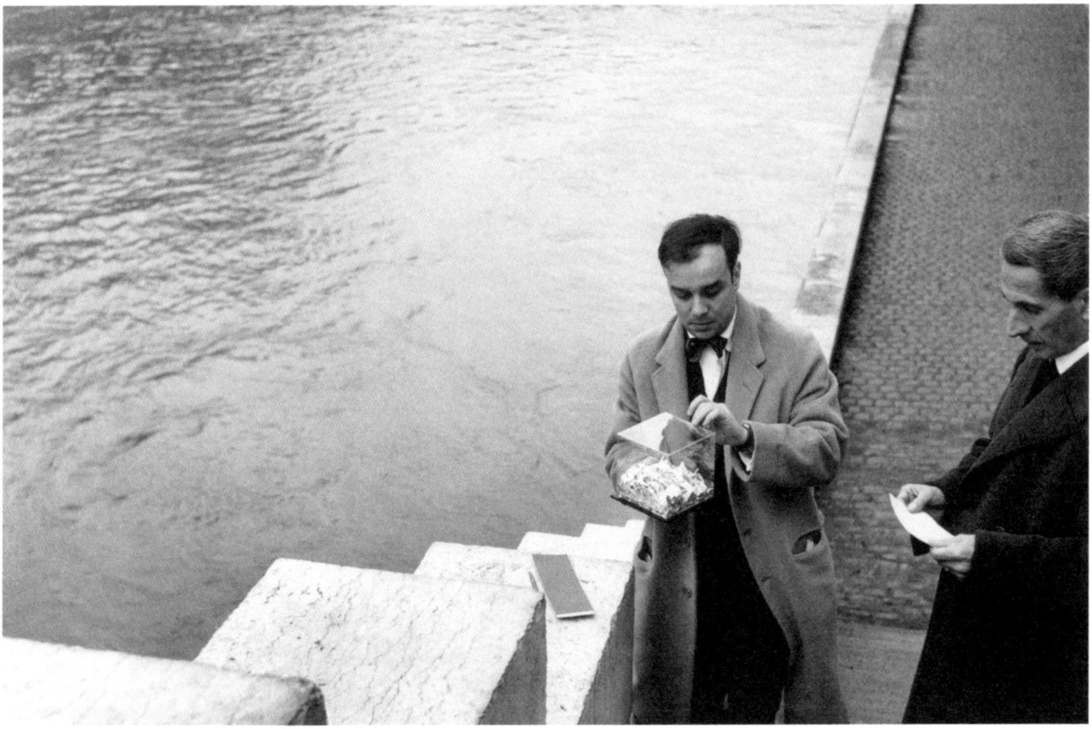

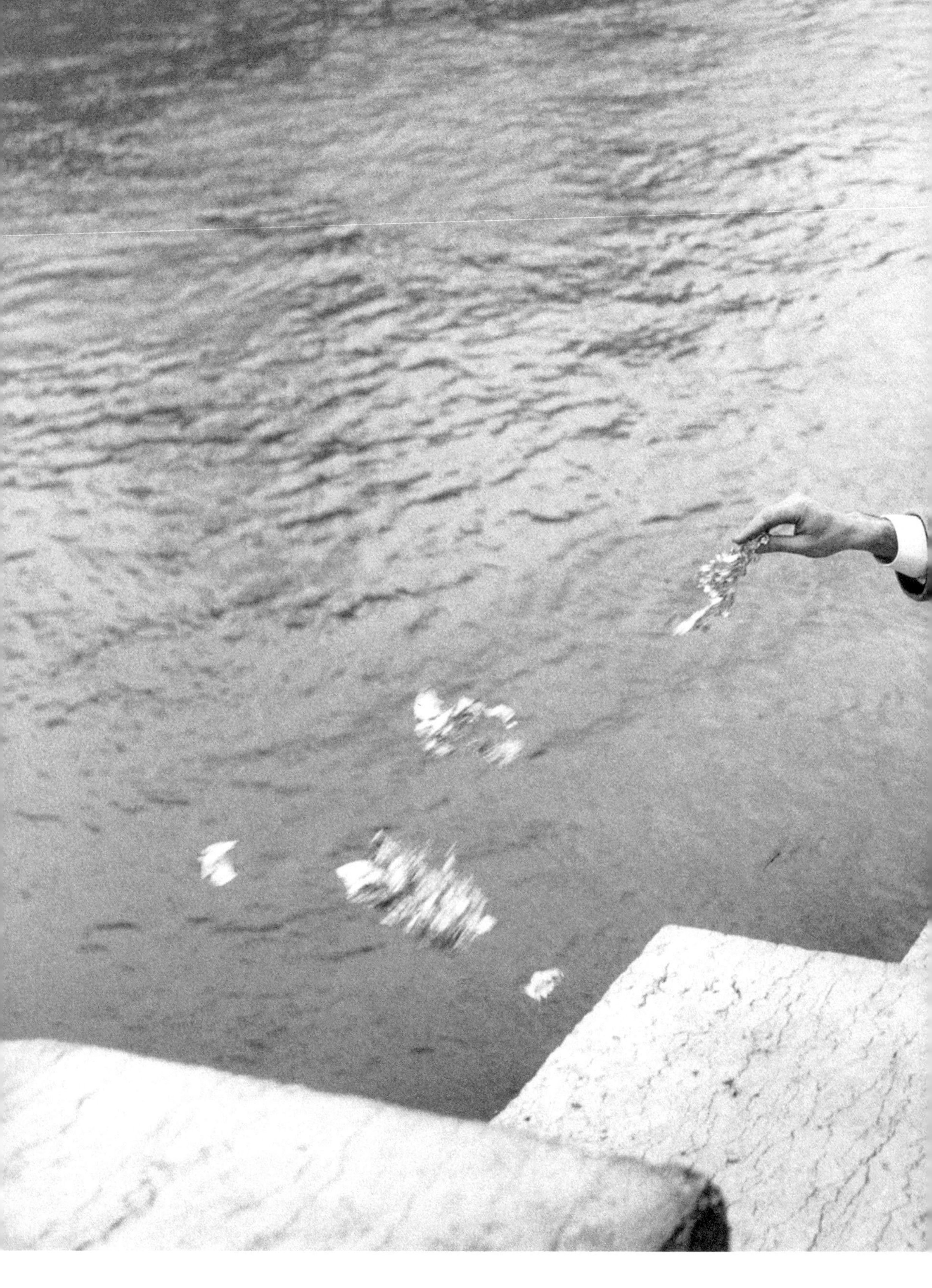

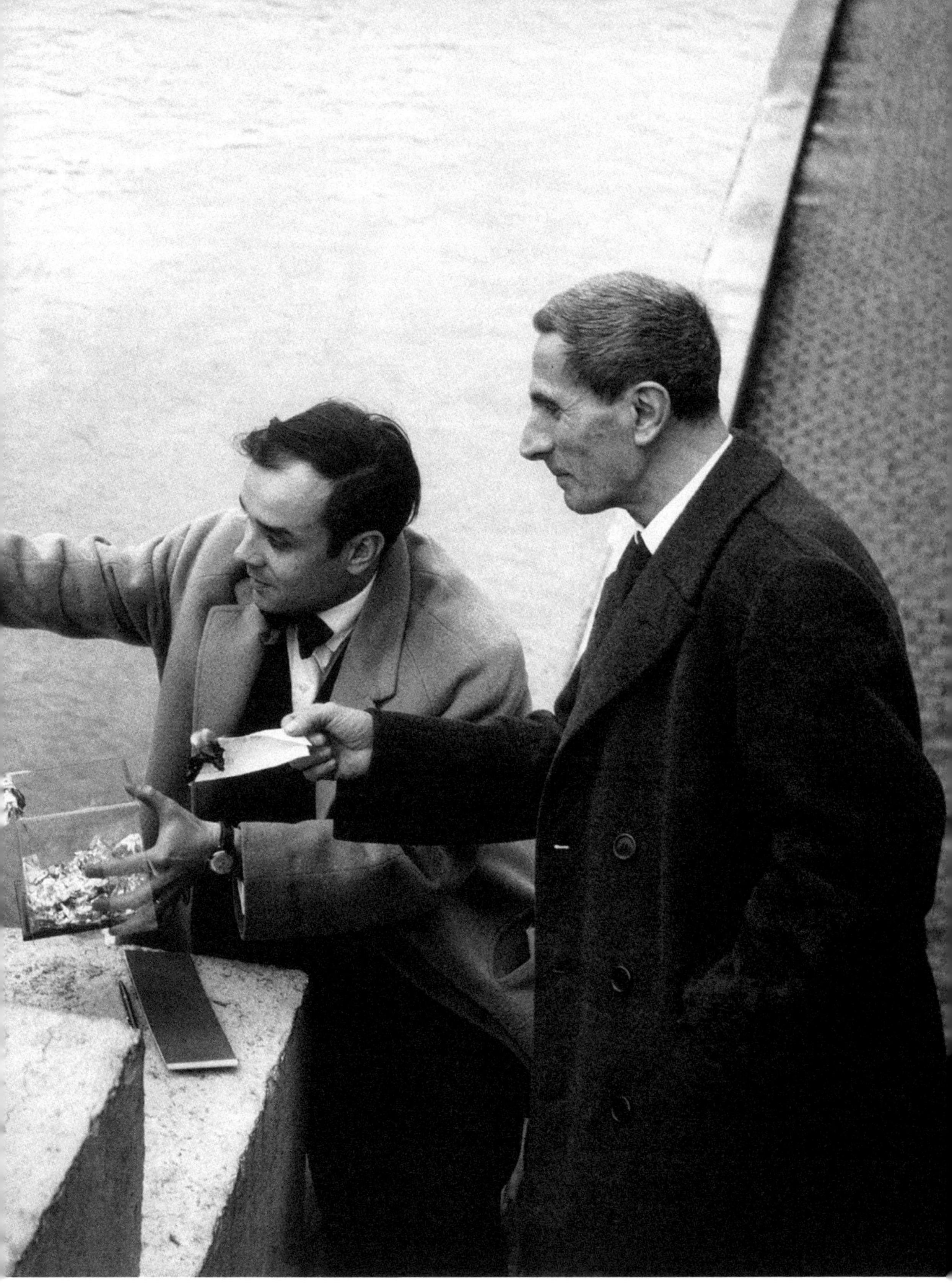

Yves Klein's press book, with the article
"Sortilegio a Notre-Dame" by Dino Buzzati,
in the *Corriere della Sera*, 4 February 1962
Translation pp. 225-227

Anno 87 - N. 30 - L. 40 (Arretrato L. 80)

CORRIERE DELLA SERA

Milano, Domenica 4 febbraio 1962 - L. 40

Domenica 4 febbraio 1962

SORTILEGIO A NOTRE-DAME

Parigi, febbraio.

Yves Klein voleva darmi un suo quadro. Parecchio tempo fa avevo scritto un articolo su Yves Klein, detto il Monocromo, e adesso lui per gratitudine voleva farmi un regalo.

Yves Klein è colui che nel gennaio 1957 espose a Milano venti quadri, perfettamente uguali, costituiti da una superficie blu assolutamente uniforme senza un segno, senza un'ombra, senza una screpolatura. La dissoluzione della pittura classica qui arrivava al limite. Dopodiché come si poteva andare oltre? (Era nato veramente il blu dipinto di blu cioè l'International Klein Blue — IKB —, e giusto due mesi dopo, chissà come, venne fuori la famosa canzone di Modugno).

Yves Klein è anche colui che fece immergere delle bellissime modelle nude in un bagno di colore blu e poi, ai suoi comandi, le ragazze premevano sulla tela bianca questa o quella parte del corpo, lasciandovi le impronte, oppure sulla tela, distesa sul pavimento, sempre ai suoi comandi, strisciavano come serpi, senza usare nè mani nè piedi, come bisce; e lasciavano le impronte.

Yves Klein è un uomo sui trent'anni, dall'aspetto molto gentile, e dalla faccia un po' da bambino, ben vestito ed estremamente civile. Chi sentiva parlare delle sue prodezze era portato a immaginarlo un folle, o un istrione, o un esibizionista che volesse épater le bourgeois. Chi lo avvicinava invece era portato a giudicarlo un puro, strepitosamente lanciato verso traguardi irraggiungibili.

Yves Klein, l'ho capito alla fine, è Peter Pan. Meravigliosamente invisibile alla razionalità del nostro mondo, proprio con gli strumenti che il nostro mondo gli offre, risuscita la fantasia della fanciullezza perduta, conservando la invincibile fantasia dei bambini, capaci di creare.

«Sa l'unica cosa di sbagliato nel suo articolo? Lei parlava della mia epoca pneumatica come se fosse quella dei quadri fatti con le modelle nude. Invece non era così».

«Anche in questa faccenda delle modelle — dissi — c'era, mi sembra, qualcosa di pneumatico, dopo tutto».

«E' vero — e fece un'altra delle sue lievi risate — Ma pneumatico, nel mio caso, è usato in senso filosofico. Pneumatico nel senso di vuoto. Pneumatico nel senso di abolizione di ogni essenza materiale».

«Come sarebbe a dire?».

«Vede? Nel '58, alla Galleria Iris Clert, in Faubourg Saint Honoré, ho tenuto una mostra. La sala della mostra era completamente vuota, non c'era neppure una cornice, neanche un chiodo».

«E allora che cosa era esposto?».

«C'era, in quella sala, la pura immaterialità della mia sensibilità pittorica. E naturalmente fu una specie di scandalo. E alla porta dovette venire la guardia repubblicana per garantire l'ordine pubblico».

«Ma — dissi — se per caso fosse venuto un collezionista a fare acquisti, lei cosa gli rispondeva?».

«Gli rispondevo che infatti la mia sensibilità pittorica immateriale, concentrata nella sala, era in vendita. E, se ne vendevo, in corrispettivo di un valore assolutamente immateriale, io volevo ricevere qualcosa che fosse materiale al cento per cento. Niente carta moneta o assegni, dunque. Sarebbe stato un compromesso. In cambio della mia sensibilità pittorica immateriale dovevo ricevere delle barrette d'oro, dei minuscoli lingotti. E avevo preparato una serie di moduli stampati, come quelli degli assegni. Ce n'erano per venti grammi d'oro, per quaranta, per ottanta, per centosessanta e così via, sempre moltiplicando per due. Uno mi portava una barretta d'oro e io gli davo la corrispondente ricevuta».

«Beh — io dissi facendomi coraggio — ma la gente non poteva pensare che questo fosse una specie di... mi perdoni la franchezza... una specie di turlupinatura?».

«Nemmeno per idea. Perchè il trasferimento, da me al cliente, di questa sensibilità immateriale, non avveniva che a una sola condizione. Che lui, il cliente, appena in possesso della ricevuta, la bruciasse. Altrimenti l'immaterialità dove sarebbe andata a finire?».

«Intanto però lei si teneva l'oro, senza fare nessuna fatica».

«Nemmeno per idea. Come il cliente bruciava la ricevuta, io tagliavo un pezzettino d'oro dal lingotto e lo consegnavo al proprietario della Galleria, il quale deve pur vivere; e il resto, alla presenza di testimoni, lo buttavo nella Senna, o nel mare, dove nessuno l'avrebbe mai potuto ricuperare».

«E se uno non bruciava la ricevuta?».

«Peggio per lui. Finora, e sono passati quattro anni, ci sono stati sette acquirenti. E uno di questi, un collezionista di Milano, invece di bruciarla, ha messo la ricevuta in cornice. E così ha defraudato se stesso. La mia sensibilità pittorica immateriale non gli è stata infatti trasmessa, non ha mai fatto corpo con lui. Intendiamoci, il compratore può girare la ricevuta, può cederla a un terzo, trasferendogli così la corrispondente zona di sensibilità pittorica immateriale, ma, naturalmente anche il terzo, per impossessarsene veramente, dovrà bruciare la ricevuta».

«Bè, sa cosa le dico, caro Klein? — io feci — Lei mi voleva gentilmente regalare un suo quadro? Perchè invece non mi regala una di queste zone immateriali? Non sarebbe molto più elegante?».

Giuro che non avevo la più lontana intenzione di prenderlo in giro. Oltre al resto, l'idea di avere uno dei suoi quadri non mi dispiaceva per niente. A parte i dipinti monocromi, a parte le impronte delle modelle anche colorate di blu, Klein, con una specie di lanciafiamme e con degli spruzzi d'acqua, ottiene degli effetti bellissimi ed emozionanti; una cosa del genere, in casa mia, me la terrei molto volentieri. Voglio aggiungere che tutti i suoi lavori sono, nel loro genere, di una ineccepibile perfezione artigiana. Eppure quel gioco, ne vogliamo chiamarlo così, quel baratto di una quid immateriale contro una certa quantità d'oro che poi veniva per sempre sommersa, aveva un suo fascino esoterico. A questo modo basta crederci, basta illudersi. Anche nell'aria sono contenuti tesori.

Peter Pan alle mie parole ebbe un fremito. «Ma è stupendo! Ma è meraviglioso! Sì, sì — esclamò — faremo tutto domattina!». Era, in quel momento, un uomo felice.

E andammo, all'indomani mattina, in tassì, fino al ponte della Senna proprio a fianco di Notre-Dame. C'era lui, Yves Klein, e poi Jean Larcade, direttore della Galerie Rive Droite e due fotografi per documentare la scena.

Il cielo era scuro. Un freddo cane, un vento che soffiava dal nord. L'acqua del fiume di colore senape scura. Yves Klein fra le mani teneva una scatola cubica in plexiglas piena di foglie d'oro, come quelle che adoperano i doratori: esattamente diciannove grammi.

Dal ponte scendemmo qualche gradino lungo la scala che porta alla banchina. Sul ponte non passava quasi nessuno. Dalle cuspidi di Notre-Dame, i mostruosi dragoni di pietra, le «gargouilles» dall'umida gola protendevano sull'abisso, guardavano, piacevolmente eccitati.

Io stavo per ricevere in dono un pezzetto di sensibilità pittorica immateriale che sarebbe entrata dentro di me per non lasciarmi più, in un giorno della morte, e forse oltre. Un'operazione di occultismo artistico. In pratica, cosa significava tutto questo? Forse niente. Oppure anche qualcosa di eccezionale e di bello, tutto dipendeva da me. Pensai ai lontanissimi giorni in cui giocavo, bambino, al predone tuareg o allo strangolatore della giungla drappeggiato con un vecchio lenzuolo, in groppa a un cavallo di legno; ed era così forte l'illusione che tutto diventava vero. A sette-otto metri di distanza passavano le automobili con sopra uomini animati di soldi, di potenza, di gloria. Invece io, Peter Pan di nome Klein mi invitava a una specie di rito deliziosamente spirituale ed assurdo: al quale però lui credeva.

La scatola in plexiglas passò nelle mie mani. Era mia. Avrei potuto andarmene, se avessi voluto, con diciannove grammi di oro zecchino in dono. E Klein non avrebbe fatto obiezioni (il ventesimo grammo, chiuso in una scatolina di cartone, fu dato a Larcade, per la percentuale dovuta al «gallerista»).

Io allora consegnai l'oro al giovane mago. E lui trasse di tasca un blocchetto simile ai libretti di chèques. Sul fondo del foglietto campeggiavano in mezza tinta le lettere IKB: International Klein Blue. E sopra, in nero c'era stampato: «Cachet di garanzia. Serie n. 1, Zona n. 05. Ricevuta di venti grammi d'oro fino in corrispettivo di una zona di sensibilità pittorica immateriale».

Il folletto di nome Yves Klein, questo personaggio vivo e incredibile, firmò con una biro la ricevuta e io gli consegnai l'oro. Poco sopra di noi un signore con gli occhiali di circa cinquant'anni che passava a piedi sul ponte si fermò, preoccupato.

Allora con notevole fatica a motivo del vento io accesi un fiammifero e diedi fuoco al cartiglio, che cominciò a bruciare. Nello stesso tempo Yves Klein aprì il coperchio della scatola di plexiglas e cominciò ad estrarre i quasi impalpabili foglietti d'oro, abbandonandoli all'aria.

Anche una donna tipo massaia, oltre al signore con gli occhiali, si fermò sul ponte a guardare. A Parigi le cose più strambe passano inosservate. Quei due però sembravano in grave sospetto.

Manciate su manciate, gli aurei foglietti furono strappati via dal vento, erano così leggeri. Volavano via nell'aria grigia, si perdevano sotto l'ombra nera del ponte.

Erano diciannove grammi, mica diecimila. Ben presto la scatola di plexiglas restò vuota; e il foglio della ricevuta era bruciato, non me ne restava fra le dita che un moncherino. Forse ingenuamente, io avevo sperato — datemi pure dell'idiota — di sentirmi un poco diverso, diverso per un infinitesimo, ma diverso. Invece niente. Ero lo stesso identico sciagurato di prima. Yves Klein viveva nella sua aura di poetica stregoneria, e io non ero riuscito ad entrarci.

Non restava che andarsene. Feci due gradini, o tre, non mi ricordo bene, e allora Klein mi chiamò: «Guardi, guardi».

Guardai. La Senna, non dico proprio tutta la Senna nell'intera sua larghezza d'acqua, ma il cuore del fiume, il filone della corrente centrale, si era trasformato in oro. Un rilucente rivo spiccava col suo giallo splendore sulle acque colore di mota, e scendeva lentamente verso il mare lontano. I foglietti d'oro, sparsi dal vento, erano discesi lentamente come fanno gli svogliati fiocchi di neve nelle notti di venti gradi sotto zero. Ad uno ad uno erano calati sull'acqua, lasciandosi portare via. E ora andavano, spensierate ed irrequiete farfalle, scivolavano verso il loro destino, a raccontare la favola.

Sembrava che non finisse più, quel rivolo d'oro. Per una lunghezza di forse cinquecento metri la Senna luccicò di mistero, di magnificenza, di incantesimo, di follia.

«Quest'oggi dovrà accadere qualcosa di straordinario» disse Klein, profondamente convinto. Anch'io, non saprei dire con precisione il perchè, mi sentivo contento.

Ma la cosa straordinaria non avvenne, che almeno io sappia. E la colpa è mia. E prego Yves Klein di scusarmi. Se il suo sortilegio, se l'incantesimo di Puck è fallito, la colpa è completamente mia, del mio meschino spirito borghese. Perchè il foglio della ricevuta non bruciò completamente e me ne rimase in mano la coda. E a titolo di souvenir mi piacque tenerlo, e, senza che Klein se ne accorgesse, me lo infilai in una tasca. E ancora adesso lo tengo, nel portafogli. E mi piace pensare di averne una specie di talismano, una piccola riserva di poesia, o di felicità, o di illusione, che potrò consumare un giorno a mio capriccio.

E' un lembo di carta con su scritto: «Série n. 1 - Reçu Vingt ...contre une Zone de... Cette ne transférable ne peut être dée par son propriétaire qu'au double de sa valeur d'achat initiale. (Signatures et dates pour transférer au dos). Le transgresseur s'expose à l'annihilation totale de sa propre sensibilité».

Trasgressore sono io, dunque, perchè ne ho conservato un pezzetto. E la sensibilità immateriale, logicamente, non è ancora entrata in me. Ma un giorno, se sarò triste e stanco, caverò quel lembo di carta dal portafogli e gli darò fuoco. E in quel che modo sarò consolato, forse. Yves Klein mi perdoni.

Dinanzi a Notre-Dame, senza aspettare tanto, trovammo un tassì.

Dino Buzzati

Yves Klein – and I only understood
this right at the end – is none other
than Peter Pan. Wonderfully indifferent
to the rationality of our world, but using
the tools that it offers him, he revives the
make-believe of childhood by preserving
that invincible imagination of children,
able to create paradise with just a stick
or a piece of paper.

Dino Buzzati

Klein, il pittore che dipinge con la pioggia e col fuoco

Vende il nulla a prezzo d'oro

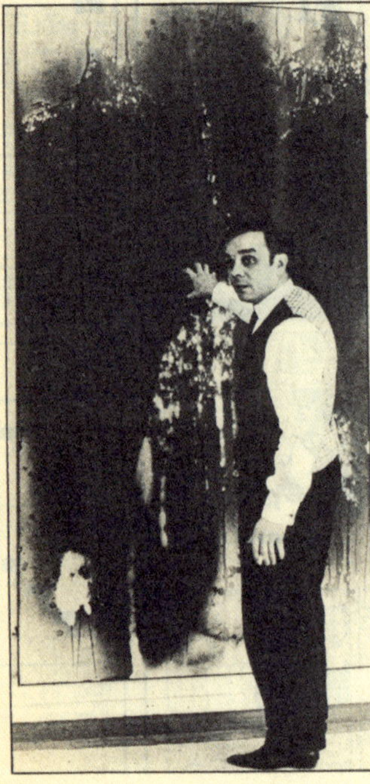

YVES KLEIN davanti a una sua tela realizzata servendosi di lanciafiamme e idranti al posto del pennello. Nato a Nizza nel 1928, Klein ha allestito le sue prime mostre a Parigi nel 1955, e a Milano nel 1957. Dall'esposizione milanese egli afferma che Modugno rubò l'idea per la sua famosa canzone: « Nel blu dipinto di blu ».

nostro servizio

PARIGI, marzo

YVES KLEIN è un uomo che suscita antipatie invincibili o ammirazione sfrenata: per gli uni è un ciarlatano che sfrutta qualsiasi mezzo per farsi della pubblicità; per gli altri è una specie di profeta dei tempi nuovi, il pioniere dell'« arte invisibile ». Tutte le sue ricerche nei più svariati campi tendono a dimostrare la preminenza e la realtà dell'« immateriale ». Chi è Klein? Orgogliosamente egli si presenta: « Io sono "il pittore", io sono "l'attore", "il compositore", "l'architetto", "lo scultore". Tengo ad affermare: "Io sono" ». Cerchiamo di ricondurlo a una dimensione ragionevole, ripercorrendo la sua estrosa biografia. E' nato trentaquattro anni fa a Nizza: il colore del Mediterraneo sarà il primo motivo profondo che condizionerà la sua formazione artistica. Da ragazzo, sdraiato in un prato, fissava lo spazio azzurro dicendosi: "Sono il re del cielo". Era un gioco, ma già un presagio. Vent'anni dopo (nel frattempo aveva appreso in Giappone il judo e le arti marziali antiche), presentava le sue "proposte monocrome": dei quadri di un azzurro profondo, uniforme, fette di mare o di cielo, che l'immaginazione deve prolungare all'infinito.

Era "l'epoca blu" (Klein dice che dalla sua mostra a Milano, alla Galleria Apollinaire, Modugno gli ha rubato l'idea del suo famoso: « Nel blu dipinto di blu »).

Due altri colori figurano nella tavolozza di Klein: l'oro e il rosa, il « monogold » e il « monopink ». Non sono colori scelti a caso da questo appassionato di simboli: l'oro significa la perennità della legge, il rosa l'amore e la carne, l'azzurro l'immateriale; insieme prefigurano la Santissima Trinità. I tre colori si fondono nei bagliori della fiamma, con cui Klein realizza sculture in movimento o anche, servendosi alternativamente del fuoco e dell'acqua, dei quadri astratti che sono fra le sue opere più impressionanti.

Klein odia il pennello che falsa i rapporti fra l'artista e la sua opera. Perciò ricorre a una serie di strumenti naturali — come appunto il fuoco, o la pioggia, con cui ha creato delle curiose « cosmogonie » — o il « pennello vivente ».

UNA SEDUTA di pittura vivente è uno dei più singolari spettacoli a cui si possa assistere: Klein, che ammette di avere una « vocazione contrastata » di uomo di teatro, sa indiscutibilmente curare i suoi effetti. Tele bianche sono disposte lungo le pareti e sul pavimento. Dalla sommità di una scala, il pittore, in smoking, dirige come un direttore d'orchestra i movimenti delle modelle che devono cospargere di colore i bellissimi corpi ignudi e poi, secondo le indicazioni dell'artista, applicare il fianco, un seno, le natiche, una guancia o il palmo della mano sulla tela, ora sfiorandola appena, ora appoggiandosi con forza, di striscio o di piatto. Talvolta il risultato è ottenuto con la leggerezza di un movimento di danza, tal altra con un corpo a corpo forsennato che evoca l'erotismo delle « donne maledette » di Baudelaire. Queste composizioni, che danno l'impressione di allucinanti radiografie poetiche, si intitolano « sudari » e rappresentano una delle cento forme di ricerca dell'« invisibile » in cui è impegnato Klein.

Come si potrebbe enumerarle tutte? Klein è l'autore di una « sinfonia monotona », costruita cioè su un'unica nota tenuta fino al limite della sopportazione, dopo di che quel che conta è « il silenzio ». Ha presentato al Festival dell'avanguardia, nel 1960, una teoria del « teatro del vuoto », che presuppone una sala vuota, l'essenza di spettacolo e un attore pagato soltanto « per sopportare la grave responsabilità di essere un attore e sparire nella folla ». Ha progettato architetture aeree, fondate sul principio dei « tetti d'aria », che dovrebbero rivoluzionare le condizioni climatiche e, modificando la fisionomia della terra, capovolgere anche le strutture sociali.

Ma è sul piano pittorico che Klein porta le sue teorie alle estreme conseguenze. Fin dalle prime esperienze monocrome, aveva avvertito che il blu è « l'invisibile che diviene visibile ».

NEL 1957 ebbe l'audacia di presentare la prima mostra di « sensibilità pittorica immateriale »: nella sala dalle pareti bianche e lisce, il nulla. Una manifestazione che fece epoca, con guardie repubblicane in alta tenuta all'ingresso, e una folla enorme venuta per ridere. Poi, racconta Klein, nel vuoto perfetto gli spettatori furono colpiti da una specie di mistico fervore, come in una cappella nuda, alcuni si misero a piangere, altri, attoniti, non se ne volevano più andare.

Se si espone il vuoto, si deve poterlo anche vendere, ma non per vile danaro: perciò Klein cominciò a vendere a prezzo d'oro delle « zone di sensibilità pittorica immateriale ». Ha già trovato una decina di clienti: il più generoso di questi mecenati è uno scrittore americano, soggettista a Hollywood, Michael Blankford, che di recente gli ha acquistato una striscia « immateriale » per 160 grammi d'oro fino, pari a 260 dollari. L'operazione si svolge secondo un rituale preciso, ispirato a un antico rito celtico. Sulle rive della Senna l'acquirente consegna all'artista dei minuscoli lingotti d'oro (in presenza del conservatore del Museo delle Arti decorative Francis Mathey, il quale autentifica la transazione e avrà la sua brava percentuale), e ne riceve in cambio una ricevuta che dovrà poi bruciare « perchè lo immateriale si integri in lui ».

Klein tiene per sè la metà dei lingotti, e con un ampio gesto lancia gli altri nel fiume perchè torni all'universo quel che appartiene all'universo. Mi permetto di chiedergli ingenuamente come giustifichi l'appropriazione di una metà dell'oro. Mi risponde con una frase di Goethe: « Dal momento in cui un artista ha scelto il suo soggetto, esso non appartiene più alla natura ma all'artista ». I lingotti lanciati nel fiume sono insomma una specie di offerta votiva. Un barbone che assiste alla scena li guarda sparire, con stupore e malinconia, inghiottiti dalle acque della Senna.

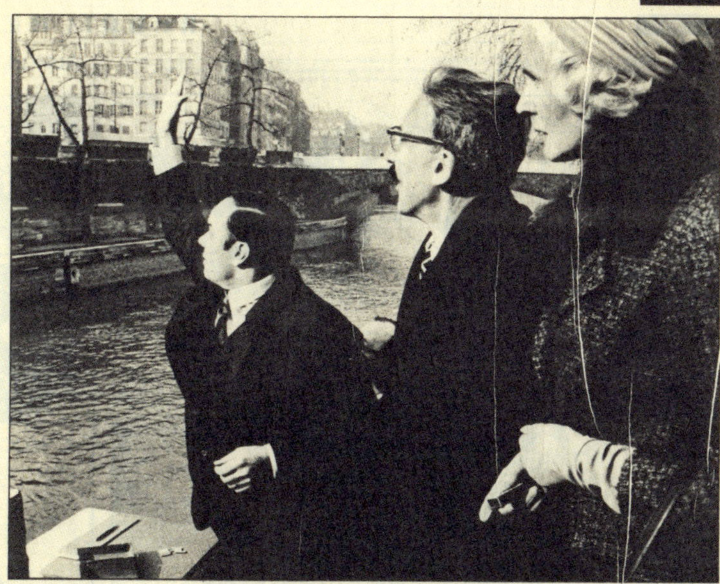

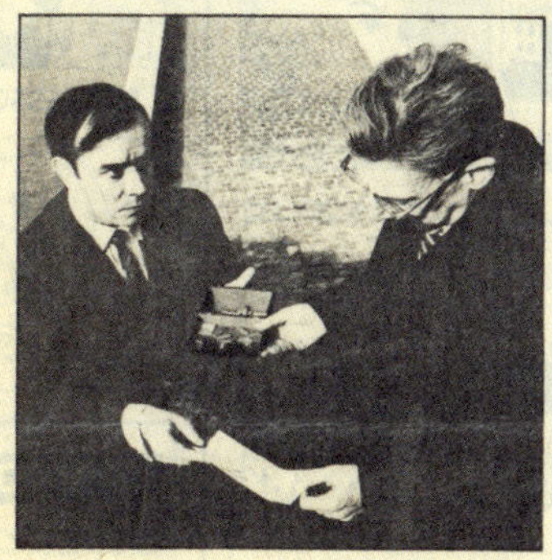

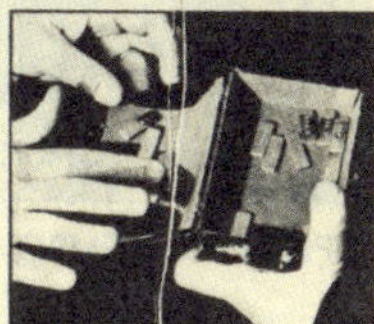

L'OPERAZIONE di vendita del « vuoto » di Yves Klein. Il pittore del nulla porta il suo cliente (qui, foto a sinistra, il soggettista hollywoodiano Michael Blankford), sulle rive della Senna; il cliente, in cambio di una « striscia immateriale », gli versa il prezzo in piccoli lingotti d'oro (qui 160 grammi, pari a 156.000 lire: foto a destra). Il pittore restituisce una ricevuta che il cliente brucerà, e dopo avere intascato la metà dei lingotti, disperderà l'altra metà nelle acque (fotografia sopra), spesso sotto gli occhi dei barboni della Senna.

Yves Klein's press book, with the article
"Vende il nulla a prezzo d'oro", published
in *Il Giorno*, 21 March 1962
The article makes reference to the *Zones
of Immaterial Pictorial Sensibility*.
Translation pp. 227-228

197

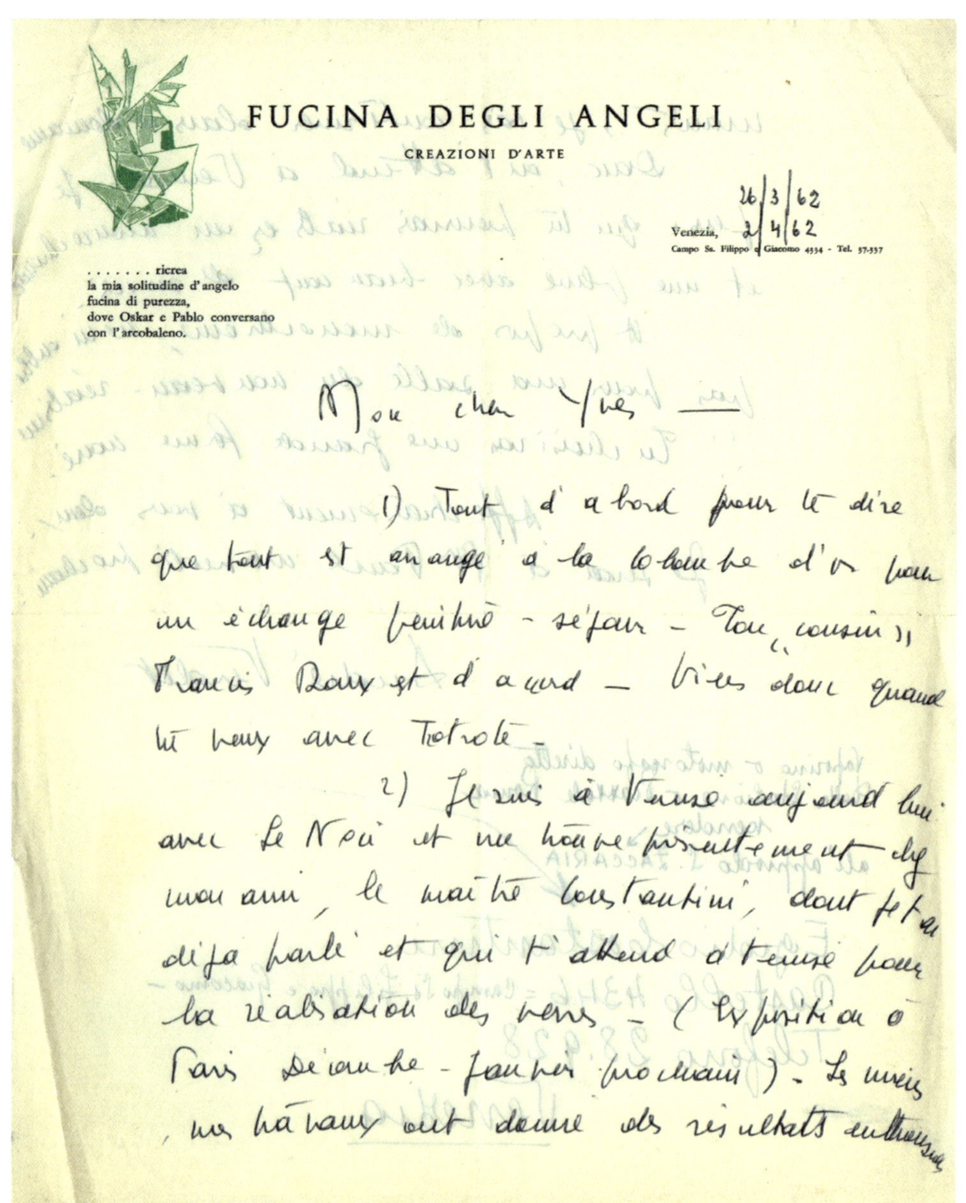

FUCINA DEGLI ANGELI

CREAZIONI D'ARTE

. . . . . . ricrea
la mia solitudine d'angelo
fucina di purezza,
dove Oskar e Pablo conversano
con l'arcobaleno.

Venezia, 26/3/62 — 2/4/62
Campo Ss. Filippo e Giacomo 4334 - Tel. 57-337

In 1960, Yves Klein met Egidio Costantini in Venice, through André Verdet. Founder of the Fucina degli Angeli - Venetian art gallery and glassworks, whose name was devised by Jean Cocteau - Costantini wanted to update art glass by calling on the artists of his time to create sculptures directly inspired by their artworks. Enjoying the support of Peggy Guggenheim, he collaborated with Arp, Picasso, Braque, Ernst, Cocteau, Le Corbusier, Calder, Kokoschka, and others. The works were created by the finest master glassmakers, such as Aldo Bon (Polo), Archimede Seguso, Angelo Tosi, and Ermanno Nason, and were often presented at major international exhibitions, thus elevating Fucina degli Angeli and its founder among the great names in international art glass. In 1960, Egidio Costantini and Yves Klein designed together a glass sculpture project inspired by the *Anthropometries*.

198

Letter from
André Verdet to
Yves Klein, April 1962
Translation
p. 228

Yves Klein, *Untitled Anthropometry*
(ANT 163), 1960
Dedication: "To Egidio Costantini
della Fucina degli angeli with
the friendship of Yves Klein"
An artwork given to Egidio Costantini
by Yves Klein, to serve as a model for
the glass sculpture that was to be created
at the Fucina degli Angeli

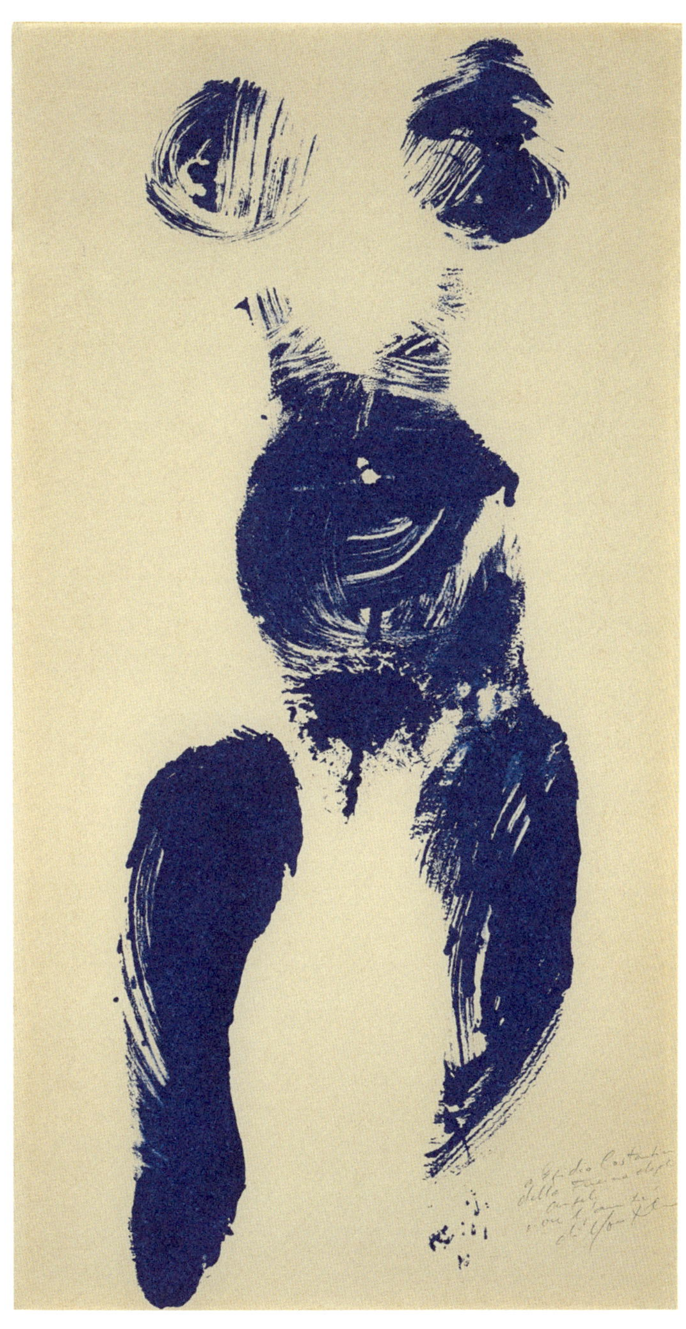

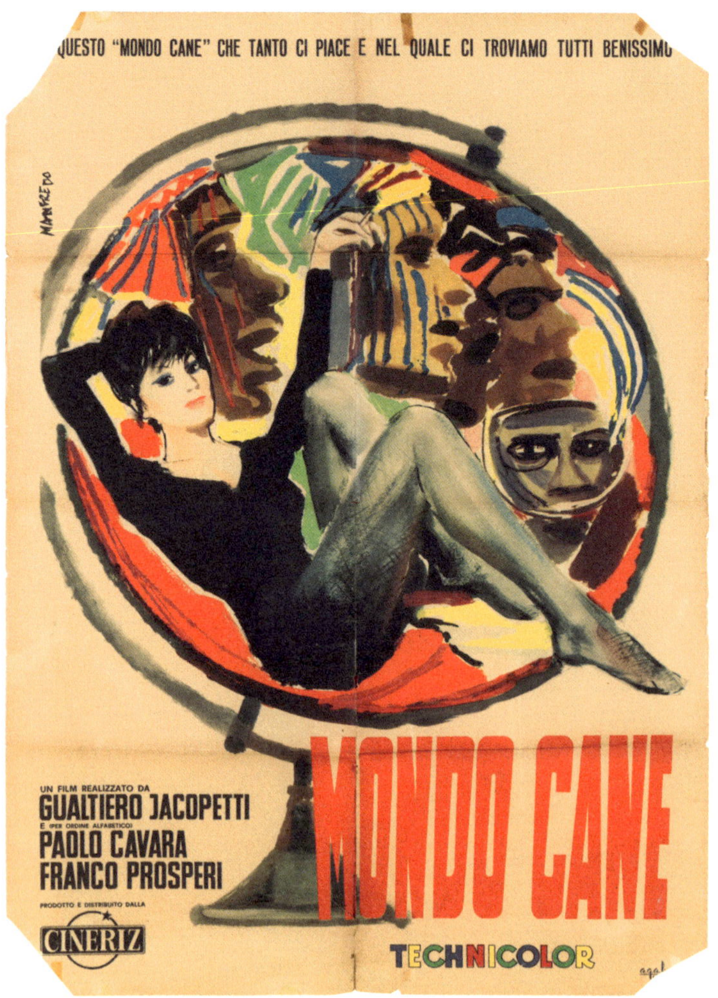

XVe FESTIVAL INTERNATIONAL DU FILM
CANNES 1962

LE CONSEIL D'ADMINISTRATION
DU FESTIVAL INTERNATIONAL DU FILM
VOUS PRIE DE BIEN VOULOIR LUI
FAIRE L'HONNEUR D'ASSISTER A
LA SOIRÉE DU SAMEDI 12 MAI
A 19 HEURES.

Mr YVES KLEIN

CORBEILLE **B** 15

TENUE DE SOIRÉE

Italian poster of
the film *Mondo Cane*,
designed by Manfredo
Acerbo, 1962

Invitation to the
screening of the film
Mondo Cane at the
Cannes Film Festival,
May 1962

Still from the film *Mondo Cane*

The film was presented at Cannes
on the evening of 12 May. The sequence
on Yves Klein lasted just a few minutes
and was a complete caricature
of the message of his oeuvre.
Yves Klein left the auditorium,
deeply wounded.

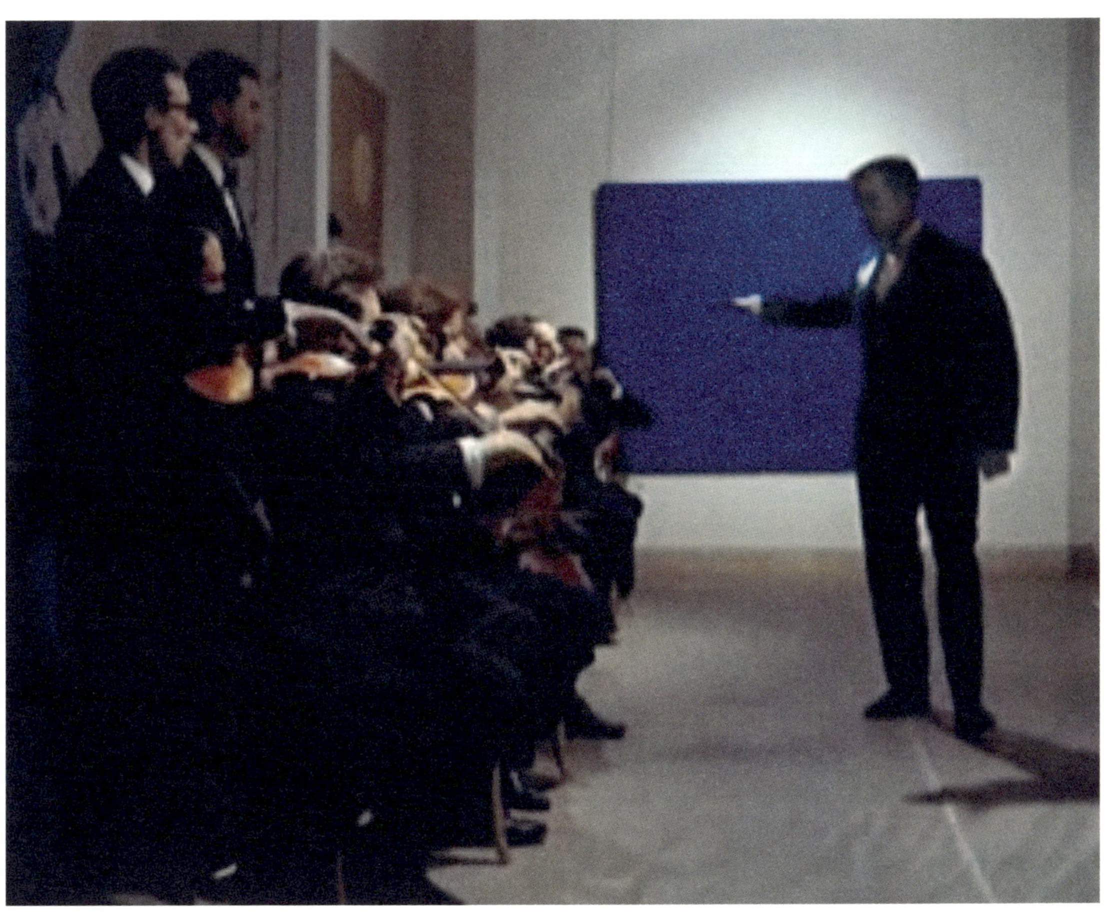

Monsieur Yves KLEIN
14, rue Campagne Première
PARIS 14ème - FRANCE

PARIS, le 5 Juin 1962

Monsieur Pablo CAVARA
Cineogi Via Cernaia, 1.

ROMA
Italie

Cher Paolo,

Cette lettre pour te demander instamment de bien vouloir m'envoyer, cette fois-ci sans faute, la copie 16 m/m de ma séquence complète telle qu'elle a été prise à PARIS (en somme telle qu'il était convenu dans notre petit contrat).

J'en ai absolument besoin pour le montage de mon petit film privé, comme je te l'avais dit déjà au Festival de CANNES.

D'autre part, tu m'avais promis une réponse définitive pour notre projet de grand film : j'attends aussi cette réponse parce que je désire passer à l'action dès septembre 1962.

En dehors de cela, mon Cher Paolo, je te souhaite de passer de bonnes vacances et te reposer; et encore une fois, je te demande de ne pas oublier de m'envoyer immédiatement la copie du film 16 m/m promise.

Meilleures amitiés.

Yves KLEIN

P.S: J'aimerai aussi que tu m'envoie la Bande que je t'avais envoyé avec ma séquence... merci

Yves Klein died of a heart attack the next day. Several days earlier, he had confided to Rotraut: "I will enter the greatest studio in the world. And I will only make immaterial artworks."

Look at Klein's *Void*, the idea of
infinite blue … Not an object nor a form …
Art will become infinity, immensity,
immateriality, philosophy …

Lucio Fontana

YVES KLEIN AND ARTE POVERA

Bruno Corà

Influence in painting and, more generally speaking, in the arts is inherent. It doesn't appear out of nowhere.

During his talk at the Sorbonne on 3 June 1959, Yves Klein stated:

> The external influences that have made me pursue this monochromatic path to this immaterial are manifold: first, the reading of the journals of Delacroix, the champion of colour, whose work lies at the source of contemporary lyrical painting; … and above all, I received a profound shock when I discovered in the Basilica of Saint Francis of Assisi frescoes that are scrupulously monochromatic, uniform and blue, which I believe may be attributed to Giotto.[1]

However, one year earlier, in April of 1958, Klein, in his writings, had already addressed the subject of "influences" or precursors in "Writings on Monochromatic Painting", where he wrote:

> Young painters such as Alberto Burri, Tàpies, Mack, Dawing, Jonesco [sic], Piene, Manzoni, Mübin, and others still that I do not know have now come to paint in an almost monochrome manner. But this is not a grave matter for me, quite to the contrary. It is not important who first composed a monochrome painting … It is the fundamental idea that counts, through the centuries. I consider Giotto as the real precursor of the monochrome painting that I practice, for his blue monochromes in Assisi (called decoupages of the sky by art historians, but they are clearly unified monochrome frescoes).[2]

However, if Giotto or Burri and Fontana can be considered precursors of Klein's extraordinary adventure, the question that this way of thinking gives rise to remains: how did Yves Klein influence the generation of Italian artists who came after him,

1. Yves Klein, "The Evolution of Art Towards the Immaterial", lecture at the Sorbonne, 3 June 1959, Paris, in *Yves Klein. Towards the Immaterial*, ed. Denys Riout (Paris: Éditions Dilecta, 2006), 64.
2. Yves Klein, "Writings on Monochromatic Painting", in *Yves Klein*, ed. Jean-Yves Mock, exh. cat. (Paris: Centre Georges-Pompidou, 1984), 193–194. Published in conjunction with the exhibition of the same title, organised and held at Centre Georges-Pompidou – National Museum of Modern Art, Paris, 3 March–23 May 1983.

and in particular, those of the Arte Povera movement? In my opinion, to tackle the subject organically, in an attempt to offer an objective appreciation of such a question, one must go back to the manifesto signed by Enrico Baj, Piero Manzoni, Ettore Sordini, Gianni Bertini, Angelo Verga, the Pomodoro brothers, Klein, Arman, and Restany himself, among others, entitled "The End of Style" (1957). That document explicitly outlines the desire to destroy the last of conventions, style, and yet it states, "The last stylistic works that we recognise are the 'monochromes' of Yves Klein (1956–1957); only the bare boards – or Capogrossi's rolls of textile – can follow them."[3]

One must not forget that in January of that same year, there was an exhibition at the Apollinaire Gallery in Milan entitled *Yves Klein. Proposte monocrome, epoca Blu* [Yves Klein. Monochrome Propositions, Blue Period], presented by Pierre Restany, whose critical introduction is dated November 1956. It was reprinted in the catalogue of the anthological exhibition, *Yves Klein le Monochrome. Il nuovo realismo del colore* [Yves Klein the Monochrome. The New Realism of Colour], which was presented in the same gallery again in November 1961. As for the significant presence of Klein's works in Italy and his influence on the art world, we must keep two important things in mind: the first involves the full-page publication of one of Klein's blue monochromes in the first issue of *Azimuth* (1959), a magazine created and published in Milan by Enrico Castellani and Piero Manzoni, which focused on a new artistic realm; in a short essay in the second and final issue of this magazine, Udo Kultermann, the historical curator of the exhibition entitled *Monochrome Malerei* [Monochrome Painting, Städtisches Museum, Leverkusen, 1960], refers not only to Fontana, Castellani, Manzoni, Klein, and Tinguely as being among the "pioneers" of this new concept of painting, but he also includes a long quote of Klein's where he speaks of "giving freedom to the state of the original material" along with another one of Klein's blue monochromes prominently displayed on the facing page.

One of the fundamental elements of the Arte Povera poetry that appeared on the scene in the second half of the 1960s by way of the various contributions from its active members, primarily in the cities of Turin, Rome, Milan, and Genoa, is the new appreciation for the materials and a new ethical and poetic attitude towards the artistic process itself with an aesthetic-existential sensibility.

While Burri and Fontana constituted shared references as cornerstones of the previous generation for the entire group of "Poverists", each of the artists that Germano Celant brought together under the banner of Arte Povera (1967), however, contributed to bringing forth a diversity of approaches regarding how the materials were considered and the various ways these techniques and results were expressed.

3. "The End of Style" (1957), in *Yves Klein: Long Live the Immaterial*, exh. cat. (New York: Delano Greenidge Editions, 2000), vi. Published in conjunction with the exhibition *Yves Klein: La vie, la vie elle-même qui est l'art absolu*, curated by Bruno Corà and Gilbert Perlein, held at the Musée d'Art moderne et d'Art contemporain, Nice, 28 April 2000–4 September 2000, and Centro Pecci, Prato, 23 September 2000–10 January 2001.
4. Jannis Kounellis, interview by Bruno Corà, in *Yves Klein: Long Live the Immaterial*, xv.
5. Ibid.
6. Jannis Kounellis, "Cavolo! Che bella donna!", *La Città di Riga* 1, 1976, 43–49.

In addition to Burri and Fontana, the experiences and examples of artists such as Francesco Lo Savio and Piero Manzoni must also be considered along with, for some of his behavioural attitudes and compelling productions, Pinot Gallizio, a pharmacist by trade and a resident of Alba in the Piedmont region, and the leading outsider among the exponents of the emerging European Situationist movement. Lo Savio and Manzoni were contemporaries of Klein and occasionally participated in the same exhibitions together with artists of the Spatialism movement or those of the ZERO Group, as was the case at the aforementioned monochrome painting exhibition curated by Kultermann or at the one that Lo Savio himself curated in Rome at the La Salita Gallery (1961). It is therefore not possible to confirm, as Pierre Restany himself occasionally stated, that Manzoni was a student of Klein's. One simply cannot deduce this from a few photos where the Milanese artist is caught in the act of intently observing Klein's work and looking amazed! It is well known by all, in fact, that he admired Klein, whether it be for having written about him in the magazine he co-edited with Castellani, or when he made the famous statement referring to Klein: "He's the blue monochrome, I'm the white one, we need to work together." But both Manzoni's and Lo Savio's artistic expressions, as well as Klein's, were established during 1958 to 1962. The situation is quite different, however, for the majority of the "Poverists", whose artistic language successfully emerged after the period of 1964 to 1965 and took on distinctive and poetic characteristics that became firmly defined during that time and up to 1972, which is the year that marks the beginning of a slow dissolution and is the point after which they strengthened their respective poetry and even deepened their mutual differences.

But returning to a discussion of the work of some of the prominent Arte Povera artists and certain claims they made in writing or in comments about their action regarding the supposed influence that Yves Klein had on them, I find rather interesting what Kounellis said in an interview given at the time of the Italian exhibition *Yves Klein. La vita, la vita stessa che è l'arte assoluta* [Yves Klein: Life, Life Itself, Is Absolute Art] (MAMAC, Nice, and Centro Pecci, Prato, 2000). In response to my first question, "What is your possible connection to the work of Yves Klein?", Kounellis replied, "I have never conceived a work based on all of it. … I would be opposed to the whole and therefore different than Klein."[4] To a subsequent question, "Between Klein and Manzoni, who do you think has had the most influence on how your work has developed?", Kounellis replied, "I understand Manzoni better, but Klein embodies adventure. … Manzoni lacks the mystical feeling that Klein has."[5]

One must note that, several times and in various circumstances, Kounellis's thoughts turned to the work of Klein. For example, in his important piece in the *La Città di Riga* magazine (1976), he raises questions such as "Is Klein's blue a colour or the representation of totality? Is Klein's blue pre- or post-impressionist? But Klein also used gold: Duchamp's *Bottle Rack* is undoubtedly much closer to Klein's blue-gold than to Manet's *The Luncheon on the Grass*."[6]

In 1978, in an interview with Marlis Grüterich, who asked him about his attitude towards the abstract art of the 1950s, Kounellis replied, "I've always considered, then and now, that the French painter, Yves Klein, has the same figurative intensity as the stained-glass windows of the Notre-Dame Cathedral in Paris."[7] Lastly, when I pointed out, in one of the many conversations I had with Kounellis, "Like him, you loved blue; like him, you used gold and fire; but moving beyond the dialogue that exists between you, where is the difference?", Kounellis stated, "Klein and I have a shared admiration for Delacroix. As for the blue, I never used it, but I love how he used it. Whenever someone mentions gold, I always think of Verrocchio, who was a goldsmith."[8]

But when reflecting on Klein's supposed influence on the leading Arte Povera artists, one must certainly not overlook the international colloquium entitled "Spirituality and Materiality in the Work of Yves Klein", which I curated with Gilbert Perlein, that took place in conjunction with the aforementioned exhibition *Yves Klein: Life, Life Itself, Is Absolute Art* at the MAMAC museum in Nice and the Centro per l'Arte Contemporanea Luigi Pecci in Prato in two successive showings on 19 May and 18 November 2000.

Among the numerous scientific contributions of interdisciplinary scholars that were invited, here one must take a moment to consider, in particular the presentations made by Anne-Marie Sauzeau, French art critic and wife of Alighiero Boetti, the leading exponent of "Poverism" from Turin. She participated in both study sessions and presented a rather varied array of readings and rereadings of foundational texts of the Arte Povera movement: the writings of Germano Celant from 1967 to 1980; texts published by the artists Fabro, Pistoletto, Penone, and Zorio; along with some interviews that she conducted with Calzolari, Paolini, and Celant himself.

During her presentation, after mentioning Klein's numerous exhibitions and travels in Italy, highlighting most importantly the relationship between Klein and Manzoni from 1958 to 1961, when both innovated artistically "in timely synchronicity and affinity" but with philosophical and aesthetical differences, Sauzeau analysed the theoretical-critical Restany-Celant "core" (calling to mind, however, the appreciation the Genovese critic had for Klein, whom he often cited in his essays on Fontana or Manzoni). Sauzeau also discussed Celant's opinions and advice gathered during their colloquia; the theorist of Arte Povera, after acknowledging that the contemplative void and Klein himself may have had an impact on Arte Povera, suggested, however, in that colloquium, that one must be "prudent" when investigating and rigorous when verifying facts and evidence, an approach that Sauzeau claims to have taken. "I took his advice: I noted specific details (in the writings of Fabro, Pistoletto, and Penone); I asked pointed questions and dated them (in meetings with Paolini and Calzolari, with confirmation from Raymond Hains)."[9]

The results of Sauzeau's work are worth remembering. Regarding the statements made by Luciano Fabro during the personal retrospective exhibition at the Centre Georges Pompidou in 1996–1997 and published in that exhibition's catalogue, the artist, who was working primarily in Milan, stated,

> Manzoni is an artist to whom I was very connected, very close. His work is fundamental for my entire generation. … Klein was very important, even if it's not correct to say that it was he who was behind the work of Manzoni.

> I rather believe that they helped each other; there was emulation. But what
> separated them was the different way they approached their work. Manzoni is
> a secular artist; Klein is a religious artist. That which has a materialistic scope
> for one has a transcendent one for the other.[10]

In 1981, an exhibition entitled *Identité italienne. L'art en Italie depuis 1959* [Italian
Identity: Art in Italy since 1959], curated by Germano Celant, was held at the Centre
Georges Pompidou. In a piece for the catalogue of that exhibition, Michelangelo
Pistoletto, after clearly articulating his own thoughts on the fate of the prospect and
its final outcome as demonstrated by the works of Pollock and Fontana, which both
hit a wall that the art of these two great painters would fail to break through,
the Piedmontese artist states,

> I found the work of Yves Klein to be very interesting. … I discovered Manzoni
> after that, and I thought that he was a good student of Klein's, just as I think
> the Milanese man would never have made it as an artist had he not gone
> to France and seen Klein (but maybe it's because I discovered him afterwards).
> Getting back to Klein, I think, however, that his work represented the end
> of this long journey, the matter of perspective hit its historical impasse,
> like lyrical abstraction. With the monochrome, the wall itself was sublimated:
> the sublimation of the wall by means of the canvas, and that's that![11]

Conversely, at the same exhibition in Paris in 1981, Giuseppe Penone focuses on
a few aspects of Klein's work that clearly catch most of his attention, because they
involve nature:

> Klein never displays the energy process; in fact, he treats the colour blue
> as energy. He continues to produce paintings, things to contemplate, but he also
> produced actions, gestures. For example, when he put a canvas on the roof
> of a car to drive all the way to Nice. This takes the painting well beyond just being
> a painting![12]

The questions that Sauzeau directly asked Calzolari in August of 2000 bring forth a
series of observations that quite clearly confirm his interest in Klein. Calzolari states,

7. Jannis Kounellis, interview by Marlis Grüterich, in *Echoes in the Darkness: Jannis Kounellis;
Writings and Interviews 1966–2002*, ed. Mario Codognato and Mirta d'Argenzio (London: Trolley, 2002), 155.
8. Jannis Kounellis, interview by Bruno Corà (1980), in *Echoes in the Darkness*, 178.
9. Anne-Marie Sauzeau, "Tracce di Yves Klein nell'arte povera? Una verifica tra i protagonisti", in *Spiritualità
e materialità nell'opera di Yves Klein* (Prato: Gli Ori, 2002), 192–207. Anne-Marie Sauzeau's essay includes
and expands on the presentation given in Nice on 19 May 2000 entitled "De Yves Klein à l'Arte Povera
en passant ou non par Piero Manzoni".
10. Luciano Fabro, *Spiritualità e materialità*, 199. First published in *Luciano Fabro: Habitat*, exh. cat.
(Paris: Centre Georges Pompidou, 1996). Published in conjunction with the exhibition of the same title,
organised and held at Centre Georges Pompidou, Paris, 9 October 1996–6 January 1997.
11. Michelangelo Pistoletto, in *Identité Italienne. L'art en Italie depuis 1959*, ed. Germano Celant, exh. cat.
(Paris: Centre Georges Pompidou, 1981). Published in conjunction with the exhibition of the same title,
organised and held at the Centre Georges Pompidou, Paris, 7 June–24 September 1981.
12. Giuseppe Penone, "La nature n'est pas séparée de l'homme", in *Ligeia, dossiers sur l'art*, nos. 25–28,
October 1998–June 1999, 161–176.

When I was young, I had no mental connection with Manzoni, while Klein's
presence was always there for me, as was, in a way, the whole Nouveau Réalisme
movement. Yves Klein presented the imaginary with a dynamic that projected
it into the future, and that's how it touched me … especially through my great
friend Raymond Hains in 1964. For me, it ignited the essence of the
phantasmagorical. After that, Yves Klein was always with me.

Calzolari concludes, "Yves Klein never directly inspired me in that he is my master,
my guardian angel, the voice that shall not be named."[13]

In closing, in the letters she exchanged with Giulio Paolini, Anne-Marie Sauzeau
successfully obtained strongly empathetic statements that could be summed up
as follows: from the moment Paolini first saw one of Klein's small blue monochromes
in the Apollinaire Gallery in Milan as part of a collective Nouveau Réalisme exhibition
(1960), the French artist joined the circle of those artists, from the oldest to
the contemporaries, that Paolini will always associate with. Furthermore, he agrees
on the existing affinities and differences in the parallel journeys Sauzeau notes
in the two artists. Finally, these are his words:

> My tendency to "establish order" in Klein's captivating and daring cosmogonies
> places me in an area adjacent (and perhaps complementary) to the fired-up,
> boundless, and planetary imagination of his absolute gestures: in a separate but
> adjoining room, the door left ajar so as not to disturb, yet ready to open for
> whatever the reason, to be able to listen to a voice, so crystal clear and yet
> delicate that perhaps, without getting too upset, is also crying out for help.[14]

Regarding the observations put forth by various sources and Anne-Marie Sauzeau's
essay over twenty years ago, one can confirm that, along with a decent number
of "Poverists", other artists in Italy recognised for their focus on the immaterial
as developed and promoted by Klein – such as Claudio Parmiggiani, Ettore Spalletti,
and Giovanni Rizzoli – ultimately shared and conveyed his sensibility and artistic vision
in incisive, poetic interpretations of their own.

March 2024

---

13. Pier Paolo Calzolari, interview by Anne-Marie Sauzeau, in *Spiritualità e materialità*, 201–203.
14. Giulio Paolini, correspondence with Anne-Marie Sauzeau, in *Spiritualità e materialità*, 203–204.

APPENDIX

—

Editor's Note: the transcripts and translations below retain the written and typographical bias used by the various authors.
Unless otherwise mentioned, all transcripts are translated from the French.

25, 30

Dear Papa Dear Mama
Here is the long-awaited account of the Journey!
A thousand details are still missing but … I'm out of paper!

Departure – Tuesday 3 August at 10 am
I stood on the roadside at the Port of Nice in Menton, I signalled to several cars, a jeep picked me up and took me as far as the Border, I crossed the border on foot and once my passport had been sighted, I once again settled in on the roadside. I started out in a minivan, as far as Ventimiglia. There, I swapped for a Buic that took me as far as San-Remo. Speaking with the people in the car, I told them I'm an art student and also that I have fifteen thousand lire in my pocket for a one-month trip; aghast, the American who was driving slipped a pack of cigarettes and a thousand lire into my pocket. I put all of it back in his pocket, refusing, In short, a great fight ensued… I accepted!
I knocked back a few cocktails in San-Remo, then set out once again on the road to Genoa; I absolutely wanted to reach Genoa by the evening, it was five o'clock, I stuck my thumb out, but nothing and still nothing….. until Ten o'clock. I'd really had enough of being in the same spot for nearly five hours, I'd even given up thumbing, and so to console myself I got a sandwich, I bit into it… and just then (it's always like that) a car stopped and asked me for "the road to Genoa" and with my mouth full, I replied I was going there too and that if they had room for me, I'd take care of finding Genoa like a needle in a Haystack. They agreed, so I was off. I arrived at three in the morning, but I made it!!
– I slept in the waiting room at the train station and at 7 am I left in a truck, I did fifteen kilometres, stopped, and once again, a little two-hour wait, then another Buic stopped and the guy who I asked in English to take me to Pisa answered me in English that it was a crime to go to Pisa directly without going via Rapallo; that it was a short detour, but that it was well worth a look… Etc……. suddenly he offered to speak French, seeing that I had a few difficulties in English. So I asked him what his nationality was: Italian…. He spoke English like an Englishman and French like a Frenchman. I stuffed his head full of art student's history and, delighted, he took me to his home, after showing me an incalculable number of splendid curiosities and locations, telling me that he loves painting and that

he has a whole collection of Matisse, Picasso, Braque works, etc… I saw the collection, I congratulated him, and over lunch, we discussed painting, while a horde of kids yelled and argued at the table. In the afternoon he apologised that he would be too busy to continue the visit by car, but if I'd like to, I could take his motorbike and visit alone, but on a motorbike.
So I visited Rapallo, St Margherita, and Portofino, the most ~~chic and~~ elegant beaches in Italy – In the evening I dined at his place and the next day I left for Pisa, via "la Spezia" I arrived in Pisa in the afternoon – in two cars.
In Pisa for the first time, I took a hotel room, I visited the tower, the Baptistery, the cemetery, in short all the celebrities, including the museum – a very pretty city but rather affected by the shelling – the next day in the afternoon I left for Florence, a single car on a splendid autostrada –
in Florence, I set myself up again at a hotel, a little inexpensive hotel (just three hundred lire) I wandered about a bit in the evening and turned in very early because I was very tired. The next morning: visits. I visited the church on the main square whose name I already can't recall – there, again, there was a Baptistery, this time with doors made of solid "gold" then I visited the Medicis Palace, the Uffizi Gallery, Pitti Palace, all of it crammed with Paintings by Raphaels, Michelangelos, Titians, Botticellis, Giottos, Filippino Lippis etc… then more various churches, and, all of these churches as well as a great deal of palaces and houses were made of marble inlaid with marbles of various colours, so a kind of marble marquetry! Finally I visited Fiesole, a small village near Florence full of Roman ruins –
My overall impression of Florence is fantastic, because everything there is harmonious and subtle – I've been here for four days already I've spent little, the Hotel three hundred lire, the restaurant (ristorante popolare) at most two hundred lire. I left the fourth day in the evening with two Belgians I met who are travelling like me – a truck took us to Rome – I travelled by night and went to Siena without being able to stop or see anything at all.
I arrived in Rome at six in the morning – The Belgians and I decided to request hospitality at a convent to thus eliminate hotel expenses – while visiting the court of the Vatican we asked all the priests that we met if they might know of a convent where we could spend the night. We stumbled on a little priest who spoke very good French, he eventually told us that he is Belgian, and even that he is quite simply the Bishop of Antwerp; he wrote us a note for a convent that he knew and sent us there – we were very well received when we got there and besides lodgings, they even offered us food for the eye. The convent is Splendid – it's a modern construction, we have truly palatial bedrooms with large bay windows with a View over all of Rome, since the monastery is in the upper part of the city, there are Baths, Showers adjoining each bedroom, the food is very Good – our hosts are Benedictine and we wash our hands very ceremoniously with Holy Water before each meal! Visit of Rome: for the visit, every other day, a very erudite monk was foisted on us, as a guide, and we had in-depth visits of Basilicas, churches, and obviously catacombs ~~(obviously)~~ the rest of the time we stroll ~~among~~ through the ancient city. ~~things seen:~~
Roman Forum, with the Basilica of Maxentius and

Constantine, Arch of Septimius Severus, Arch of Titus,
the Palatine Hill, Palazzi Imperiali, Arch of Constantine
near the Coliseum, thermal baths of Caracalla – Temple
of Vesta, Pantheon – Saint Mary Major, Saint Cecilia,
the Quirinale Palace in Saint Paul's Bay, beyond the walls
on the Appian Way, the catacombs, tomb of Cecilia
Metella completely round like the Castel Sant'Angelo
– the villa Doria Pamphili – the Vatican, the Vatican
Museum which is a wonder, an inestimable treasure,
firstly in terms of its paintings:
all the Byzantines and Primitives, the Sienese School –
the Fra Angelicos, Bellinis – Raphaels in paintings
and tapestries with the Sistine Chapel and a few rooms,
each twenty to thirty metres long, decorated with
frescoes by Raphael –
– secondly – all the famous statues, Discobolus,
all the Venuses, Juno, and Hercules with Olympian Zeus –
– thirdly – the rooms of Greek vases, those marvellous
red vases painted black, in their thousands!!
– fourthly – the Egyptian rooms – Wonders – sarcophagi
in wood painted in hallucinatory colours, statues,
tombs, basically more wonders piled upon wonders –
Once I left Rome after five days of intense visiting
I was utterly exhausted and incapable of saying a word
about anything that I'd seen, only now am I starting
to discern it.
————

The journey from Rome to Naples now: it was splendid,
we were able to take a truck and this truck was
transporting mattresses, so we undertook the journey
lying on these mattresses and nonchalantly watching
the landscape – once arrived in Naples, we dined
with the truck drivers then we continued as far
as Pompeii by the autostrada, setting up at a Hotel
for two days –
Pompeii is the most fantastic evocation of the
prestigious Latin past –
– we strolled around the ancient city for the entire day
and even in the evening by moonlight – we absolutely
had the sense of strolling through a modern city
(besides a few details) that had been bombarded the
day before and that would now be emptied of all
its inhabitants – it is really striking and then there are
the very famous Frescoes, which are splendid,
and the petrified corpses that still have captivating
facial expressions –
we also visited Herculaneum, which is, with few
deviations, the same similar to Pompeii –
We ascended Vesuvius twice in a row – once by Night,
once by Day – we visited Pazuoli, where the lava is
liquid and boiling –
naturally, we visited Naples and set off for Capri
to Sorrento after seeing Amalfi –

Finally Capri, the Goal of the journey I'd offered myself,
I made it there!! There I could finally have a restful
holiday, without being debilitated by the compulsory
visit of several unmissable wonders on pain of being
treated as an American – Since all of us intended to
base ourselves in Capri for a while, we then had
to find another convent to economise hotel expenses,
so we enquired on the boat: there are Carthusians –
arrived in Capri: a landscape of a thousand colours
and yet full of softness, huge Rocks that plunge into
the water, and this water is no longer the sea, because
through a special play of light it gives the impression
of being a mixture of colours in several different tones
that occasionally break apart and form green, red,

blue, grey beaches hither and thither – we berthed
at the wharf of a charming little Port called Marina
Grande, where several fishing houses can be seen and
at first you think it's Capri, but not at all, to go to Capri
you take a little cable car and ten minutes later you
find yourself at: La Piazzetta!! La Piazzetta is the heart
of Capri, it's a wonderful little square with pretty shops,
pretty cafés, a pretty church and bell tower, all of which
has a charm that immediately takes hold and won't
let go, as I wrote to you already it's like Cagnes-sur-Mer
in miniature with very narrow streets that all depart
from this famous little square that is clearly the centre
of the whole island: in the evening the whole village
is illuminated by the very elegant shops selling fashion,
knick-knacks, and the streets are bustling with people;
a world of all that is as strange and varied as possible –
The entire earth, all nations are represented there –
We found the charterhouse and the monks (who are
only there to create chartreuse liqueur), they Agreed
and we are staying in a small disused chapel, except
that it is impossible to eat there every day, they have
not planned for more than themselves! We were only
invited three or four times, however every evening
a monk in a state of advanced inebriation brought us
a Bottle of chartreuse, and the three of us drank it
all the same –
Every evening as well (as actually resting) we went
Dancing, in the most chic dance halls of the City,
always with our Bottle of chartreuse under the arm –
we started to get noticed! Plus I still have my shirt
with Feet and hands which was a big hit, even in Capri
(which is a very eccentric place) I have a lot of Rivals –
During the day: swims, strolls by the sea, a tour
of the island in a kayak and frenetic visit of the caves
– These caves are the most marvellous mystery of
the island – how were they formed? There's no point
wondering, all you can do is contemplate. It's the
most fantastic play of colours that I've ever seen
in all of nature. The general impression of Capri is that
it's a real dazzle of colours, and yet never overpower-
ing, but rather gentle and at all events always pleasant –
Capri – Anacapri – Blue Cave – Grotta Meravigliosa – etc
in Capri, after 7 days of delights we met a Belgian
by chance who has a little eight-metre-long sailboat
and he was bored by himself, he didn't dare to confront
the sea or undertake long treks, so we changed his
mind and off we went!!
This time it is a sea voyage, a bit harder all the same,
as we cling to one side of the boat while the mast and
sail lean towards the other – and so we travelled for
four days in this way seeing: Ischia, the coastline of the
Gulf of Naples, as far as Reggio Calabria, which is at the
extreme tip of Italy, Messina, Palermo – Stromboli and
the surrounding islands, basically a really spectacular
expedition!!
————

————

Back in Capri, I rested for one night and then headed
for Venice – Naples – – Rome – Rome – Florence – –
Florence – Bologna – Venice, in a single car!!
and the guy was in a rush – so here I am in Venice
after a day and a half's journey –
Here in Venice, there's another dazzling array of artistic
Wonders, both paintings and architecture, I settled
into a Hotel for two days for three hundred lire again
(whereas everyone had said it'd be Five to Six hundred)
and I visited: obviously by boat, because everything is
on the water like in Amsterdam! I even took a gondola

ride, but it did make me think twice (paying for half
an hour: 400 lire) that I ~~had to~~ must think about
my return trip – I ~~had~~ have had enough of hitchhiking
and I decided to take the train back, I bought my ticket
and then I realised that I only had fifty lire left – I got
a refund on the cost of the room where I'd already
spent one night, I had a massive meal and left at
midnight after spending two days in the unforgettable
Venice and its jewel, Saint Mark's Square – I took
the train to Nice! with two lire in my Pocket – I ~~felt~~ was
feeling quite poor and felt the need to talk about it
in the conversation of my compartment – and that
was enough to then be assailed with sandwiches, wine,
and cigarettes – so here I am now in Nice, no longer
hungry, thirsty, or needing to smoke – a bit tired,
but satisfied by my little trek – and that's the end
of the Story!!!!

It's very badly written but I hope that you will
understand I couldn't get to the end of it and by
getting annoyed I made mistakes, deletions,
and wrote poorly! a thousand excuses and Much Love,
Yves

27

Dear Papa and Mama
In Rome for three days, I've been constantly circulating
from one wonder to the next.
Tomorrow or the day after I'll leave for Naples.
Love,
Yves

34

Yves Klein
116 rue d'Assas
<u>Paris 6th arrondissement</u>

Paris, 22 September 1951.

CINZANO
Mr Ariès
30, Avenue Kléber
<u>Paris</u>

Dear sir,
At the recommendation of Mr Villequey, an employee
in your advertising department, I would be honoured
to be considered for the role of Representative
or Propagandist.
I am French, aged 23 and single.
I have undergraduate training which, however, is not
sanctioned by a diploma. Visits to England and Spain
allowed me to learn these languages, which I speak
fluently. I also hold a driver's license for trucks
and tourism.
Thank you for your time, I remain at your disposal
for any further information you may require.
Yours respectfully.

36

Yves Klein
34 boul. Raimbaldi
(Raimbaldieu!
like Restany)
Nice A.M.

10 July

And your article "The Monochrome Proposition"
in *i Cuatri Soli* with Parizot?? for July!

My dear tato and my dear Pierre

Today I'm sending you a mandate of 8000 FF to thank
you infinitely my dear old Restany! You're an incredible
guy! I had a good trip and now I'm on the coast…
Every day I swim in my Blue Period – what pleasure
to dive and move about like this in my colour!!
Excuse me for having stood you up on Sunday but
I was very sad and very jumpy – I had concerns!
Tell tato that she is the most delicious little married
woman I know (that is said with no untoward
ulterior motive)
Think of the Film – I only live now for this great battle
of line and colour – The War!![1] I shall retreat by myself
and work Rendez vous in Venize on 1st September!
You must make a big effort my dear Restany so that
I obtain the gold medal in Phys Ed[2] and Sports because
then I'll be much more admissible with respect
to "others", have "Contractual" employment at the
ministry next year or even next autumn, remember
old friend that without the Judo club (they're selling
the Clichy hall) I would have no income other than
that of the American Students Center – But no more
Chatter…. The Gold Medal is ultra-necessary
to the health of monochromy!
Console Bernadette about my departure, Tell her the
truth…: that I love her very much but that I must pull
myself together alone, without her, so as to better
deserve and appreciate her upon my return.
I sent the large red painting to the Marseille festival!?!?
I'll endeavour to be there at the vernissage on 4 August
and I'll tell you about it – write to me at 34 Boul
Raimbaldi – Nice.
Que pasa for Lenocci? Will my exhibition in Milan
go ahead or not?
Anyway, Viva Restany el màs grande critico de arte
del mundo! y tato sù Dama elegante y divina
Yves

45

Translated from the Italian

My dear Pierre,

I agree with you completely. If you think it's necessary
to hold Yves's exhibition this year, we will not fail
to do so, in which case we could schedule it from 2
to 11 January. That way, we would begin the year
with a <u>sensational exhibition.</u>
If you then think that another exhibition is necessary,

in addition to the ones you are planning, we will do that too.
More than prudence or wisdom on my part, I am at the moment concerned about meeting my material commitments and moving forward. But when I am a little more at ease, when it comes to the exhibitions you are planning, I will do not one, but three of them a year.
Please go see Bryen and start getting him to set aside the material for the exhibition.
A fraternal embrace to you and Tato. You figure things out with Yves.
Yours, Guido.
31 Oct 56

57

Translated from the Italian

A PHENOMENON AT THE APOLLINAIRE GALLERY
Blue Blue Blue
—

Yves Klein, a judo champion and a super avant-garde painter, has presented the most paradoxical painting exhibition this world has ever seen.
Due to the fortuitous unavailability of the official art critic, yours truly, who is not a critic, was asked to visit a solo show and to report on it as a journalist.
And because chance has a rich imagination, it turns out that this art exhibit is one of the most unique, if not the most unique and disconcerting since people have been making art on earth.
So much so that the official critic who was unable to come will say to himself: "What do you know, I see hundreds of exhibits a month that more or less look the same, such that they end up forming a single show in my mind, which makes writing about them an extremely tiresome problem. And then there is one that is totally out of the ordinary, about which there would be so much to say, and I can't go, and I lose the opportunity to look really good." (But how does a simple journalist manage to look good, however industrious and diligent he may be?)
The exhibit is open until 12 January at the Apollinaire Gallery, at Via Brera 4, the lair – or so I was told – of the most extremist avant-garde, the most polemical space in Italy, which shows the living stars, the crazies, the anarchists, the revolutionaries, the terrorists, and the most frenetic yet-to-be-discovered talents there are.
It's a small space with a small window onto the street. Ironically, further up the street is another art space with its own window, loyal to the best-known kinds of well-meaning painting. The result being that people coming out of Piazza della Scala, in the brief span of six or seven metres, stumble upon (or rise up from) a decent but conventional landscape fit for a waiting room at the dentist's office to the most blazing abstraction.
People might think that the owner of such a gallery must be a kind of psychological monster, a hallucinatory creature that, who knows, smokes hash or marijuana, some kind of turbulent character who stays up all night building infernal machines, or some gloomy fanatic steeped in his own subterranean asceticism.

Guido Le Noci is instead the most gentle, courteous, and friendly person imaginable. Of course, he would make a personal sacrifice to convert you, the reluctant, to what we call non figurative art. But he exerts this passionate pressure with such discretion that you only realise it later, after the fact.
Be that as it may, there is no doubt that the most unsettling and esoteric rituals of modern art are celebrated at the Apollinaire Gallery. Le Noci's faith in this field is as solid as the Egyptian pyramids. Asking him whether he believes that Mondrian is indeed a great artist is tantamount to going to the Vatican to ask the Pope whether God really exists.
Yet even this man, who is all too used, we might say, to acrobatic recklessness, the leader of the most daring, captain of the fine arts "commandos", this time, in looking at the works of the French painter Yves Klein, to be honest, even he was astounded.
Astounded, but we should also say, extremely interested. He opened the door for him immediately, had him sit down, and he showed his paintings on the walls.
How many times, in the face of the unbridled frenzy of modern art, have people said, "Now everything has been subverted. We can't go any further." And yet, we have continued to push ahead further.
So, in Yves Klein's case, it would be impossible to be mistaken. The renunciation of figurative art, formal purity, abstraction – we will not be able to go further than this for centuries and centuries.
Let's get into some specifics.
First of all, Yves Klein is an extraordinary fellow, as a person, not just as an artist. Born in Nice twenty-eight years ago, he studied nautical sciences and Asian languages. He has trained racehorses. He is a judo champion in Japan, where he won the "fourth dan of the Kodokan black belt" in Tokyo two years ago – and in fact, he will give a martial arts exhibition here in Milan on Saturday night at 9:00 pm., at the Jijoro Kano Club at Via San Senatore 5, close to Via Sant'Eufemia.
But his paintings are the most extraordinary of all. He is showing twelve of them at the Apollinaire Gallery. The first, rectangular in shape, 56 centimetres wide and 78 centimetres high, depicts … oh, I'm sorry. The undersigned journalist, indulging in old habits, was about to make a terrible gaffe. Talking about "depicting something" at The Apollinaire Gallery is like talking about rope in a hanged man's house.
So, the first painting, which is of the above-mentioned size, consists of a smooth, uniform surface, a uniform blue colour, a beautiful blue, actually, ultramarine in tone. There isn't a single mark, dot, spot, or interruption on this surface, just a blue that is entirely the same, slightly and regularly rippled like the cementite in our apartment buildings. And now, let us move on to the second painting. The second painting, rectangular in shape (56 cm by 78 cm) consists of a smooth, uniform surface, a uniform blue colour, a beautiful blue, ultramarine in tone, without a mark, line, spot, etc. See above. The same goes for the third painting. And for the fourth painting, and so on. Eleven absolutely identical paintings (at least in appearance) consisting of blue rectangles without the slightest mark on them. There isn't even a signature.
Only the twelfth one is different; it is square instead of rectangular, and red instead of blue. One might

ask oneself, is it possible that there isn't the slightest
difference between one painting and the next?
The answer is that Yves Klein made these paintings in
different states of mind. So, is there any way to identify
these varying states of mind in the paintings? No,
absolutely not. To make a literary analogy, it would be
like writing a poem like this:

Mmmmmmmm
mmmmmmmm
mmmmmmmm
etc.

(given that, with all due respect to Rimbaud, the colour
blue is represented in the alphabet by the letter "m"
and not "o", which is famously red).
We should now turn the floor over to the presenter,
Pierre Restany, who says: "Careful, these monochrome
utterances demand from you, the reader, that entire
reservoir of willingness necessary to carry out
revolutions and overthrow tyrants." And, further on:
"Blue dominates, lives. We are before the Blue Lord,
the absolute master of the most definitive of all
liberated frontiers, the Blue of the frescoes in Assisi;
this utter void, this Nothing that asserts the Everything
Possible, this supernatural, feeble silence of colour,
this infinite X that, above and beyond the anecdotal
and the formal pretext, determines the immortal
greatness of Giotto."
What do people say? They react in one of three ways.
Most sneer or complain that it's time to stop pulling
people's legs, and so on. A minority recognises
that the matter is, at the very least, extremely amusing.
A minority of that minority ruminates over whether,
in a very distant future, one of these paintings might
not be hanging in the Louvre (as far as these things go,
after everything we've seen in the last several decades,
who's willing to bet against that?).
Actually, while we're on that topic, the price. It's very
low: 25,000 lire per painting. Two buyers so far:
a well-known tailor who collects abstract art and the
painter-sculptor Lucio Fontana – the guy who makes
those holes, just so we're clear – who has shown with
this purchase that he has a good sense of humour
and sport.
Dino Buzzati

58

Translated from the Italian

What Blue Courage!
ART or courage? That is the question you ask yourself
when you step into the Apollinaire Gallery at Via Brera 4,
where Nice-born painter Yves Klein is showing
right now. Look at the paintings, next to the artist
who painted them.
They're blue, completely blue, without so much as a
dot or a smattering of another colour. People walk in,
look, are dumbfounded. Then, they either leave
annoyed or start to laugh. And there's a few folks
who are buying them, for the small sum of 25,000 lire
per painting. And you should hurry up and get in line
to buy one, because it seems that, following this "blue
period", the painter will begin a "red period", and you
risk not having something from this "early period".

61

Restany's answer to Valescchi in *Giorno*

Dear Sir,
Accused by your associate Mr VALESCCHI in the article
that he dedicated to the Yves KLEIN exhibition (issue
of *Il Giorno* from last Tuesday 6 January), I'd be grateful
if you would please publish the following clarifications:
– Mr VALESCCHI seems to use and abuse a very basic
psychology, regarding which he is more than a little
proud, to the point of believing himself very naturally
authorised to read between the lines of a preface all
of the author's so-called hidden agendas. A confidence
that is this blind to its own capacities for judgement
and such a methodical absence of doubt are very
dangerous states of mind: Mr VALESCCHI should be
concerned about it, if he were however capable
of sincerity with himself.
– Whether he likes it or not, we are not provocateurs.
This exhibition follows a series of analogous events that
I organised in France, notably in Paris and Marseille.
Yves KLEIN's approach is profoundly original and
current. As I said in my preface to this exhibition in
Milan (which Mr VALESCCHI took pains not to reference),
no confusion is possible here with Mondrian
and Malevich.
The evolution of these two painters, and particularly
that of Malevich, can only be completely illuminated
through the cubist ideology with which they were
contemporaneous. Malevich's very beautiful gesture
that led him to the 1913 black square against a white
background and to the 1919 white square against
a white background was the result of a wonderful
pictorial intuition, the illustration of his suprematist
theory. Through this revolutionary act (to whose
logical and material justification the artist then devoted
his life, until his death in 1935), Malevich wished to
establish once and for all, and against any system of
cubist analysis, the supremacy of the simple geometric
form, the pictorial obviousness of the square.
Malevich therefore sought to impose, in its absolute
and total purity, a certain formal vision.
Yves KLEIN's approach, on the other hand, is essentially
of a chromatic nature. It is based on a lyrical postulate,
that of the immense affective possibilities of pure
colour, that is, of colour liberated of any representative
or formal pretext.
The monochrome propositions are coloured spatial
projections, presented to the viewer in the most sober
of contexts. Everything that appears to be architectural
integration is also refused: the colour is projected
beyond the picture rails, since the monochrome
propositions are set at variable distances from
the support wall.
At a time when the viewer is subjected to the daily
avalanche of often gratuitous forms and designs, due
to today's inflation of abstract art, Yves KLEIN's attempt,
giving the floor to pure colour, assumes the meaning
of a bona fide intellectual cleanse.

I have the honour to remain, Sir, yours faithfully.

P. RESTANY
The Director of IL GIORNO
Via Settala 22
MILANO – ITALY

62

Translated from the Italian

Avant-Garde in the Tram by Adele Cambria

IT WAS 9h15 in the evening. Via Manzoni was completely
empty, swept clear by a cold wind. The number 16 tram
was almost empty. Three men were sitting in a row,
one behind the other, talking loudly in French.
One of them was very young, pale, with protruding
temples, and his head as closely shaved as his cheeks.
He was wearing a black bowler hat, an old, black frock
coat, and he carried a round, Chamberlain-style
umbrella.
He looked like an orphan dressed up as a gentleman.
The three of them talked about Florence, what a
marvellous city, but it was clear that they were thinking
about something else. Suddenly, the man with the
bowler hat asked, "Can we do a show in Rome too?"
"Of course we can", the older of his two friends
answered, adding, "We are inviting a bishop to the
opening, along with Zavattini and De Sica …
These folks always make an impression, but let's talk
about the Milan show …" "We're opening on Monday,
right?" the other youngster asked. He said, "In that
case, you can come watch me on Saturday evening at
Via Senatore … I will be doing judo, but just for a few
close friends!"
The youngster who would be doing judo for just a few
friends was a painter too. He was immediately
recognisable. Several papers had published his
photographs, and he had even been on the radio.
He said he was born in Nice, and that he had
a bookstore on the Côte d'Azur for a period of time.
"So, is literature another one of your passions?" the
radio host asked, unsuspectingly. "For goodness' sake,
Miss, don't say such things", he answered. "I haven't
opened a book in years!" The radio host exacted
her revenge. "Oh, I understand … and that's why
you started raising horses in Ireland!"
The painter's name is Yves Klein. He's thirty years old
and he has a black belt in judo. He paints paintings
that are blue, all blue, without any drawing or any
other colour appearing on the canvas. Logically,
these paintings belong to the artist's "blue period",
but he also has a "red period", which means that he has
painted paintings that are completely red and nothing
but red. In a gallery downtown, he is currently showing
eleven blue paintings and one red one.
Monday, this same gallery will host the solo show
of another painter, the one with the bowler hat who
– of course – is English. His name is Ralph Rumney. He is
twenty-three years old, and he has lived in Cornwall,
Paris, and Sicily. In 1955, he published an avant-garde
journal called *Other Voices*. Some of his paintings
are in Japan.
Ralph Rumney presents himself in this Milan show.
He writes, "I try to materialise the fetishes of the
machine age. We are looking forward to a time when
artists will no longer be tied to a personal style.
To a time when we – anonymously – will be free to work
without an obligation to repeat or 'develop' what
has already been achieved."

66

Dear Tato
Dear Restany
It's fantastic, the affluence of visitors is becoming more
apparent daily. There are now 2 paintings sold and
perhaps a third – sensational discussions are underway.
Tomorrow I'll be on the Radio and television. Long live
taTo and Restany. Yves

67

First part translated from the Italian

Dear Pierre, Here is a first sample of the new gallery
postcard.
I thought I would print the caption on the back.
Hugs, Guido

Here is sample no. 1 of the "Blue Period" monochrome
postcard!
Viva Restany!
and TATO.
Yves

68

Monochrome Proposition

In the month of February 1956, at Collette Allendy's
gallery, Yves exhibited a dozen paintings in diverse
formats, painted in a single flat colour, without
variations or nuances in the tones, and set at different
distances from the support wall (in short, projected
beyond the picture rail).
Following the controversies that were sparked
regarding this rather new concept of chromatic
expression, based on a veritable act of faith in the
possibilities of affective resonance of colour in and of
itself, I believe it is necessary to expand on the notion
of "monochrome proposition" that I chose to use
in my preface to this exhibition.
Why speak of a "monochrome proposition"? The fact
of the matter is that here, each time, we are in the
presence of a plain colour offered for contemplation.
In that respect, the colour is proposed.
The proposition is an equation: it is therefore
a balanced system, based on a certain notion of zero,
appropriately represented by the theoretical basis of
an optimum visual field, which it determines for itself.
A "monochrome proposition" is reduced to the
balance of a format-colour system. It involves the
abstraction of the artist's personal creation. But, once
this balance is reached, the proposition must naturally
form a whole, an entity, and must be considered
as such with its spatial imperatives – it gives rise to
an "aura" of development, and thus poses a situational
problem – the situation of the reader with respect
to the artwork.
The problem that we are broaching is that of colour
in context, which also involves a radical exclusivity (just
as two situations are mutually excluded in drama).

It is possible to imagine that for the painter himself,
the research ends with this contextualisation. But there
undeniably emerges from then on a host of complex
developments that are the manifestation of a second
existence. Architecture now intervenes and its role
is to anticipate the potential adjustments for
this survival, its channelling towards co-existence,
the determination of the geometric location
of the "zero degrees" that we mentioned earlier.
At the limit we arrive at – in opposition to the synthetic
pretentions of architectural polychromy – a rigorously
analytic conception of monochromy. Colour thus
proposed becomes the rhythmic tuning fork of an
ensemble devised in accordance with it, an elementary
raison d'être, and no longer a pretext for the use
of the support.
It is only from this perspective that monochromy can
avoid the pitiless retaliation of matter,
the misunderstanding arising from the terrible
"objective" contamination of our visual sense,
and above all the definitive failure, the disintegration
of the colour field within the ambient space that
is expressed by the sensation of a direct relationship
(generative of synthetic "values") between the artwork
and the support, the canvas and the picture rail.
P. Restany

72

The monochrome propositions of Yves KLEIN now seal
the artistic fate of pure pigment. This great history
of the blue period will be retraced, simultaneously,
on the picture rails of Colette Allendy and Iris Clert.
RESTANY

77

My dear Baj,
It's hopeless, your letter arrived very urgently and
Charles Estienne isn't here! still not here even after all
these recent days passed. So if you like, I've just
obtained his holiday address and I can write to him but,
as I know the man, he can either be late in replying
or he may respond immediately. What's to be done?
I have other critics on hand, if you like. Tell me,
if it's urgent I can contact a bunch of people for you.
My phone number in Paris is: DANTON 63.22
If you call me, do it via notification, that is, you ask
the Post Office to notify me when you are telephoning,
at what time exactly and with enough warning for
me to be present.
A thousand fond thoughts for you and your Wife
Your friend
Yves K.

Critics that I can contact:
Restany
Ragon
J. Alvard
L.P Favre

82

Original in English

THE END OF STYLE

In February 1952 the first nuclear manifesto stated our
intention of doing away with the last remaining
concessions to academism. Our revolt against
the reign of the right angle, against the dominion
of the machine, and against the glacial geometry
of abstraction had found its voice.
And in our experimentations since then we have used
every technical ressource [*sic.*] — going from the
tachisme of objective automatism to the graphism,
action painting, calligraphying, emulsifying,
polymaterialism and flottages of subjective automatism
— to finally arrive at the "h e a v y   w a t e r" colours
of Baj and Bertini in January 1957.
These technical experimentations have naturally
brought their own vocabulary with them: we have
gone from "Imaginary Spaces" (cf. Pierre Restany)
and "States of matter" (Baj and Dangelo, 1951)
to "P r e f i g u r a t i o n s" (Baj, Dangelo, Colombo
and Mariani, 1953), "New Flora" (Dangelo), "Puppets,
Animals and Fable" (Baj and Jorn, 1956) and "Atomised
Situations" (Baj and Pomodoro, 1957).
But every invention turns into convention: it gets
imitated and copied for purely commercial reasons.
That is why we must begin a vigorous antisylistic [*sic.*]
action in the cause of an eternally "other" art
(cf. Michel Tapié).
"De Stijl" is dead and buried, and it is now up to
its opposite — a n t i s t y l e — to break down the last
remaining barriers of cliché-ridden convention
that official stupidity still dares to oppose against
this liberation — that has finally discovered its verbal
definition — of art.
Once upon a time impressionism helped painting get
rid of conventional subject-matter; cubism and
futurism later got rid of the need for the realistic
reproduction of objects; and abstraction finally
removed the last traces of representational illusion.
A new — and final — link today completes this chain:
we, nuclear painters, denounce, in order to destroy,
the final convention, s t y l e.
The last stylistic works that we recognize are the
"monochromes" of Yves Klein (1956-1957); only the bare
boards — or Capogrossi's rolls of textile — can follow
them.
Decorators or painters: we have to choose. And we
choose to be painters, creating something new and
unique every time; painters for whom the virgin canvas
is the constantly self-renewing scene for an
unpredictable "c o m m e d i a   d e l l ' a r t e".
We state that in a world in which the artifices of
celebration are rejected, a work of art should be known
by the unity of its character, by the effective influence
of its appearance and for the simple reality of its
living presence.

Milan, September 1957.

Signed by: Armand, Enrico Baj, Bemporad,
Gianni Bertini, Jaques Calonne, Stanley Chapmans [sic],
Mario Colucci, Dangelo, Enrico De Miceli,
Reinhout [sic] D'Haese, Wout Hoeboer, Hundertwasser,

Yves Klein, Théodore Koenig, Piero Manzoni, Nando,
Joseph Noiret, Arnaldo Pomodoro, Gio Pomodoro,
Pierre Restany, Saura, Ettore Sordini, Serge Vandercam,
Angelo Verga.

91

Dear Iris, In the Basilica of St Francis of Assisi there are
monochrome paintings that are entirely Blue!
It's really quite incredible to perceive the imbecility
of art historians who have still never noticed this yet.
They are all signed "Giotto". What a Precursor!!
Now that's a Precursor! Long live Giotto, Long live Iris,
see you soon
Yves

92

My dear Mama,
Tantine and I have decided to take a little trip together
to Italy from 1st September to the 15th – There you
have it! There is no possibility of doing this before
– If you come, then come around the 16th –
Here is a photo and a catalogue with a Blue stamp!
You must have an ultra-wonderful extraordinary stay!
Iris will be in Athens on 8 or 10 August – I hope you're
having magnificent holidays, I'm having very good ones
here. I'd really like to go to Greece but I don't have
enough –
I'm actively concerned with causing Tantine a lot
of worry, All is Well –
Ever so much love and See you soon
Yves

I'll add a word. In the end, Yves apparently cannot leave
before 1 Sept. I could've been free on 24/8, you know
how hard it is to organise something with him
– he is very categorical, try as I might to tell him that
you were about to arrive, that he should leave earlier to
get back sooner, it was impossible. also my maid is tired
and she absolutely has to take a few days off – while
Yves is here it's impossible with all the washing to do,
and the meals and all – so because of him I'm obliged
to leave on the 1 Sept and we can only return by
the 15th – we need at least a fortnight, both for ourselves and the maid – it's really hard to reconcile it all!!
So arrange as best you can for passage around the 15th
of September – or the 16th, rather – because of him
there's no other way for me –
Much love,
hear from you soon
Rose

98

Meine grosse Rotraut,
Ich bin dein und dein gross and dick bear!
I'll be back in Nice on 19 September – Make some very
pretty paintings – I want one for my personal collection
in Paris – You are a true artist and ich lie be dich serh
fiel! tell Héléna I'm counting on her for Paris and
if possible for two months without fail, I just turned
down a young Italian woman for her.
See you soon
Yves

101

Translated from the Spanish

<u>Milan 2/5/59</u>

Dear Klein –
The material I'm sending will be used for the Triennale
di Milano that I believe you know: it's an international
art and architecture event. The commission called me
to give them ideas and organise an exhibition in
the open air in the park of the Triennale. On Thursday
I attended a meeting to explain to the commission
what your concept is and that of the architect
Werner Ruhnau,[3] together with other artists we could
do a demonstration of art nouveau. On principle,
the commission has agreed, but it asked me for more
concrete ideas, so we will need to meet and speak,
to specify as much as possible the form of
the production, the costs, basically a more established
programme and present it to the commission. I am
sure that it'll be a wonderful thing for the next
Triennale, which will be inaugurated in June of next
year, 1960 – If you agree, write to me and the best thing
would be that you come to Milan –
More soon
Best wishes
Fontana

106

Madam Iris Clert
I am delighted to inform you that on the list of guest
artists to feature at the 11th Lissone Prize there is
a painter who belongs to your Gallery; Yves Klein.
As you well know, our Prize is dedicated to avant-garde
painting; and the École de Paris, as usual, will be
presented with its best names.
Since I will take charge of extending the official
invitation to the artist, would you please give me his
personal address?
I am attaching the Regulations, and I am giving you
the address of our transport company, responsible
for collecting and delivering the artworks, who is
Mr Henri Walbaum – 49 rue Marx Dormoy – Paris 18
Tel. Bot. 6870
Furthermore, may I request that you send me,
before the end of July, the artist's documentation,
in accordance with article 7 of the Regulations.

I look forward to your prompt response, dear madam,
and please accept my warmest greetings.
Guido le Noci
17 June 1959

107

13 July 1959
Segr/TF/ms

The sculptor Lucio Fontana – who told us at length
about your great initiatives – and the sculptor Agenore
Fabbri (member of the Executive Technical Committee
of this Institute) informed us about what you may
present on the occasion of the Twelfth Triennale.
It would be really interesting to learn and hear detailed
information directly from your perspective, since
we would like our Executive Technical Committee to
definitively rule on the question of your presentations.
We would be delighted to be able to discuss directly
with you in order to bring to fruition what these
same friends, Fontana and Fabbri, described to us.
However, we would like to know what costs would be
incumbent on us.
I look forward to hearing from you and meeting you
if possible.
Best regards,

Il Segretario dell'Ente
T. Ferraris

109

I regret my belated reply and to inform you that the
members of the Executive Technical Committee of the
Twelfth Triennale, including myself, cannot complete
the initiative proposed by the sculptors Fabbri
and Fontana. The financial commitment is so great
that we cannot even envisage a partial presentation.
I wish to impart once again my regret and that of my
friends.
Yours truly,

Il Segretario dell'Ente
T. Ferraris

110

Original in English

Camaiore, 10 Settembre 1959

Dear Klein,
I write you in English because my English is very poor:
anyhow I hope you may understand English.
I have a magazine of art and poetry, Direzioni, and I am
interested with your works, even if I don't agree with
your position.
Anyhow I think that what you have done and what you
are doing now is at least very important: for this reason

I beg you to send me quelques reproductions,
or something you have written.
Which I would like to reproduct dans ma revue.
I expect a letter from you; yours sincerely
Fabrizio Mondadori, Via Locatelli, I Milan.

I sent by return the article on the "Realism" in my work
YK.

<u>**Not reproduced, but mentioned in the transcript above**</u>

Today's Authentic Realism
Paris, September 1959

Figurative painting and the kind known as abstract
are doomed!
There is a lot of talk about a return to figurative realism
today … That is true, it is underway, but it is very naive
to immediately think, as some do, of the return to
still life and landscape!
On the fringes of my monochrome attempt, in a deeply
classical spirit, I have long conducted a return to
realism, to an authentic realism of today and tomorrow,
by way of THE IMMATERIAL!
My *zones of immaterial pictorial sensibility*, stabilised,
transferable, and expandible beyond infinity
are created through a dynamic and awestruck
contemplation of nature in all of its aspects
and periods.
For me, it is a question of no longer painting canvases
but rather of establishing in a permanent and rather
enduring way, between myself and nature (which are in
fact inseparable) the NEOFIGURATIVE canvas that is at
once the most real and the most intangible that exists
and that provides readers – or, better still – "VIVEURS"
[enthusiasts] with such pictorial climates or events
based on pure behaviours, providing them
with a spectacle, or more precisely a "state" of virtue,
permanency, and transparency akin to that which
works by VERMEER, REMBRANDT, GIOTTO,
and MICHELANGELO furnished in their time!

My position with respect to contemporary art is
the "RECUMBENT" position! Yes, I am now searching
for this very first sleep. A great sleep without dreams
or nightmares, which creates blinding daylight
in the middle of the night, down to our very bones,
through its power and potential, and which,
upon awakening next morning, allows us to recover
genuine *joie de vivre*!
Yves Klein

112

Dear Yves,
I wrote to you, but I haven't yet received a reply.
So now there is an exhibition in Antwerp to organise.
In this exhibition, there would be Vanderbraun,
Verheyen, Fontana, and me (all more or less
the same trend).
The organiser is Verheyen; we hope to have your
participation with two or three works. Do you want to
write to Verheyen about this? We'd also like to exhibit

the German artist you told me about and whose work
is also similar to our trend. Would you like to write
to him and give his address to Verheyen and me?
After Antwerp, we could transport the exhibition
to Milan: I could do that in a small gallery; but you told
me that for you it would be easy to arrange that at
Le Noci's? Do you want to do that? That way would be
much better.
The exhibition in Antwerp is in February and it will be
the opening exhibition for a new gallery.
See you soon then and please arrange all of this
as quickly as possible.

Piero Manzoni   Via Cernaia 4 Milano
Jef Verheyen Rue Rubens 14 Antwerp Belgium

116

20.1.59
Dear Mr Palazzoli,

Yves Klein is delighted that you were <u>the first to buy
a painting</u> *zone of sensibility* !!!
We are studying the project of this receipt and as soon
as it's ready, we will send it to you. You'll see, it will
be <u>very good</u>.

See you soon.
Warm regards,
Iris Clert

118

21.9.59
Dear Sir,
Bravo for your decision to buy a *zone of sensibility.*
We are currently establishing the receipt, which will
be a true masterpiece, and as soon as it's ready,
I'll let you know.
Mr Palazzoli has already bought one and is <u>also</u>
awaiting his receipt.
See you soon I hope.
Warm regards,
Iris Clert

120

Dear Yves,
Please excuse me for this late missive, but I didn't
have your address. I only got it a few days ago.
As you know, we have opened a little central gallery
that has been very successful: we would like to hold
an event for you there. Would that be possible?
Now the monochrome affair is starting to gain
popularity in Milan.
In a few days' time issue 2 of *Azimuth* will be released,
with a blue page, as always!
See you soon and all the best with your work.
Piero Manzoni
Via Cernaia 4 Milano

133

Translated from the Italian

THE NUDE, NO OBJECTIONS

PARIS. There were just a few guests: a few painters,
writers, businessmen who love art, collectors, elegant
gentlemen, not more than forty people. Everyone
in evening wear. The guest, the painter Yves Klein,
who was doing the honours at the Contemporary Art
Gallery on Rue du Faubourg Saint-Honoré, received
them coolly and politely, inviting them to sit down
in the seats that were lined up as in a movie theatre,
before a blank, white wall. He remained standing,
somewhat aloof.
The lights dimmed slightly, just enough to signal the
start of the performance. A record began to play. It was
of musique concrète, which means that it was made
not with the usual, impersonal instruments such as
violins, violas, trumpets, and contrabasses, instead with
actual objects, such as jars, tins, plates, pieces of wood,
or living beings, such as dogs, frogs, crows, and even
humans. No one seemed surprised – a sign of the "class"
that these spectators have. Like abstract painting,
organic architecture, or a new-wave film, musique
concrète forms part of the cultural heritage of anyone
who keeps up to speed with what is going on in
the world, for whom it provokes neither stupor nor
indignation, instead just an amused smile. At a certain
point, the host gave the signal. The musique concrète
stopped, and six or seven serious-looking youngsters
entered with violins and cellos. They sat down and
began to play Paisiello's *Regina Proserpina*.
Klein clapped his hands, and at that signal, three totally
nude young women walked in, each holding a bucket
full of paint. They were all well put together and
graceful, as fashion models generally are, even when
they're not wearing any clothing. The paint in the
buckets was blue, Klein's favourite colour, actually the
only one he uses when he paints. The paintings in his
last exhibition were all of that colour, without any
intrusions of white, yellow, or green: pure blue surfaces
of the same tone, from top to bottom. The paintings
were distinguishable from one another only because of
their dimensions: some were rectangular, some wider,
some taller, and others were square. The exhibition
was a huge success. All the paintings sold at very high
prices and now occupy an important place in the
collections of those who don't let such first fruits
get away from them.
With a signal from Klein, the girls faced the audience
and then used sponges to cover themselves in paint,
from their shoulders to their calves, transforming
themselves into large fishes from the depths.
After completing that operation, always adapting their
movements to the actual sounds that bounced about
the room, they went up to the white wall and began
to press themselves against it. Pressing their chests,
then their bums, their thighs, their knees, and their
elbows, they remained on close terms with the wall
for some twenty minutes, until it was largely
covered with big blue spots.
At that point Klein discreetly gave the signal for them
to stop. They picked up their buckets and, smiling like
models at the end of a runway show, they left.

The music stopped, the lights came back on, and all the guests admired the work.
No one stood up to criticise the painting's aesthetic foundations. Just one lady very politely observed that Klein's merit was relative, because the painting had ultimately been made by the three models, each one of whom had brushed up against the wall as she saw fit. Klein answered that he didn't care about that. The lady responded, "Of course." Klein then said, "And this way I have more fun." The lady asked him, "Are you going to paint again?" "No", Klein answered, "*painting bores the hell out of me.*"
With his exhibition, Klein has certainly outdone Mathieu, as well as the Surrealists who thought they were going to revive the group's wavering fortunes with their last exhibition.
The beautiful part of the show was entirely in the last room. You got there after walking down a dark hallway with echoes of sighs and moans of women in sexual ecstasy, and you were almost blinded by the bright light that rained down on a table that had been laid. But instead of a tablecloth, a naked woman was lying down on the table between those who were seated (six well-known figures from the art world in Paris). Plates and food were placed on her, and the people seated at the table wiped their fingers on her. One of them, who had a big, black beard, sprayed sauces and spilled wine on her. At a certain point, a lobster (a large shrimp from the English Channel), slid – we don't know if intentionally or by chance – off a plate and landed precisely on the stomach of the woman-tablecloth. That was the most intense moment. But overall, this gathering of Surrealists seemed quite insipid. Today, people prefer things that are more immediate, such as Klein's women-paintbrushes, whom one could reproach at the very most for having made a few concessions to the past by using colour. In this sense, Klein was outdone by Jeanine Fleury, a young painter who only paints with her mouth, passionately kissing her canvasses. In terms of their concreteness, it is undeniable that this represents a step forward that opens up interesting possibilities. These events are mainly worth it for comparing and judging people. The classy folks, the ones who understand everything, never ask questions that might give rise to a problem. The whole is never discussed; they instead limit themselves to making brief observations about details. In looking at Klein's monochrome paintings, they might, for example, say that they would have preferred a different arrangement, perhaps proposing for the next show that he put them on the ground instead of on the walls. If you conduct yourself in this manner, you will be immediately accepted by the elite.
To the contrary, anyone who ingenuously gives in to the temptation to invoke principles, be they aesthetic or moral, will come up against a wall of disdain. They will be called petty bourgeois, moralists. And in the world of these beautiful people, there is no worse insult. The difference between Paris and other European capitals is essentially that. People in Paris don't discuss general principles; they accept everything that happens and at the most, they advise some retouching. Elsewhere the petty bourgeois and the moralists, however insulted they may be, still have the courage to object.

MANLIO CANCOGNI

142

In the case of series no. 4 entrusted to Mr Lenoci, for the Group Exhibition organised by Mr Pierre Restany at the Apollinaire Gallery in Milan, in May 1960, take into account the fact that zone no. 1 of this series no. 4 is already reserved and sold; so only show zone no. 2 from this series no. 4.
Thank you.
Yves Klein.

148, 149

Translated from the Italian

Yves Klein
Yves, you must rescue me!
I have sacrificed so much to have one of your works.
I am an employee.
Look what this cursed high water in Venice
Did to your painting!
Rescue me!

My home had become noble and suggestive:
everything reverberated
with the chromatics
of your painting.
I was happy.
I was proud.
I was.

Help me. Restore
The painting for me or exchange it for me,
Please!
I believe in your painting
You are the new
You will be the most primitive
Of this new school of painting

156, 157

The BLUE, the GOLD, the PINK, the IMMATERIAL, the VOID, the architecture of air, the urbanism of air, the climatisation of vast geographical spaces for a return of human life to the legendary Edenic state. The three bars of fine gold are the proceeds from the sale of the first four ZONES OF IMMATERIAL PICTORIAL SENSIBILITY.
To God the Almighty Father in the name of the Son, Jesus Christ, in the name of the Holy Spirit, and in the name of the Holy Virgin. Through Saint Rita of Cascia under her guardianship and protection, with all my infinite gratitude. Thank you.
Y. K.
Saint Rita of Cascia, I ask you to intercede with God the Almighty Father that He may always grant me, in the name of the Son, Jesus Christ, the Holy Spirit, and the Holy Virgin, the grace of living in my works and that they may always become more beautiful; and that He may also grant me the grace that I may discover continually and regularly new things

in art, each time more beautiful, even if, alas, I am not
always worthy to be a tool for creating Great Beauty.
May all that emerges from me be beautiful. So be it.
Y. K.
Under the earthly guardianship of Saint Rita of Cascia:
pictorial sensibility; the monochromes; the I.K.B.; the
sponge sculptures; the immaterial; the static, negative
and positive anthropometric prints; the shrouds;
the fountains of fire and water; the architecture of air;
the regulating of geographic spaces, thus transformed
into constant Edens rediscovered on the surface
of our globe; the Void.
The theatre of the vold; all the particular marginal
variations of my work; the Cosmogonies; my blue sky ;
all my theories in general. May my enemies become my
friends, and if that is impossible, may any attempt
against me never harm me. Make me and all my works
invulnerable. So be it.
May my work in Gelsenkirchen always be beautiful,
more and more beautiful, and be recognised as such
and as soon as possible. May the fountains of fire and
walls of fire be executed by me without delay in front
of the Gelsenkirchen opera house; may my exhibition
in Krefeld be the greatest success of the century
and be recognised by all.
Saint Rita of Cascia, saint of impossible and desperate
cases, thank you for all the powerful, decisive,
marvellous aid that you have granted me up to now.
Thank you infinitely. Even if I am personally unworthy
of it, grant me your aid again and always in my art and
always protect everything that I have created so that
even in spite of myself it should always be of great
beauty.
Y. K.

158

My Dearest Rotraut
I hope that you arrived safely in Paris after my
departure – My journey was magnificent – all is well and
in my absence please do a few paintings. There is white
paper at the studio on top of your paintings, you'll see.
Work a bit and see? See you soon, sending much love,
Yves

162

<u>AGREEMENT</u>

Mr. Paolo CAVARA, of the Cie CINERIZ, Viale Castrense, 9,
ROMA (Italy) formally agrees to adhere to the following
scenario written by Mr. Yves KLEIN.
SCRIPT:

<u>FIRST SCENE</u>

Set: A big workshop.
a)   On the walls are hung, only at the start:
–   a large blue monochrome
–   a large blue relief
b)   On the floor, a large surface of white paper
        which is in the centre (4 m x 2 m 80).

–   On this white surface the girls are stretched
        out (nude models). They are posing.
c)   Beside them, a kind of liquid blue swimming pool
        – depth 3 cm. (2m 50 x 1m 20) – the idea:
        A single palette, a single colour.
d)   An easel with a white canvas (60 Fig.)
e)   On the floor, beside the easel: two 60 Fig.
        canvases
f)   Beside the pool:
–   A large paintbrush
–   A large roller
–   A large sponge
–   An average-sized sponge
Action:
a)   Yves paints the monochrome on the easel
        with the large paintbrush (Views of his wrist)
b)   Yves paints the 2nd monochrome on the floor
        with the roller.
c)   Yves paints the 3rd monochrome with the
        two sponges – (Effect: handprints,
        furiously erased afterwards)
d)   Each time, to paint his monochromes,
        he successively dips the big paintbrush,
        the roller, and the sponges into the blue
        of the swimming pool. – Palette!
–   While he paints, at first, the camera only films
        the monochrome hung on the wall, in the field
        of action.
–   Yves occasionally looks at the models and
        also the monochrome on the wall.
–   At the end, after Yves finishes his last
        monochrome with the sponges, he looks at
        the sponges that are all blue, hesitates,
        and then places them on the last,
        fresh monochrome.
–   The camera can then film the large relief
        on the wall.
–   All of Yves's clothes are stained blue,
        as are his hands.
–   Satisfied looks at the paintings.
–   Annoyed looks at his hands covered in blue
        and his stained clothes.
–   Views of the models posing in the centre.
Second Action:
1: Yves leaves.
2: <u>The scene:</u> The models come to see the paintings
and the blue in the pool.
The models start to play with the paint. They stain
themselves.
3: Yves returns in a tuxedo and sees the scene
(possibly looks at the orchestra who are now in place).
Director Yves.
4: <u>Idea of the living paintbrush:</u> The models then receive
the order to completely immerse themselves in the
blue of the swimming pool and paint the large white
canvas on the floor in the centre with their bodies.
5: They could also paint one of the canvases on the wall.
6: They also create *La Grande Glace* [Big Mirror] thing.[4]
7: Yves, throughout the scene, directs them from the
top of a ladder, yelling specific orders for all of the
movements.

Mr. Yves KLEIN formally agrees to allow Mr. CAVARA
to judge the time sequences devoted to each take.
Mr. Yves KLEIN reserves the right to be present
at the final cutting before the première of the film.
Mr. CAVARA promises to handle the montage and

cutting of the film, according to the indications
set down in the scenario of Mr. KLEIN.
For his participation in the film, Mr. Yves KLEIN
will receive from the Cie CINERIZ:
1°/ A copy of the sequence regarding Mr. KLEIN,
of the film in colour, 16 mm.
Mr. Klein will utilise this copy uniquely to illustrate
his private conferences and lectures.
2°/ The sum of N.F. 3.000, from which N.F. 1.500 will
be versed before, and N.F. 1.500 at the completion.
All materials, models, orchestra, lighting, equipment
and other expenses will be borne entirely by M. CAVARA
and Cie CINERIZ.
Mr. Yves KLEIN declares that, after having received
the copy of the sequence of the film in 16 mm,
and the sum of N.F. 3.000, he considers himself
completely remunerated, and will have no present
or future claims relative to the film *La Donna
del mondo*,[5] or the Cie CINERIZ.

PARIS,
Paolo CAVARA   Yves KLEIN
12 July 1961

166

Paris, 17 October 1961

To the Honourable Mayor of Tivoli,
        I am pleased to submit the following projects
to your high authority:
–   To include fire jets in the cascatelles and
        in the TIVOLI Gardens, during the great
        summer season. –
        These arrangements would be undertaken
        by Yves KLEIN, the Monochrome [artist],
        who has already constructed Fire Fountains
        at the KREFELD Museum (Germany) during
        the retrospective exhibition in early 1961.
        This artist also presented these Fire Fountains
        in front of the Werner RUHNAU Theatre on
        the grand plaza of GELSENKIRCHEN (Germany),
        and he has held several other events in
        the United States.
        Please find enclosed a map of the cascatelles
and fountains with the fire jets, to give you an idea
of the grandiose project that this fire and water
ensemble might represent in TIVOLI.
        As a further illustration, I am sending you
the plans for the Trocadero fountains that have been
prepared by Yves KLEIN.
        In the hope that these projects might draw
your attention, please accept, Sir, the assurance
of my highest consideration.

Jean LARCADE

172

Listen: I've already sent the invitations to Rome.
Watch out for the conductor of the fast train arriving
at 2:50 pm from Milan, he is bringing you the parcel
of catalogues. Please ensure you are there to wait for
this fast train with a piece of blue paper in your hand.
You can arrive at midnight Saturday, there is a fast train
leaving at 6. Ciao, ciao, Guido.

173

Dear Madam, Dear doctor,
This short note from Rome to tell you that all is well
for Rotraut and myself. We are presenting an exhibition
in Milan on Tuesday – Kindest regards to you and all
of your lovely family
Your Yves Klein

174

Rome, 24 November 1961
Dear Mr Klein,

I wanted to tell you again what a great pleasure it was
to make your acquaintance and apologise once more
for the incident with your painting. I greatly appreciated
your kindness and handling of the restoration of said
painting. It has been consigned for delivery and I hope
that it will arrive soon for you.
I wrote to Mr Larcade, hoping to have better and
more ample occasions to present your works in Rome
in future and telling him how sorry I am for the
customs accident. A human lack of understanding
can sometimes be more noticeable than enthusiasm.
I hope to have the possibility of going to Milan to see
the paintings from your exhibition. I'll write to you
afterwards.
Thank you once again, dear sir.
Yours faithfully,

G.T. Liverani

188

Obliged to postpone journey toothache regret not
to be there for your wedding I'll see you from here
in a blue sky on a flying carpet smiling with your
Trototte = Guido +

194

Translated from the Italian

A SPELL AT NOTRE-DAME

Yves Klein wanted to give me one of his paintings.
A long while back, I had written an article about
Yves Klein, titled "The Monochrome", and so,
he wanted to make me a gift as a sign of his gratitude.
Yves Klein is the artist who exhibited twenty paintings
in Milan in January 1957 that were all the same,

consisting of an absolutely uniform blue surface, without a mark, without a shadow, without a single crack. The dissolution of classical painting had arrived at its limit. How could one go any further? (It gave rise to the "blue painted in blue", the International Klein Blue – IKB –, and two months later, what do you know, Modugno's famous song was released.)

Yves Klein is also the artist who immersed beautiful naked models in a bath of blue colour, who then, at his orders, pressed this or that body part against the canvas, leaving their imprint on it. Or, again at his orders, they squirmed around on a canvas laid down on the ground, without using either their hands or their feet, like snakes, leaving their imprints.

Yves Klein is a man going on thirty, very kind in his appearance, with somewhat of a baby face, well dressed, and extremely polite. Anyone hearing of his feats might have been tempted to imagine a madman, a pretender, or an exhibitionist who wants to *épater le bourgeois*.

Anyone who approached him was instead led to think of him as a pure spirit hurtling towards unreachable horizons.

Yves Klein – and I only understood this right at the end – is none other than Peter Pan. Wonderfully indifferent to the rationality of our world, but using the tools that it offers him, he revives the make-believe of childhood by preserving that invincible imagination of children, able to create paradise with just a stick or a piece of paper.

Yves Klein told me, laughing, "Do you know what the only mistake was in your article? You talked about my pneumatic period as if it were the one with the paintings made with the nude models, but that's not true." I told him, "In the end, I thought there was something pneumatic even with the models." "It's true", he replied, giving another one of his light laughs, "but I was using pneumatic in a philosophical sense. Pneumatic as a void. Pneumatic as the abolition of any tangible essence." "What do you mean?" "Do you see? In 1958, I had an exhibition at the Iris Clert Gallery on Faubourg Saint-Honoré. The exhibition room was completely empty. There wasn't even a frame, not even a nail." "So, what was showing then?" "That room held the pure intangibility of my pictorial essence. And of course, it caused somewhat of a scandal. The Republican Guard had to stand at the door to keep the peace." I said, "If a collector came to buy something, what did you tell them?" "I told them that my intangible pictorial sensibility, which was concentrated in that room, was for sale. And, if I were to sell any of it, in consideration of an utterly intangible value, I wanted to receive something that was 100% tangible. In other words, no paper currency or cheques. That would have been a compromise. In exchange for my intangible pictorial sensibility, I was supposed to receive small gold bars, tiny ingots. And I had prepared a series of printed forms, like the ones we use for cheques. There were some for twenty grams of gold, forty, eighty, one hundred and sixty, and so on, always multiplying by two. Someone would bring me a small gold bar, and I would give them the corresponding receipt." I mustered up the courage to tell him, "Well, didn't people think that this was a kind of … forgive me my bluntness … a bit of a swindle?" "Not for one second. Because the transfer from me to the client of this intangible sensibility happened on one sole condition, namely that he, the client, had to burn the receipt as soon as he received it. Otherwise, what would have happened to the intangibility?" "But in the meantime, you kept the gold, no problem." "Not even for one second. When the client burned the receipt, I cut off a small piece of the gold from the ingot and gave it to the gallery owner. He had to make a living too. The rest, in the presence of witnesses, I threw into the Seine, or the ocean, where no one could fish it out again." "And if someone didn't burn their receipt?" "Too bad for him. Four years have passed, and there have been seven buyers. One of whom, a collector from Milan, framed the receipt instead of burning it. And that way, he defrauded himself. My intangible pictorial sensibility was in fact not transmitted to him. It never became real for him. Just so we're clear, the buyer can pass the receipt on to a third party, like a cheque, thereby transferring the corresponding zone of intangible pictorial sensibility to him, but of course, even this third party, to possess it truthfully, would have had to burn the receipt." I told him, "You know what I think, dear Klein? You kindly wanted to give me one of your paintings. Why don't you give me one of these intangible zones? Wouldn't that be much more elegant?"

I swear that I had absolutely no intention of making fun of him. After all, the idea of having one of his paintings certainly appealed to me. Aside from the monochrome paintings, aside from the imprints made by the nude models coloured blue, Klein, in using a kind of flamethrower and spraying water, creates beautiful, very inspiring effects. I would love to have something of the sort in my house. I would like to add that all his works are, for their genre, of an impeccable perfection in terms of their craftsmanship. And yet, that game, if we want to call it that, that bartering of an intangible something for a certain quantity of gold which was then dispersed in the waters for eternity, there was something fascinating about it, in an esoteric kind of way. All you have to do is believe in that world to fool yourself. Even the air contains treasures.

Peter Pan quivered at my words. "That's stupendous! It's magnificent! Yes, yes!" he exclaimed. "We'll do everything tomorrow morning!" And he was, at that moment, a happy man.

The next morning, we went in a taxi to the bridge over the Seine right next to Notre-Dame, him, Yves Klein, Jean Larcade, director of the Galerie Rive Droite, and two photographers to document the scene. A grey sky, freezing cold, a wind blowing out of the north, the water a dark mustard colour. Yves Klein held a Plexiglas cube box full of gold leaf in his hand, the kind of sheets that gilders use. Exactly nineteen grams. We went down a few steps from the bridge on the stairs that lead to the river's edge.

There was almost no one walking across the bridge. From the spires of Notre-Dame, monstrous dragons in stone, the gargoyles, with their wet throats opening onto the abyss, looked on, excited and happy. I was about to receive the gift of a small piece of intangible pictorial sensibility that would enter me and never leave me, until the day I die, and maybe even past that. A transaction of artistic occultism. In practice, what did all this mean? Perhaps nothing. Or perhaps something exceptional and beautiful. It all hinged on me. I thought

of long-ago days when, as a child, I played the Tuareg
marauder or the jungle strangler, draped in an old
sheet, riding a wooden horse. And the illusion was
so strong that it all became true. Seven, eight metres
away, cars were passing by, driven by men worrying
about money, power, women, success, glory. I was
instead being invited by a Peter Pan named Klein
to a kind of ritual that was delightfully spiritual and
absurd all at once, but in which he believed.
The Plexiglas box was placed in my hands. It was
"mine". I could have gone off if I wanted, with the gift
of 19 grams of gold. And Klein would not have objected
(the twentieth gram, closed in a small cardboard box,
was given to Larcade: the percentage owed to
the "gallerist". I then handed the gold to the young
magician. And he pulled a booklet out of his pocket
that looked like a cheque book. At the bottom
of the page, printed in half-tone were the letters IKB:
International Klein Blue. Above, in black, was printed:
"Warranty Cachet. Series No. 1, Zone No. 05. Receipt
of twenty grams of gold in consideration for
a zone of intangible pictorial sensibility".
This madman named Yves Klein, this lively, incredible
character, signed the receipt with a ballpoint pen
and I gave him the gold. A little way above us,
a bespectacled gentleman of about fifty who was
walking across the bridge stopped, looking concerned.
So, with some difficulty, due to the wind, I lit a match
and put it to the paper, which began to burn. At the
same time, Yves Klein opened the lid of the Plexiglas
box and began to pull out the almost impalpable sheets
of gold and dispersed them into the air. A woman who
looked like a housewife stopped on the bridge to look,
next to the bespectacled gentleman.
The strangest things go unnoticed in Paris.
But those two were deeply suspicious.
Handful by handful, the golden sheets were swept
away by the wind; they were so light. They flew off into
the grey air and disappeared under the bridge's dark
shadow. It was nineteen grams, not ten thousand.
The Plexiglas box was soon empty, and the receipt
had been burned. All that was left was a stub
in between my fingers.
Perhaps ingenuously, I had hoped – feel free tell me
I am an idiot – that I would feel a little different,
different for a split second, just different. But no,
nothing. I was the same wretch as before. Yves Klein
lived within his aura of poetic sorcery, and I hadn't
managed to penetrate it.
It was time to go. I took two, maybe three steps.
I don't remember. And then Klein called out to me:
"Look, look." I looked. In the Seine, not all the way
across, but at the heart of the river, the central stream
of its current had turned to gold. A glistening rivulet
stood out in its yellow splendour against the
silt-coloured waters, slowly making its way towards
the distant sea. The gold leaves scattered in the wind
had slowly fallen like listless snowflakes on a night
of below-zero temperatures. One by one, they settled
on the water and let themselves be carried away.
And now they went off like carefree and
restless butterflies, sliding towards their destiny
to tell their fable.
That golden rivulet seemed without end.
For a length of perhaps five hundred metres, the Seine
glittered with mystery, magnificence, enchantment,
and madness.

"Something extraordinary is bound to happen today",
Klein said, with utter conviction. I wouldn't know how
to explain it, but I also felt happy. But the extraordinary
thing did not come to pass, at least as far as I know.
And it was my fault. I ask Yves Klein to forgive me.
If Puck's spell, if his incantation failed, the fault was
all mine, due to my petty bourgeois spirit. Because the
receipt didn't burn fully and the tail end of it remained
in my hand. And I was happy to keep it as a souvenir,
so I put it in my pocket when Klein wasn't looking.
I still keep it in my wallet. And I like to think that I have
a kind of talisman, a small reserve of poetry, or of
happiness, or illusion that I can consume one day,
whenever I feel like it. It's a paper strip with the words
in French: "Series No. 1 - Received Twenty …
in exchange for a Zone of … This transferable zone
may only be transferred by its owner at twice its initial
purchase value. (Signatures and dates for the transfers
on the back). Transgressors risk total annihilation
of their own sensibility".
So, I am the transgressor, because I kept a small piece.
And, logically, the intangible sensibility has not yet
entered me. But some day, if I am sad and tired,
I will pull that strip of paper out from my wallet and
set it aflame.
And in some way, that will bring me consolation,
perhaps. May Yves Klein forgive me.
We found a taxi in front of Notre-Dame, without having
to wait too long.

Dino Buzzati

196

Translated from the Italian

He Sells Nothing for the Price of Gold

YVES KLEIN is a man who elicits infinite dislike or
unbridled admiration. For the former, he is a charlatan
who uses any means to promote himself; for others,
he is a kind of prophet of our new age, the pioneer of
"invisible art". All his investigations in the most diverse
fields demonstrate the pre-eminence and the reality
of the "intangible". Who is Klein? He proudly introduces
himself with "I am 'the painter', I am 'the actor',
'the architect', 'the sculptor'. I must assert, 'I am.'"
Let's try to look at him rationally, by perusing his
whimsical biography. He was born thirty-four years ago
in Nice. The colour of the Mediterranean was the first
deep motif that conditioned his artistic education.
As a young boy, he would lay down in the grass and
look at the blue above him and tell himself, "I am
the king of the sky." It was a game, but it foretold
something. Twenty years later (after learning judo and
ancient martial arts in Japan), he presented his
"monochrome proposals": paintings of a deep,
uniform blue, slivers of the sea or the sky that the
imagination is supposed to extend to infinity. It was his
"blue period" (Klein says that it was from his exhibition
in Milan at the Apollinaire Gallery that Modugno stole
Klein's idea for the famous line *Nel blu, dipinto di blu*,
"In a blue painted in blue"). Two other colours appear
on Klein's palette: gold and pink, the "monogold"
and the "monopink". These colours were not chosen

at random by this devotee of symbols: gold signifies
the eternity of the law, pink, love and flesh, and blue,
the intangible; together they constitute the Holy
Trinity. The three colours merge in the flickering
of a flame, with which Klein creates moving sculptures
or even, alternately using fire and water, abstract
paintings that are among his most impressive works.
Klein hates the paintbrush, which he believes falsifies
the relationship between an artist and his work.
Which is why he makes use of a series of natural
instruments, such as fire or rain to create very curious
"cosmogonies", or the "living paintbrush".

A LIVING PAINTING SESSION is one of the most unique
performances one will ever see. Klein, who admits to
having a "conflicted vocation" as a man of the theatre,
unquestionably knows how to manipulate his effects.
White canvasses are arranged against the walls and
on the floor. From atop a ladder, the painter, dressed in
a tuxedo, like a conductor, directs the movements
of the models, who cover their gorgeous bodies with
colour and then, according to the artist's instructions,
press their haunches, breasts, buttocks, cheeks,
or palms of their hands on the canvas, now barely
grazing against it, now leaning hard, in a swiping or
a static pressing motion. At times the result is yielded
with the lightness of a ballet movement, at others
with a charged body-to-body interaction that evokes
the eroticism of Baudelaire's "damned women".
These compositions, which feel like hallucinatory,
poetic X-rays, are entitled "shrouds", and they
represent one of hundreds of forms of Klein's quest
for the "invisible". How could we list them all?
Klein is the author of a "monotone symphony", built
on one note sustained to the limits of the bearable,
after which what matters is "the silence".
At the Avant-Garde Festival in 1960, he presented a
"theory of the void", which involves an empty room,
the lack of a performance, and an actor who is paid
simply "to bear the grave responsibility of being
an actor and disappearing into the crowd". He has
designed aerial architectures based on the principles
of "air roofs" that are supposed to revolutionise climate
conditions and, by changing the Earth's physiognomy,
our social structures as well. But it is with painting that
Klein takes his theories to their furthest conclusions.
From the first monochrome experiences, he said
that blue is "the invisible that becomes visible".
IN 1957, he dared to present the first exhibition of
"intangible pictorial sensibility": in a room of smooth,
white walls, there was nothing. This event caused
an uproar, with the Republican Guard in uniform
at the entrance and a huge crowd that had come
to sneer. Klein described how then, in that perfect void,
viewers were struck by a kind of mystical fervour,
as if in a naked chapel. Some of them began crying,
others, astonished, didn't want to leave. If you exhibit
emptiness, you also have to be able to sell it, but not
for lowly money, which is why Klein began selling
"zones of intangible pictorial sensibility" for the price
of gold. He has already found some ten clients.
The most generous of these patrons is an American,
the Hollywood screenwriter Michael Blankfort,
who recently bought an "intangible" strip from him
for 160 grams of fine gold, equal to 260 dollars.
The transactions are conducted according to a precise
ritual inspired by an ancient Celtic rite. On the banks

of the Seine, the buyer gives the artist miniscule gold
ingots (in the presence of Francis Mathey, curator
of the Museum of Decorative Arts, who certifies
the transaction and earns a percentage on it),
and in exchange, he is given a receipt that he then
has to burn, "so that the intangible can enter him".
Klein keeps half the ingots for himself, and with a
broad gesture, he throws the rest into the river so that
what belongs to the universe can be returned to
the universe. I took the liberty of ingenuously asking
him how he justifies appropriating half of the gold.
He responded with a phrase from Goethe:
"The moment an artist has chosen his subject,
it no longer belongs to nature, rather to the artist."
The ingots thrown into the river are a kind of votive
offering. A *clochard* who was a witness to the scene
watched with sad astonishment as they disappeared,
swallowed by the waters of the Seine.

197

Translated from the Italian

THE TRANSACTION-CESSION of the sale of the "void"
by Yves Klein. The void painter brings his client (here,
in the photo to the left, Hollywood screenwriter
Michael Blankfort) to the banks of the Seine.
In exchange for an "intangible strip", the client pays
him the price in small gold ingots (here 160 grams,
equal to 156,000 lire: photo to the right). The painter
provides a receipt, which the client will burn,
and after pocketing half of the ingots, he disperses
the other half in the water (photo above), often under
the eyes of *clochards* who live along the Seine.

198

My dear Yves —

1) Firstly to tell you that everything is arranged at
the Colombe d'Or for a painting exchange – visit – your
"cousin" Francis Roux has given permission – So come
whenever you like with Trotrot.
2) I am in Venice today with Le Noci and find myself
currently at my friend's house, Mr Constantini, whom
I have already told you about and who expects you
in Venice for the creation of glass works – exhibition
in Paris next December–January). The [unreadable],
my works have turned out beautifully, I will master
this field yet.
So we are waiting for you in Venice … I think that
you might make a monochrome and a rain[6] very
successfully.
While we're on the subject of monochromes,
don't forget the one for my Nouveau Réalisme room!
You will choose a large black form.
Warmest regards to you both.
I'll be in Saint-Paul next Wednesday.

André Verdet.

202

Dear Paolo,

I write to ask you instantly to please send me, this time
without fail, the 16 mm copy of my complete sequence
as it was shot in PARIS (in short, as it was agreed
in our little contract).
It is absolutely essential for editing my little private
film, as I already told you at the CANNES Festival.
Secondly, you promised me a definitive answer
regarding our major film project: I am also awaiting
this response because I would like to start this
in September 1962.
Besides that, my Dear Paolo, I hope you have good and
restful holidays; and once again, please do not forget
to immediately send me the promised copy of
the 16 mm film.
Warmest regards.

Yves KLEIN

PS: I'd also like you to send me the tape that I sent you
with the *Monotone Symphony.*
thanks

Editor's Notes:
1. *La Guerre (de la ligne et de la couleur)* [The War
(of Line and Colour)] is a scenario written by Yves Klein
in 1954 in which he retraces the history of art
since Lascaux, from the angle of the line /
colour contradiction.
2. Abbreviation for "physical education".
3. The project mentioned is that of the *Architecture
de l'air* [Air Architecture] co-developed by Yves Klein
in 1958 with German architect Werner Ruhnau.
4. A support, made of glass or plexiglass,
had been mounted against the gauze canvas in order
to withstand the models' imprints and allow the
director to film transparently through it.
5. The title of the film was changed to *Mondo Cane*
prior to release.
6. *Pluie* [Rain] is a sculpture by Yves Klein made
of wooden rods.

LIST OF WORKS

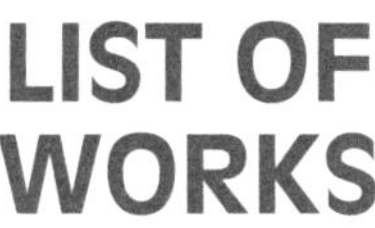

—

Editor's Note: the transcripts of the dedications retain Klein's written and typographical bias.

List of works by Yves Klein

Ex-voto dédié à sainte Rita de Cascia [Ex-voto
Dedicated to Saint Rita of Cascia], 1961
Dry pigment, gold leaf, gold bars, and manuscript
in Plexiglas
14 × 21 × 3 cm
Saint Rita Monastery, Cascia
Cover, pp. 156, 157

Monochrome bleu sans titre [Untitled Blue
Monochrome] (IKB 259), 1956
Dry pigment and synthetic resin on canvas mounted
on wood panel
14.2 × 18 cm
p. 38

Monochrome bleu sans titre [Untitled Blue
Monochrome] (IKB 104), 1956
Dry pigment and synthetic resin on gauze mounted
on wood panel
78 × 56 cm
Dedication on the back: "Yves 56,
to the uncompromising Guido Le Noci"
p. 46

Monochrome bleu sans titre [Untitled Blue
Monochrome] (IKB 100), 1956
Dry pigment and synthetic resin on gauze mounted
on wood panel
78 × 56 cm
On the back: "* Yves 56 Collection Lucio Fontana Milan"
p. 50

Monochrome rouge sans titre [Untitled
Red Monochrome] (M 62), 1956
Dry pigment and synthetic resin on wood panel
51 × 39 cm
On the back: "* Yves 56 Collection Count
Giuseppe Panza Milan"
p. 65

Monochrome bleu sans titre [Untitled Blue
Monochrome], 1957
Dry pigment and synthetic resin on gauze mounted
on wood panel
50 × 50 cm
MAMC – Musée d'art moderne et contemporain,
Saint-Étienne
p. 78

Monochrome bleu sans titre [Untitled Blue
Monochrome], 1958
Dry pigment and synthetic resin on gauze mounted
on wood panel
55.7 × 46.5 cm
Dedication on the back from Yves Klein:
"In Recognition of Saint Rita / 15 September 1958 /
Yves Klein aka The Monochrome"; and from
Rose Raymond: "From Paris / thanks to Saint RITA /
Rose-Marie Raymond"
p. 93

Relief éponge bleu sans titre [Untitled Blue Sponge
Relief] (RE 51), 1959
Dry pigment and synthetic resin, natural sponges
and pebbles on wood
106 × 105 cm
p. 102

Sculpture éponge bleue sans titre [Untitled Blue Sponge
Sculpture] (SE 203), 1959
Dry pigment and synthetic resin on natural sponge,
metal rod
20 × 13 × 10 cm
p. 103

*Zone de sensibilité picturale immatérielle, série n° 1,
reçu n° 1* [Zone of Immaterial Pictorial Sensibility, series
no. 1, receipt no. 1] (IMMA 8), 18 November 1959
Printed paper
8.7 × 19.3 cm
Signed on the back: "Zone transferred to Mr. Peppino
Palazzoli of Milan on 18 Nov 1959 Yves Klein"
p. 117

*Zone de sensibilité picturale immatérielle, série n° 1,
reçu n° 3* [Zone of Immaterial Pictorial Sensibility,
series no. 1, receipt no. 3] (IMMA 10), 7 December 1959
Printed paper
8.7 × 19.3 cm
p. 118

Anthropométrie sans titre [Untitled Anthropometry]
(ANT 133), 1960
Dry pigment and synthetic resin on paper mounted
on wood panel
129 × 37 cm
p. 128

Héléna (ANT 111), 1960
Dry pigment and synthetic resin on paper mounted
on canvas
218 × 151 cm
p. 129

L'Exilé d'Ischia [Ischia's Exile] (ANT 122), 1960
Dry pigment and synthetic resin on paper mounted
on canvas
181 × 115 cm
On the back: "Ischia's Exile / Yves Klein / Paris 1960"
p. 134

Anthropométrie sans titre [Untitled Anthropometry]
(ANT 175), February 1960
Dry pigment, undetermined fixative, and gold painted
on paper mounted on canvas
204 × 132,5 cm
Dedicated below on the left: "To Guido Le Noci with
all the esteem and true friendship of Yves Klein, Paris,
February 1960"
p. 135

Monochrome bleu sans titre [Untitled Blue
Monochrome] (IKB 271), 1960
Dry pigment and synthetic resin on gauze mounted
on wood panel
50 × 50 cm
Dedication on the back: "to Bertini with the friendship
of Yves Klein 1960"
p. 138

Book of receipts for the *Zones de sensibilité picturale
immatérielle, série n°5* [Zones of Immaterial
Pictorial Sensibility, series no. 5], 1959
Printed paper
8.7 × 29.8 cm
p. 143

Monogold "Âge d'or" ["Golden-Age" Monogold] (MG 42),
1960
Gold leaf on wood panel
21.5 × 12.5 cm
Dedicated on the back: "to Fontana a golden-age
monogold 1960 Yves Klein"
p. 145

Gold board from the *Triptyque de Krefeld*
[Krefeld Triptych] dedicated to Saint Rita of Cascia, 1961
Gold leaf on cardboard
32 × 23.5 cm
Dedication on the back: "To Saint Rita / of Cascia /
Yves Klein / the monochrome / 1961"
Saint Rita Monastery, Cascia
pp. 152,153 (detail)

Suaire de Mondo Cane [Mondo Cane Shroud]
(ANT SU 8 I, ANT SU 8 II), 1961
Dry pigment and synthetic resin on gauze
234 × 297 cm
Walker Art Center, Minneapolis
pp. 164-165

Jets d'eau et de feu [Water and Fire Fountains]
(D 92), 1959
Watercolour, gouache, and ballpoint on tracing paper
24 × 31 cm
p. 167

Relief planétaire "Région de Grenoble"
[Planetary Relief "Grenoble Region"] (RP 10), 1961
Dry pigment and synthetic resin on plaster mounted
on wood panel
86 × 65 cm
p. 180

Monogold sans titre [Untitled Monogold] (MG 11), 1961
Gold leaf on wood panel
75 × 60 cm
Kunstsammlung NRW, Düsseldorf
p. 181

Relief planétaire rose "Lune II" [Pink Planetary Relief
"Moon II"] (RP 21), 1961
Dry pigment and fixative on plaster
95 × 65 × 7 cm
p. 183

Peinture de feu "Carte de Mars par l'eau et le feu"
[Fire Painting "Map of Mars by Water and Fire"] (F 83),
1961
Burnt cardboard
69 × 49 cm
On the back: "Yves Klein 1961"
p. 184

Sculpture éponge bleue sans titre [Untitled Blue Sponge
Sculpture] (SE 181), 1960
Dry pigment and synthetic resin, natural sponge on
plaster and metal base
53 × 33 × 27.5 cm
p. 185

Transfer of the *Zone de sensibilité picturale
immatérielle, série n°1, zone n°5* [Zone of Immaterial
Pictorial Sensibility, series no. 1, zone no. 5] (IMMA 13)
to Dino Buzzati, 26 January 1962
Artistic action by Yves Klein on the Pont au Double,
Paris
pp. 190, 191, 192–193

Anthropométrie sans titre [Untitled Anthropometry]
(ANT 163), 1960
Dry pigment and synthetic resin on paper
87.5 × 45.4 cm
Dedication below on the right: "To Egidio Costantini
della Fucina degli angeli with the friendship of
Yves Klein"
p. 199

Other artworks

Enrico Baj, Untitled, 1957
Mixed media on canvas
30 × 40 cm
p. 79

Marie Raymond, *Composition*, 1957
Gouache on paper
50.5 × 33 cm
Dedication on the back from Yves Klein: "To Madame
Marieda / Boschi on / behalf of my mother / Yves Klein /
Paris, 7 July / 1957"
Museo del Novecento, Milan
p. 81

Lucio Fontana, *Concetto spaziale* [Spatial Concept], 1960
Canvas with holes
61 × 50 cm
Signed on the back: "al amigo Yves Klein"
p. 144

CITATIONS

—

Dino Buzzati, "Spell at Notre-Dame", in *Corriere della Sera*, 4 February 1962: p. 195

Lucio Fontana, *Art et Création*, no. 1 (January–February 1968): pp. 146, 203

Yves Klein, "The Evolution of Art Towards the Immaterial", Lecture at the Sorbonne, 3 June 1959: p. 53

Yves Klein, letter to Tommaso Ferraris, director of the Milan Triennale, 2 October 1959, Yves Klein Archives, Paris: p. 108

Guido Le Noci, handwritten notes, January 1957, Yves Klein Archives, Paris: p. 63

Guido Le Noci, gallery introduction for *Yves Klein le Monochrome. Il nuovo realismo del colore* [Yves Klein the Monochrome. The New Realism of Colour], Apollinaire Gallery, November 1961: p. 177

Manifesto "The End of Style", Milan, 1957: p. 83

Adriano Parisot, *Possibilità della materia* [The Potential of Matter] (Turin: Canale Edizioni, 1998): p. 41

Pierre Restany, *Yves Klein* (Paris: Éditions du Chêne, 1982): p. 44

INDEX

—

AUTHOR BIOGRAPHIES

—

Cecilia Braschi is an independent art historian and exhibition curator. She is an expert on Italian, French, and South American art as well as artistic and critical circulations between Latin America and Europe. Within the framework of her university studies, she initially focused on abstract Italian and French art movements of the 1940s and 1960s, then on the Brazilian and Argentinian scenes of the same period, as well as on the debate concerning the "synthesis of the arts" and on social, multidisciplinary, and collective models of art; she has published numerous studies on these subjects.

An exhibition assistant at the Centre Georges Pompidou (Paris) in 2000–2001 (*Denise René l'intrépide. Une galerie dans l'aventure de l'art abstrait*), she was also the head of art book publications for Il Cigno Galileo Galilei publishing house and exhibition coordinator at the San Salvatore Museum in Lauro, Rome, where she notably prepared exhibitions on Kinetic Art and Programmed Art, between 2002 and 2004 (featuring artists such as Julio Le Parc, Horacio Garcia Rossi, Hugo Demarco, Ennio Finzi, and Alberto Biasi).

As a conservation attaché and head of documentation at the Alberto and Annette Giacometti Foundation (Paris) between 2005 and 2012, she co-ordinated research for the artist's catalogue raisonné and assisted on the curation of several exhibitions in France and abroad, including *L'Atelier d'Alberto Giacometti* (Centre Pompidou, 2007) and the first Giacometti retrospective in Argentina and Brazil (Pinacoteca de São Paulo / MAM Rio, Rio de Janeiro / Fundación Proa, Buenos Aires, 2012–2013). She published many essays and books on Giacometti between 2007 and 2024, including *Alberto Giacometti. Les copies du passé* (Lyon: Fage Publishing, 2013).

Head of research on Latin America at the Centre Georges Pompidou in 2013–2014, she then become exhibitions manager at the Hôtel de Caumont–Centre d'art, in Aix-en-Provence, between 2015 and 2022. Among other exhibitions, she curated *Yves Klein intime*, in 2022.

While continuing to carry out her research, she now works as an exhibition curator for various institutions, such as BAM – Musée des Beaux-Arts de Mons, Belgium (*Fernando Botero, au-delà des formes*, 2021), the Grand Palais-RMN (Paris), and the Guggenheim Museum (Bilbao), where she is currently preparing the first European retrospective of Brazilian artist Tarsila do Amaral.

Bruno Corà is a historian, art critic, essayist, exhibition curator, and author of art monographs published in Italy and many countries around the world. He began his career as a critic and curator in the mid-1960s in Milan before moving to Rome. In 1970, he helped found the Incontri Internazionali d'Arte in Rome and curated exhibitions such as *Contemporanea* in 1973.

From 1979 to 1999, he was a professor at the "Pietro Vannucci" Academy of Fine Arts in Perugia, of which he is also an honorary member, as he is of the Florence Design Academy. He also taught at the University of Cassino from 1999 to 2006 and at the University of Florence for two years, from 2007 to 2009. Currently President of the Burri Foundation, he has been the director of Palazzo Fabroni Arti Visive Contemporanee in Pistoia, the Luigi Pecci Contemporary Art Centre in Prato, the La Spezia Modern and Contemporary Art Centre (CAMeC), and the Lugano Museum of Modern and Contemporary Art, as well as being the founder and director of the Cassino Museum of Contemporary Art.

Corà has curated various international art biennials, including those of Dakar, Gubbio, and La Spezia. He has curated exhibitions of the work of international artists such as Alberto Burri, Louise Nevelson, Yves Klein, Alighiero Boetti, Lucio Fontana, Giuseppe Uncini, Vincenzo Agnetti, Michelangelo Pistoletto, Fausto Melotti, Enrico Castellani, Luciano Fabro, Giulio Paolini, Francesco Lo Savio, Gerhard Richter, Antoni Tàpies, Jannis Kounellis, Georg Baselitz, Dadamaino, Costas Tsoclis, and Sigmar Polke. In 1970, he founded the international review *AEIOU* and acted as its editor-in chief until 1987, and he was the editor-in-chief of the *MozArt* review from 2012 to 2016; both were dedicated to contemporary art and over the years featured interviews with artists such as Enrico Castellani, Jannis Kounellis, Bill Viola, Christian Boltanski, Claudio Parmiggiani, and Jaume Plensa, among many others. He is currently a member of the advisory committee of the archives of the following artists: Burri, Calzolari, Uncini, Kounellis, Agnetti, J. P. Bertrand, and Spagnulo.

He has curated the general catalogues, replete with specific scholarly essays, of the works of Alberto Burri, Marco Gastini, and Enrico Castellani. He is currently editor and curator of the general catalogues raisonnés of the work of Emilio Isgrò and Jannis Kounellis. His more than three hundred critical essays on contemporary art have been published in many languages in monographs, daily newspapers, and journals specialising in art and museology worldwide.

CREDITS

—

ACKNOWLEDGEMENTS

—

The editor expresses his warmest gratitude to the Yves Klein Archives, to Rotraut Klein-Moquay and Daniel Moquay, as well as to Cecilia Braschi, Bruno Corà, and Elena Palumbo Mosca. Many thanks to all those who helped with the research undertaken for this book, in particular:

The Yves Klein Archives: François Roulin, Anne Anthony, Marilou Barbanti, Dorothée Dujardin, Louis Thelier

Charlotte Ménard

Thierry Bertini
Simona Bordone — Domus Archive, Milan
Andrea Camuffo
Michele Casamonti — Tornabuoni Arte
Letizia Castellini Baldissera and Ferruccio Luppi — Piero Portaluppi Foundation, Milan
Antonio Comelli and Luigi Costantini — Fucina degli Angeli, Venice
Father Andrea Dall'Asta and Luca Ilgrande — Fondazione Culturale San Fedele, Milan
Duccio Dogheria — MART, The Museum of Modern and Contemporary Art of Trento and Rovereto
Catherine Fabry — Succession Decock-Restany
Antonella Felicioni and Debora Demontis — Centro Sperimentale di Cinematografia, CSC, Rome
Cristina Filippi — Casa Museo Boschi Di Stefano, Milan
Barbara Könches and Rebecca Welkens — ZERO Foundation, Düsseldorf
Judith Kranitz — The Venice Biennale Foundation
Sandra Laupa — Picture library of the Cinémathèque française, Paris
Laurence Le Poupon — Association for the Archives of Art Criticism, Rennes
Alessia Locatelli and Giuliano Manselli — Enrico Cattaneo Photographic Archive, Milan
Jean-Pierre Mattei and Gabrielle Merlini — Cinematheque of Corsica, Porto-Vecchio
Valeria Morandi — Lucio Fontana Foundation, Milan
Emiliano Neri — Corraini Edizioni, Mantua
Daniele Palazzoli
Libera Pennacchi — State Archives, Latina
Alessandra Pozzati — Ugo Mulas Archives, Milan
Silvio Ruffert Veronese — Solomon R. Guggenheim Foundation, Venice
Federico Sardella — Enrico Castellani Foundation, Milan
Tracey Schuster, Getty Research Institute, Los Angeles
Paolo Senna and Francesco Tedeschi — Università Cattolica del Sacro Cuore, Milan
Philippe Siauve
Silvana Sperati and Bruno Munari — Bruno Munari Association, Milan
Rosalia Pasqualino di Marineo and Irene Stucchi — Piero Manzoni Foundation, Milan
Elisa Testori
Tommaso Tofanetti — Triennale di Milano
Francesca Tramma — Corriere della Sera Foundation, Milan
Giuseppe Valtorta — Famiglia Artistica Lissonese, Lissone

Edited by
Charlotte Ménard

Éditions Dilecta

Editorial Direction
Grégoire Robinne

Editorial Management
Sirrine Laalou

Editorial Coordination
Chris Marie Tyan

Transcription of the interviews
with Rotraut Klein-Moquay
and Elena Palumbo Mosca
Charlotte Ménard

Translations
Claudio Cambon (Italian-English)
Anna Knight (French-English)
Charles Penwarden (French-English)

Proofreading
Julia Monks

Photoengraving
Christian Demare

Graphic Design
Grégoire Romanet

The text of this book is set in Antique Olive
(1962, by Roger Excoffon), the captions
in Prestige Élite bold (1953,
by Clayton Smith), and the dates and folios
in Van Dijk (1986, by Peter O'Donnell).

This book was also published in French
as *Yves Klein Italie* (978-2-37372-199-7)
and in Italian as *Yves Klein Italia*
(978-2-37372-204-8).

49 Rue Notre-Dame-de-Nazareth
75003 Paris
www.editions-dilecta.com

ISBN: 978-2-37372-200-0
Price (France): 32 €
Printed by Graphius, in Ghent (Belgium)
Legal Deposit: September 2024

Diffusion-Distribution
France, Belgium, Switzerland
Belles Lettres – Diffusion Distribution
25 Rue du Général Leclerc
F – 94270 Le Kremlin-Bicêtre
T +33 1 45 15 19 70
www.bldd.fr

International
Garzón Diffusion internationale
10 Rue de la Maison Blanche
F – 75013 Paris
T +33 1 45 82 01 14
contact@garzondi.com
&
North America, UK, Asia, Australia
ARTBOOK | D.A.P.
75 Broad St., suite 730
New York, NY 10004
www.artbook.com